Byzantium in the Popular Imagination

New Directions in Byzantine Studies

This series showcases the work of writers who are setting new agendas and working at the frontiers of the field, exploring Byzantium's peripheries (geographically, socially), promoting innovative research methods and demonstrating the empire as dynamic, complex and fluid – the crossroads between East and West.

Series editor

Dionysios Stathakopoulos, University of Cyprus

Advisory board

Kostis Smyrlis, New York University (NYU)
Vlada Stanković, University of Belgrade
Claudia Sode, University of Cologne

New and forthcoming titles:

Politics and Government in Byzantium: The Rise and Fall of the Bureaucrat Class, Jonathan Shea

From Byzantine to Norman Italy: Mediterranean Art and Architecture in Medieval Bari, Clare Vernon

Byzantium in the Popular Imagination: The Modern Reception of the Byzantine Empire, edited by Markéta Kulhánková and Przemysław Marciniak

Theodore Metochites: Patterns of Self-representation in Fourteenth Century Byzantium, Ioannis D. Polemis

Byzantine Spain: A History of Spania, Jamie Wood

Byzantine Sardinia: A History, Salvatore Cosentino

Byzantium in the Popular Imagination

The Modern Reception of the Byzantine Empire

Edited by
Markéta Kulhánková and
Przemysław Marciniak

I.B.TAURIS
LONDON • NEW YORK • OXFORD • NEW DELHI • SYDNEY

I.B. TAURIS
Bloomsbury Publishing Plc
50 Bedford Square, London, WC1B 3DP, UK
1385 Broadway, New York, NY 10018, USA
29 Earlsfort Terrace, Dublin 2, Ireland

BLOOMSBURY, I.B. TAURIS and the I.B. Tauris logo are trademarks
of Bloomsbury Publishing Plc

First published in Great Britain 2023
This paperback edition published in 2025

Copyright © Markéta Kulhánková and Przemysław Marciniak, 2023

Markéta Kulhánková, Przemysław Marciniak and Contributors have asserted their right under the Copyright, Designs and Patents Act, 1988, to be identified as Editors of this work.

For legal purposes the Acknowledgements on pp. 41, 100, 221, 236, 258 constitute an extension of this copyright page.

Series design by Rebecca Heselton
Cover image © Byzantine Tales

All rights reserved. No part of this publication may be reproduced or transmitted in any form or by any means, electronic or mechanical, including photocopying, recording, or any information storage or retrieval system, without prior permission in writing from the publishers.

Bloomsbury Publishing Plc does not have any control over, or responsibility for, any third-party websites referred to or in this book. All internet addresses given in this book were correct at the time of going to press. The author and publisher regret any inconvenience caused if addresses have changed or sites have ceased to exist, but can accept no responsibility for any such changes.

A catalogue record for this book is available from the British Library.

A catalog record for this book is available from the Library of Congress.

ISBN: HB: 978-0-7556-0728-0
PB: 978-0-7556-5195-5
ePDF: 978-0-7556-0729-7
eBook: 978-0-7556-0730-3

Series: New Directions in Byzantine Studies

Typeset by Integra Software Services Pvt. Ltd.

To find out more about our authors and books visit www.bloomsbury.com and sign up for our newsletters.

Contents

List of Figures   vii
List of Contributors   ix

Introduction: The Many Faces of the Reception of Byzantium
Przemysław Marciniak   1

Part 1   Byzantium on Display: Scholarly Debates, Political Uses, Modern Reconstructionism

1. Popularizing Byzantine Architecture: The 1900 Paris World Exhibition, Balkan Nationalisms and the Byzantine Revival   *Fani Gargova*   11
2. East or West? Byzantine Architecture and the Origins of French Medieval Architecture in the Scholarly Debate, Nineteenth Century   *Francesco Lovino*   33
3. Byzantium as a Political Tool (1657–1952): Nations, Colonialism and Globalism   *Ivan Foletti and Adrien Palladino*   45
4. The Prince and the Greeks: The Byzantine Baptizers of Prince Vladimir in Modern Russian Sculpture, Mosaic and Church Architecture *Roman Shliakhtin*   67
5. Museum Interpretations of Byzantium   *Sofia Mali*   81

Part 2   Byzantium and Modern Media

6. Byzantium in Comics   *Lilia Diamantopoulou*   109
7. Games of Byzantium: The Image of the Empire in Three Strategy Videogames   *Marco Fasolio*   123
8. From History to Propaganda and Back: Byzantium in the Romanian Historical Cinema   *Florin Leonte*   147
9. Imagination of Byzantium and the Byzantines in Modern Turkish Popular Literature and Cinema   *Buket Kitapçı Bayrı*   159
10. Byzantium in Greek Cinema and Television   *Konstantinos Chryssogelos*   177

Part 3   Byzantium and Literature

11. 'Beware of Greeks Bearing Gifts': Byzantium in Czech Historical Fiction *Markéta Kulhánková*   193

12 Imagining Action: Explanation in Twentieth-Century Historiographical
    and Fictional Rewritings of the *Chronicle of Morea* Matthew Kinloch   207
13 The Barbarians Will Always Stay: Rose Macaulay and the Futility of
    Empire *Olof Heilo*   225
14 M. Karagatsis's Byzantinism in his *Sergios and Bacchos* (1959)
    Katerina Liasi   239
15 Fantastic(al) Byzantium: The Imagery of Byzantium in Speculative
    Fiction *Przemysław Marciniak*   249

Conclusion: No Longer a Forgotten Empire? *Przemysław Marciniak*   261

Afterword: Forging Textual Realities, or How to Write a 'Byzantine Mystery
Story' *Panagiotis Agapitos*   264
Index   272

Figures

1.1 General Plan of the Exhibition Grounds of the 1900 Paris World Exhibition. Source: *L'exposition de Paris (1900)*, vol. 1 Encyclopédie du siècle, Paris: Montgredien et Cie, supplément n. 16, provided by Smithsonian Libraries and Archives, https://library.si.edu/digital-library/book/expositiondepar1   13

1.2 Rue des Nations and Pavilions of the Sovereign Powers at the 1900 Paris World Exhibition. Source: Baschet, L. (1900), *Exposition Universelle de 1900. Guide Lemercier. Dictionnaire pratique des objets exposés et des Attractions*, Paris: Imprimeries Lemercier et Cie, plan G, provided by Bibliothèque nationale de France, https://gallica.bnf.fr/ark:/12148/bpt6k5496328d/f12.item   14

1.3 View of the Italian Pavilion from the Pont des Invalides at the 1900 Paris World Exhibition. Source: Baschet, L., ed. (1900), *Le Panorama. Exposition Universelle 1900*, Paris: Librairie d'art, Ludovic Baschet, provided by Universitätsbibliothek Heidelberg, https://digi.ub.uni-heidelberg.de/diglit/baschet1900/0110   15

1.4a View of the Serbian Pavilion at the 1900 Paris World Exhibition. Source: Baschet, L., ed. (1900), *Le Panorama. Exposition Universelle 1900*, Paris: Librairie d'art, Ludovic Baschet, provided by Universitätsbibliothek Heidelberg, https://digi.ub.uni-heidelberg.de/diglit/baschet1900/0046   16

1.4b View of the Greek Pavilion at the 1900 Paris World Exhibition. Source: Baschet, L., ed. (1900), *Le Panorama. Exposition Universelle 1900*, Paris: Librairie d'art, Ludovic Baschet, provided by Universitätsbibliothek Heidelberg, https://digi.ub.uni-heidelberg.de/diglit/baschet1900/009   17

1.4c View of the Romanian Pavilion at the 1900 Paris World Exhibition. Source: Baschet, L., ed. (1900), *Le Panorama. Exposition Universelle 1900*, Paris: Librairie d'art, Ludovic Baschet, provided by Universitätsbibliothek Heidelberg, https://digi.ub.uni-heidelberg.de/diglit/baschet1900/0032   18

1.4d View of the Bulgarian Pavilion at the 1900 Paris World Exhibition. Source: *L'exposition de Paris* (1900), vol. 2 Encyclopédie du Siècle, Paris: Montgredien et Cie, p. 201, provided by Smithsonian Libraries and Archives, https://library.si.edu/digital-library/book/expositiondepar2   19

viii *Figures*

2.1 Entrance of the Abbey of Saint-Gilles, Gard, after A. de Laborde (1818–36), *Les Monuments de la France classés chronologiquement et considérés sous le rapport des faits historiques et de l'étude des arts*, 2 vols, Paris: Jules Didot l'aîné, II: pl. CXXV 35
2.2 Church of St. Theodore, Athens, after A. Couchaud (1842), *Choix d'églises byzantines en Grèce*, Paris: Lenoir, pl. 8 37
2.3 The cathedral of St. Front, Périgueux, after F. de Verneilh (1851), *L'Architecture byzantine en France. Saint-Front de Périgueux et les églises à coupoles de l'Aquitaine*, Paris: V. Didron, pl. I 39
3.1 Costanzo da Ferrara, medal: Sultan Mehmed II, 1481. © Metropolitan Museum, New York 47
3.2 Portrait of Charles du Fresne, Sieur du Cange, 1698. From Charles Perrault (1698), *Les hommes illustres qui ont paru en France pendant ce Siècle: avec leurs Portraits au naturel*, Paris: chez Antoine Dezailler, not paginated 48
3.3 Aleksandr Vitberg, design of the Cathedral of Christ the Savior, 1817. Authors' photo 50
3.4 Konstantin Thon, design of the Cathedral of Christ the Savior, 1832. Authors' photo 51
3.5 Paul Abadie, Basilique du Sacré-Cœur, Paris, 1875–1923. © Private collection 53
3.6 Hermann Schaper, Mosaic of Wilhelm II and his family approaching the Cross, Kaiser-Wilhelm memorial church, Berlin, 1891–95. © N. Bock 54
3.7 David Grimm, Alexander Nevsky Cathedral, Tbilisi, 1871–72/1889–97. © Private collection 55
3.8 *Vizantija: uroki prošlogo i budušego dlja Rossii* [Byzantium: duties of the past and of the future for Russia], 2016. © KATEHON.com 60
4.1 Viktor Vasnetsov, baptism of Prince Vladimir (sketch). Courtesy of Nizhny Novgorod State Art Museum 70
4.2 Relief of Salavat Scherbakov behind the monument to St. Vladimir in the Kremlin (2016). Courtesy of Nina Arkhipova (2020) 73
4.3 The cathedral in Kubinka, lower church, the baptism of Vladimir Mosaic. Author's photo (2020) 76
9.1 Cover photo of Abdullah Ziya Kozanoğlu, *Battal Gazi Destanı* (1946). Public domain 160
13.1 Static components engendering a dynamic whole: the interplay of Byzantinism, classicism, orientalism and barbarism in 'Dirge for Trebizond'. Drawing by the author 233

Contributors

Panagiotis Agapitos is currently Gutenberg Research Fellow of Byzantine Studies at the University Mainz, having worked for twenty-five years at the University of Cyprus as Professor in the Department of Byzantine and Modern Greek Studies. His research interests focus on Byzantine literature, narratology, theory and practice of rhetoric, genre studies and cultural history. He has published over eighty papers on these topics, while his most recent book is a translation into English of the *Tale of Livistros and Rodamne* (2021), a Byzantine love romance of the thirteenth century. He is currently writing a narrative history of Byzantine literature.

Buket Kitapçı Bayrı's research interests are late Byzantine and early Ottoman social and cultural history, hagiography, medieval epics, identity, spatial studies, foundation stories of medieval cities, food history, perception of Byzantium in modern Turkish popular culture and Byzantine studies in Turkey. Her most recent monograph is *Warriors, Martyrs, and Dervishes. Moving Frontiers, Shifting Identities in the Land of Rome (13th–15th Centuries)* (2020).

Konstantinos Chryssogelos is Assistant Professor at the University of Patras (Department of Philology) in the Division of Byzantine and Modern Greek Studies. His research interests include Byzantine and post-Byzantine literature (fourth–eighteenth century) and the reception of the Byzantine past in modern Greece (nineteenth–twenty-first century). His most recent book is the critical edition of Constantine Manasses's *Hodoiporikon* (2017).

Lilia Diamantopoulou is Professor for Modern Greek Studies at Ludwig-Maximilians-University in the Department of Cultural Studies. Her research focuses on intermediality in modern Greek literature, visual poetry and comics and the practices of forgery and mystification in modern Greece. She is currently researching Greek migration in Germany and Black History in Greece.

Marco Fasolio is Lecturer in Latin Palaeography and Postdoctoral Fellow in Byzantine history at the University of Eastern Piedmont. His main research interests are within the field of Byzantine studies, with special focus on the relationships between Byzantium and northwestern Italy, Byzantine aristocracy, Byzantine splinter-states after the Fourth Crusade and Byzantine political ideology. He has published extensively on these topics and his first monograph, *Ai margini dell'Impero. Potere e aristocrazia a Trebisonda e in Epiro da Basilio II alla quarta crociata* (2022), deals with power and aristocracy in Trebizond and Epirus between Basil II and the Fourth Crusade.

Ivan Foletti is Full Professor at the Masaryk University. His research focuses on the history of art history and of Byzantine studies, the late antique and medieval art around the Mediterranean and in the south Caucasus. He uses social and anthropological approaches to explore the impact of migrations and pilgrimage on visual cultures. He is the Head of the Centre for Early Medieval Studies at the Masaryk University and editor-in-chief of the scholarly journal *Convivium*. His most recent monograph is *Objects, Relics, and Migrants: The Basilica of Sant'Ambrogio in Milan and the Cult of its Saints (386–972)* (2020).

Fani Gargova is Postdoctoral Researcher for the interdisciplinary project 'Synagogen-Gedenkbuch Hessen' at the Goethe University Frankfurt am Main. Previously, she was a Postdoctoral Assistant in Art History at the University of Vienna, Byzantine Research Associate at the Image Collections and Fieldwork Archives of Dumbarton Oaks, Harvard University, and project coordinator of the Digitales Forschungsarchiv Byzanz (DiFaB) at the University of Vienna. Her research interests include synagogue architecture and Jewish spaces, architectural Byzantinisms, medievalisms and orientalisms, as well as the historiography of Byzantine art history.

Olof Heilo is Director of the Swedish Research Institute in Istanbul. He earned his PhD at the Department of Byzantine and Modern Greek Studies in Vienna in 2010 and later taught history at the Centre for Middle Eastern Studies in Lund. In his research, he focuses on political narratives and the historical reception of empires in a wide sense, with particular attention given to the Eastern Christian and Islamic worlds. Together with Johanna Chovanec, he has edited the volume *Narrated Empires* (2021).

Matthew Kinloch is Research Fellow in the history of ideas at the University of Oslo. He is currently leading a comparative narratological and historiographical project, 'Narrative Hierarchies: Minor Characters in Byzantine and Medieval History Writing', funded by the Research Council of Norway. His principal research interests are Byzantine historiography, narratology, philosophy of history and gender/queer history.

Markéta Kulhánková works as Researcher at the Czech Academy of Sciences and Associate Professor at Masaryk University in Brno, Czech Republic. Her research focuses mainly on Byzantine narrative, both in verse and in prose, and she is currently working on the narratological commentary of the *Digenis Akritas* poem. She is also interested in the reception of Byzantium in modern culture and translates Byzantine and modern Greek literature into Czech. She published a monograph entitled *Das gottgefällige Abenteuer. Eine narratologische Analyse der byzantinischen erbaulichen Erzählungen* (2015).

Florin Leonte is Assistant Professor at the Department of Classics, Palacký University of Olomouc. Previously, he held teaching and research positions at Harvard University and Villa I Tatti, Florence. He has published articles and studies on late Byzantine rhetoric and society, epistolography, and the reception of classics. His new monograph is titled *Ethos, Logos, and Perspective Studies in Late Byzantine Rhetoric* (2023).

Katerina Liasi obtained her PhD from the Faculty of Humanities and Social Sciences of Open University of Cyprus. Her research interests focus on the reception of Byzantium by modern Greek literature, especially by the prose of the post-war and modern eras. Her research interests also include the developments of fictional biography, historical novel, historiographical metafiction, metahistorical novel and detective literature in Greek region.

Francesco Lovino is Research Fellow at the Università degli studi di Ferrara, Italy, where he is working on a project on Neo-Byzantine architecture in France and Italy in the nineteenth and twentieth century. He earned his PhD at the University of Padova in 2015. His research interests span from Byzantine illumination, medieval cartography and the reception of Byzantine art and imagery in the nineteenth and twentieth century.

Sofia Mali is Senior Lecturer in Contextual and Theoretical studies at the University of the Arts London. She was previously a Senior Lecturer in Cultural Theory at Buckinghamshire New University, and has also worked as a lecturer at the universities of Loughborough, Nottingham, Derby, Southampton Solent and Middlesex. Sofia is Section Editor for the Visual Culture section of the Open Cultural Studies Journal (De Gruyter). She has research and teaching interests in visual culture, art, design, fashion, curation and communication. She is also a curator and an exhibited artist with contributions to national and international art exhibitions.

Przemysław Marciniak is currently Gastprofessor für Kulturgeschichte des Altertums at the Münchner Zentrum für Antike Welten at Ludwig-Maximilians-University and Professor of Byzantine Literature at the University of Silesia in Poland. His research interests focus on Byzantine humour, the reception of Byzantium and recently on historical animal studies.

Adrien Palladino is Assistant Professor at the Department of Art History, Masaryk University, Brno, at the Centre for Early Medieval Studies. His interests include the history of art history, with a focus on 'Byzantium', the Caucasus and 'Romanesque' France in the nineteenth and first half of the twentieth century, as well as the study of late antique and early medieval material cultures, with a special interest in the interaction between objects, stories, spaces and people. His most recent book is *Inventing Late Antique Reliquaries* (2022).

Roman Shliakhtin is Postdoctoral Research Associate in the Research Training Group 2304, 'Byzantium and the Euro-Mediterranean Cultures of War. Exchange, Differentiation and Reception' at the University of Mainz. His research interests focus on Byzantine–Seljuk relations of the twelfth and thirteenth centuries, the history of medieval landscapes in Anatolia, perceptions of space in Byzantine rhetoric and the political history of twelfth-century Byzantium. He has published articles on the history of Byzantine-Seljuk relations of the twelfth century. He is also interested in the uses of Byzantium in Russian discourse from the fifteenth century to the present.

Introduction: The Many Faces of the Reception of Byzantium

Przemysław Marciniak

The reception of Byzantium, its culture and literature, is not a completely untouched phenomenon, even if considerably less popular than the reception of antiquity and the Western Middle Ages. Art and literature are undoubtedly two privileged areas of research – scholars have looked into how Eastern Empire art was imitated and how it inspired artists throughout the centuries (see, for instance, Bullen 2003) and how Byzantine motifs were recycled and used in literature (Konstantinou 1998). A recently published volume demonstrated a significant interest in Byzantine culture in pre-modern Europe (Aschenbrenner and Ranshoff 2022). Still, one area of Byzantine reception remains underrepresented – the (re)use of Byzantine motifs and inspiration in popular culture. Such a gap is, however, understandable – engaging with Byzantine reception in popular culture means exploration of a plethora of phenomena in diverse cultures and languages. Not to mention that we deal with a constantly expanding corpus. As a result, no study of the reception of Byzantium in the modern world can be complete.

In 2021, Istanbul's Pera Museum launched a successful exhibition titled '"What Byzantinism is this in Istanbul!" Byzantium in popular culture.' In the catalogue which accompanied the exhibition, scholars from across the globe discuss the presence of Byzantine motifs in cinema, metal music, video games, comics and speculative fiction. They demonstrate that Byzantium's acceptance spans modern culture's diverse media, and its reception has also entered popular culture. However, while the catalogue's authors offer varying definitions of Byzantinism, their understanding of popular culture is to be extrapolated by their choice of subject, which ranges from architecture through graphic novels to education.[1]

Popular culture and Byzantinism are indeed two terms critical for surveying the presence of the Eastern Empire in the modern period. However, both terms are difficult to pinpoint. Popular culture is often defined in opposition to *high culture*. It is a relatively recent phenomenon (Danesi 2019: 14); however, today the rigid distinction between 'high' and 'low' (popular) culture is less assured as concepts and ideas can travel both ways. Products of popular culture can contribute to a better understanding of a given phenomenon in the same way as (or even more efficiently than) scholarly efforts. Similarly, academic and non-academic perceptions of Byzantium are two intersecting areas. Charles Diehl previously noted this, remarking that people such as Victorien Sardou, Sarah Bernhardt and Jules Massenet (the author of the opera *Esclaramonde*) did more for Byzantium than many academic books (Diehl 1900: 11–12).

However, this volume more cautiously opts for a different, perhaps even fuzzier term, 'popular imagination'. This is an elusive concept that scholars have only recently conceptualized. Sven-Erik Klinkmann argues that 'a marking of imagination as popular imagination should be seen as a special, more limited kind of imagination; an imagination that resonates with an ambivalent Other, embedded both in cultural history and in the mass media of today' (2002: 60). Moreover, some researchers sharply contrast 'historical reality' and 'popular imagination' (Cufurovic 2018). It seems, however, that popular imagination could function as a collective mirror for an image of a particular event, historical period or geographical location, which is, to some extent, based on historical facts. Simultaneously it is culturally 'processed' (explained) and anchored in the contemporary reality of potential or implied receivers, a phenomenon 'popular' or influential enough to trigger a response in the broader public. This could include specific motifs in cinema and their presence in school textbooks, architecture and politics.

Therefore, the 'popular imagination' concept is more encompassing than 'popular culture'. Moreover, it seemed more fitting for the present volume since not all contributions here discuss the phenomena directly related to popular culture as such. For example, the first part of the volume surveys the presence of Byzantium and Byzantine motifs in architecture and museums. These are stories about the (re)construction of Byzantium, be it for political (Shliakhtin, Foletti and Palladino), aesthetic (Gargova) or educational purposes (Mali). These contributions also demonstrate that 'the popular' is rooted in various trends belonging to higher culture and scholarly endeavours, they explore how Byzantium, beginning in the nineteenth century, started playing a more prominent role in the popular imagination.

The many dangers of Byzantinism

The second term, which typically appears within discussions of Byzantium reception, is Byzantinism. This is a complex concept (at least for Byzantinists) as it is viewed as simultaneously anachronistic (as the appellation 'Byzantium' is a retronym), ideologically charged (since it was given to the empire rather than adopted by its inhabitants) and finally, somewhat comparable to or utterly different from orientalism. The 'n-gram-viewer', a tool developed to trace the frequency of words in books, available through Google Books, indicates how often this term was employed in books.[2] A more detailed look proves that when employed outside Byzantine studies, Byzantinism may mean virtually anything: it is used to describe the post-war political situation in the (future) communist countries; luxurious tendencies of the Sun King in France; to express the opposition to Levantinism; or listed among theocracy theism, and monarchism as a somewhat similar notion.

Consequently, any attempt to find a proper definition for this term recalls the story of the city Zangle ... *[sic!]* from the sci-fi novel *A Million Adventures* (1976), penned by the famous Russian writer Kir Bulychev. The committee responsible for naming the new city decided that anyone could call it as they saw fit, provided the name started with the word *Zangle*. Byzantinism has the same elasticity; it can take any shape and meaning depending on cultural and political circumstances.

This volume deliberately uses the appellation 'Byzantium' despite some contributors addressing the tension created by such a name (see the chapter by Foletti and Palladino). While academic discussions regarding the implications of using the anachronistic name of the Greek Empire might be of great importance for students of this period, they do not, at least not yet and not to a great extent, resonate in the world outside academia. Nevertheless, as foggy and artificial as it is, the notion of 'Byzantium' reigns supreme in the popular imagination.

Because of several negative connotations associated with the term Byzantium and its cognates, including Byzantinism,[3] students of Byzantium have a love-hate relationship with the latter concept. This is best summarized by Jan Olof Rosenqvist, who remarked that depending on one's evaluation of Byzantine culture, it can be seen as positive or negative, but mostly negative (Rosenqvist 2007: 214). Consequently, there is no room for a neutral definition of the concept, like 'Medievalism' or 'Neomedievalism', which would describe the field of studies rather than the emotional approach to the discipline.

Medievalism can be construed as the presentation and representation of the Middle Ages in various media and as the process of the intellectual examination of such presentations/representations (Coote 2010: 25). In 1977, Hedley Bull coined the term 'Neomedievalism' to describe an aspect of modern political relations. But more importantly, this concept was used – and popularized – by Umberto Eco. On the most general level, the difference between 'Medievalism' and 'Neomedievalism' is that the former 'implies a genuine link – sometimes direct, sometimes somewhat indirect – to the Middle Ages' while the latter 'invokes a simulacrum of the medieval' (Toswell 2010: 44). The difference between these two is sometimes explained, even if not always convincingly, by the fact that 'Neomedievalism' involves modern media and technology. Even though scholars debate both concepts, they serve as methodological frameworks to examine the medieval presence in contemporary culture.

Interestingly, there was no similar attempt to name and tackle the Byzantium phenomenon in modern/popular culture from the methodological point of view. The only chapter on Byzantium included in the volume on 'Neomedievalism' penned by Glenn Peers (2010: 77–113) does not even mention 'Byzantinism' or 'Neobyzantinism'. Regardless of whether this was intended, such caution is understandable as it may arise from a reluctance toward the heavily loaded term 'Byzantinism'. On the other hand, the adjective 'Neo-Byzantine' is used regarding the architectonic style of buildings inspired by Byzantine churches – and it is employed in precisely this sense by Gargova, Lovino and Shliakhtin in this volume. However, it can also have political undertones and can be used, for instance, to signify the revival of Byzantine or Constantinopolitan religious influences.[4] This complex heritage, coupled with recent attempts to eliminate the appellation 'Byzantium' altogether, does not make it simple to find the Eastern Roman counterpart of '(Neo)medievalism'.

Perhaps it is time to reset the meaning of 'Neobyzantinism' and start using it as a purely technical term describing the imagery of Byzantium in modern culture as broadly conceived. Like 'Neomedievalism', 'Neobyzantinism' could be construed as a representation of Byzantium in modern or digital media, as evidenced in the second part of this volume in the chapters written by Fasolio (videogames), Kitapçı Bayrı, Leonte, and Chryssogelos (cinema) and Diamantopoulou (graphic novels). The contributions included in the third part tackle a more traditional medium: literature. However, the authors often engage not so much with the presentation of Byzantium but rather, as Toswell put it, with the simulacrum, 'a neomedievalist text is one that is presented as a copy of an absent original, a sign that no longer speaks to a semiotic' (2010: 46). Texts discussed by Kulhánková, Kinloch, Heilo, Liasi and Marciniak demonstrate that the Byzantium image is mediated through and filtered by earlier (chronological) lenses, texts and preconceptions. They refer to a reality that is absent for most of their readership (which is why many of the novels include various authorial explanations and glossaries). Therefore, these texts might reflect the Byzantine reality, but they also build on earlier retellings and 'versions' of Byzantium.

There is some method to this madness

Volumes which deal with developing subfields of research in complicated and sometimes controversial topics cannot promise to deliver complete cohesion. This is the case with our collection as well. We chose instead to see our volume in terms of the 'mosaic novel' approach. In literature, a mosaic novel is one wherein individual chapters share a setting or a set of protagonists; it might be written by many authors, depict various viewpoints and present multiple styles and stories. As Jo Walton, a fantasy and science fiction writer, remarked in the introduction to the novel *China Mountain Zhang* by Maureen McHugh (1999), 'a mosaic novel builds up a picture of a world and a story obliquely, so that the whole is more than the sum of the parts'.

Various chapters in this collection tell different stories of one main protagonist – Byzantium (Eastern Roman Empire) – using different methodologies, materials and definitions of Byzantinism. They are as polyphonous as using and recycling Byzantine motifs in various media. However, they depict a fragment of a bigger story.

This volume is divided into three parts which cover three important areas of interaction with Byzantine cultural heritage: art/architecture, new media (cinema, graphic novels) and literature. We have opted for a thematic rather than geographical approach, focusing on the different media types.

As mentioned above, contributions from the first part demonstrate how Byzantium entered popular imagination through architecture, and how architecture can be used today to shape popular imagination and political propaganda. The chapter by Sofia Mali also tackles the presence of Byzantium in museums as perhaps the most obvious – but also not wholly unproblematic – way of creating points of contact with the Byzantine legacy.[5] The second part of the volume addresses the presence of the Eastern Empire in new media: from comics to cinema to videogames. The three contributions on cinema focus on the imagery of Byzantium in cultures with different types of relationships with Byzantium: Greece, Turkey and Romania. Understandably, the image of Byzantium is shaped by past relationships and political propaganda.

Interestingly enough, the presentation of the Eastern Empire in graphic novels and videogames seems to be much less influenced by local political and social conditions (but there are always exceptions to the rule, as in the case of graphic novels published in Greece). The third part of the collection focuses on Byzantine motifs in literature. This is perhaps the most diversified part of the volume as it encompasses the chapters on British, Greek and Czech literature and a more general contribution on speculative literature. These contributions demonstrate how Byzantine elements were recycled under different socio-historical conditions and in various languages. All the chapters in this part discuss either texts not easily accessible to a broader readership or which were once popular but today have fallen into oblivion.

This volume is rounded out by the text penned by a prolific Byzantinist, Panagiotis Agapitos, who also authors detective stories set in Byzantium. He is not an isolated exception, however; Arkady Martine (the pen name for AnnaLinden Weller), the author of the Hugo award-winning novel *A Memory Called Empire* (2019), holds a PhD in Byzantine Studies. Her novel is, in fact, based on her research on medieval Armenia. It is also worth recalling that the great Isaac Asimov penned a history of Byzantium titled *Constantinople. The Forgotten Empire* (1970), wherein his vision of the Empire is undeniably positive:

'So few westerners realized that in the centuries when Paris and London were ramshackle towns, with streets of mud and hovels of wood, there was a queen city in the East that was rich in gold, filled with works of art, bursting with gorgeous churches, busy with commerce – the wonder and the admiration of all who saw it' (Asimov 1970: 1).

This volume hopes to demonstrate the similarities and differences in Byzantium's reception in modern culture. These approaches build on earlier ideas and stereotypes, which can be similar for numerous cultures and languages because they originate from earlier popular texts. On the other hand, these chapters show that the imagery of Byzantium can be modified to serve various purposes, but it also evolves. Modern imagination does not feed on one singular, heavily influential text portraying Byzantine history. In pre-modern times there was a popular work by Cardinal Baronius (*Annales Ecclesiastici*, 1588–1607, heavily criticized by Protestants), which was later superseded by Edward Gibbon's *Decline and Fall of the Roman Empire* (1776–89). The picture became more varied from the nineteenth century onwards, with certain texts enjoying more popularity than others. There is no single guide, no one dominant narrative anymore – works become more polyphonous because they are based on various textbooks. And finally, one cannot underestimate the increased access to translations and information afforded by the internet. As with the mosaic novel, the chapters of this volume offer a view of the reception of the Byzantium/Eastern Empire that is larger than the sum of its parts.

***

This volume arises from a conference that took place in Brno in 2017 and was part of the activities of the network of scholars working on the reception of Byzantium funded by the Alexander von Humboldt Stiftung (2014–18). The University of

Silesia also generously supported its preparation under the programme 'Initiative of Excellence (IDUB)'. We are also grateful to Yasmin Garcha and Rory Gormley, our editors, for their patience and help. We extend our gratitude to Chrysa Sakel and Theocharis Spyros, the creators of *Byzantine Tales*, for allowing us to use an image from one of their graphic novels.

It is desirable to achieve some sort of cohesion while transliterating Byzantine names. However, such a cohesion was hardly possible in this volume. The contributors often use forms as they were employed by the authors whose works are referred to. We have decided that this degree of inconsistency is permissible and, what is perhaps even more important, it also shows one more aspect of the reception of Byzantium.

Notes

1. Alışık (2021: 15): 'A number of the authors here suggest coining a term to define Byzantinism in the material they have evaluated [...] Betancourt calls this Byzantinism paratextual; Lifshitz, incidental; Fasolio, quasi.'
2. This tool is of course imperfect and can only be used to indicate some tendencies as the results will include second editions of the books and, of course, there is no way to differentiate between the modern uses and quotations of older authors.
3. On this term, see Aerts (1993: 311–24).
4. See, for instance, Mikaberidze (2020: 374–75) regarding the attempt of the Phanariots 'to revive Byzantine practices by empowering the Orthodox Patriarchate of Constantinople'.
5. For a useful catalogue of Byzantine exhibitions see Chondrogiannis (2018).

Bibliography

Aerts, R. (1993), 'Dull Gold and Gory Purple: Images of Byzantium', in H. Hokwerda, E. R. Smits and M. M. Woesthuis (eds.), *Polyphonia Byzantina: Studies in Honour of Willem J. Aerts*, 311–24, Groningen: Forsten.

Alışık, E., ed. (2021), *'What is This Byzantinism in Istanbul!': Byzantium in Popular Culture*, Istanbul: Kasım.

Aschenbrenner, N. and Ranshoff, J., eds. (2022), *The Invention of Byzantium in Early Modern Europe*, Washington, DC: Dumbarton Oaks Research Library and Collection.

Asimov, I. (1970), *Constantinople: The Forgotten Empire*, Boston: Houghton Mifflin.

Bullen, J. B. (2003), *Byzantium Rediscovered: The Byzantine Revival in Europe and America*, London: Phaidon Press.

Chondrogiannis, S. T. (2018), *Byzantium in the World: Artistic, Cultural and Ideological Legacy from the 19th to 21st Century*, Thessaloniki: Centre for Byzantine Research, Aristotle University of Thessaloniki.

Coote, L. (2010), 'A Short Essay about Neomedievalism', in K. Fugelso (ed.), *Defining Neomedievalism(s)*, 25–33, Cambridge: D.S. Brewer.

Cufurovic, M. (2018), 'Popular Imagination versus Historical Reality. What Does HBO's Rome Reveal about the Practice of History?', *Public History Review*, 25: 1–11.

Danesi, M. (2019), *Pop Culture: Introductory Perspective*, Lanham, MD: Rowman & Littlefield.
Diehl, Ch. (1900), 'Les études byzantines en France', *Byzantinische Zeitschrift*, 9: 1–13.
Klinkmann, S.-E. (2002), 'Theorizing Popular Imagination', in S.-E. Kirkmann (ed.), *Popular Imagination: Essays on Fantasy and Cultural Practice*, Turku: Nordic Network of Folklore.
Konstantinou, E., ed. (1998), *Byzantinische Stoffe und Motive in der europäischen Literatur des 19. Und 20. Jahrhunderts*, Frankfurt a. M.: Peter Lang.
Mikaberidze, A. (2020), *The Napoleonic Wars: A Global History*, Oxford: Oxford University Press.
Peers, G. (2010), 'Utopia and Heterotopia: Byzantine Modernisms in America', in K. Fugelso (ed.), *Defining Neomedievalism(s)*, 77–113, Cambridge: D.S. Brewer.
Rosenqvist, J. O. (2007), *Die byzantinische Literatur: vom 6. Jahrhundert bis zum Fall Konstantinopels 1453*, Berlin and New York: De Gruyter.
Toswell, M. J. (2010), 'The Simulacrum of Neomedievalism', in K. Fugelso (ed.), *Defining Neomedievalism(s)*, 44–57, Cambridge: D.S. Brewer.

Part One

Byzantium on Display: Scholarly Debates, Political Uses, Modern Reconstructionism

1

Popularizing Byzantine Architecture: The 1900 Paris World Exhibition, Balkan Nationalisms and the Byzantine Revival

Fani Gargova

The World Exhibitions of the late nineteenth and early twentieth centuries can be considered as *the* events synonymous with the popularization of ideas of 'progress' and the modern imagination (Geppert 2010). They were attended by millions of international visitors and, as such, acted as the most effective, wide-ranging and far-reaching forums for the dissemination of trends, knowledge and ideologies. Therefore, the means of representing the 'nation' and its technological, cultural and artistic accomplishments for those invited to partake as sovereign countries was of paramount and lasting importance.[1]

This chapter deals with the impact of the 1900 Paris World Exhibition on the reception, research and revival of Byzantine architecture and shows how this particular event acted as a watershed moment in the historiography of Byzantine art and architecture, the importance of which stemmed, in particular, from the role Byzantine references played in the new 'national' styles of the young Balkan states. Unlike previous studies that focus on the years leading up to the World Exhibition and the event proper (Dobreva 2007; Hajdu 2015; Ignjatović 2015), I argue that the primary importance of the 1900 Paris World Exhibition derived from the discussions, initiatives and buildings that ultimately shaped the Balkan nations in the following two decades.[2]

In the long series of World Exhibition events, the one in Paris in 1900 holds a special place for the popularization of 'the Byzantine' in architecture, the arts and the general discourse, because of its sheer grandiosity and the fact that, for the first time, all countries whose territory once constituted the Byzantine Empire were presenting themselves with their own pavilions and additional participation in numerous fair competitions.[3] Also for the first time, a great number of structures and artistic objects from various countries extensively used Byzantinizing elements and motifs to denote a certain idea of the 'national'. There had been only singular instances of the employment of the Byzantine revival earlier, such as the Tiffany chapel for the 1893 Chicago World's Fair (Bullen 2005: 200–10). The important distinction, however, is that in 1900 several countries claimed Byzantium, or at least its architectural and artistic legacy, as their own 'national' heritage and, therefore, exhibited a wide variety of Neo-Byzantine buildings next to each other.

The 1900 Paris World Exhibition

Plans for this World Exhibition began as early as 1889, during the previous World Exhibition which took place in Paris, with authorities officially deciding in 1892 that the city would host another grand event in 1900.[4] Its main purpose was to act as an overview of human accomplishments of the nineteenth century and give an outlook into the progress that was believed to come during the twentieth century. First architectural competitions for the varied thematic and monumental buildings and gardens were opened in 1894, albeit only for French architects.[5] Large-scale constructions for the 1900 event began as early as 1896. Some of these then-new structures still define the urban landscape of Paris today. Prominent examples include the Pont Alexandre III, the Grand Palais and the Petit Palais (*Volume Annexe Du Catalogue Général Officiel 1900*: 9–23).

The official invitation to 'foreign' nations to participate in the World Exhibition was sent out in 1897.[6] To be included in this list of perceived 'equal' nations was a great honour for many of the young and small Balkan states who saw it as confirmation that they were considered sovereign states by the 'great powers' even when, in fact, they were still not entirely independent from a sovereign empire. This was the case, for instance, with Bulgaria and Bosnia-Herzegovina.[7] It was a unique opportunity to showcase their commitment and belonging to the 'progress'-oriented and 'civilized' nations.[8] They were given their own voice, unlike many 'foreign' and especially Indigenous cultures which were only represented through the eyes of French 'explorateurs' and, therefore, exhibited through much Othering, exoticism and orientalism (*L'exposition de Paris (1900)* 1900a: 1:118–200 *passim*). This Othering stance, which was mirrored in the exhibition layout, divided the world into, broadly speaking, those that were considered 'civilized' people and those seen as 'non-civilized', 'savage' or 'primitive' (Figure 1.1) (*L'exposition de Paris (1900)* 1900b: 2:231–32, 316–18).[9] It was especially reinforced by the area of the exhibition that was devoted to the colonies (*L'exposition de Paris (1900)* 1900a: 1:211–51 *passim*; *L'exposition de Paris (1900)* 1900b: 2:79–280 *passim*). In this bigoted presentation of the 'world' in the World Exhibition, Greece, Serbia, Bulgaria, Romania, Bosnia-Herzegovina and Hungary were given a space and thus the possibility to show their belonging to the 'foreign powers'[10] along the Rue des Nations (Figure 1.2).

This spatial separation is clearly emphasized in the plans of the exhibition grounds (Figure 1.1): from the main entrance on the Place de la Concorde on the northern bank of the Seine, visitors were first directed toward the Grand and Petit Palais with exhibits of French art,[11] then by passing the Pont Alexandre III they reached the Esplanade des Invalides, whose eastern end was reserved for the showcasing of French craft and industrial accomplishments, while the western side housed the 'foreign' crafts section.[12] Continuing further west along the southern Seine river bank followed the Rue des Nations proper with the national pavilions of the 'foreign powers'. It was divided into a front row, which was more visible as it lay on the bank of the Seine, and a second, more hidden, row along the Quai d'Orsay behind it. Those national pavilions that employed Byzantine elements were the highly visible ones of Italy, Greece and Serbia along the front row, as well as Bulgaria and Romania along the second row.[13] Further to the west followed the pavilions devoted to hygiene and the army and navy.

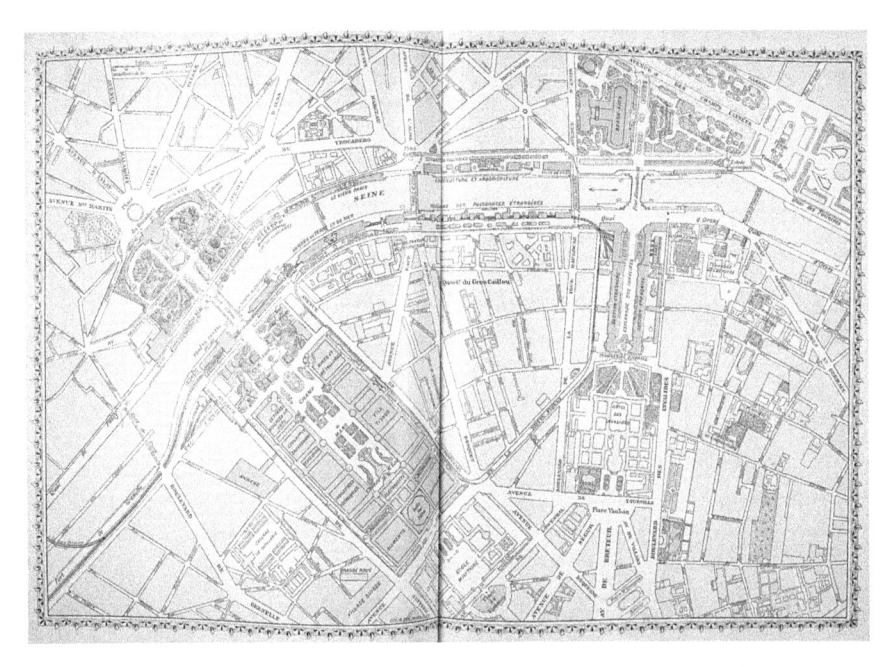

Figure 1.1 General Plan of the Exhibition Grounds of the 1900 Paris World Exhibition. Source: *L'exposition de Paris (1900)* (1900a), supplément n. 16, provided by Smithsonian Libraries and Archives, https://library.si.edu/digital-library/book/expositiondepar1.

Then, along the Champ de Mars, the host and the 'great powers' were given additional space to showcase their technological, industrial, commercial or cultural singularities and accomplishments.[14] (Colonial) mechanisms of amazement and Othering were also combined in the pavilions closest to the river banks by including a Cour des Miracles, Venise à Paris, but also a special Palais de la Femme, and the pavilions of Morocco, Siam, St. Martin and Ecuador (Baschet 1900a: map K). The latter countries were thus denied the status as 'foreign powers' along the Rue des Nations. Then, passing over the Pont d'Iéna, visitors arrived at the area called Trocadéro, the vast space reserved for the French and 'foreign' colonies.[15] Orientalist attitudes were also well served and stirred in this section with additional attractions such as an entirely anachronistic 'Moorish Andalusia' (Baschet 1900a: 184–86; *L'exposition de Paris (1900)* 1900b, 2: 191–92).[16] On the same northern river bank continuing to the east followed a reconstruction of 'Old Paris', another Othering instance; in this case, however, a medievalism toward the own Parisian medieval 'Other' within (*L'exposition de Paris (1900)* 1900a, 1: 65–66, 78–80, 95–98; *L'exposition de Paris (1900)* 1900b, 2: 25–26, 47–48).[17] Finally, passing by the horticulture and arboriculture exhibition and the pavilion of the city of Paris, visitors returned to the main entrance. Therefore, the distinction between 'civilized' and 'progressive' on the southern bank and 'backward' or 'primitive' on the northern bank of the Seine was spatially emphasized, and visitors were constantly reminded of this separation.

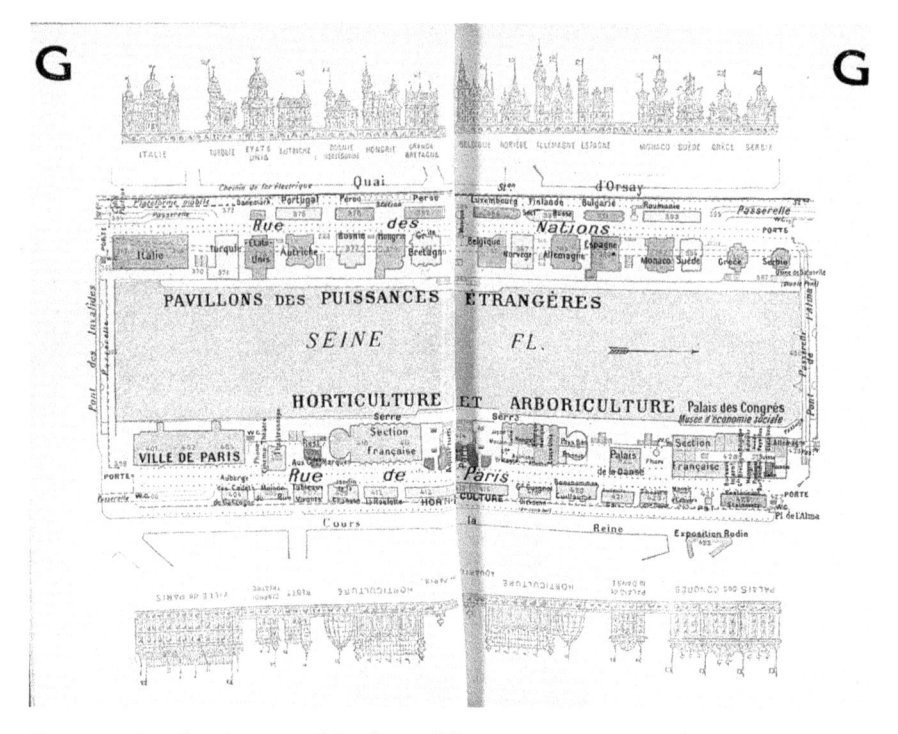

Figure 1.2 Rue des Nations and Pavilions of the Sovereign Powers at the 1900 Paris World Exhibition. Source: Baschet (1900a), plan G, provided by Bibliothèque nationale de France, https://gallica.bnf.fr/ark:/12148/bpt6k5496328d/f12.item.

The national pavilions of the Balkan States

The invitation to the Balkan countries to take part in the 1900 Paris World Exhibition through 'national' pavilions prompted the question of what constitutes and how to define a 'national' architecture, an architecture that would unmistakably differentiate the 'I',[18] or the own nation, from the other neighbouring countries. In this respect, Romanian and Serbian architects were better equipped to address this issue, as they had been dealing with the question of a 'national' style since the 1860s and 1870s. Romanian professionals became aware of the question of style in relation to the representation of the nation through the influence of their training at the Parisian École des Beaux-Arts and the country's participation through a national pavilion at the previous World Exhibition in Paris in 1889 (Hajdu 2009; Popescu 2013; Minea 2015). French scholarship also exercised great influence through particularly early architectural surveys and studies in Romania, which soon identified the Episcopal Church in Curtea de Argeș and the Stavropoleos church in Bucharest as exceptional for the Balkan region and emblematic within Romanian architectural historiography (Popescu 1998; Minea 2016). On the other hand, Serbian architects studied in Vienna with Theophil Hansen and made his understanding of the Byzantine style their programmatic standard (Jovanović 1985; Pantelić 1997; Ignjatović 2014; Kadijevic 2016). In both the Serbian and Romanian cases, with minor variations, a recurrence of Byzantine motifs as a sign of belonging to Orthodox Christianity seemed fitting. Therefore, in a gesture very common in Western Europe, or, more specifically, in works derived from the architectural schools of Paris and Vienna, the earliest 'national' buildings employed a generic Neo-Byzantine style that was identified through domes, round arches and a striped façade. These characteristics also became common motifs at the 1900 World Exhibition and, therefore, beyond differentiating strategies, made the common reference to Byzantine architecture apparent.

Located at the corner of the Pont des Invalides and the Seine riverbank, the pavilion of Italy was the largest and most visible one showing Byzantine elements (Figure 1.3). The structure, reminiscent of San Marco and general Venetian architecture, was designed by three Italian architects: Carlo Ceppi, Constantino Gilodi and Giacomo Salvadori. Although the reference to San Marco and consequently to Byzantine architecture is conspicuous, exhibition guides, press and overall feedback characterized the Italian pavilion as a structure in the Southern Gothic style, mainly because of the extensive Neo-Gothic ornamentation on the façade of the structure (Baschet 1900a: 92; *L'exposition de Paris (1900)* 1900b, 2: 159–60; *Paris exposition 1900: guide pratique du visiteur de Paris et de l'exposition* 1900; Picard 1903, 5: 64–66). Therefore, this stylistically eclectic structure was clearly not perceived as Byzantinizing

Figure 1.3 View of the Italian Pavilion from the Pont des Invalides at the 1900 Paris World Exhibition. Source: Baschet (1900b), provided by Universitätsbibliothek Heidelberg, https://digi.ub.uni-heidelberg.de/diglit/baschet1900/0110.

by contemporaries as it operated with the specific reference of the city of Venice as a whole and consequently incorporated the entire spectrum of Ruskinian forms, which have ever since oscillated between orientalism, Byzantinism and an Othered Gothic (Crinson 1996: 48–61, 81–87; Bullen 2003: 119–31; Nelson 2010).

On the other end of the front row of the Rue des Nations, the Serbian and Greek pavilions stood next to each other, with the Serbian one being more prominent, as it was directly visible from the Pont de l'Alma. For the Serbian pavilion, as for the Serbian 'national' style in general, the use of the Byzantine style was preferred because of its connotation with a glorious Christian Orthodox history during the Middle Ages. In the wake of the 1900 Paris World Exhibition, Serbian architects expanded their Hansenian Byzantine style by turning to vernacular cultural heritage for inspiration and possible models, which would conveniently be associated with a great Serbian medieval history. The World Exhibition pavilion by the architect Milan Kapetanović, with final modifications by Ambroise Baudry[19] (Figure 1.4a), was consequently a precursor of what would later form the so-called 'Serbo-Byzantine style', which shared motifs with the 'Byzantine style', but which was enriched with distinct Serbian vernacular elements, such as the smaller domes on the four corners (*L'exposition de Paris (1900)* 1900b, 2: 161–62; Picard 1903, 5: 86–87).[20] Therefore, the Serbian pavilion is noteworthy as being one of the first buildings to fulfil the goal of showcasing a Serbian 'national'

Figure 1.4a View of the Serbian Pavilion at the 1900 Paris World Exhibition. Source: Baschet (1900b), provided by Universitätsbibliothek Heidelberg, https://digi.ub.uni-heidelberg.de/diglit/baschet1900/0046.

architecture (Pantelić 1997, 2007; Ignjatović 2014, 2016; Kadijevic 2016; Merenik, Simić and Borozan 2016).

Guidebooks often remark that the Serbian and Greek pavilions (Figure 1.4b), which stood side by side, perfectly complemented each other because of their common recurrence to Byzantine architecture (e.g. *L'exposition de Paris (1900)* 1900b, 2: 162). During the same period, Greece, unlike its Balkan neighbours, did not seem interested in its Byzantine heritage. Consequently, the country's participation at the World Exhibition with a Neo-Byzantine structure is most surprising (Magouliotis 2018).

The Greek pavilion was designed by a French architect, Lucien Magne (Baschet 1900a: 122–24; Picard 1903, 5: 60–61). Neither the appointment of this architect, who was already a professor at the École des Beaux-Arts, nor his decision to erect a Neo-Byzantine building are coincidental. Following two fieldwork campaigns in 1894–95, Magne created a study on the state of preservation of the Parthenon in Athens commissioned by the French government in consultation with the Greek government.[21] During this time, he also actively chose to visit a good number of Byzantine monuments in Athens, Hosios Loukas and Daphni, as well as Corinth, Argos and Mistra in the Peloponnese (Magne 1895: v). Magne was aware of and fascinated by Gabriel Millet's work on the Byzantine monuments of Mistra, and his personal interest in the site led to him publishing two articles detailing his own observations both in written form and in original photographs (Magne 1897a, 1897b). The latter

Figure 1.4b View of the Greek Pavilion at the 1900 Paris World Exhibition. Source: Baschet (1900b), provided by Universitätsbibliothek Heidelberg, https://digi.ub.uni-heidelberg.de/diglit/baschet1900/009.

he also exhibited at the Musée du Trocadéro. Therefore, it is apparent that the Greek pavilion at the 1900 World Exhibition drew on the architect's local studies in Athens[22] and Mistra rather than Greece's wish to portray a supposed 'national style'.

Along the second row stood the Romanian pavilion (Figure 1.4c), also designed by a leading French architect, Jean-Camille Formigé. Similarly to Magne, Formigé's significant architectural accomplishments included surveys and restorations of antique and medieval buildings, albeit in this case on French soil.[23] Significant for the reception and revival of Byzantine architecture, however, is his design for the crematorium in the

Figure 1.4c View of the Romanian Pavilion at the 1900 Paris World Exhibition. Source: Baschet (1900b), provided by Universitätsbibliothek Heidelberg, https://digi.ub.uni-heidelberg.de/diglit/baschet1900/0032.

Cimetière du Père-Lachaise built in 1887–89 (see the original plans in Musée d'Orsay ARO 1992 21, 1992 34 and 1992 35), which exhibits common motifs such as a striped façade, a central dome and round-arched openings derived from a late nineteenth-century French academic understanding of the Byzantine style.[24] Therefore, otherwise unfamiliar with specifically Romanian architecture,[25] Formigé used his familiarity with the Byzantine style in combination with the established idea of Romanian architecture derived from French and Romanian scholarship for his design of the 1900 Romanian pavilion (Minea 2014: 89–102). The resulting solution was not straightforward, as evidenced by the variety and number of preliminary projects that Jean-Camille Formigé prepared.[26] Conveniently, the resulting appearance coincided well with the conception of a Romanian 'national' style, even though it was dismissed as a false pastiche and a foreign invention by Romanian intellectuals (Hajdu 2015: 57). The pavilion's design remained overall Neo-Byzantine by exhibiting a large central dome and a striped façade. Still, it skilfully incorporated unmistakably Romanian markers: twisted drums, elaborate sculptural relief work showing rosettes framed by arches, a cornice of blind interlacing arches and three-lobed arch corbels. All these motifs were drawn from signature Romanian buildings such as Curtea de Argeș (Popescu 1998, 2013, 2009; Minea 2016; Hajdu 2017: 416–28).

Finally, the last pavilion of a Balkan country, Bulgaria (Figure 1.4d), was also designed by two French architects, Henri Saladin and Henri de Sévelinges

Figure 1.4d View of the Bulgarian Pavilion at the 1900 Paris World Exhibition. Source: *L'exposition de Paris (1900)* (1900b), p. 201, provided by Smithsonian Libraries and Archives, https://library.si.edu/digital-library/book/expositiondepar2.

(Picard 1903, 5: 47), despite the fact that the debate on what constitutes an appropriate 'Bulgarian national style' was already in full swing among Bulgarian architects of the time (see, e.g. Kozarov 1900). Saladin was an orientalist architect (Bacha 2009).[27] Notably, he also designed the Tunisian and Moroccan pavilions for the 1900 World Exhibition.[28] De Sévelinges had mostly been involved in archaeological work in modern-day Iraq.[29] Consequently, neither familiar with Bulgarian local architecture nor with the Bulgarian architectural debates, the two architects created an idiosyncratic mixture of Byzantine and Ottoman elements, which by the French press and public was perceived as particularly successful through the combination of the history of the country (Baschet 1900a: 116; Picard 1903, 5: 47). The Bulgarian reviews, on the other hand, saw it as tasteless and completely foreign to their identity (Tornyov 1900: 234; Dobreva 2007: 132–43).

In particular, the Bulgarian press felt that the 'oriental' elements were not appropriate to represent the country because the direct visual comparison on the grounds of the 1900 World Exhibition showed that 'oriental' elements were markers of a Muslim country, as was the case with the pavilions of Turkey or Bosnia, in opposition to Byzantine elements that were used as markers for Christian countries (Popescu 2011: 825). The relevance of this context has been pointed out by a good number of recent studies on the Byzantinizing pavilions at the Paris World Exhibition, which conclude that the use of the Neo-Byzantine in the pavilions of the Balkan countries was a matter of conscious competition (Dobreva 2007; Hajdu 2015; Ignjatović 2015; Minea 2015). While this aspect seems like a plausible explanation, I would argue that in none of the four Balkan pavilions was any use of Byzantine elements determined from within, but rather from the point of view of the French architects commissioned to design these pavilions. Reactions from, for instance, Bulgarian architects and intellectuals confirm this complex of not being adequately represented, as they praise the pavilions of the neighbouring countries for their appropriate use of Byzantine elements. They expressed that such a Byzantine appearance would also have been appropriate for the Bulgarian pavilion because of the shared Christian heritage (Dobreva 2007: 136–38). Ultimately, this consciousness of and insistence on deriving much of their own heritage from a common shared and, above all, Christian history remained a recurrent motif in all 'national' architecture debates of Serbia, Romania, Greece and Bulgaria.

From the perspective of the French architects tasked with designing the national pavilions, the Byzantine revival seemed to be the most accurate characterization of those countries by way of their historical and confessional specificities. Even though they did not have much previous first-hand knowledge and, except for Magne, who designed the Greek pavilion, had only once visited the country they were representing with their pavilions, the French architects seemed to have a preliminary idea that they could project on their structures. Whether this projection was correct and appropriate is debatable. However, these clear preconceived ideas point to an already large enough corpus of scholarly and theoretical material on Byzantine architecture available in French that served as the basis and inspiration and gave the necessary architectural motifs.[30] Ultimately, the mere existence of five pavilions using Neo-Byzantine motifs or variations thereof, some of which were highly visible, meant that an idea of the 'Byzantine' was seen by nearly fifty million French and international visitors. Therefore, beyond Sardou's *Theodora* or Ruskin's *Stones of Venice* (Nelson 2004: 51–72; Boeck 2015), the far-reaching popularization of Byzantium among the diverse public in Paris in 1900 should not be underestimated.

The aftermath of the 1900 World Exhibition: defining national cultural heritage

Once the first reactions from the press at the World Exhibition reached the individual Balkan countries, a more intensified debate on how to identify the vernacular, 'national' or 'local' by way of architecture set in, the special question being how to accomplish differentiating the own country and its medieval and Byzantine legacy from that of the neighbouring countries (Stoilova and Yokimov 2002; Ignjatović 2016; Hajdu 2017; Loyer 2020). It is apparent that this was prompted by the direct comparison with other representational pavilions on-site in Paris. The discourse among Bulgarian architects will, in this second part of the chapter, serve to exemplify this point in the Bulgarian context. Slightly modified, though, the discourse also applied to Serbia or Romania; the outcome of these debates was, however, fundamentally different.

As soon as the perceived 1900 World Exhibition disaster was digested, the *Journal of the Bulgarian Engineering-Architectural Society* (*BIAD*) published comprehensive critiques on the lack of a style that Bulgarians could call their own (Tornyov 1900). By 1902, this critique was also contextualized through the more theoretically focused discussion on aesthetics and their meaning in architecture. This internal debate was guided by Western European discourses and the adoption of Western architectural theories (cf. Koychev 1902).

During the same period, a major new concern among architectural theorists and practitioners became the need to get acquainted with the historical monuments on Bulgarian soil. In 1904, this quest culminated in the first book ever dealing with the history of Bulgarian architecture (Chamardjieff 1904). The occasion and motivation for this publication was, unsurprisingly, a World Exhibition, the one at Saint Louis in the United States. There, Bulgarian architects once again competed and contrasted with other nations. However, the overarching architectural questions prompted in Paris remained a matter of concern: what constitutes the country's cultural and architectural heritage? And how can Bulgarian architects employ this heritage to create a Bulgarian 'national' style? I argue that a key reason for this problem to remain unsolved was that the focus of the quest had always been on a foreign target audience and their perception of Bulgarian architecture. The 'Bulgarianness' of cultural heritage was not a question of a vernacular need defined from within for the local circumstances. At its core, this quest was a representational device aimed to show belonging to the 'civilized world'.[31]

Consequently, this first book on the history of Bulgarian architecture was not published in Bulgarian but only in French. The author detailed a wide range of architectural heritage on Bulgarian soil, from prehistoric to modern. In this, he does not shy away from defining all Bulgarian medieval Christian heritage, which would have ideally constituted the Bulgarian 'national' highlight, as being in the 'Byzantine style'. He concludes that, for instance, the architecture of the churches in Pliska, Tarnovo or Nesebar 'ont été construites en style purement byzantine. C'est là qu'on peut voir le développement graduel du style byzantin en Bulgarie [...] parmi les monuments les plus importants de la Bulgarie' (Chamardjieff 1904: 7). Therefore, the comparably few preserved medieval monuments were not 'purely' or 'uniquely' Bulgarian, and they were quickly vanishing (Tornyov 1904: 99). The reasons for the problem of finding a suitable Bulgarian 'national' style thus became apparent: the characteristics of most preserved or known architecture on Bulgarian soil could only be attributed to foreign cultural imprints or foreign sovereignty, such as the Byzantine.

The author also detailed contemporary reasons for the lack of suitable model buildings for the 'national' style: much of the 'old' heritage had been destroyed in the years following Bulgaria's independence in the name of modernization and 'progress'. Only through the intensified phase of new church construction that set in by the mid-1890s did Bulgarian architects start researching Bulgarian historical church architecture, which resulted in the employment of the 'Byzantine style' but defined as 'local' (Chamardjieff 1904: 28).

The discourse on the question of national heritage and the publication of relevant monuments continued in the *BIAD* throughout the rest of the decade. At this point, however, the underlying question of national heritage and its fundamental relevance for establishing a 'national' style gained centre stage. Consequently, because of their 'national importance' and their possible model character for future architecture, these debates were accompanied by a call for the preservation and thorough study of the relevant medieval monuments (see Usta-Genchov 1905, 1906; Koychev 1907a, 1907b, among the many examples).

In 1910, during the second congress of Bulgarian engineers and architects, the architect Koychev gave a presentation on the importance of preserving 'national monuments' of 'Bulgarian culture', 'tradition' and 'character' (Koychev 1910b: 10). According to him, this architectural, artistic and folklore heritage was in danger of being completely lost because of neglect and the aggressive urban regulation plans of the time. As a consequence, he called for a collective resolution by the congress to ensure that the Bulgarian government creates a 'committee for the preservation of the artistic treasures in the country' (Koychev 1910a: 189), which would take on the responsibility to classify and document the cultural heritage and ensure its preservation. As expected, Koychev's argument of importance ultimately came back to helping inspire the 'national character' of future architecture in Bulgaria.

In this quest, the Byzantine heritage of Bulgaria was eventually embraced because it was unmistakably linked to a glorious medieval and, above all, Christian past, even though the 'Byzantine style' yielded little uniqueness in comparison with the neighbouring Balkan nations. This happened against the backdrop of the recent independence from the Ottoman Empire and, therefore, a profound negation that anything Ottoman or Muslim could ever be associated with the Bulgarian character, identity or culture (cf. for instance Stanoeva 2013).

The idea of a 'Bulgarian national style' did, of course, not remain only theoretical. Starting in 1900, a good number of prominent and monumental structures were erected in a supposed 'national style', above all, in the capital Sofia (Stoilova and Yokimov 2002; Hajdu 2017; also Hajdu 2022 for an unrealized project). Among those are the Holy Synod, the Central Baths and the Central Market Halls. Looking at these buildings, however, the struggle to define what is 'national' is evident, as they remain, with few exceptions, overall generically Neo-Byzantine.

While in Bulgaria, a 'national' style could ultimately not be defined, the years following the Paris 1900 World Exhibition saw Serbia and Romania rediscover their vernacular unique heritage, which, contrary to Bulgaria, they, indeed, had preserved (Pantelić 1997; Kallestrup 2002; Ignjatović 2014, 2016; Hajdu 2017: 409–39). There, it resulted in constructions mimicking, in detail, the proud local heritage, which there, too, was identified and considered as worthy of national heritage protection. These developments, notable throughout the Balkans, saw an abrupt end with the two Balkan Wars and the First World War, which left the entire region, more or less, in a state of ruin.

In conclusion, the 1900 Paris World Exhibition was a watershed moment for the reception of Byzantine architecture and modern Byzantine revival buildings. To the international public in the French capital, this World Exhibition gave the opportunity to extensively engage, for the first time, with 'Byzantium' through the lens of Neo-Byzantine structures, raising the awareness for both the history of Byzantine heritage, but also, more specifically, for the ways that the Balkan successor states defined themselves through their common Orthodox Christian heritage. For Bulgaria, Greece, Romania and Serbia, the direct comparison with neighbour states raised many questions on the appropriateness of what they had designated as a 'national style'. It opened up the question of how to deal with common heritage while at the same time claiming forms and motifs as their own. In this, the importance of truly owning their 'national' heritage and defining their 'national' style from within gained prime importance through the painful experience of the Othering designs of those French architects tasked with the national pavilions. Therefore, ultimately, and probably most importantly, the 'national style' discussion prompted an awareness of national heritage and, therefore, resolutions for its documentation and preservation.

Notes

1   The flipside to the question of whether a country or a people were considered 'sovereign' is the overt (re)presentation of power and subjugation by the colonial powers in the form of colonial exhibits and pavilions. These racist practices were inscribed in the popular and academic discourse by the establishment and use of exoticisms and orientalisms, as well as notions that characterized the colonized as 'barbarian', 'primitive' or 'savage'. The most atrocious manifestation of these practices was the dehumanization of the colonized subjects in the form of 'human zoos' at these World Exhibitions (Blanchard, Bancel, Boetsch, Deroo and Lemaire 2011; Bancel, David and Thomas 2014: 185–280).
2   Unfortunately Hajdu (2022) came too late to be incorporated into this chapter's discussion.

3   The status of the 1900 Paris Exhibition for the Byzantine Revival is much like the status of the 1851 London Exhibition for the so-called 'Moorish' revival owing to the impact of Owen Jones' Alhambra Court (cf. Ferry 2007; Jones, Calatrava and Tito Rojo 2010; Calatrava 2011; Varela Braga 2017: 25–55).
4   The official publication of the 1900 Paris World Exhibition details the decision-making in all its intricacies (*L'exposition de Paris (1900)* 1900a, 1: 1–9).
5   It is remarkable, how readily the World Exhibition commissioners and competitors embraced the destruction of earlier exhibition structures in favour of new, more 'modern' and larger buildings. At one point, officials even considered dismantling the Eiffel Tower (*L'exposition de Paris (1900)* 1900a, 1: 3–4).
6   The invitation was sent out to fifty-six countries, of which, eventually, only thirty-nine participated because of different reasons. The thirty-nine remaining nations were Andorra, Austria, Belgium, Bosnia-Herzegovina, Bulgaria, China, Congo, Denmark, Ecuador, Germany, Great Britain, Greece, Hungary, Italy, Japan, Korea, Liberia, Luxembourg, Mexico, Morocco, Monaco, Montenegro, the Netherlands, Norway, Paraguay, Peru, Persia, Portugal, Romania, Russia, Saint-Martin, Serbia, Siam, South Africa, Spain, Sweden, Switzerland, Turkey, the United States. The seventeen nations that did not take part were Argentina, Bolivia, Brazil, Chile, Costa Rica, Dominican Republic, Egypt, Ethiopia, Guatemala, Haiti, Hawaii, Orange Free State, Uruguay (*L'exposition de Paris (1900)* 1900b, 2: 35–36).
7   Bosnia-Herzegovina was occupied by the Austro-Hungarian monarchy from 1878 to 1918 (Oberhuber 2003; Sparks 2014: 33–72; Reynolds-Cordileone 2015). Bulgaria remained, even after the state's quasi-independence of 1878, an autonomous principality under Ottoman suzerainty until 1908 (Crampton 2007: 96–189; Kuneralp and Tokay 2008).
8   Compare, for instance, this reasoning for Bulgaria's participation: 'C'était, pour la jeune Principauté, en effet, un grand honneur que de pouvoir prendre part, après une existence politique de vingt-deux ans, à une manifestation de cette importance, et d'exposer dans la capitale d'une grande nation les produits de son sol, de son commerce et de son industrie, en montrant au monde civilisé les progrès réalisés par elle à divers points de vue [...]' (*La Bulgarie à l'exposition universelle internationale de 1900 à Paris* 1900: 5–6).
9   In recent years, scholarship has revealed and highlighted the mechanisms of constructing the 'primitive', the modes of presenting their supposed inferiority and France's 'mission civilisatrice' throughout the World and Colonial Exhibitions (Morton 2000; Jones 2007; Tran 2007; Blanchard, Boetsch and Thuram 2011; Hodeir and Pierre 2011; Hodeir 2014). Fuelled by such modes of presentation at the World Exhibitions, the notion of the 'primitive' also gained a major impetus in the sphere of avant-garde art, where it was appropriated and misused as a mere stylistic device by artistic movements such as Les Fauves or Die Brücke, whose year of inception has commonly been dated to 1905 (see, most recently, Wilhelm 2022: 40–45). Thus, just like I argue in this chapter that the aftermath of the Byzantinism of the 1900 World Exhibition gains special importance in the Balkans of the 1900s–1920s, so can the same conclusion be drawn for the reception of the primitivism presented at this event.
10 'Puissances étrangères' was the official term used throughout.
11 Belgium, Portugal, Spain, Italy, Norway, the Netherlands, Russia, Switzerland, Sweden, the United States, Great Britain, Japan, Austria and Denmark were given smaller rooms in the northern wing of the Grand Palais (Baschet 1900a: 77–78 and map B).

12   Once again, it was only specific countries that were given the possibility to exhibit: Belgium, Russia, Austria – with one entire pavilion dedicated to Vienna, Hungary, Japan, Italy, Spain, Portugal, Sweden, Switzerland, the Netherlands, Great Britain, Germany, the United States, Denmark and Norway (Baschet 1900a: 85 and maps E and F).

13   The pavilions in the front row were, from the Pont des Invalides toward the Pont de l'Alma, those of Italy, Turkey, the United States, Austria, Bosnia, Hungary, Great Britain, Belgium, Norway, Germany, Spain, Monaco, Sweden, Greece, Serbia, and passing the Pont de l'Alma also Mexico. The pavilions in the second row, following the same direction, were Denmark, Portugal, Peru, Persia, Luxembourg, Finland with a Russian section, Bulgaria and Romania (Figure 1.2).

14   The countries represented in the commercial section were Italy, Great Britain, the United States, Germany, Russia; in the forestry, hunting and fishing section: Russia, Hungary, Austria, Denmark, Great Britain, Romania, Belgium, the United States; in the metallurgy section: Austria, Hungary, the United States, Belgium, Norway, the Netherlands, Russia, Great Britain, Germany, Luxembourg, Sweden, Italy, Japan, Spain, Portugal; in the mechanics section: Great Britain, Sweden, Persia, the United States, Italy, Austria, Hungary, Russia, Germany, Belgium, Japan, Switzerland, Spain; in the textiles section: Austria, Belgium, Switzerland, Spain, the Netherlands, Romania, Denmark, Italy, the United States, Great Britain; in the chemical industries section: Germany, Spain, Belgium, Switzerland, Sweden, Great Britain, Russia, Italy, the Netherlands, Hungary, Austria, the United States, Great Britain, Norway, Denmark, Romania, Japan, Spain, Portugal; in the transportation section: Switzerland, the Netherlands, Great Britain; in the education section: Belgium, Switzerland, Great Britain, the Netherlands, Denmark, Norway; in the arts and science section: Russia, Italy, Hungary, Austria, Germany, the United States, Portugal, Spain, Japan, Sweden, Guatemala; in the agriculture section: Denmark, Romania, Sweden, Italy, Hungary, Spain, Andorra, Liberia, Switzerland, Austria, the Netherlands, Russia, Portugal, Turkey, Germany, Japan, Great Britain, Belgium, the United States, Norway; in the electricity section: Austria, Hungary, Denmark, Norway, Russia, Sweden, the Netherlands, the United States, Italy (Baschet 1900a: maps L, M and N).

15   Notwithstanding their status as sovereign states, the pavilions of Japan, Russia, China, as well as Egypt as an autonomous principality of the Ottoman Empire were also placed in this section. The area further housed the exhibits of the British and Portuguese colonies, and the Dutch East Indies. The French colonies taking up the great majority of the area included Madagascar, Algeria, Tunisia, Côte d'Ivoire, Guinea, Dahomey, Sudan, Senegal, French West Indies, French Polynesia, Indochina, Tonkin, Cambodia, Guiana, Martinique, Guadeloupe, Réunion, New Caledonia and Congo. Other colonial agencies such as the French Catholic missions were also given exhibition space (Baschet 1900a: 154–92).

16   There was an overall great prevalence of structures and motifs at the World Exhibitions that reinforced orientalist prejudices (Çelik 1992; Ganim 2002).

17   The interrelatedness of orientalism and medievalism as Othering mechanisms have been aptly shown by Ganim (2005), cf. 'If the European past of the European host countries was sometimes represented as if it were a colonized past, the present of the colonies was often presented as if it were the Middle Ages' (Ganim 2005: 102–3).

18   In the Bulgarian architectural press of the late 1890s, there is a widespread discourse surrounding the question of how to represent the 'national' self by

26   *Byzantium in the Popular Imagination*

specifically employing the term 'I' in the sense of an acting subject (cf., for instance, Nenov 1899: 100).

19   As a matter of fact, French 1900 World Exhibition reports and guides, as well as archival materials only indicate Ambroise Baudry's name, who also signed all official documents (*L'exposition de Paris (1900)* 1900b, 2: 161; Picard 1903, 5: 86; Minea 2014: 87–88). The only exception to this is the 'Volume annexe du Catalogue général officiel' (1900: n.p. [98]), which mentions both Kapetanović and Baudry. The Serbian press, on the other hand, omits Baudry's involvement and adds Milorad Ruvidić as a second collaborator (Nova Iskra 1900).

20   These elements were, however, also highly ambivalent, as some guidebooks identify them as 'Muslim' domes (Baschet 1900a: 124).

21   During his Parthenon fieldwork, Magne met Nicolas Delyannis, who later as Greek ambassador to Paris decided to entrust Magne with building the Greek pavilion (Magne 1895, vi; Minea 2014: 80).

22   The pavilion was planned from its inception to be transferred to Athens after the exhibition to serve as a museum. In 1901, it was decided that the pavilion would still be reconstructed in Athens, however, to serve as a church (Magouliotis 2018: 55–56; Loyer 2020).

23   Notable such examples include the Arènes de Lutèce (the Parisian Roman arena) or the abbey church of Sainte-Foy in Conques (cf. the original plans preserved in the Médiathèque de l'architecture et du patrimoine of the French Ministère de la culture, files 0082/075/1005 and 0082/013/2036).

24   Formigé experimented with different domed solutions also in the designs for his Palais des Beaux-Arts for the 1889 Paris World Exhibition (cf., for instance, Musée d'Orsay ARO 1991 25).

25   Formigé visited Romania at least once in preparing to design the Romanian pavilion (Hajdu 2015: 57).

26   The original plans for these and the final projects are preserved in the Musée d'Orsay (ARO 1991 26, ARO 1991 19, ARO 1992 23–ARO 1992 26, ARO 1992 28–ARO 1992 29, ARO 1992 33, ARO 1992 43 2–ARO 1992 43 18, ARO 1992 43 21–ARO 1992 43 44). In addition, the architect was given the possibility to exhibit an additional aspect of Romanian 'traditional' architecture in the structure of the Romanian restaurant, for which he drew from examples of domestic architecture (*Volume Annexe Du Catalogue Général Officiel* 1900: n.p. [198]). For the restaurant there are also several projects preserved (Musée d'Orsay ARO 1992 43 19, ARO 1992 43 20, ARO 1992 42 1–ARO 1992 42 14, ARO 1992 27, ARO 1992 30–ARO 1992 32).

27   Saladin published several books on Tunisian art and architecture, and a highly influential overview of Islamic architecture from the seventh century to the early nineteenth century and from Morocco to India (Saladin 1907).

28   The western north African coast, the 'Maghreb', was considered to be the same geographic, climatic and above all cultural sphere, a Muslim 'Orient', whose only demarcation lines were to be sought in the amount of colonization and 'civilization': 'Entre le Maroc et l'Algérie, entre l'Algérie et la Tunisie, les lignes de démarcation sont fictives, et si, la frontière franchie, il semble que l'on aborde une autre région, un examen, même superficiel, montre qu'il n'en est rien et que le contraste résulte, non du relief du sol, des conditions climatériques, de la nature des produits, mais du degré de colonisation et de civilisation. Il y a peu d'années encore, Bône semblait marquer la limite entre deux contrées distinctes: à l'ouest, l'Algérie, semée de villes et de villages, traversée par de grandes routes, florissantes et cultivées; à l'ouest, la

Tunisie, relativement aride et déboisée, personnifiant l'immobile Orient à côté de l'Orient moderne et cultivé' (*L'exposition de Paris (1900)* 1900b, 2: 146). In this understanding, Algeria played a special role as the earliest French colony, and therefore considered to be the most 'modern' and 'cultivated'. This is what created its difference, and consequently the need for a distinguished architectural solution for its pavilion by the architect Albert Ballu: 'French colonizers presented the Algerian palace as a "didactic and demonstrative" exposition' (Çelik 1992: 130). Consequently, it was a logical decision to have the same architect, Henri Saladin, design the pavilions of both Morocco and Tunisia, the two countries still thought to be stuck as being the same indistinguishable 'immovable Orient'.

29   Cf. Archives nationales de France F/21/2289 dossier 4 and F/17/3005/2. Sévelinges was responsible for drawing site plans and taking photographs (Pillet 1958: 59; González Reyero 2001: 174).

30   Lucien Magne's own involvement in this process was already discussed above. One of the most influential corpuses of such material, Gabriel Millet's photographic documentation of Byzantine monuments, was, in fact, also exhibited at the 1900 World Exhibition (Kourelis 2007: 391).

31   Cf. the review of Chamardjieff's book by Tornyov (1904: 99): 'It is lamentable that it was necessary for the American Exhibition to happen for us to be compelled to be now interested in our vernacular architecture.'

Archival Sources

Archives nationales de France, Paris
Ministère de la culture of France, Paris
Musée d'Orsay, Paris

Bibliography

Bacha, M. (2009), 'Henri Saladin (1851–1923). Un architecte «Beaux-Arts» promoteur de l'art islamique tunisien', in N. Oulebsir and M. Volait (eds.), *L'orientalisme architectural entre imaginaires et savoirs*, 215–30, Paris: Picard.

Bancel, N., Th. David and D. R. D. Thomas, eds. (2014), *The Invention of Race: Scientific and Popular Representations*, New York: Routledge.

Baschet, L. (1900a), *Exposition Universelle de 1900. Guide Lemercier. Dictionnaire pratique des objets exposés et des Attractions*, Paris: Imprimeries Lemercier et Cie.

Baschet, L., ed. (1900b), *Le Panorama. Exposition Universelle 1900*, Paris: Librairie d'art, Ludovic Baschet.

Blanchard, P., N. Bancel, G. Boetsch, É. Deroo and S. Lemaire, eds. (2011), *Zoos humains et exhibitions coloniales: 150 ans d'inventions de l'autre*, Paris: La Découverte.

Blanchard, P., G. Boetsch and L. Thuram, eds. (2011), *Human Zoos: The Invention of the Savage*, Arles: Actes Sud.

Boeck, E. (2015), 'Archaeology of Decadence: Uncovering Byzantium in Victorien Sardou's Theodora', in R. Betancourt and M. Taroutina (eds.), *Byzantium/Modernism: The Byzantine as Method in Modernity*, 102–32, Leiden: Brill.

Bullen, J. B. (2003), *Byzantium Rediscovered: The Byzantine Revival in Europe and America*, London: Phaidon.

Bullen, J. B. (2005), 'Louis Comfort Tiffany and Romano-Byzantine Design', *The Burlington Magazine*, 147 (1227): 390–98.
Calatrava, J., ed. (2011), *Owen Jones y la Alhambra*, Granada: Patronato de la Alhambra y Generalife.
Çelik, Z. (1992), *Displaying the Orient: Architecture of Islam at Nineteenth-Century World's Fairs*, Berkeley: University of California Press.
Chamardjieff, J. (1904), *L'Architecture en Bulgarie*, Sofia: Imprimerie de la Cour, Prošek frères.
Crampton, R. J. (2007), *Bulgaria*, Oxford: Oxford University Press.
Crinson, M. (1996), *Empire Building: Orientalism and Victorian Architecture*, London: Routledge.
Dobreva, D. (2007), 'Bulgarien auf der Pariser Weltausstellung 1900. Bilder von Eigenem und Fremdem in den zeitgenössischen publizistischen Debatten über die Ausstellung', in P. Petrov, K. Gehl and K. Roth (eds.), *Fremdes Europa? Selbstbilder und Europa-Vorstellungen in Bulgarien (1850–1945)*, 101–52, Berlin: Lit-Verlag.
Ferry, K. (2007), 'Owen Jones and the Alhambra Court at the Crystal Palace', in G. Anderson and M. Rosser-Owen (eds.), *Revisiting Al-Andalus: Perspectives on the Material Culture of Islamic Iberia and Beyond*, 225–46, Leiden and Boston: Brill.
Ganim, J. M. (2002), 'Medievalism and Orientalism at the World's Fairs', *Studia Anglica Posnaniensia: International Review of English Studies*, 38: 179–90.
Ganim, J. M. (2005), *Medievalism and Orientalism: Three Essays on Literature, Architecture, and Cultural Identity*, New York: Palgrave Macmillan.
Geppert, A. C. T. (2010), *Fleeting Cities: Imperial Expositions in Fin-de-Siècle Europe*, Houndmills and New York: Palgrave Macmillan.
González Reyero, S. (2001), 'Los usos de la fotografía en favor de la arqueología como ciencia moderna. Francia 1850–1914', *Cuadernos de Prehistoria y Arqueología Universidad Autónoma de Madrid*, 27: 163–82.
Hajdu, A., ed. (2009), *Architecture and National Project: The Romanian National Style*, Bucharest: NOI Media Print.
Hajdu, A. (2015), 'The Pavilions of Greece, Serbia, Romania and Bulgaria at the 1900 Exposition Universelle in Paris', in M. Couroucli and Tch. Marinov (eds.), *Balkan Heritages: Negotiating History and Culture*, 47–78, Farnham: Ashgate.
Hajdu, A. (2017), 'The Search for National Architectural Styles in Serbia, Romania, and Bulgaria from the Mid-Nineteenth Century to World War I', in R. Daskalov, D. Mishkova, Tch. Marinov and A. Vezenkov (eds.), *Entangled Histories of the Balkans*, vol. 4, 394–39, Leiden and Boston: Brill.
Hajdu, A. (2022), 'Bulgarian versus Byzantine: The Unrealized Museum of the Bulgarian Revival and National Style Debates in Architecture, ca. 1900', in S. Kallestrup, M. Kunińska, M. A. Mihail, A. Adashinskaya and C. Minea (eds.), *Periodization in the Art Historiographies of Central and Eastern Europe*, 88–102, New York: Routledge.
Hodeir, C. (2014), 'Human Exhibitions at World's Fairs: Between Scientific Categorization and Exoticism? The French Colonial Presence at Midway Plaisance, World's Columbian Exposition, Chicago, 1893', in N. Bancel, Th. David and D. R. D. Thomas (eds.), *The Invention of Race: Scientific and Popular Representations*, 222–32, New York: Routledge.
Hodeir, C. and M. Pierre (2011), *L'exposition coloniale de 1931*, Bruxelles: A. Versaille.
Ignjatović, A. (2014), 'Byzantium Evolutionized: Architectural History and National Identity in Turn-of-the-Century Serbia', in D. Mishkova, B. Trencsényi and M. Jalava

(eds.), *'Regimes of Historicity' in Southeastern and Northern Europe, 1890-1945*, 254-74, London: Palgrave Macmillan.
Ignjatović, A. (2015), 'Competing Byzantinisms: The Architectural Imaginations of the Balkan Nations at the Paris World Exhibition in 1900', in M. Székely (ed.), *Ephemeral Architecture in Central-Eastern Europe in the 19th and 20th Centuries*, 107-22, Paris: L'Harmattan.
Ignjatović, A. (2016), 'Byzantium's Apt Inheritors: Serbian Historiography, Nation-Building and Imperial Imagination, 1882-1941', *The Slavonic and East European Review*, 94 (1): 57-92.
Jones, D. V. (2007), 'The Prison House of Modernism: Colonial Spaces and the Construction of the Primitive at the 1931 Paris Colonial Exposition', *Modernism/Modernity*, 14 (1): 55-69.
Jones, O., J. Calatrava and J. T. Rojo (2010), *El Patio Alhambra en el Crystal Palace*, Madrid and Granada: Abada/Patronato de la Alhambra y Generalife.
Jovanović, M. (1985), 'Théophile Hansen, "la Hansenatique" et les disciplines serbes de Hansen', *Zbornik Za Likovne Umetnosti*, 21: 235-58.
Kadijevic, A. (2016), *Byzantine Architecture as, vol. 1, Inspiration for Serbian New Age Architects*, Belgrade: Serbian Academy of Sciences and Arts.
Kallestrup, S. (2002), 'Romanian "National Style" and the 1906 Bucharest Jubilee Exhibition', *Journal of Design History*, 15 (3): 147-62.
Kourelis, K. (2007), 'Byzantium and the Avant-Garde: Excavations at Corinth, 1920s-1930s', *Hesperia: The Journal of the American School of Classical Studies at Athens*, 76 (2): 391-442.
Koychev, P. (1902), 'Neshto varhu estetikata', *Spisanie na Balgarskoto inzhenerno-arhitekturno druzhestvo v Sofiya*, 7 (3-4): 48-51.
Koychev, P. (1907a), 'Hudozhestveni bogatstva na Balgariya', *Spisanie na Balgarskoto inzhenerno-arhitekturno druzhestvo v Sofiya*, 12 (3-4): 40-43.
Koychev, P. (1907b), 'Hudozhestveni bogatstva na stranata ni', *Spisanie na Balgarskoto inzhenerno-arhitekturno druzhestvo v Sofiya*, 12 (1-2): 1-3.
Koychev, P. (1910a), 'Znachenieto na starite balgarski postroyki i tyahnoto zapazvane. (Referat za II kongres na balg. inzhen. i arhitekti)', *Spisanie na Balgarskoto inzhenerno-arhitekturno druzhestvo v Sofiya*, 15: 188-89.
Koychev, P. (1910b), 'Znachenieto na starite balgarski postroyki i tyahnoto zapazvane', *Spisanie na Balgarskoto inzhenerno-arhitekturno druzhestvo v Sofiya*, 15: 10-34.
Kozarov, G. (1900), 'Nashite predshestvennitsi - maystora Kolyu Ficheto', *Spisanie na Balgarskoto inzhenerno-arhitekturno druzhestvo v Sofiya*, 5 (1-2): 15-23.
Kuneralp, S. and G. Tokay, eds. (2008), *Ottoman Diplomatic Documents on the Origins of World War One. I: The Road to Bulgarian Independence. September 1908-May 1909*, Istanbul: The Isis Press.
La Bulgarie à l'exposition universelle internationale de 1900 à Paris: catalogue spécial du pavillon bulgare et de la section bulgare au Palais des Beaux-Arts (1900), Paris: Imprimerie et Librairie Centrales des Chemins de Fer.
L'exposition de Paris (1900) (1900a), vol. 1, *Encyclopédie du Siècle*, Paris: Montgredien et Cie.
L'exposition de Paris (1900) (1900b), vol. 2, *Encyclopédie du Siècle*, Paris: Montgredien et Cie.
Loyer, F. (2020), 'Athènes ou Byzance?', in F. Loyer, *L'Architecture de la Grèce au XIXe siècle (1821-1912)*, 107-40, Athens: École française d'Athènes.

Magne, L. (1895), *Le Parthénon: Études faites au cours de deux missions en Grèce (1894–1895)*, Paris: Imprimerie nationale.

Magne, L. (1897a), 'Mistra (deuxième article)', *Gazette des beaux-arts*, 17 (4): 301–13.

Magne, L. (1897b), 'Mistra (premier article)', *Gazette des beaux-arts*, 17 (2): 135–48.

Magouliotis, N. (2018), 'Byzantium, to and fro: The "Pavillon de la Grèce" from the Paris 1900 Expo to Athens', *Future Anterior*, 15 (2): 46–60.

Merenik, L., V. Simić and I. Borozan, eds. (2016), *Imagining the Past: The Reception of the Middle Ages in Serbian Art from the 18th to the 21st Century*, Byzantine Heritage and Serbian Art, vol. 3. Belgrade: Službeni glasnik.

Minea, C. (2014), 'An Image for the Nation: Architecture of the Balkan Countries at 19th Century Universal Exhibitions in Paris', MA diss., Central European University, Budapest.

Minea, C. (2015), 'New Images for Modern Nations: Creating a "National" Architecture for the Balkan Countries at Paris Universal Exhibition of 1889', in M. Székely (ed.), *Ephemeral Architecture in Central-Eastern Europe in the 19th and 20th Centuries*, 91–106, Paris: L'Harmattan.

Minea, C. (2016), 'The Monastery of Curtea de Argeş and Romanian Architectural Heritage in the Late 19th Century', *Studies in History and Theory of Architecture, Marginalia. Architectures of Uncertain Margins*, 4: 181–201.

Morton, P. A. (2000), *Hybrid Modernities: Architecture and Representation at the 1931 Colonial Exposition, Paris*, Cambridge, MA: MIT Press.

Nelson, R. S. (2004), *Hagia Sophia, 1850–1950: Holy Wisdom Modern Monument*, Chicago: University of Chicago Press.

Nelson, R. S. (2010), 'The History of Legends and the Legends of History: The Pilastri Acritani in Venice', in H. Maguire and R. S. Nelson (eds.), *San Marco, Byzantium, and the Myths of Venice*, 63–90, Washington, DC: Dumbarton Oaks Research Library and Collection.

Nenov, G. (1899), 'Arhiologiya', *Spisanie na Balgarskoto inzhenerno-arhitekturno druzhestvo v Sofiya*, 4 (4–5): 100–01.

Nova Iskra (1900), 'Sa Pariske Izlozhbe', 16 May.

Oberhuber, F. (2003), 'Zur Konstruktion bürgerlicher imperialer Identität. Gustav Ratzenhofers Vorträge zur Okkupation Bosniens und der Herzegowina', in J. Feichtinger, U. Prutsch and M. Csáky (eds.), *Habsburg Postcolonial: Machtstrukturen und kollektives Gedächtnis*, 277–88, Innsbruck: Studienverlag.

Pantelić, B. (1997), 'Nationalism and Architecture: The Creation of a National Style in Serbian Architecture and its Political Implications', *The Journal of the Society of Architectural Historians*, 56: 16–41.

Pantelić, B. (2007), 'Designing Identities Reshaping the Balkans in the First Two Centuries: The Case of Serbia', *Journal of Design History*, 20 (2): 131–44.

Paris exposition 1900: guide pratique du visiteur de Paris et de l'exposition (1900), Paris: Hachette.

Picard, A. (1903), *Exposition universelle internationale de 1900 à Paris. Rapport général administratif et technique*, vol. 5, Paris: Imprimerie nationale.

Pillet, M. (1958), 'Ernest de Sarzec, explorateur de Tello (1832–1901)', *Comptes rendus des séances de l'Académie des Inscriptions et Belles-Lettres*, 102 (1): 52–66.

Popescu, C. (1998), 'André Lecomte du Nouÿ (1844–1914) et la restauration des monuments historiques en Roumanie', *Bulletin de la Société de l'Histoire de l'Art français*, 287–308.

Popescu, C. (2009), 'Le paradoxe de l'orientalisme balkanique: entre géopolitique et quêtes identitaires. Lecture à travers le cas roumain', in N. Oulebsir and M. Volait (ed.), *L'orientalisme architectural entre imaginaires et savoirs*, 253–72, Paris: Picard.
Popescu, C. (2011), 'Being Specific: Limits of Contextualising (Architectural) History', *The Journal of Architecture*, 16 (6): 821–53.
Popescu, C. (2013), 'Digging Out the Past to Build Up the Future: Romanian Architecture in the Balkan Context 1859–1906', in P. J. Geary and Gábor Klaniczay (eds.), *Manufacturing Middle Ages: Entangled History of Medievalism in Nineteenth-Century Europe*, 189–216, Boston: Brill.
Reynolds-Cordileone, D. (2015), 'Displaying Bosnia: Imperialism, Orientalism, and Exhibitionary Cultures in Vienna and Beyond: 1878–1914', *Austrian History Yearbook*, 46 (April): 29–50.
Saladin, H. (1907), *Manuel d'art musulman*, vol. 1, *l'architecture*, Paris: Librairie Alphonse Picard et Fils.
Sparks, M. (2014), *The Development of Austro-Hungarian Sarajevo, 1878–1918: An Urban History*, London and New York: Bloomsbury Academic.
Stanoeva, E. (2013), 'Interpretations of the Ottoman Urban Legacy in the National Capital Building of Sofia (1878–1940)', in E. Ginio and K. Kaser (eds.), *Ottoman Legacies in the Balkans and the Middle East*, 209–30, Jerusalem: Hebrew University Press.
Stoilova, L. and P. Yokimov (2002), 'The Search for Identifiably National Architecture in Bulgaria at the End of the 19th and During the Early 20th Century', in C. Popescu and I. Teodorescu (eds.), *Genius Loci: National et régional en architecture – entre histoire et pratique*, 96–105, Bucharest: Simetria.
Tornyov, A. (1900), 'Vsesvetskata izlozhba v kraya na 19-to stoletie', *Spisanie na Balgarskoto inzhenerno-arhitekturno druzhestvo v Sofiya*, 5 (12): 225–35.
Tornyov, A. (1904), 'L'Architecture en Bulgarie, par J. Chamardjieff', *Spisanie na Balgarskoto inzhenerno-arhitekturno druzhestvo v Sofiya*, 9 (7–10): 98–102.
Tran, V. (2007), 'L'éphémère dans l'éphémère: la domestication des colonies à l'Exposition universelle de 1889', *Ethnologies*, 29 (1–2): 143–69.
Usta-Genchov, D. (1905), 'Nasheto zlatarstvo', *Spisanie na Balgarskoto inzhenerno-arhitekturno druzhestvo v Sofiya*, 10 (3): 37–39.
Usta-Genchov, D. (1906), 'Belezhki po razkopkite pri selo Aboba', *Spisanie na Balgarskoto inzhenerno-arhitekturno druzhestvo v Sofiya*, 11 (1–2): 13–15.
Varela Braga, A. (2017), *Une théorie universelle au milieu du XIXe siècle: la grammar of ornament d'Owen Jones*, Roma: Campisano Editore.
Volume annexe du Catalogue Général Officiel (1900), Paris: Imprimeries Lemercier et Cie.
Wilhelm, M. (2022), *Vjera Biller und das Kindliche: Primitivistische Entwürfe von Künstlerinnenschaft in der Avantgarde der 1920er Jahre*, Bielefeld: transcript.

2

East or West? Byzantine Architecture and the Origins of French Medieval Architecture in the Scholarly Debate, Nineteenth Century

Francesco Lovino

On the evening of the 16 August 1806, on his (long) way to Jerusalem, François-René de Chateaubriand reached Mystras, in Laconia. Lying on the couch of his host, the Turk Ibraïm Bey, Chateaubriand glimpses the peak of the Taygetos: he had finally reached Sparta, the city of Menelaos and Helen. The day later, accompanied by a local Cicero – 'très-bonhomme, mais très-ignorant' (Chateaubriand 1811: 79) – and his dragoman Joseph, Chateaubriand first visited Amyclae, but while looking for the remains of the Heroic Age, he found only a dozen of Greek chapels, ravaged by the Albanians (80). Chateaubriand knew how to arouse his reader's curiosity, lingering on the description of a papas, singing litanies, with worshippers in front of the image of a Virgin, smeared in red, over a blue background (81). His guides pressed him to return, fearful of Maniots brigands; on the route back to Mystras, he encountered the mountain views, the fountains a traveller ran into while approaching the town, and then the neighbourhoods, the Gothic castle and the view from that castle: 'Ma quand parlerez-vous de Sparte, me dira le lecteur?' (87). Chateaubriand found himself in an impasse: he knew that modern Mystras did not correspond to ancient Sparta, but at the same time, he was unable to recognize even the remains of the legendary city. The conundrum is solved during a nonsense dialogue with the local Cicero, who revealed that Palaeochôri, the old city, is down in the valley, along the way to Amyclae, and indicated a white farmhouse far away. Now, Chateaubriand began to run to the spot in the distance, avoiding the guides who try to show him other modern ruins and tell him stories about the pasha, but he was finally forced to stop by a group of papas, who invited him to meet the archbishop in the cathedral. The description he left of the cathedral of Saint Demetrius is harsh, and reflects his attitude towards Byzantine culture, and its architecture in particular:

> l'église […] fort célèbre dans nos géographies, n'a pourtant rien de remarquable. La mosaïque du pavé est commune; les peintures, vantées par Guillet, rappellent absolument les ébauches de l'école avant le Pérugin. Quant à l'architecture, ce sont

toujours des dômes plus ou moins écrasés, plus ou moins multipliés. Cette cathédrale [...] a pour sa part sept de ces dômes. Depuis que cet ornement a été employé à Constantinople dans la dégénération de l'art, il a marqué tous les monuments de la Grèce. Il n'a ni la hardiesse du gothique, ni la sage beauté de l'antique. Il est assez majestueux quand il est immense; mais alors il écrase l'édifice qui le porte: s'il est petit, ce n'est plus qu'une calotte ignoble qui ne se lie à aucun membre de l'architecture, et qui s'élève au-dessus des entablemens, tout exprès pour rompre la ligne harmonieuse de la cymaise.

(Chateaubriand 1811: 87)[1]

A matter of vocabulary

Chateaubriand's disdain leaned on the rooted view of Byzantium as a period of general decadence, especially in comparison with the highest moments of the Roman Empire (Bianco 2015). His repulsion appears even more clearly while reading his pages on Constantinople, where he described merely all his efforts to leave the Bosphorus as soon as possible, before confessing how he felt oppressed by the city (Chateaubriand 1811: 87).[2]

Nonetheless, in the same years French attitude toward Byzantine architecture was slowly changing, on different levels. The notion of 'Byzantine' in itself was a floating concept, even more than today, and used with discretion by scholars and amateurs while referring to architecture. There were neither geographical boundaries nor specific elements to define it, as was well explained by the *Inspecteur général des monuments historiques*, Prosper Mérimée, who in one passage declared the interchangeability of the adjective Byzantine with 'roman, lombard, saxon, quels que soient les noms qu'on donne' (1838b: 289). The statement deserves further attention. Mérimée was well aware of the different implications of each attribution, and none of the accepted definitions was omitted: *roman* emphasized the link with Roman architecture, deteriorated throughout the centuries;[3] *lombarde* and *saxon* leaned on historical geography. *Byzantine*, however, has no direct connection besides a generic, oriental influence on Western medieval architecture. Mérimée himself was unable to deepen this idea. In the following pages, he mentioned a general 'imitation des architectures néo-grecque et orientale, importée par des étrangers ou par des artistes nationaux' (1838b: 293), whose elements of distinction were the domes, a few details of the ornamentations and a taste for mosaics and encrustations. Then, Mérimée mentioned, as examples, the plans of several churches along the Rhine, and the portals of the churches of Sélestat, Treviri and Maguelone. The case of Maguelone clearly illustrates how weak these oriental attributions were. Mérimée was famous for being a tireless traveller: after his appointment as *Inspecteur général* (1834), he embarked on a long mission throughout the country, meticulously reporting on his travels in the *Notes* he published in the following years (Mérimée 1835, 1836, 1838a, 1840). The first mission took him to Maguelone, a small island in Occitanie that was an archbishopric under siege since the sixth century. While describing the façade of the cathedral of Saint Peter and Paul, Mérimée highlighted the oriental taste of the windows, just because its archivolts were made of alternating black and white stones (1835: 377).

This (mis)use of the adjective Byzantine was deeply rooted in volumes on architecture of the early nineteenth century: Alexandre de Laborde, author of the massive *Les Monuments de la France classés chronologiquement et considérés sous le rapport des faits historiques et d'étude des arts* (Laborde 1816-36), even entitled a section of his second volume 'Monuments du style byzantin ou roman', although the only church labelled as Byzantine is the twelfth-century abbey church of Saint-Gilles-de-la-Gard, along the pilgrimage route to Compostela (Figure 2.1) (Laborde 1816-36, II: 3). Nonetheless, the mere taxonomy could mislead our current understanding of the nineteenth-century approach towards Byzantine architecture, as the same two volumes of *Les Monuments de la France* show. Laborde had paid his respects to Byzantine architecture since the very beginning, and even in its highest form: already on page iii of the *Discours préliminaire*, he stated that 'l'arc ogive, cette innovation heureuse dont on ignore l'auteur, vient de Constantinople, ainsi que toutes les traditions du Moyen Âge' (Laborde 1816-36, I: ii-iii].[4] Constantinople thus acted as a primigenial source of the architecture of the Middle Ages, or rather, as its core: where all traditions converged before being

Figure 2.1 Entrance of the Abbey of Saint-Gilles, Gard, after A. de Laborde (1818-36), *Les Monuments de la France classés chronologiquement et considérés sous le rapport des faits historiques et de l'étude des arts*, 2 vols, Paris: Jules Didot l'aîné, II: pl. CXXV.

widespread again.[5] The superb basilicas built at Ravenna, Pavia, Modena and Monza under Theodoric were exemplary in this regard, and were the model for those built in Constantinople since the sixth century, as well as of those made under Clovis and his successor Childeric in the *Regnum Francorum* (Laborde 1816–36, I: 37–40).

Frenchmen in Byzantium

French architects and scholars thus focused mainly on the interval between the third and the twelfth century, that is, between the establishment of Christian architecture and the coming of Gothic. The monuments built in this period, almost completely ignored (when not despised), became the inspirational source for a group of radical architects, like Léon Vaudoyer, Felix Duban, Louis Duc and Henri Labrouste, the so-called 'génération romantique' (Van Zanten 1987). They were impressed by the ideas of socialist philosopher Henri de Saint-Simon, who considered Byzantium as a 'critical' period of change and instability, in opposition to ancient Greece and the Middle Ages from the twelfth and the fifteenth century, which were both considered cohesive, 'organic' periods. To these architects, Byzantium was energetic, innovative, modern and exotic – although not remote from the French tradition, as scholars were demonstrating. This group was joined by Albert Lenoir: another Saint-Simonien, Lenoir was researching the relationship between social and political history and architectural styles. He was convinced that, in the early Middle Ages, architecture separated into two different branches, the *style byzantin* and the *style latin*: the synthesis of which would eventually become Gothic architecture (Lenoir 1840; Bergdoll 1994: 122; Thomine-Berrada 2009). In 1836, Lenoir departed to the Orient to confirm his intuition: he visited Athens and Constantinople, the Cyclades, the Adriatic coast up to Venice. His travel did not led to a specific publication, but lay the foundations for several initiatives: with Vaudoyer and the architect Léonce Reynaud, Lenoir published a series of essays on the popular *Magasin pittoresque*, 'Études sur l'architecture en France', covering specifically the period between the fall of the Roman Empire and the flourishing of Gothic architecture (Lenoir and Vaudoyer 1839–52); he was appointed professor of Byzantine architecture at the *Bibliothèque royale*, organizing with Adolphe-Napoléon Didron a complete course of Christian archaeology (Loyer 2017: 115); he supported the research of another young architect, André Couchaud, who spent a year in Athens carrying out surveys of the Byzantine monuments. The outcome of Couchaud's research was one of the first books specifically dedicated to Byzantine architecture, *Choix d'églises bysantines en Grèce* (Couchaud 1842). The volume is a short description (only 32 pages) of eighteen churches (Figure 2.2), with three entries dedicated to sculptures, manuscripts and painted ornamentations that Couchaud had the chance to see during his stay. Couchaud justified his interest in medieval Greece, highlighting that its heritage was unknown, and introducing several recurrent topoi of Byzantine architecture: the *genius loci* of Greece, the reinterpretation and evolution of an architectural type born in Rome (the basilica), the impact of Christianity and the role of Byzantium in connecting the antiquity to the Gothic (Couchaud 1842: 1–2). His conclusions are slightly different from those of Lenoir: instead of two different

Figure 2.2 Church of St Theodore, Athens, after A. Couchaud (1842), *Choix d'églises bysantines en Grèce*, Paris: Lenoir, pl. 8.

styles, Couchaud suggested that the lucky encounter between Greece and Christianity inspired the creation of a Byzantine style, which would later be dispensed throughout Europe, leading to several local, Western styles ('donner naissance au roman, au normand, au saxon et au lombard': Couchaud 1842: 13).

The Grand Tour of the former Byzantine Empire was replacing the traditional eighteenth-century trip to Italy, and knowledge of Byzantine architecture benefitted of several expeditions *outremer*. Charles Texier, inspector at the public works in Paris, was appointed foreign correspondent of the École des Beaux-Arts, and travelled throughout Turkey from 1833 to 1836 on behalf of the Ministry of Education.[6] Inspired by the sixteenth-century *De Topographia Constantinopoleos* by Petrus Gyllius and the recent *Constantiniopolis und der Bosphorus*, published in 1822 by the German orientalist Joseph von Hammer-Purgstall (Hammer-Purgstall 1822; Gilles 1986). Texier later planned to publish a survey of Constantinople, richly illustrated with mosques, churches, cisterns and other public buildings (Pedone 2016: 1670–71). Therefore, during his travels, he realized hundreds of drawings, sketches and watercolours of local monuments, today preserved at the Archive de l'Institut de France in Paris, and at the Royal Institute of British Architects in London. The survey of Constantinople was never accomplished, but the material merged fifteen years later in a volume on Byzantine architecture that

Texier published in London with the English architect Richard Popplewell Pullan. In the preface, Pullan described himself as editor of the immense portfolio of Texier, who chose the material to publish and confided it to his English co-author (Texier and Pullan 1864: 2). Pullan also suggested that other volumes may have been published, if this first one had met the favour of the public, a possible explanation for why Texier decided not to publish any of the drawings of Constantinople, save for a further volume that was never published (Pedone 2016: 1675).

Byzantium in France

While Couchaud and Texier were deepening actual Byzantine architecture in the Orient, in France, the debate focused on the role of Byzantium in the development of Western medieval architecture – and, in particular, on its role in defining Gothic architecture. The question was initially raised by Ludovic Vitet, first *Inspecteur général des monuments historiques* since 1830, who continued a discussion begun in Germany. In 1829, Vitet met in Cologne with German architect Sulpiz Boisserée, who at that time was promulgating the idea that Rhenish medieval churches were *byzantin-roman* (Dubois 2003). Boisserée's enthusiasm infected Vitet, who wrote two widely read articles on how the late Romanesque Church of St. Cunibert in Cologne and the Lombard architecture in Italy should be considered as bridges between Byzantium and Gothic architecture (Vitet 1830, 1867). Vitet even translated the terminology of Boisserée, so the German term *neo-griechischen*, became in French *néo-grec*, a word that served, for a time, as a synonym for *byzantin* (Levine 1977; Brownlee 1991).

The idea of Byzantine architecture as a vector between antiquity and the Gothic resonated in the work of the aforementioned Prosper Mérimée, Vitet's successor as General Inspector. Through his multiple interests and his tireless travels, Mérimée gained direct knowledge of dozens of churches and monuments throughout France. While Byzantium seems almost neglected in his major works,[7] in a long essay published in 1837, he mentioned the idea of Byzantine architecture as a connection between the main architectural styles, classical and Gothic. Nonetheless, Vitet and Mérimée (and Lenoir as well) did not encapsulate the evolution of Western medieval architecture into a mere plagiarism of Byzantium, but rather as a 'compromis entre l'Orient et l'Occident' (Lenoir 1852: 215), a renewal of the French national architecture (without altering its originality) (Vitet 1853: 270), with an 'infusion' of Byzantium into France (Viollet-le-Duc 1845: 76).

A different position, however, was suggested a decade later by Félix de Verneilh. Born aristocratic, de Verneilh was a collaborator of the *Annales archéologiques*, directed by Adolphe-Napoléon Didron and dedicated to French cultural heritage. In its pages, the *Annales* supported the rediscovery of a Middle Ages 'chrétienne et nationale', according to the conception of its director (Nayrolles 2005). De Verneilh agreed, and debuted in 1844 with an article on the ancient meaning of the term *ogive* (1844),[8] followed a year later by an essay explicitly entitled 'Origine française de l'architecture ogivale' (de Verneilh 1845). In 1851, de Verneilh published *L'Architecture byzantine en France. Saint-Front de Périgueux et les églises à coupoles de l'Aquitaine*, which suggested the direct influence of Byzantium on a distinctive group of domed churches in Aquitaine (de Verneilh 1851). In particular, de Verneilh focused on the cathedral of St. Front at Périgueux (Figure 2.3), whose domes were still hidden in 1851. The author proposed a restoration of the cathedral to unveil the domes and confirm his deductions, that St. Front was a copy of the basilica of St. Mark in Venice. Venice served as mediator between Orient and Occident – 'n'est ce pas toute l'histoire de Venis au moyen age?' asked de Verneilh, before stating that St. Front and the basilica of St. Mark must be considered sisters, with a few differences resulting from local materials and from substitutions of local systems of measurement (de Verneilh 1851: 18). The importation of an oriental architectural type in the southwest of France was probably due to an architect active in St. Mark, Byzantium or Venice, who moved to Périgueux and decided to build a copy of the Venetian basilica. St. Front is thus a Byzantine church in all its aspects, and served as a model for other churches built in Périgord in the following decades. The volume was highly influential: the restoration of St. Front began in 1853, under the direction of Paul Abadie (Wittmann-Englert 2011), and the cathedral was still labelled as Byzantine in the 1930s by local guidebooks (Mayjonade 1935) and postcards.

The dispute over Byzantine architecture's role in France re-erupted. Ludovic Vitet responded to de Verneilh in a long article appearing in 1853, arguing how the

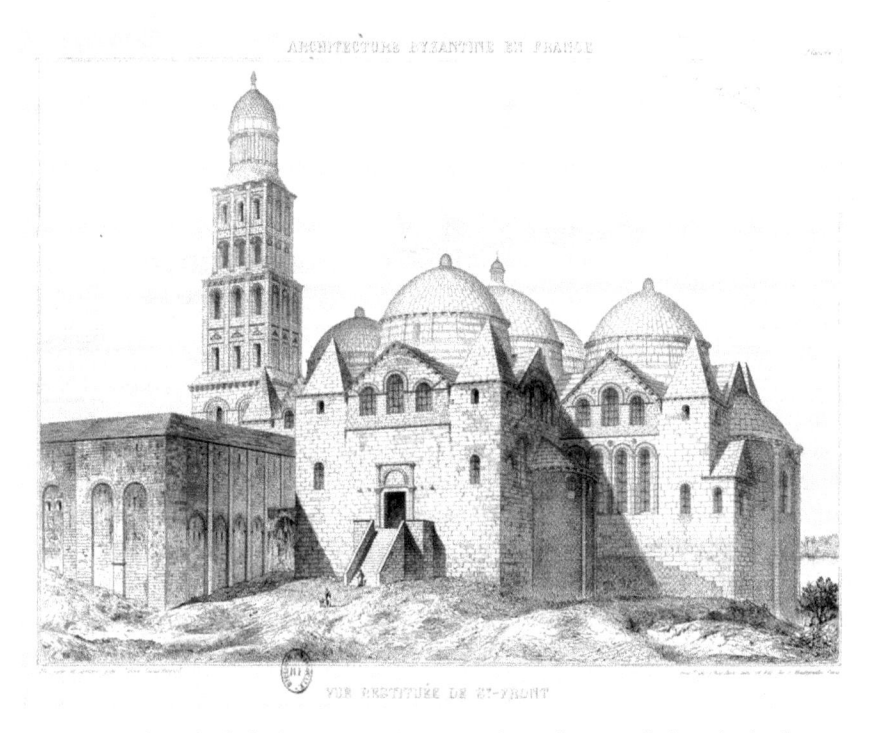

Figure 2.3 The cathedral of St. Front, Périgueux, after F. de Verneilh (1851), *L'Architecture byzantine en France. Saint-Front de Périgueux et les églises à coupoles de l'Aquitaine*, Paris: V. Didron, pl. I.

plan and geometry of St. Front may be Byzantine, but its soul is definitely French (Vitet 1853: 342).[9] Léonce Reynaud, *Inspecteur général des édifices diocésains*, expanded Vitet's theories on the Byzantine influence over French medieval architecture, arguing that the cathedral of St. Pierre at Angoulême, rather than St. Front, was the cornerstone in the relationship between the two architectures (Reynaud 1853). Twenty years later, the debate was still tied with the dispute over the establishment of Gothic architecture. By describing a corpus of churches 'étrangère à notre climat, isolée de notre art national' (de Verneilh 1851: 8), de Verneilh was in fact reducing the impact of Byzantine architecture to a singular episode. From this perspective, de Verneilh took a stand against the common idea of an oriental influence over Gothic architecture, adopting the sceptical attitude already expressed by Adolphe Berty in his *Dictionnaire de l'architecture du Moyen âge* (Berty 1845): with the notable exception of Périgueux, the influence of Byzantine architecture is negligible not only in France but also in Germany and in Italy (Passini 2000; Thomine-Berrada 2008: 328).

Conclusion

While condemning the volume of de Verneilh, Vitet deepened another fundamental topic, that is, the contemporary historicist practice in architecture. The positive roles played by Byzantine architecture in modifying and reinvigorating French architecture occurred in both the Middle Ages and the nineteenth century, as the aforementioned 'génération romantique' of Duban, Labrouste and Vaudoyer. The latter, in particular, was a passionate supporter of the Byzantine in France. Since the 1830s, he was reflecting on the notion of Romanesque and Byzantine architecture, corresponding with local archaeologists and amateurs alike about the Byzantine sources of French medieval architecture, and turning directly to the French Ambassador in Istanbul to get information about Fossati's restoration of Hagia Sophia (Bergdoll 1994: 240). The outcome of his research is the Neo-Byzantine cathedral of Sainte-Marie-Majeure in Marseille, designed in the midst of the dispute (1852), but consecrated only in 1896 (Bergdoll 1986). The cathedral is not only a manifesto of the relationship between Byzantium and France, but intertwined with several influences, including the revival of Catholicism under the Second Empire; the idea of Marseille as a 'Porte d'Orient', an outpost for the arrival of Christianity in France; and also, a sign of the triumph of Mediterranean architecture over the Northern European Gothic style (Bullen 2003: 66–67). The bold structure was flanked by another Neo-Byzantine church, Notre-Dame-de-la-Garde, which was constructed nearby on the highest point of the city, also on a project by Vaudoyer and his pupil, Henri-Jacques Espérandieu.

It is remarkable how the debate over the origins of French medieval architecture, its transformation from Romanesque into Gothic and the alleged Byzantine influence each played a direct part in the design of important, new buildings in France. After Sainte-Marie-Majeure, Neo-Byzantine buildings spread throughout the country, from the Sacré-Coeur on the hill of Montmartre by Paul Abadie, to the crypt of

Louis Pasteur by Charles Girault, from the Orthodox Churches in Paris, Lyon and Reims, to the churches built for the *Chantiers du Cardinal*, during the 1920s and 1930s (Kampouri-Vamvakou 2003: 94–96; Pigafetta and Mastrorilli 2004: 140; Nelson 2015: 27–29). Architects were driven by the desire for a style which was neither Gothic nor classical, rather than for a direct link to French traditions. Nonetheless, although the dispute on Byzantine architecture in France lasted for only a few years, surpassed by a new season of studies,[10] Neo-Byzantine buildings still stand as a symbol of French interest in Byzantium.

Acknowledgements

This article was carried out as a part of the project 'Modern Byzantiums. Receipting and Reinventing Byzantine Architecture in France and Italy, XIX-XX centuries' (Provincia Autonoma di Bolzano, decreto nr. 17444/2021).

Notes

1. 'the church [...] much lauded in our geographies, nevertheless possesses nothing of note. The mosaic pavement is common; the paintings, praised by Guillet, exactly resemble rough drafts of the school preceding Perugino. As for the architecture, there are always domes, more or less overwhelming, more or less multiplied. The cathedral [...] possesses, for its part, seven of these domes. Since this ornament was employed in Constantinople in a degenerate artistic period, it has marred all the monuments of Greece. It has neither the boldness of the Gothic nor the wise beauty of the antique. When immense it is sufficiently majestic; but then it overwhelms the building that bears it; if it is small, it is merely an ignoble skullcap, which fails to link to any element of the architecture, and that rises above the entablature for the express purpose of break the harmonious line of the cymatium.'
2. 'Le séjour à Constantinople me pesoit. Je n'aime à visiter que les lieux embellis par les vertus ou par les arts, et je ne trouvois dans cette patrie des Phocas et des Bajazet ni les unes ni les autres.'
3. The term *roman* was introduced into the vocabulary in 1818, thanks to the intuition of the naturalist Charles de Gerville who translated the word from linguistic into the art historical debate (Nayrolles 2001).
4. At the same time, his opinion of Byzantium as political entity is negative: in the second volume, he blamed Greeks for the failure of Louis VII's crusade in the twelfth century (Laborde 1816-36, II: 8).
5. 'On a beaucoup écrit pour établir l'origine de ce genre d'architecture. Les uns l'ont attribué aux Goths, aux Arabes, aux Allemand. On l'a voulu trouver dans l'imitation des forêts, dans la copie des mosquées arabes antérieures des croisades, dans l'intersection des courbes. Les divagations auxquelles on s'est livré à cet égard proviennent d'une première erreur, celle de croire que ce genre d'architecture était une invention particulière, un goût nouveau.'

6   Texier would later return to Asia: he travelled through Persia, Armenia and Mesopotamia between 1839 and 1841, publishing an account in 1842 (Texier 1842), while a third expedition was financed by the Count Tanneguy Duchâtel in 1842, to rescue the marbles from the temple of Artemis Leucophryene in Magnesia, described in Strabo *Geographia* (XIV. I. 40).
7   Nonetheless, Mérimée demonstrated an overall curiosity toward Byzantium. In his eclectic activity, in 1841 he even translated from Spanish a description of Constantinople, written in 1403 by a member of the Castilian court on the occasion of an embassy of Henry III to Tamerlan (Mérimée 1875).
8   After an inquiry on the technical terminology used by medieval theorists, the definition given by de Verneilh is 'arcs diagonaux d'une voûte d'arêtes'.
9   De Verneilh leaned especially on the historical studies of Maurice Ardant and Charles-Nicolas Allou about the commercial relationship between Venice and Limoges, a connection that Vitet considered misleading: why the Byzantine churches were thus erected in Périgord and not in Limousin? Again, Vitet preferred a soft comparison and wrote about a generic 'génie hellénique' (Vitet 1853: 357).
10   In 1870, Alfred Rambaud published *Constantin Porphyrogénète*. Its introduction is an unapologetic manifesto praising Byzantium. '*L'Empire byzantine a été chez nous sévèrement jugé*', wrote Rambaud, who asked, '*d'ou vient cet oubli ou cette ingratitude de l'Europe?*' (Rambaud 1870: xii). Gustave Schlumberger, commenting the publication of Rambaud's book, described it as an epiphany for the scholars of his generation, who afterwards decided to dedicate works to Byzantium (Schlumberger 1934).

Bibliography

Bergdoll, B. (1986), 'La cathédrale de Marseille: fonctions politiques d'un monument éclectique', *Bulletin de la Société de l'Histoire de l'Art Français*: 129–43.
Bergdoll, B. (1994), *Léon Vaudoyer: Historicism in the Age of Industry*, New York: The Architectural History Foundation.
Berty, A. (1845), *Dictionnaire de l'architecture du Moyen âge*, Paris: A. Derache.
Bianco, E. (2015), *La Bisanzio dei Lumi. L'Impero Bizantino nella cultura francese e italiana da Luigi XIV alla Rivoluzione*, Bern: Peter Verlag.
Brownlee, D. B. (1991), 'Neugriechisch/Néo-Grec: The German Vocabulary of French Romantic Architecture', *Journal of the Society of Architectural Historians*, 50: 18–21.
Bullen, J. B. (2003), *Byzantium Rediscovered*, London: Phaidon.
Chateaubriand, F.-R. de. (1811), *Itinéraire de Paris à Jérusalem et de Jérusalem à Paris, en allant par la Grèce et revenant par l'Egypte, la Barbarie et l'Espagne*, 2 vols, Paris: Le Normant.
Couchaud, A. (1842), *Choix d'églises byzantines en Grèce*, Paris: Lenoir.
Dubois, I. (2003), 'La réception française des théories de Sulpiz Boisserée sur les primitifs allemands', in U. Fleckner and T. W. Gaehtgens (eds.), *De Grünewald à Menzel. L' image de l'art allemand en France au XIXe siècle*, 17–37, Paris: Éditions de la Maison des Sciences de l'Homme.
Gilles, P. (1986), *The Antiquities of Constantinople*, transl. J. Ball, New York: Italica Press.
Hammer-Purgstall, J. von (1822), *Constantinopolis und der Bosporos: örtlich und geschichtlich beschrieben*, Pesth: Hartleben.

Kampouri-Vamvoukou, I. (2003), 'L'Architecture de style néo-byzantin en France', in M.-F. Auzépy (ed.), *Byzance en Europe*, 87–100, Saint-Denis: Presses Universitaires de Vincennes.

Laborde, A. de (1818–36), *Les Monuments de la France classés chronologiquement et considérés sous le rapport des faits historiques et de l'étude des arts*, 2 vols, Paris: Jules Didot l'aîné.

Lenoir, A. (1840), 'De l'architecture byzantine', *Revue générale de l'architecture et des travaux publics*.

Lenoir, A. (1852), 'Influence de l'architecture byzantine dans toute la chrétienté', *Annales archéologiques*, 12: 177–85, 209–18.

Lenoir, A. and L. Vaudoyer (1839–52), 'Études d'architecture en France', *Magasin pittoresque*, Paris: Lachevardière.

Levine, N. (1977), 'The Romantic Idea of Architectural Legibility: Henri Labrouste and the Neo-Grec', in A. Drexler (ed.), *The Architecture of the École des Beaux-Arts*, 325–416, Cambridge, MA: MIT Press.

Loyer, F. (2017), *L'Architecture de la Grèce au XIXe siècle (1821–1912)*, Athens: École française d'Athènes.

Mayjonade, J. B. (1935), *Une basilique byzantine: Saint-Front de Périgueux. Guide du touriste*, Périgueux: Syndicat d'Initiative du Périgord.

Mérimée, P. (1835), *Notes d'un voyage dans le Midi de la France*, Paris: Fournier.

Mérimée, P. (1836), *Notes d'un voyage dans l'Ouest de la France*, Paris: Fournier.

Mérimée, P. (1838a), *Notes d'un voyage en Auvergne*, Paris: Fournier.

Mérimée, P. (1838b), 'Essai sur l'architecture religieuse du Moyen Âge', *Annuaire historique pour l'année 1838*: 283–327.

Mérimée, P. (1840), *Notes d'un voyage en Corse*, Paris: Fournier.

Mérimée, P. (1875), 'Constantinople en 1403' (1841), in *Études sur les arts au moyen âge*, 305–33, Paris: Calmann Lévy.

Nayrolles, J. (2001), 'Sciences naturelles et Archéologie médiévale au XIXe siècle', in *L'Architecture, les Sciences et la Culture de l'histoire au XIXe siècle*, 25–50, Saint-Étienne: Publications de l'Université de Saint-Étienne.

Nayrolles, J. (2005), *L'invention de l'art roman à l'époque moderne (XVIIIe – XIXe siècles)*, Rennes: Presses Universitaires.

Nelson, R. S. (2015), 'Modernism's Byzantium Byzantium's Modernism', in R. Betancourt and M. Taroutina (eds.), *Byzantium/Modernism: The Byzantine as Method in Modernity*, 15–36, Leiden and Boston: Brill.

Passini, M. (2000), Vernehil, Félix (de), in P. Sénéchal and C. Barbillon (eds.), *Dictionnaire critique des historiens de l'art actifs en France de la Révolution à la Première Guerre mondiale*, [https://www.inha.fr/fr/ressources/publications/publications-numeriques/dictionnaire-critique-des-historiens-de-l-art.html, last accessed 07.03.2023]

Pedone, S. (2016), 'I monumenti di Costantinopoli della prima età bizantina nei disegni di Charles Texier (1802–1871)', in S. Cresci, J. Lopez Quiroga, O. Brandt and C. Pappalardo (eds.), *Episcopus, civitas territorium, Proceedings of the conference (Toledo, 2008)*, 1669–82, Rome 2013: Arbor Sapientiae Editore.

Pigafetta, G. and A. Mastrorilli (2004), *Paul Tournon architecte (1881–1964). Le 'moderniste sage'*, Sprimont: Mardaga.

Rambaud, A. (1870), *L'empire grec: Constantin Porphyrogénète*, Paris: A. Franck.

Reynaud, L. (1853), *Traité d'architecture*, Paris: Carilian-Goeury.

Schlumberger, G. (1934), *Mes Souvenirs*, Paris: Plon.

Texier, C. (1842), *Description de l'Arménie et de la Perse, de la Mésopotamie*, 2 vols, Paris: F. Didot frères.

Texier, C. and R. P. Pullan (1864), *Byzantine Architecture Illustrated by Examples of Edifices Erected in the East During the Earliest Ages of Christianity*, London: Day & Son.

Thomine-Berrada, A. (2008), 'Art d'Orient/Art d'Occident. Les débats sur l'apport oriental dans l'architecture médiévale française au XIXe siècle', in R. Recht, P. Sénéchal, C. Barbillon, and F.-R. Martin (eds.), *Histoire de l'histoire de l'art en France au XIXe siècle*, 321–38, Paris: La Documentation française.

Thomine-Berrada, A. (2009), 'L'Orient d'Albert Lenoir (1801–1891). Voyages, lectures, écritures', in N. Oulebsir and M. Volait (eds.), *L'Orientalisme architectural entre imaginaires et savoirs*, 21–35, Paris: Publications de l'Institut national d'histoire de l'art.

Verneilh, F. de (1844), 'Ogive. L'ancienne signification de ce mot', *Annales archéologiques*: 209–210.

Verneilh, F. de (1845), 'Origine française de l'architecture ogivale' *Annales archéologiques*: 1–7.

Verneilh, F. de (1851), *L'Architecture byzantine en France. Saint-Front de Périgueux et les églises à coupoles de l'Aquitaine*, Paris: V. Didron

Vitet, L. (1830), 'De l'architecture lombarde', *Revue française*, 15: 151–73.

Vitet, L. (1853), 'L'Architecture byzantine en France', *Journal des savants*: 5–16, 80–93, 261–79.

Vitet, L. (1867), 'Église Saint-Cunibert à Cologne' [1830], in *Études sur l'histoire de l'art. II. Moyen Âge*, 316–26, Paris: Michel Lévy frères.

Viollet-le-Duc, E.-E. (1845), 'De la construction des édifices religieux en France depuis le commencement du christianisme jusqu'au XVIe siècle', *Annales archéologiques*, II: 69–76, 134–41, 318–30.

Wittmann-Englert, K. (2011), 'Konstruiertes Mittelalter: Paul Abadie restauriert', *Insitu. Zeitschrift für Architekturgeschichte*, 3: 87–104.

Zanten, D. van (1987), *Designing Paris: The Architecture of Duban, Labrouste, Duc, and Vaudoyer*, Cambridge, MA: MIT Press.

3

Byzantium as a Political Tool (1657–1952): Nations, Colonialism and Globalism

Ivan Foletti and Adrien Palladino

The Empire of Constantinople – which we will call here the 'Byzantine Empire', as it is commonly referred to – disappeared as a political entity in 1453. Its history, however, did not end with this date. Quite the contrary: the notion of the 'Byzantine Empire' is the product of incessant religious, cultural and political rewritings throughout the centuries after its demise. Paradoxically, this phenomenon starts with the very name attributed to the empire, 'Byzantine' (Spieser 1991). Practically absent in medieval sources, the name became an element of identity for Greek humanists under Ottoman rule, after 1453, before being 'canonized' into scholarly research by the German Protestant humanist Hieronymus Wolf (1516–80) (Beck 1984; Reinsch 2016). It would be thus possible to argue that 'Byzantium' only started to exist when the actual empire disappeared. What followed would be the transformation of a vanished entity into a perfect instrument for expressing the uses and abuses of the historical past (Cameron 1992). Becoming a perfect historiographical myth, 'Byzantium' remained a 'floating signifier' (Bodin 2016: 13), creating an ideal blank canvas for all kinds of projections and narratives.

The goal of this article is to focus on one of the possible lines for rewriting 'Byzantium': politics. Its starting point will be what is most likely the first explicit use of the dissolved Empire of Constantinople to promote coeval politics, during the reign of Louis XIV. The end point of our account will be the suppression of the Kondakov Institute in Prague, probably the most influential centre for Byzantine studies, between the two world wars. Our investigation will, however, not follow a chronological order. As suggested by the paper's subtitle ('Nations, Colonialism and Globalism'), we will try to analyse how the very notion of 'Byzantium' has been used by scholars and policymakers as a tool for promoting national, colonial and 'global' constructions of the world.

Considering the extremely large scope of this reflection, we have, of course, no pretension of exhaustivity. By putting forth a perspective on the longue durée, we would like, however, to propose an impressionist image of this broad phenomenon (Braudel 1958). Like an Impressionistic painting, certain details are invisible from up close but, looking from afar, it is possible to see not only the general framework emerge but also the points that connect this framework. This is why our discourse will be constructed around selected case studies, which we believe can put forward arguments supporting such an image. We will be following the three main lines suggested in the subtitle of this chapter, namely the question of 'nations', 'colonial' views on the past and concluding with a reflection on the interpretation of 'Byzantine heritage' as a tool to support a transnational perspective.

Byzantine nations?

Before entering into the heart of this section, one premise is fundamental: the issue of how we understand the word 'nation'. Its meaning has indeed varied in time and space. We would thus like to follow the most general definition of the term, namely, describing a state that does not necessarily need anything more than political unity. Following this interpretation, in a pre-modern way, we consider seventeenth-century France, the Russian Empire of the nineteenth century and contemporary Greece as 'nations'.

Following on from this definition, it is not surprising that the heritage of the Byzantine Empire was not immediately adopted by the Greeks, since what would become the modern Greek state was part of the Ottoman Empire until the nineteenth century. Even when Greece emerged as a state in the War of Independence, perhaps due to the support of its 'Romantic' allies, this brand-new country constructed its identity around its classical Hellenistic heritage – despite the existence of the ambivalent and utopic *Megali Idea* (Argyropoulos 2001; Lassithiotakis 2007). An interest in the Byzantine past would progressively emerge, but this would retain only a marginal role until the beginning of the twentieth century (see the essays in Niehoff-Panagiotidis 2011; Delouis, Couderc and Guran 2013).

To a certain extent, immediately after the fall/conquest of Constantinople, its imperial heritage was taken up by Sultan Mehmed II (1451–81). This is clearly visible in a very well-known medal cast by Costanzo da Ferrara, depicting the Sultan as 'SVLTANI·MOHAMMETH·OCTHOMANI·VGVLI·BIZANTII·INPERAT ORIS·1481' (Figure 3.1) and other medals, such as one executed by Gentile Bellini or Bertoldo di Giovanni (Belting 2018). If, from a political point of view, continuity with the Eastern Roman Empire was 'preserved' in the eyes of the Ottomans, then from a 'European' perspective, the rupture was total, since Constantinople had lost its Christian identity (Pertusi 2004). This essentially colonial perspective on the Ottoman, and later Turkish, reappropriation of the 'Byzantine' past has been recently questioned (see, Malcolm 2019). For our purposes, this is, however, not significant, since the Ottomans perceived its continuity as not only natural but also 'marginal' at the same time, in terms of actual politics (Vryonis 1969/70; Akasoy 2004; Pippidi 2006).

Paradoxically, the first evidence of 'Byzantium' used as a reference point for the ambitions of a modern nation appears in France, a country never directly included in the historical Empire of Constantinople. This paradox is not hard to explain: it formed around the king of France's desire for imperial authority, and even more around the mythical narrative of authority transferred to the French rulers after the sack of

Figure 3.1 Costanzo da Ferrara, medal: Sultan Mehmed II, 1481. © Metropolitan Museum, New York.

Constantinople in 1204 and the subsequent establishment of the Latin Empire. It is in this context that Charles du Fresne, Sieur du Cange (1610–88), who had trained as a lawyer, started to work on the history of the Eastern Empire (Figure 3.2) (Spieser 2000). His position is already clear in the *Histoire de l'Empire de Constantinople sous les empereurs français* (1657), where he suggests that the history of a Latin presence in Constantinople was the product of French heroism and identity (du Cange [1657] 1729). In his dedication to King Louis XIV, du Cange writes explicitly:

> Sire I do not present to Your Majesty foreign lands, and new worlds, when I offer Him the empire of Constantinople, since it is a Throne on which value and virtue have raised your Ancestors [...] Your subjects, Sire, who never give in to one or the other in promises and generosity, will hardly have left the harness when you will have led peace on earth, that they will burn with ardour and impatience to put it back on to make this trip themselves, and to carry Your Majesty covered with laurels on this Throne, which is now the seat of the harshest tyranny which ever was.[1]

Considered, at least in the nineteenth century, as a text with few literary qualities, due to Du Cange's excessive erudition and juridical training, its political meaning is,

Figure 3.2 Portrait of Charles du Fresne, Sieur du Cange, 1698. From Charles Perrault (1698), *Les hommes illustres qui ont paru en France pendant ce Siècle: avec leurs Portraits au naturel*, Paris: chez Antoine Dezailler, not paginated.

however, explicit (Buchon 1826). The author invites Louis XIV to take back for France what, according to him, had rightfully belonged to the nation before. For du Cange, there is no question that seventeenth-century France was the direct successor of the medieval French kingdom, and of an even earlier state, that of the Franks. In a brief introduction, the French scholar uses the term *français* – French – to describe the fifth-century Franks arriving in Gallia, and then at different stages throughout the region's history (du Cange 1826: xxi–xxxi). Du Cange would repeat, no less explicitly, the same concept in his subsequent monumental opus devoted to Byzantine history: in his dedication to Colbert (1619–83), Louis XIV's secretary of state, he urges the king to take back Constantinople from the Ottomans (du Cange 1680).

It is debatable what impact these texts had on actual French politics. According to Jean-Michel Spieser (2000), it represented a marginal issue. On the other hand, it must be noted that military conflicts between European states and the Ottoman empire were frequent in these years, and that Louis XIV had tangible plans to besiege Constantinople (Omont 1893; Grélois 2003; Faruk 2004). While these belligerent projects remained merely wild dreams, what is fundamental for us is the rhetorical use of 'Byzantium' as a measure of France's legitimate right to potential imperial honours. Another crucial point is certainly the concept of what has been called, already in the Middle Ages, the *translatio imperii* (Goez 1958; Schmoll 2007). In the dedication of his 1657 volume, du Cange does not mention this theory, which holds that Roman imperial tradition moved from Rome to Constantinople with Constantine, only to return to the 'West', to Charlemagne, because the crown entered Greece in the hands of a woman – the Empress Irene. Indeed, du Cange mentions the inability of the Greeks – the schismatic Christians – to perpetuate a stable imperial dynasty several times. In this way, because of the tradition of Charlemagne and, even more because of the Latin Empire of Constantinople in the thirteenth century, France should be seen as the true moral and religious recipient of imperial dignity. This is even more important if we consider the seventeenth-century tensions between the French kingdom and the Holy Roman Empire, which were centred on Carolingian succession (Tellenbach 1982; Brühl 1995; Schieffer 2006). In other words, Du Cange's work does not mirror any *realpolitik*, but its symbolic meaning is significant.

Less than two centuries later, in Russia, Byzantine heritage underwent another important and emblematic phase. After the tragic events of the French invasion of Russia, the country was going through an intense moment of self-reflection (Heller 1997: 661; Lieven 2009). Starting with Peter the Great (1682–1725), the general orientation of the country, represented by its elites, was turning towards the 'West', with particular attention to Prussian and French cultures. It is no coincidence that Peter, when declared emperor, explicitly referred to the heritage of the Roman West – implicitly rejecting 'Greek-Byzantine' influences. This was also true in terms of the political structure of his empire, which had shifted from the theocratic structure of the Empire of Constantinople toward the lay model of Rome (Heller 1997: 444–45, 453). On the other hand, it has been assumed that one of the reasons for the prodigious growth of the Russian Empire during the reign of Catherine the Great (1762–96) was the country's Orthodox/Byzantine heritage. This would be especially visible during the war with the Ottoman Empire (1762–74). According to Michel Heller, Catherine – together with the prince Alexis Orlov – dreamt of supporting all of the Orthodox Slavs of the Ottoman Empire in raising themselves up against the Turks in order to renew, to a certain extent, the Empire of Constantinople (Heller 1997: 582–83). However, we would argue that this dream was unrealistic, and that the reference to the Empire of Constantinople was essentially a political tool in the hands of the empress (Heller 1997: 571–75, 582–84).

The Napoleonic invasion can be seen as an event that radicalized these two perspectives (Nivat 1992; Rouleau 1992; Aizlewood 2000). While vehemently rejected by some intellectuals, such as Piotr Čadaeev (1794–1855) in his famous 'Philosophical Letters' (1836), conversely, 'Byzantium' became the 'promised land' for others (Heller 1997: 712–15). This would open up a double perspective on Russian identity, with opposing groups defined as 'Slavophiles' and 'Occidentalists'. And while such a binary vision is, of course, far too simplistic, the relationship with 'Byzantine' heritage seems to have played a significant part in it. This can be seen clearly when considering the construction of the Cathedral of Christ the Saviour in Moscow. Conceived as a temple celebrating victory over Napoleon, it was first designed by Alexander L. Vitberg (1787–1855) in 1816 (Figure 3.3). This neoclassical project, which was never actually constructed, was later replaced by a design by Konstantin Thon (1794–1881), on which work started in 1839 (Foletti 2019). This new building was executed in a style defined as Russo-Byzantine (Figure 3.4). This impressive aesthetic movement can be best understood when examining the transition from the reign of Alexander I (1801–25), who represented a pre-Napoleonic perspective, to Nicholas I (1825–55), who openly promoted a very different outlook (Heller 1997: 696–750). The latter can be characterized, following Sergej Uvarov (1786–1855), by the three keywords on which the tsarist worldview was constructed: autocracy, orthodoxy and nation (Heller 1997: 718–21). It is precisely the first two of these that connected Russia and the Empire of Constantinople. During the same time, this Russo-Byzantine style became the visual rhetoric of the Empire and a mandatory pattern for new religious buildings (Foletti 2019).[2] Furthermore, interest in Russo-Byzantine antiquities became a trend supported by the ruling elites (see, e.g. Sacharov 1841–49).

This slow process reached an apex in the second half of the century, when, starting with the Russo-Turkish War of 1877–78, official propaganda publicly defined Russia as the heir of Byzantium (Heller 1997: 814–16). This idea was, of course, not entirely new to the Russian environment after the fall of Constantinople and was present in the political fantasies of many rulers, such as noted above for Catherine the Great. It

Figure 3.3 Aleksandr Vitberg, design of the Cathedral of Christ the Savior, 1817. Authors' photo.

Figure 3.4 Konstantin Thon, design of the Cathedral of Christ the Savior, 1832. Authors' photo.

is, however, precisely in the last quarter of the nineteenth century that this perspective became the official *doxa*, notably in the reflections of Konstantin Leontiev (1831–91) and Nikolaj Danilevskij (1822–85), as well as in coeval mass media (Rakitin 2013; Stamatopoulos 2013). It is also no coincidence that it is in this very period, the legendary fifteenth-century writings of the monk Filofej were published for the first time, defining Moscow as the 'Third Rome' – heir of the first two, Rome and Constantinople, which had collapsed (Meyendorff 1991; Ivanov 2016; Boček 2019). In preparing for the above-mentioned war, the ambitions of the Empire of the Tsars are clearly stated: to free Constantinople from Turkish rule. What was a dream for Catherine, and what was not possible to achieve during the Crimean War (1853–56), appeared now as a realistic goal for the empire, stabilized by the important reforms of Alexander II (1855–81). We will encounter this ambition again in 1916, when Nicholas II (1896–1917) announced that one of the major objectives of the First World War was to 'take back' Constantinople (Heller 1997: 928–29).

The geopolitical background of the conflicts with the Ottoman Empire is evident: Russia wanted access to the Mediterranean. Moreover, while becoming the hegemon of the Euro-Asiatic zone during the late eighteenth and throughout the nineteenth century, the country also wished to control the Balkans (directly or indirectly). The role of 'Byzantium' in this case is quite different to the one presented above, when speaking of seventeenth-century France. Orthodox tradition and the historical link with the Empire of Constantinople, after more rhetorical uses prior to this, became the pretext on which Russia could justify concrete political (and military) actions during the nineteenth century. All instruments of late nineteenth-century propaganda are involved in the promotion of such a viewpoint: visual culture, diplomacy, newspapers and scholarship. When examining the history of Byzantine studies, it is fundamental to underline this last aspect. History, art history, philology and archaeology begin to interact profoundly with the country's political ambitions. Figures such as Fëdor Buslajev (1818–97), Nikodim Kondakov (1844–1925) and Alexander Veselovskij (1838–1906) present a viewpoint of the Byzantine past which now appears clearly determined by and intertwined with their present (Kyzlasova 1985; 'Veselovskij' 1989; Foletti 2017). The last point worthy of mention is, on the contrary, something that unites the court of Louis XIV with the last Romanovs: the evident imperial authority associated with the notion of 'Byzantium'. It is no surprise that the Russian Tsars used the medieval Slavic term to describe Constantinople – 'Tsargrad'.

Two other minor episodes are worthy of a brief mention to complete this viewpoint. First, the situation at the court of Napoleon III (1852–70) in Paris. According to coeval sources, the king's personal chapel was built in a 'Neo-Byzantine' style by Sébastien Cornu (1804–70) (Jolles, Cummings and Landais 1978; Granger 2005: 70, 230). Moreover, it is in this very period that we see, in France, the first studies devoted to positive analysis of Byzantine art and architecture. This is the case, for example, for studies by Jules Labarte (1797–1880), but also for studies on 'Byzantine architecture' such as those by Auguste Choisy (1841–1909) (Labarte 1861; Labarte 1864–66; Choisy 1883; Tomasi 2009). Furthermore, a 'Byzantine revival style' (Figure 3.5), with all the limits that this notion evokes, appeared in architecture across the country (Kampouri-Vamvoukou 2003). At the same time, works of art history seeking to prove the 'Byzantine' origins of 'French medieval architecture' (Thomine-Berrada 2008) appear on the horizon. Strangely enough, it is in this same period that historical research on the Roman Empire, with a clear focus on the notion of *translatio imperii,* is published by Henry Dunant (Auzépy 2001: 16). This certainly does not follow the dominant trend of French culture and historiography in the 1850s and 1860s, yet an imaginary 'Byzantium' appears when France wants to represent itself as an empire again.

It is well known that the dream of the French Empire was shattered by the Franco-Prussian war of 1870. Just a year later, Prussia would be integrated into the newly

Byzantium as a Political Tool (1657–1952) 53

351. PARIS — MONTMARTRE — Le Sacré-Cœur
et le Funiculaire   C. M.

Figure 3.5 Paul Abadie, Basilique du Sacré-Cœur, Paris, 1875–1923. © Private collection.

Figure 3.6 Hermann Schaper, Mosaic of Wilhelm II and his family approaching the Cross, Kaiser-Wilhelm memorial church, Berlin, 1891–95. © N. Bock.

founded German Empire (recently, see Arand 2018). It is not therefore surprising that, when looking for an ideal model of self-representation, only a few years later, Emperor Wilhelm II (1888–1918) chose the imperial 'Byzantine' mosaics of San Vitale in Ravenna (Figure 3.6) to represent himself and his father Wilhelm I (1871–88) at the Kaiser-Wilhelm Memorial Church in Berlin (Bock 2018; Frantová 2019: 17–30). Once more, this is not the dominant trend of late nineteenth-century German visual culture, even though Ludwig II of Bavaria (1864–86) had used similar 'Byzantine/Imperial' references in his political ambitions. In this case, it is worth mentioning that the 'Byzantine' reference seems to have been mediated by Norman Sicily (Berger 2003; Schellewald 2008). Yet, 'Empire' and 'Byzantium', in these cases, become almost synonymic within a very limited circle.

Unlike in Russia, where it gradually assumed an official and public aspect, the Empire of Constantinople became a 'generic' evocation of past glory and imperial splendour in Germany and France. In both cases, a historical justification was given for this use: the French Kingdom of Constantinople and the Norman/Hohenstaufen Kingdom of Sicily, a mythology that was revived after 1871 (e.g. Kaul 2009). In addition, for Russia, 'Byzantine' heritage became a tool of imperial and colonial policy in the Balkans, while Germany and France had no real ambitions to compete with the decadent Ottoman Empire in the nineteenth century. For them, 'Byzantium' was a visual and intellectual paradigm utilized to assert their new, imperial identity.

Colonizing through Byzantium

When the Russian Empire conquered the Caucasus in 1878, the decision was made to build a church dedicated to Alexander Nevskij in Tbilisi (1871–97) (Savel'ev 2005). When looking at the image of this building (Figure 3.7), we cannot help but notice a striking resemblance with buildings from the Middle Byzantine period. When colonizing a previously autonomous region, the Russian Empire presented its new power by using the visual patterns of Byzantine Orthodoxy (Wortman 2003, 2006: 251). This made perfect sense in Georgia, which was one of the few Christian countries of this region. It is not surprising that when, several decades before in 1801, Russia decided to annex Georgia into the empire, this act was presented as the logical consequence of a shared Orthodox identity (see 'Manifest' 1830). Visual culture was, in this case, used consciously as evidence to support a supposed shared past.

In 1856, Grigorij Gagarin (1810–93), an incredibly eclectic figure – politician, architect, painter and scholar – published a book devoted to Byzantine art (Gagarin 1856; Bertash 2011). Monuments from late antique Italy, Constantinople, Armenia, Georgia and Russia are included in this volume. The concept that he was implicitly supporting was the artistic coherence uniting Rome with Constantinople, and both cities with Moscow. What is, however, more delicate, is the place held by the Southern Caucasian region in his work. This area is seen as the place where the Empire of Constantinople overlaps with the territory of the Russian Empire. As with the Alexander Nevskij Church, shared Orthodox identity plays a key role in the perception

Figure 3.7 David Grimm, Alexander Nevsky Cathedral, Tbilisi, 1871–72/1889–97. © Private collection.

of Georgia as belonging the empire, as it does also in art and architectural history (Foletti and Rakitin 2018).

In 1890, the above-mentioned Nikodim Kondakov published an important book on Russian medieval art. It featured the subtitle 'Crimea, Caucasus, and Kiev' (Kondakov, Tolstoj 1891). In the part dedicated to the art of Georgia and Armenia, Kondakov explicitly suggests that they should be considered as an expression of Byzantine provincial reception (Kondakov and Tolstoj 1891: 36). What was already implicitly present in Gagarin's research here becomes evidence: the Southern Caucasus is considered an artistically and culturally inferior province when seen from Constantinople (or from Saint Petersburg). Such an idea was already inherently visible in the writings of Dimitri Bakradze (1873). Bakradze had devoted a survey to the arts of the region, where Armenian and Georgian monuments were ordered alphabetically – thus indirectly negating any particularism to Armenian and Georgian artistic cultures. When speaking about the medieval architecture of these regions, this is anything but true: the artistic production of medieval Armenia and Georgia is a demonstration of the highest cultural level, certainly in contact with Constantinople but in no way a passive and provincial recipient of Byzantine influences (Foletti and Thunø 2016; Bacci, Kaffenberger and Studer-Karlen 2018; Foletti and Riccioni 2018). Gagarin, Kondakov and Bakradze seem to be projecting the Russian present onto the past (Foletti 2016). To do this, they affirm the dependence of the cultures of the Southern Caucasian region on Byzantium, thus distorting historical reality. In the writings of intellectuals, as well as in contemporary political attitudes, the Byzantine past is used to justify a colonial policy.

This use of Byzantium as a colonial entity was not limited to the newly annexed provinces of the Russian Empire. It is mirrored in the attitude of scholars through the popular concept of the 'Byzantine Commonwealth', a term coined by the Russian émigré Dimitri Obolensky (1918–2001) in his 1971 *opus magnum* (Obolensky 1971), but already present in his studies from the 1950s (Obolensky 1950; Korenevskiy 2016). His 'Commonwealth' encompasses a wide chronological and geographical perspective, which specifically considers Byzantium's areas of influence beyond its 'formal borders'. One of the overarching issues in Obolensky's studies is the 'soft power' exerted by the Eastern Roman Empire, based on its standing and reputation (Cameron 2014: 38–40). Looking at the map of lands composing this 'Commonwealth', we notice two important elements. On the one hand, it encompasses many lands which had formed part of the Russian Empire, and until the 1991 fall of the Soviet Union, had been united within the 'Eastern Communist Block'. On the other hand, these are overwhelmingly lands of Orthodoxy. As such, 'Byzantium' is posited by the scholar as the home and champion of Eastern Orthodoxy. Therefore, one of the commonalities of the lands of this commonwealth is the fact that they had adopted Christianity through Byzantine hands, while at the same time benefiting from the technical, cultural and artistic skills brought by Byzantine 'missions'. This perspective can be, without a doubt, characterized as a continuation of the colonial attitude promoted by Russian scholars: under the influence of Byzantium, this perspective minimizes historical and national specificities (Raffensperger 2004; Shepard 2006).

What is particularly interesting is that Obolensky's own life story matches this vision of history. As an émigré, Obolensky had arrived in England in 1919 as a small child, and had come from an aristocratic Russian family whose roots could be traced back to the Muscovite aristocracy of the late Middle Ages (Obolensky 1999). Having received his intellectual training entirely in Great Britain, but within a traditional Russian elite milieu, it is not surprising to see Obolensky apply the conceptual framework of 'Commonwealth' – a notion deeply linked with British colonial tradition, although presenting decolonizing ambitions – to his history of Eastern Europe. We can mention here the 1926 creation of the 'British Commonwealth of Nations', forming a consortium of sovereign states which are almost all former British colonies (see 'British Commonwealth' 1991; Srinivasan 2006). Obolensky, while speaking of the influence of the Empire of Constantinople, was thus using language that was clearly understandable from the point of view of coeval political thought. He projected his present as an émigré, and of subsequent historical moments, such as the start of the Cold War, onto 'Byzantium' (Korenevskiy 2016). While Obolensky's work had no direct political weight, he formed a bridge between the British colonial conception of cultural influence and the existing Russian perspective, focusing on the dependence of 'provincial' cultures on a Byzantine centre. In this perspective, rooted in the early nineteenth century, 'Byzantium' is presented as the historical counterpart of Russia.

'Byzantium' without borders

As stated in the introduction, there is, however, a third signifier 'applied' to 'Byzantium' from a broader political perspective: its definition as a supranational entity not belonging to any one nation-state. Paradoxically, this perception appears in the writings of Russian scholars during the interwar period. However, like Obolensky, these scholars were all émigrés, forced to leave the country by the Bolshevik Revolution. Some of them, such as one of the most important art historians of the twentieth century, André Grabar, were trained in Russia with a traditional colonial and, at the same time, national viewpoint (Smirnova 1999; Medvedkova 2016). Once forced to acculturate themselves to Europe, they adapted their writing and thought to their new reality of emigration (e.g. Raeff 1990; Schlögel 1994).

The first example worth mentioning in this context is a group of Russian émigrés who gathered in Prague around the figure of Kondakov, who was an émigré himself. After his death in 1925, this informal company was transformed into an institute bearing Kondakov's name: the *Institutum Kondakovianum* (Beißwenger [2001] 2005; Dmitrieva 2018; Foletti 2019; Lovino 2019; Foletti and Palladino 2020). For almost thirty years, this institute was one of the most influential and creative research centres focused on Byzantine studies. Its world fame was promoted on the one hand by its outstanding members, such as Georgij Vernadskij, Nikolaj Toll and Georgij Ostrogorskij, and on the other, through the publication of the journal *Seminarium Kondakovianum* (Lovino 2016a, 2016b, 2017; Foletti and Palladino 2020). When reading through this periodical, the image of Byzantium that appears is quite different to the one previously described: in an outlook similar to that of Obolensky, Byzantine culture does not belong to a unique nation, but goes beyond the borders of the Empire of Constantinople. Slavs, Greeks and Latins all participated in this cultural epicentre, formed by visual culture and Orthodoxy. In a few decades, a colonial empire thus became a cultural aggregation in the writings of these scholars.

Such a transformation is hard to imagine without a very specific context: the situation of Russian émigrés in Czechoslovakia. They had lost their homeland, Imperial Russia, but had found a new safe harbour in a young democracy, which also had the explicit ambition of becoming a uniting point between East and West. This was one of the main ambitions of the 'Russian Action', promoted by the Czechoslovak government, to welcome Russian intellectual émigré elites (Chinyaeva 1993; Bobrinskoy 1995; Chinyaeva 2001: 41–68). The goal of such a project – never achieved – was to train young Russian elites who would then, once they had returned to their stabilized homeland, make up a fundamental group of allies to promote Czechoslovakia's role as mediator. This never came to be, and yet, the Russian émigrés experienced in Prague a cosmopolitan environment nourished by Pan-Slavic ideals, democratic values and multiethnic contacts.

A further element to consider when speaking about the Byzantine circles in Prague is the existence of another journal promoted directly by the Czech state and by the president Tomáš Garrigue Masaryk (1850–1937) himself. Named *Byzantinoslavica*, this journal chiefly shared interests with *Seminarium Kondakovianum*, but placed greater attention on the Slavic cultures born outside the Empire of Constantinople (Burgmann 2001; Lovino 2018). In the foreword of the journal, it is clear that this focus is promoted by the construction of the new, supposedly Slavic, Czechoslovakian nation (Bidlo et al. 1929). In a country that had serious problems with ethnic minorities, such as Germans and Hungarians, the emphasis on Byzantium as a 'trans-Slavic' cultural entity takes on a clear political meaning. Together with the Cyrillo-Methodian tradition, this turned Czechoslovakia into a place where a certain 'Byzantium' could be 'used' by the current democracy (Malíř 2016).

At the same time, the Russian diaspora was not at all limited to Czechoslovakia, but spread literally all around the globe. Colleagues from a select few Russian universities were suddenly teaching in Prague, New Haven and Tokyo. This certainly contributed to a radically different perception of the self. It is in this context that we should understand this new layer of perceiving 'Byzantium'. Following the history of a transnational diaspora, and with the very specific situation of Czechoslovakia as one of its epicentres, the vision of 'Byzantine culture' was extended beyond many borders.

This vision is also affirmed in the trajectory of the above-mentioned André Grabar. Unlike the members of the *Institutum Kondakovianum*, this individual moved from Russia to Bulgaria, and later to France (Dagron 1992; Foletti 2012). There, he would very soon go through a rapid acculturation to the French milieu, receiving French citizenship in 1928. We believe that this movement towards French Republican culture deeply impacted Grabar's writing on 'Byzantium' (Foletti forthcoming). Already during his Bulgarian exile, his view on the cultural history of the 'Byzantine Empire' arrived at similar perspectives as the members of the Kondakov Institute: his artistic 'Byzantium' goes, indeed, far beyond the borders of the Empire of Constantinople (Palladino 2020). In his thought, we find imperial identity transferred to an idea of a large and shared space. This reasoning is, of course, logical when considering the medieval paintings he studied in the Balkans, which had developed outside the political reality of the empire (Grabar 1924a, 1924b, 1928a, 1928b). However, we can argue that such a viewpoint becomes logical once Russian émigrés like Grabar were forced to live outside Russia. Their Byzantium was transformed directly by political events and their experience of emigration. Having lost their homeland, Russian émigrés adopted a 'Euro-Asiatic' gaze, which they transposed onto their visions of the past.

It is no surprise that another crucial step in the use and perception of 'Byzantium' would come in the Second World War and the progressive Soviet occupation of Central and Eastern Europe. Nazi propaganda never explicitly used Byzantine heritage, choosing Roman and Germanic appropriations instead, but was quite 'tolerant' toward 'Byzantine studies' (e.g. Agapitos 2019). This was perhaps due to the very fluidity of the notion of 'Byzantine studies'. On the other hand, because of its Christian émigré identity, 'Byzantine studies' would be marginalized in Soviet historiography (e.g. Ivanov 2003). It is thus unsurprising that one of the significant acts of the newly established regime in Czechoslovakia was the suppression of the *Institutum Kondakovianum* in 1952. We do not have space here to enter more deeply into the very complex interaction between the notion of Byzantium, Soviet scholarship and political power, however, what seems to us worthy of mention is the fact that, once again, the idea and notion of 'Byzantium' was shaped by historical events.

Conclusion

In this article, we have touched on three main lines of argument out of many. These very different perspectives, however, highlight two notable aspects. First, because of the absence of any clear 'heir' to the Empire of Constantinople, its political heritage was taken up, to a certain extent, by the Ottoman Empire, while its visual, religious and literary cultures were adopted by many regions and nations. Thus, 'Byzantium' became a sort of 'empty box'. Its imperial prestige and certain visual glamour made this past reality an ideal tool for exploring political conflicts, cultural appropriations and misuses of power. This is visible from France to Germany, and throughout Russia, but it would also be possible to extend this list beyond the few examples touched on in this essay, looking at Bulgaria, Romania or Turkey, for example.

The second impressive element is the connection established between the Byzantine past and Russian political and cultural identities. In all the perspectives investigated above, Russia is present as state, as empire and as dissolute émigré reality. It is no coincidence that, still today in Putin's and the Patriarchs Alexis and Cyril's Russia, the 'Byzantine orthodox legacy' is still a constitutive element for political ambitions and abuses (Figure 3.8).

With this research, we hope we have been able to present some valid lines of inquiry. We do, however, firmly believe that today, more than ever, 'Byzantium' requires a proper systematic historiographical investigation, to avoid the trap of over-politicized perceptions and uses.

Figure 3.8 Vizantija: uroki prošlogo i budušego dlja Rossii [Byzantium: duties of the past and of the future for Russia], 2016. © KATEHON.com.

Notes

1 'Sire je ne présente pas à Votre Majesté des terres étrangères, & de nouveaux mondes, quand je luy offre l'Empire de Constantinople, puisque c'est un Trône sur lequel la valeur & la vertu ont élevé vos Ayeux [...] Vos sieurs, Sire, qui ne cèdent ny aux un ny aux autre en promesses & en générosité, auront à peine quitté le harnois quand vous aurez ramené la paix sur terre, qu'ils brûleront d'ardeur & d'impatience de le rendosser pour faire ce voyage à leur tour, & de porter Votre Majesté couverte de lauriers sur ce Trône, qui est maintenant le siège de la plus rude tyrannie qui fut jamais' (du Cange [1657] 1729).
2 *Ustava Stroitel'nogo Svoda Zakonov izdanija 1857 g.*, Saint Petersburg 1841, Mart, 25, St. 218.

Bibliography

Agapitos, P. (2019), 'Franz Dölger and the Hieratic Model of Byzantine Literature', *Byzantinische Zeitschrift*, 112: 707–79.
Aizlewood, R. (2000), 'Revisiting Russian Identity in Russian Thought: From Chaadaev to the Early Twentieth Century', *The Slavonic and East European Review*, 78 (1): 20–43.

Akasoy, A. (2004), 'Die Adaptation byzantinischen Wissens am Osmanenhof nach der Eroberung Konstantinopels', in C. Kretschmann, H. Pahl and P. Scholz (eds.), *Wissen in Krise. Institutionen des Wissens im gesellschaftlichen Wandel*, 43–56, Berlin: De Gruyter.

'Alexander Veselovskij' (1989), in *Russkie pisateli, 1800–1917: Biografičeskij slovar'* [Russian authors, 1800–1917: biographical dictionary], vol. 1, 434–36, Moscow: Bol'šaja rossijskaja enciklopedija.

Arand, T. (2018), *1870/71. Die Geschichte des Deutsch-Französischen Krieges 1870/71 erzählt in Einzelschicksalen*, Hamburg: Osburg Verlag.

Argyropoulos, R. D. (2001), *Les intellectuels grecs à la recherche de Byzance (1860–1912)*, Athens: Institut de Recherches Néohelléniques.

Auzépy, M.-F. (2001), 'Introduction', in M.-F. Auzépy and, J.-P. Grélois (eds.), *Byzance retrouvé. Érudits et voyageurs français [XVIe-XVIIIe siècles]*, (exhibition catalogue, Paris, Chapelle de la Sorbonne, 13 August –2 September 2001), 16–9, Paris: Publications de la Sorbonne.

Bacci, M., T. Kaffenberger and M. Studer-Karlen, eds. (2018), *Cultural Interactions in Medieval Georgia*, Wiesbaden: Reichert Verlag.

Bakradze, D. (1873), 'Kavkaz' v drevnich' pamjatnikach' christianstva' [The Caucasus into the ancient Christian monuments], *Akty, sobrannye Kavkazskoj archeografičeskoj komissiej*, 5: 993–1107.

Beck, H.-G., ed. (1984), *Der Vater der deutschen Byzantinistik. Das Leben des Hieronymus Wolf von ihm selbst erzählt*, Munich: Institut für Byzantinistik und neugriechische Philologie der Universität.

Beißwenger, M. ([2001] 2005), *Das Seminarium Kondakovianum in Prag (1925–1952)*, MA diss., Humboldt-Universität, Berlin.

Belting, H. (2018), Hans Belting, 'A Venetian Artist at the Ottoman Court: An Encounter of Two Worlds', *Convivium*, V/2: 14–31.

Berger, A. (2003), 'Les projets byzantins de Louis II de Bavière', in M.-F. Auzépy (ed.), *Byzance en Europe*, 75–85, Saint-Denis: Presses Universitaires de Vincennes.

Bertash, A. (2011), 'Arhitekturnoe i hudozhestvennoe tvorchestvo knjazja G. G. Gagarina v kontekste razvitija russkogo i vizantijskogo stilej' [Architectural and artistic creations of the Prince G. G. Gagarin into the context of the development of the Russian and Byzantine styles], in *Grigorij Gagarin hudozhnik i obshhestvennyj dejatel': materialy nauchnoj konferencii, posvjashhennoj 200-letiju so dnja rozhdenija vice-prezidenta Imperatorskoj Akademii hudozhestv knjazja G.G. Gagarina, 17–18 nojabrja 2010 g.*, 74–85, Saint Petersburg: [b.i.].

Bidlo, J. et al. (1929), 'Úvodní slovo' [Foreword], *Byzantinoslavica*, 1: I–II.

Bobrinskoy, O. (1995), 'La Première République tchécoslovaque et l'émigration russe (1920–1938): la spécificité d'une politique d'asile', *Revue d'études comparatives Est-Ouest*, 26: 153–75.

Boček, P., ed. (2019), *Moskva. Třetí Řím. Od ideje k symbolu* [Moscow. Third Rome. From the idea to the symbol], Prague: Lidové noviny.

Bock, N. (2018), 'Art and the Origins of Authority: Prussia, From Ravenna to Byzantium and the Romanesque', in I. Foletti et al. (eds), *Re-thinking, Re-making, Re-living Christian Origins*, 191–208, Rome: Viella.

Bodin, H. (2016), 'Whose Byzantinism – Ours or Theirs? On the Issue of Byzantinism From a Cultural Semiotic Perspective', in P. Marciniak and D. C. Smythe (eds.), *The Reception of Byzantium in European Culture since 1500*, 11–42, Farnham: Routledge.

Braudel, F. (1958), 'Histoire et sciences sociales: La longue durée', *Annales. Histoire, Sciences Sociale*s, 13 (4): 725–53.
'British Commonwealth of Nations' (1991), in J. S. Olson (ed.), *Historical Dictionary of European Imperialism*, 79–80, London: Greenwood Publishing Group.
Brühl, C. (1995), *Deutschland – Frankreich: Die Geburt Zweier Völker*, Vienna: Böhlau.
Buchon, J. A. (1826), 'Préface', in C. du Fresne Sieur du Cange, *Histoire de l'Empire de Constantinople sous les empereurs français*, 13–20, Paris: Verdière.
Burgmann, L. (2001), 'Byzantinoslavica, Prag 1929–1999', *Rechtshistorisches Journal*, 20: 28–32.
Cameron, A. (1992), *The Use & Abuse of Byzantium: An Essay on Reception*, London: The School of Humanities, King's College.
Cameron, A. (2014), *Byzantine Matters*, Princeton, NJ: Princeton University Press.
Chinyaeva, E. (1993), 'Ruská emigrace v Československu: vývoj ruské pomocné akce' [Russian emigration to Czechoslovakia: the development of the Russian action for help], *Slovanský přehled*, 79: 14–24.
Chinyaeva, E. (2001), *Russians outside Russia. The Émigré Community in Czechoslovakia 1918–1938*, Munich: R. Oldenbourg Verlag.
Choisy, A. (1883), *L'Art de bâtir chez les Byzantins*, Paris: Librairie de la Société Anonyme de Publications Périodiques.
Dagron, G. (1992), 'Préface: André Grabar (1896–1990)', in A. Grabar, *Les origines de l'esthétique médiévale*, 5–10, Paris: Macula.
Delouis, O., A. Couderc and P. Guran, eds. (2013), *Héritages de Byzance en Europe du Sud-Est à l'époque moderne et contemporaine*, Athens: École française d'Athènes.
Dmitrieva, M. (2018), 'Towards a Trans-national History of Russian Culture: The N. P. Kondakov Institute in Prague', in C. Flamm, R. Marti and A. Raev (eds.), *Transcending the Borders of Countries, Languages, and Disciplines in Russian Émigré Culture*, 173–98, Cambridge: Cambridge Scholars Publishing.
du Cange, C. du Fresne, sieur (1680), *Historia Byzantina duplici commentario illustrata*, Paris: apud Ludovicum Billaine.
du Cange, C. du Fresne, sieur ([1657] 1729), *Histoire de l'Empire de Constantinople sous les empereurs français jusqu'à la conquête des Turcs*, Venice: Barthelemi Javarina.
du Cange, C. du Fresne, sieur (1826), *Histoire de l'Empire de Constantinople sous les empereurs français*, Paris: Verdière.
Dunant, J. H. (1859), *L'empire de Charlemagne rétabli ou le Saint-Empire romain reconstitué par Sa Majesté l'Empereur Napoléon*, Geneva: Imprimerie Jules-G^me Fick.
Faruk, B. (2004), *Louis XIV et son projet de conquête d'Istanbul*, Ankara: Türk Tarih Kurumu.
Foletti, I. (2012), 'André/Andrej Nikolajevič Grabar', in S. Heid and M. Dennert (eds.), *Personenlexikon zur Christlichen Archäologie. Forscher und Persönlichkeiten vom 16. bis zum 21. Jahrhundert*, 2 vols, vol. 1, 601–02, Regensburg: Schnell & Steiner.
Foletti, I. (2016), 'The Russian View of a "Peripheral" Region: Nikodim P. Kondakov and the Southern Caucasus', *Convivium*, Supplementum: 20–35.
Foletti, I. (2017), *From Byzantium to Holy Russia. Nikodim Kondakov (1844–1925) and the Invention of the Icon*, Rome: Viella.
Foletti, I. (2019), 'Russian Inputs in Czechoslovakia: When Art History meets History. The Institutum Kondakovianum during the Nazi Occupation', in I. Foletti and A. Palladino (eds.), *Inventing Medieval Czechoslovakia 1918–1968: Between Slavs, Germans, and Totalitarian Regimes*, 63–92, Rome: Viella.
Foletti, I. (forthcoming), 'How to Write Images about the Medieval World: André Grabar and his Byzantium. The Case of L'empereur dans l'art byzantin (1936)', *Word & Image*, 37.

Foletti, K. and I. Foletti (2019), 'Moskva nebo Řím? Rusko-byzantská architektura a *translatio imperii*?' [Moscow or Rome? Russian-byzantine architecture and the *translatio imperii*?], in P. Boček (ed.), *Moskva. Třetí Řím. Od ideje k symbolu*, 185–99, Prague: Lidové noviny.

Foletti, I. and A. Palladino (2020), *Byzantium or Democracy? Kondakov's Legacy in Emigration: The* Institutum Kondakovianum *and André Grabar, 1925–1952*, Rome: Viella.

Foletti, I. and P. Rakitin (2018), 'From Russia with Love: The First Russian Studies on the Art of Southern Caucasus', *Venezia Arti*, 27: 15–33.

Foletti, I. and S. Riccioni (2018), 'Inventing, Transforming, and Discovering Southern Caucasus: Some Introductory Observations', *Venezia Arti*, 27: 7–14.

Foletti, I. and E. Thunø, eds. (2016), *The Medieval Southern Caucasus: Artistic Cultures of Albania, Armenia, and Georgia*, with the collaboration of Palladino, A., Turnhout: Brepols (= *Convivium*, Supplementum).

Frantová, Z. (2019), *Ravenna: Sedes Imperii. Artistic Trajectories in the Late Antique Mediterranean*, Rome: Viella.

Gagarin, G. (1856), *Kratkaja hronologicheskaja tablica v posobie istorii vizantijskogo iskusstva* [Short chronological table as a handbook of Byzantine art], Tbilisi: Tipografija Kanceljarii namestnika kavk.

Goez, W. (1958), *Translatio Imperii. Ein Beitrag zur Geschichte des Geschichtsdenkens und der politischen Theorien im Mittelalter und in der frühen Neuzeit*, Tübingen: J. C. B. Mohr.

Grabar, A. (1924a), *Bojanskata cŭrkva. Architektura – živopis/L'église de Boïana. Architecture – peinture*, foreword by B. Filov, Sofia: Institut archéologique bulgare.

Grabar, A. (1924b), 'Un reflet du monde latin dans une peinture balkanique du 13e siècle', *Byzantion*, 1: 229–43.

Grabar, A. (1928a), *La peinture religieuse en Bulgarie*, foreword by G. Millet, 2 vols, Paris: Paul Geuthner.

Grabar, A. (1928b), *Recherches sur les influences orientales dans l'art balkanique*, Paris: Les Belles Lettres.

Granger, C. (2005), *L'Empereur et les arts: la liste civile de Napoléon III*, Paris: École des chartes.

Grélois, J.-P. (2003), 'Louis XIV et l'Orient: la mission du capitaine Gravier d'Ortières (1685–1687)', in M.-F. Auzépy (ed.), *Byzance en Europe*, 31–41, Saint-Denis: Presses Universitaires de Vincennes.

Heller, M. (1997), *Histoire de la Russie et de son Empire*, Paris: Plon.

Ivanov, S. A. (2003), 'Byzance rouge: la byzantinologie et les communistes (1928–1948)', in M.-F. Auzépy (ed.), *Byzance en Europe*, 55–60, Saint-Denis: Presses Universitaires de Vincennes.

Ivanov, S. A. (2016), 'The Second Rome as Seen by the Third: Russian Debates on "the Byzantine Legacy"', in P. Marciniak and D. C. Smythe (eds.), *The Reception of Byzantium in European Culture since 1500*, 55–79, Farnham: Routledge.

Jolles, A., F. J. Cummings and H. Landais, eds. (1978), *The Second Empire: Art in France under Napoleon III* (exhibition catalogue, Philadelphia, Museum of Art, 1 October–26 November 1978; Detroit, Institute of Arts, 15 January–18 March 1979; Paris, Grand Palais, 24 April–2 July 1979), Philadelphia: Philadelphia Museum of Art.

Kampouri-Vamvoukou, M. (2003), 'L'Architecture de style néo-byzantin en France', in M.-F. Auzépy (ed.), *Byzance en Europe*, 87–100, Saint-Denis: Presses Universitaires de Vincennes.

Kaul, C. G. (2009), 'Der Staufer-Mythos im Bild. Zur Stauferrezeption im 19. und 20. Jahrhundert', *kunsttexte.de*, 4.

Kondakov, N. and I. Tolstoj (1891), *Russkija Drevnosti v pamjatnikax iskusstva. Vypusk' četvertyj. Christianskija drevnosti Krima, Kavkaza i Kieva* [Russian antiquities into the monuments of art. Volume four. Christian antiquities of Crimea, Kavkaz and Kiev], Saint Petersburg: Tipografija V. Vypusk' četvertyj.

Korenevskiy, A. V. (2016), 'Russia's Byzantine Heritage: The Anatomy of Myth', *Новое Прошлое/The New Past*, 1: 62-79.

Kyzlasova, I. L. (1985), *Istorija izučenija vizantijskogo i drevnerusskogo iskusstva v Rossii. F. I. Buslajev, N. P. Kondakova: metody, idei, teorii* [The history of the study of Byzantine and ancient Russian art in Russia. F. I. Buslajev, N. P. Kondakov: methods, ideas, theories], Moscow: Izdat. Moskovskogo University.

Labarte, J. (1864-66), *Histoire des arts industriels au Moyen Âge et à l'époque de la Renaissance*, 6 vols, Paris: V. A. Morel & C. Libraires-éditeurs.

Labarte, J. (1861), *Le Palais impérial de Constantinople et ses abords, Sainte-Sophie, le forum Augustéon et l'Hippodrome, tels qu'ils existaient au Xe siècle*, Paris: Librairie archéologique de Victor Didron.

Lassithiotakis, M. (2007), 'Une Grèce chrétienne. Les lettrés grecs et la réhabilitation de Byzance dans la seconde moitié du XIXe siècle', in J.-M. Spieser (ed.), *Présence de Byzance*, 91-112, Gollion: Infolio.

Lieven, D. (2009), *Russia against Napoleon: The Battle for Europe, 1807 to 1814*, London: Penguin.

Lovino, F. (2016a), 'Leafing through "Seminarium Kondakovianum", 1: Studies on Byzantine Illumination', *Convivium*, 3 (1): 206-13.

Lovino, F. (2016b), 'Southern Caucasus in Perspective: The Scholarly Debate through the Pages of "Seminarium Kondakovianum" and "Skythika" (1927-1938)', *Convivium*, Supplementum: 36-51.

Lovino, F. (2017), 'Communism vs. Seminarium Kondakovianum', *Convivium*, 4 (1): 142-57.

Lovino, F. (2018), 'Seminarium Kondakovianum/Byzantinoslavica: A Comparison', in I. Foletti, F. F. Lovino and V. and Tvrzníková (eds), *From Kondakov to Hans Belting Library: Emigration and Byzantium – Bridges between Worlds*, 38-55, Rome: Viella.

Lovino, F. (2019), 'Constructing the Past through the Present: The Eurasian View of Byzantium in the Pages of Seminarium Kondakovianum', in M. Kinloch and A. MacFarlane (eds.), *Trends and Turning Points: Constructing the Late Antique and Byzantine World*, 14-28, Leiden and Boston: Brill.

Malcolm, N. (2019), *Useful Enemies: Islam and the Ottoman Empire in Western Political Thought, 1450-1750*, Oxford: Oxford University Press.

Malíř, J. (2016), 'Cyrilometodějská tradice na Moravě koncem 19. a počátkem 20. století ve službách politiky' [The Cyrillo-Methodian tradition in Moravia in the late 19th and early 20th century in the service of politics], in *Středověký kaleidoskop pro muže s hůlkou: věnováno Františku Šmahelovi k životnímu jubileu* [Kaleidoscope of the Middle Ages for the man with a walking stick: dedicated to Fratišek Šmahel on the occasion of his life jubilee], 394-412, Prague: Lidové noviny.

'Manifest k gruzinskomu narodu. 12 (24)sentjabrja 1801 goda' (1830), [Manifest to the Georgian nation. 12 (24)September 1801], in *Polnoe sobranie zakonov Rossijskoj imperii s 1649 goda: 1800-1801*, 26, 782-86, Saint Petersburg.

Medvedkova, O. (2016), 'André Grabar et la filiation entre l'art antique, l'art byzantin et russe ancien dans l'historiographie russe', *Revue des études slaves*, 87 (1): 95-102.

Meyendorff, J. (1991), 'Was There Ever a "Third Rome"? Remarks on the Byzantine Legacy in Russia', in J. J. Yiannias (ed.), *The Byzantine Tradition after the Fall of Constantinople*, 45–60, Charlottesville: University Press of Virginia.

Niehoff-Panagiotidis, J. (2011), 'To Whom Does Byzantium Belong? Greeks, Turks and the Present of the Medieval Balkans', in R. J. W. Evans and G. P. Marchal (eds.), *The Uses of the Middle Ages in Modern European States History: Nationhood and the Search for Origins*, 139–51, New York: Palgrave Macmillan.

Nivat, G. (1992), 'Nationalité et nationalisme russes', in M. Niqueux (ed.), *La question russe: essais sur le nationalisme russe*, 5–14, Paris: Editions universitaires.

Obolensky, D. (1950), 'Russia's Byzantine Heritage', *Oxford Slavonic Papers*, 1: 36–63.

Obolensky, D. (1971), *The Byzantine Commonwealth: Eastern Europe, 500–1453*, London: Weidenfeld & Nicolson.

Obolensky, D. (1999), *Bread of Exile: A Russian Family*, London: Harvill Press.

Omont, H. (1893), 'Projets de prise de Constantinople et de fondation d'un empire français d'Orient sous Louis XIV', *Revue d'histoire diplomatique*, 7: 195–246.

Palladino, A. (2020), 'Transforming Medieval Art from Saint Petersburg to Paris: André Grabar's Fate and Scholarship between 1917 and 1945', *Convivium*, Supplementum 2: 122–41.

Pertusi, A. (2004), *Bisanzio e i Turchi nella cultura del Rinascimento e del Barocco*, C. M. Mazzucchi (ed.), Milan: V&P Università.

Pippidi, A. (2006), *Byzantins, Ottomans, Roumains. Le Sud-Est européen entre l'héritage impérial et les influences occidentales*, Paris: Honoré Champion.

Raeff, M. (1990), *Russia Abroad: A Cultural History of the Russian Emigration, 1919–1939*, Oxford: Oxford University Press.

Raffensperger, C. (2004), 'Revisiting the Idea of the Byzantine Commonwealth', *Byzantinische Forschungen*, 28: 159–74.

Rakitin, P. (2013), 'Byzantine Echoes in the Nineteenth Century Press and in the Writings of Russian Intellectuals', *Opuscula Historiae Artium*, 18/Suplementum: 98–109.

Reinsch, D. R. (2016), 'Hieronymus Wolf as Editor and Translator of Byzantine Texts', in P. Marciniak and D. C. Smythe (eds.), *The Reception of Byzantium in European Culture since 1500*, 43–54, Farnham: Routledge.

Rouleau, F. (1992), 'Le nationalisme slavophile', in M. Niqueux, *La question russe: essais sur le nationalisme russe*, 41–48, Paris: Editions universitaires.

Sacharov, I. P. (1841–49), *Issledovanije o russkom ikonopisanii* [Research on Russian iconography], Saint Petersburg.

Savel'ev, J. (2005), *Vizantijskij stil' v architekture Rossii* [The Byzantine style in Russian architecture], Saint Petersburg: 'Liki Rossii' [u.a.].

Schellewald, B. (2008), '"Le byzantinisme est le rêve qui a bercé l'art européen dans son enfance". Byzanz-Rezeption und die Wiederentdeckung des Mosaiks im 19. Jahrhundert', *Mitteilungen des Kunsthistorischen Institutes in Florenz*, 52 (1): 123–48.

Schieffer, R. (2006), 'Konzepte des Kaisertums', in B. Schneidmüller and S. Weinfurter (eds.), *Heilig – Römisch – Deutsch. Das Reich im mittelalterlichen Europa*, 44–56, Dresden: Michael Sandstein.

Schlögel, K., ed. (1994), *Der grosse Exodus. Die russische Emigration und ihre Zentren 1917–1941*, Munich: C. H. Beck.

Schmoll, P. (2007), 'La Translatio Imperii: transmission et transformations d'un mythe politique européen', *Revue des Sciences sociales*, 2007: 118–25.

Shepard, J. (2006), 'Byzantium's Overlapping Circles', in E. Jeffreys and F. K. Haarer (eds.), *Proceedings of the 21st International Congress of Byzantine Studies* (London, 21–26 August 2006), vol. 1, 15–55, Aldershot: Ashgate Publishing.

Smirnova, E. S. (1999), 'Andrej Nikolaevič Grabar i voprosy russkoj kul'tury v ego naučnom nasledii' [Andrej Nikolaevič Grabar and problems of Russian culture in his scholarly heritage], in E. S. Smirnova (ed.), *Drevnerusskoe iskusstvo. Vizantija i Drevnjaja Rus'. K 100-letiju Andreja Nikolaeviča Grabara (1896–1990)* [Old Russian art. Byzantium and Kievan Rus'. For the 100th-birthday of Andrej Nikolajevič Grabar], 76–82, Saint Petersburg: Bulanin.

Spieser, J.-M. (1991), 'Héllénisme et connaissance de l'art byzantin au XIXe siècle', in *Hellenismos, quelques jalons pour une histoire de l'identité grecque* (Conference proceedings, Strasbourg, 25–27 October 1989), 337–62, Leiden [i.a.]: Brill.

Spieser, J.-M. (2000), 'Du Cange and Byzantium', in R. Cormack and E. Jeffreys (eds.), *Through the Looking-Glass. Byzantium through British Eyes*, 199–210, Aldershot: Ashgate Publishing.

Srinivasan, K. (2006), 'Nobody's Commonwealth? The Commonwealth in Britain's Post-Imperial Adjustment', *Commonwealth & Comparative Politics*, 44: 257–69.

Stamatopoulos, D. (2013), 'From the *Vyzantism* of K. Leont'ev to the *Vyzantinism* of I. I. Sokolov: The Byzantine Orthodox East as a Motif of Russian Orientalism', in O. Delouis, A. Couderc and P. Guran (eds.), *Héritages de Byzance en Europe du Sud-Est à l'époque moderne et contemporaine*, 321–40, Athens: École française d'Athènes.

Tellenbach, G. (1982), 'Kaiser, Rom und renovation: Ein Beitrag zu einem großen Thema', in M. Balzer (ed.), *Tradition als historische Kraft. Interdisziplinäre Forschungen zur Geschichte des früheren Mittelalters (Festschrift Karl Hauck)*, 231–53, Berlin [i.a.]: De Gruyter.

Thomine-Berrada, A. (2008), 'L'art d'Orient/Art d'Occident. Les débats sur l'apport oriental dans l'architecture médiévale française au XIXe siècle', in R. Recht, P. P. Sénéchal, C. Barbillon and F.-R. Martin (eds.), *Histoire de l'histoire de l'art en France au XIXe siècle*, 323–36, Paris: La Documentation française.

Tomasi, M. (2009), 'Labarte, Jules (23 juillet 1797, Paris - 14 août 1880, Boulogne-sur-Mer [Pas-de-Calais])', in P. Sénéchal and C. Barbillon (eds.), *Dictionnaire critique des historiens de l'art actifs en France de la Révolution à la Première Guerre mondiale*, Paris. Available online: https://www.inha.fr/fr/ressources/publications/publications-numeriques/dictionnaire-critique-des-historiens-de-l-art/labarte-jules.html?search-keywords=Labarte (accessed 2 June 2020).

Vryonis, Jr., S. (1969/70), 'The Byzantine Legacy and Ottoman Forms', *Dumbarton Oaks Papers*, 23/24: 251–308.

Wortman, R. (2003), 'The "Russian Style" in Church Architecture as Imperial Symbol after 1881', in J. Cracraft and D. B. Rowland (eds.), *Architectures of Russian Identity: 1500 to the Present*, 101–229, Ithaca, NY: Cornell University Press.

Wortman, R. (2006), *Scenarios of Power: Myth and Ceremony in Russian Monarchy from Peter the Great to the Abdication of Nicholas II*, Princeton, NJ: Princeton University Press.

4

The Prince and the Greeks: The Byzantine Baptizers of Prince Vladimir in Modern Russian Sculpture, Mosaic and Church Architecture

Roman Shliakhtin

The question of Byzantine heritage in Russia is problematic. Firstly, as every graduate student knows, Russia is the 'Third Rome'. Secondly, at least some actions of Russian government have been labelled as 'Byzantine', or as having something to do with an alleged 'Byzantine' agenda. All these factors create the image of a country obsessed with Byzantium. The present article aims to question this image and to analyse some fluctuations of the 'Byzantine' component in a historical scene that is usually associated with the interactions between the Rus and Byzantium, namely the Baptism of Prince Vladimir of Kiev in 988. This chapter analyses images of St. Vladimir created in imperial Russia, focusing on the images of the prince in modern Russia with a special focus on a relief installed in front of the Kremlin (2016), and on a mosaic in the newly built cathedral of the Russian Armed Forces in Kubinka (2020).[1] The concluding section of the chapter proposes a certain correlation between the external politics of the Russian state and fluctuations in the depictions of the prince and the Greeks.

It seems important to recapitulate the story of the 'historical' St. Vladimir. According to the present scholarly consensus, Prince Vladimir of Kiev (r. 980–1015) was pagan in the beginning of his reign, before he allegedly began considering conversion to one of the monotheistic religions (Preobrazhensky 2007). The twelfth-century *Rus Primary Chronicle* introduces a story about Vladimir making the choice between religions and receiving the ambassadors from Muslims (Volga Bulgars), from Catholics (Germans), from Khazarian Jews and from Orthodox (Byzantines) (*Rus Primary Chronicle* 1997: year 986; Griffin 2019: 136–37). A certain Greek philosopher conveyed the views of the Byzantines in a speech delivered in front of the prince and included his speech in the *Primary Chronicle*. After the meeting with the ambassadors, Vladimir allegedly sent his own embassies to the people who represented the different faiths. After visiting many cities, the ambassadors of Rus came to Constantinople, attended the Orthodox Church service and spoke highly about Christianity. Vladimir perceived this service positively, and asked the boyars whether he needs to accept baptism or not (Griffin 2019: 139).

In 987, Emperor Basil II (r. 976–1025) had to suppress the rebellion of Bardas Phocas, who had captured most of Asia Minor. Basil appealed to Vladimir for help, and Vladimir sent nine thousand men to the emperor in exchange for the hand of his sister, and for sponsorship in Christianization. The emperor did not hold to his promise, so the prince attacked the Byzantine holdings, and besieged the capital of the Prince's empire – Cherson (*Rus Primary Chronicle* 1997: year 988). After some months of the siege, says the *Primary Chronicle*, the Byzantines surrendered and fulfilled the terms of the treatise. Soon afterwards Vladimir passed baptism, receiving 'Basil' as his Christian name. The Byzantine emperor gave him the Princess Anna's hand in marriage, and provided the priests and learned men necessary to baptize the Rus. Vladimir proceeded to Kiev, where he baptized the population of the city in Dnieper, while his associates baptized the populations of other cities in Rus, including Rostov and Novgorod (Artamonov 2019: para 24). While modern historians wage long discussions about the historicity of evidence presented in the *Rus Primary Chronicle*, medieval Russian intellectuals took a different stance.

Rise and fall of the prince: Vladimir and the Greeks from 988 to 1988

The story of Vladimir's baptism in Russian sources had been criticized from many positions. The critics point out the gap between the time of the composition of the *Rus Primary Chronicle* (the main source) and the events themselves, as well as the absence of the description of these events in contemporary Byzantine sources; they also point to the problems connected with baptism in Cherson (Butler 2002: 3; Griffin 2019). This prevented neither medieval nor modern (in the historical sense) historiographers and hagiographers from creating many images of St. Vladimir. According to Griffin, already in the eleventh century, panegyrists of Rus praised Vladimir in words suitable for a saint (Griffin 2019: 184–87). The process of sanctification was complex and began not very long after the death of the historical Vladimir (Butler 2002: 32). After the dissolution of Kievan Rus, Vladimir became one of the patron saints of Grand Princes of Moscow. One of the sons of Dmitry of Donskoy, Vasily I (r. 1371–1425) whose baptismal name was Vladimir, constructed a church dedicated to St. Vladimir in his suburban palace (Cherepnin 1960: 61). In the sixteenth century, the first Tsar of Rus, Ivan the IV (r. 1530–84), counted St. Vladimir among his relatives. Prince Vladimir with his saint sons, Boris and Gleb, are present on the icon 'Blessed is the Host of the King of Heaven' that Ivan commissioned in 1652, after the creation of the regular army and successful siege of Kazan (Tychinskaya 2014: 316–18).

In the nineteenth century, the Russian monarchy 'mobilized' Prince Vladimir for the support of the regime. Tsar Nicholas I (r. 1825–55) ordered the construction of a statue of St. Vladimir in Kiev. The new statue, construction of which was begun by Vasily Demut-Malinovsky and finished by Peter Clodt von Jürgensburg in 1853, depicted the prince in medieval attire holding a straight cross and a crown. The relief on the front panel of the pedestal depicted priests in Byzantine robes, baptizing the population of Kiev. In 1859, St. Vladimir found his place in the pantheon of the 'Millennium of Russia' monument in Novgorod. The sculptor depicted him in a princely attire, holding an Orthodox Cross in hand. In the 1880s, church authorities and the local population of Kiev sponsored the construction of a new cathedral dedicated to the saint prince, a cathedral today called St. Volodymyr's. Architect Alexander Beretti built the cathedral in the Russian-Byzantine style. In 1880–90, a prominent Russian painter, Viktor Vasnetsov (1848–1926), created a series of frescoes for the cathedral. It took him ten years to accomplish this difficult task. His frescoes influenced contemporary artists, and continue to influence them to the present day (Grabar 1926: para 4).

'The Baptism of Vladimir' (Figure 4.1) depicts the Russian prince accepting his new faith. Vladimir is in water up to his breast, and he is making the sign of the cross. Byzantine warriors and officials are holding shields with Christograms, while the bishop reads from the book and blesses Vladimir in his baptismal font. Byzantine church attendants around him each carry a processional cross and a candle. The armed warriors of Rus are present in the background, and are looking at the scene cautiously. In the preliminary sketch, one can see that whole scene happens inside a single building, probably the baptistery, which has a dome with a barely discernible scene from Jesus's baptism on it. The image of Byzantium present in both frescoes is ambiguous. Vasnetsov presents Byzantium and the Byzantines as the educated people who provided Rus with religion, literacy and an imperial tradition and culture. One can note that Vasnetsov depicted the Byzantines mostly as bearded, old men or as young men — or as women — reserving more masculine and adult roles for the warriors of the ancient Rus. One can also note the difference between the sketch of 'The Baptism of Vladimir' and the final fresco, namely the absence of the Byzantine background of the baptistery (Figures 4.1 and 4.2). The final version contains less 'Byzantine' elements than does the sketch.

Vasnetsov's frescoes received critical acclaim from contemporaries. He lived long enough to see the collapse of the cult of St. Vladimir. The Soviet era saw the decline of the image of St. Vladimir and the dissipation of the cult. While other warrior princes, Dmitry Donskoy and Alexander Nevsky, became parts of the Soviet Pantheon of 'heroic ancestors', St. Vladimir remained in relative obscurity. The situation changed only in the 1970s and 1980s when Soviet historians, with the tacit agreement of Soviet leaders, became interested in the pre-Christian and early Christian past. The celebration of a thousand years of Russian Christianity in 1988 stimulated the growth of attention to the Prince's figure. At the same time, when late Soviet films discussed the adoption of Christianity by the Slavs, they avoided mention of St. Vladimir and criticized the Byzantines. A popular folk history movie, *Rus Iznachalnaya* (1989), presented the Byzantines as enemies of the Eastern Slavs, who were eager to poison pagan princes to promote their Christian faith (Beskov 2016: 14–16).

Figure 4.1 Viktor Vasnetsov, baptism of Prince Vladimir (sketch). Courtesy of Nizhny Novgorod State Art Museum.

The prince strikes back: New Vladimir for new millennium (2000–14)

The collapse of the Soviet Union was a massive, collective psychological trauma for many Russians. In the search for grounding and support in this tragedy, many flocked to the churches. The Russian Orthodox Church once again became a notable actor in all fields of Russian daily life. The return of this church signified the return of the patron saints of Old Russia, including St. Vladimir. In Crimea, in Sevastopol, Russian and Ukrainian monuments competed with one another, while in Russia per se, many churches dedicated to St. Vladimir were brought back into service. This holds true for the Church of Vladimir founded by Vasiliy I. Conveniently located in the centre of Moscow, the church signified the presence of the cult of the prince in the very centre of political power. It was (and still is) one kilometre away from the Kremlin and a few hundred metres away from the Administration of the president of Russia, a body of power that became important in the reign of Vladimir Putin.

Vladimir Putin became president of Russia in 2000. Distancing himself from the 'historical neutrality' of Yeltsin, he began to mobilize the Russian past for the aims of the present, invoking the concept of 'thousand years of Russian history' (Malinova 2019). At the same time, the president of Russia distanced himself from Byzantium, using the term only in the cultural meaning and never in its principal media releases. One might connect this with the presence of professional historians among his speech writers, who were keen to avoid any 'Third Rome' associations.

However, the situation with Russian history was different, and the state-sponsored changes in the public vision of the past. In the first decade of the new century, private authors of different media decided to dedicate their works to Prince Vladimir. In 2002, a pompous cathedral was dedicated to St. Vladimir in the southern Moscow district of Orekhovo-Borisovo. In 2006, the destiny of the prince became a subject of specialized animated movie *Prince Vladimir* which focused on the early part of Vladimir's career and his fight with nomadic Pechenegs. Originally, the movie aimed to depict the Christianization of Europe, but in the late 1990s the authors decided to focus on the Christianization of Russia. They planned to produce two instalments of the film, but despite state sponsorship, the workshop created only one animated movie, which was released in 2004 and was commercially successful (Anonymous 2020: line 6).

The animated movie depicted the pagan part of Vladimir's life and his complex relations with the many actors of the era, historical as well as imagined. For the first time in generations if not in the history of Russian Cinema, the animated movie presented Byzantium as a powerful and friendly ally of the future Russian prince. It included scenes of Constantinople, which depicted Constantine Porphyrogennetus and Princess Anna, the future wife of Vladimir. Unfortunately, the project abruptly ended after the first instalment, due to financial issues. Two years later, another film about Byzantium appeared not in cinemas, but on national TV. In 2008, Archimandrite Tikhon (Shevkunov) whom some label as a man close to Vladimir Putin, produced a film called *The Death of the Empire: A lesson from Byzantium*. The film presented Byzantium as an idealized Christian state, surrounded by barbarians and heathen neighbours, and destroyed by the oligarchs from within. In a later interview, the author stated that he hoped the film might prevent the repetition of the Byzantine mistakes in modern Russia (Danilov 2012: para 41). In 2008, Vladimir Putin ended his second term as president of the country and Dmitry Medvedev became the president (2008–12). Over the next four years, Russia did not see much activity in the state-sponsored or state-oriented rethinking of St. Vladimir.

The new rise of interest in the saint coincided with the new term of Vladimir Putin, and with significant changes in Russian external politics. In 2014, Euromaidan in

Kiev and the ensuing events in Crimea and Southern Ukraine changed the situation around St. Vladimir, and affected the Russian popular image of the prince and the Greeks. On 9 May 2014, Vladimir Putin made a trip to Crimea and visited a church there, dedicated to St. Vladimir. As usual, the monumental politics changed slowly in response to new events. It is interesting to compare the image of Vladimir present in new textbooks prepared after the events of 2014 with the statue that was erected in front of the Kremlin in 2016.

One of those new textbooks appeared in schools in 2015. It presented Byzantium and the baptism of Vladimir in a traditional way. According to the authors (Arsentyev et al. 2016), the image of Byzantium is controversial. On the one hand, Byzantium in this textbook acts as a country that gave Russia its culture and faith; on the other, it is an enemy of the early Rus princes, and thus an object of legitimate military aggression (41). In the textbook, Byzantium is described as the 'most developed and richest country of Europe', with incapable rulers and many secrets (43). It explains the baptism of Vladimir as a conscious act, and points at the necessity of 'united religion' for the young state as the main reason for the baptisms (51). It claims that the military rebellion of 987 caught Basil II off-guard, and he had to turn to the Russians for help, promising Vladimir his sister Anna as a bride. 'The emperor did not haste to follow his obligations,' states the textbook (53). This prompted the Kievan prince to occupy Cherson and accept baptism to get the princess's hand. Interestingly, the text does not provide any details on the baptism of Vladimir. It brings the reader's attention to the capture of Chersoneses in Crimea and the territorial gains that came out of the problematic alliance. Very much like the *Rus Primary Chronicle*, the textbook describes the 'Greeks' walking the streets of Kiev and propagating the new faith. Thus, one year after its 2014 publication, the image of the prince and the Greeks in the textbook remained rather traditional. The textbook presented Vladimir as an able ruler and the Greeks as weak warriors, dangerous partners in negotiation, while Christians are presented as powerful culture brokers.

Another new image of the prince was created in a different media: in 2015 an imposing monument appeared in front of the Kremlin. The formal constructor of the new statue was the Russian Military Historical Society, founded by Vladimir Putin and supported by the Minister of Culture Vladimir Medinsky, and the sculptor was Salavat Scherbakov. The original plan was to construct the massive monument on the Sparrow Hills near the Moscow River, at a place that is currently occupied by an observation platform. After significant protests from the local population, the constructors decided to change the location of the statue and chose to situate it instead in front of the Borovitskaya tower, next to the official entrance to the Kremlin. Vladimir Putin and other officials inaugurated the monument on the Day of National Unity, 4 November 2016.

As many have noted, the statue bears a striking similarity to the one built in Kiev in 1853. This depicted Prince Vladimir in royal attire with a cross in his hand overlooking the valley of the river. However, there were several important differences. To compete with Kiev sculptor Salavat Scherbakov, the statue depicts St. Vladimir in princely attire, and not only with a cross but also with a sword in his right hand. The height of the statue is 17.5 metres, making it slightly lower than the monument in

Kiev, which stands at 20.4 metres high. More interesting for us in the context of this chapter are the detailed bas-reliefs that accompany the statue. While the Kievan statue contains only one relief on a direct pedestal, the statue in Moscow contains three: two panels depict Russian warriors and saints, including St. Boris and Gleb, as well as some monastic saints, while the central panel depicts the baptism of Vladimir. As Sean Griffin noted in his recent book, the visual narrative is inspired by the *Rus Primary Chronicle* (2019: 2). It seems highly likely that the main composition took inspiration from the frescoes of Vasnetsov, thus enhancing the competition between Moscow and Kiev. The change here lies in the medium. While Vasnetsov *painted* the processional cross, Scherbakov *cast* it in metal, making it more tangible to the observer (Figure 4.2). This new dimension highlights the importance of the scene, as the sculptor (probably unconsciously) makes it more definite.

The difference lies not only in the medium but also in the many new characters present in the composition. In Vasnetsov's work, the baptism happens in a Byzantine-like rotunda, with the prince surrounded by Byzantine warriors and churchmen. The warriors of Rus are present only in the background. In Scherbakov's relief, Prince Vladimir is surrounded by heavily armed Russian soldiers, with the Trinity of Andrey Rublev located above him. Below the Trinity, one can see future Russian saints, while on the right side of the relief one can see Byzantine saints that surround the baptismal font. The names on the halos identify them as St. John Chrysostom, St. Demetrius of Thessaloniki and St. George. None of the Byzantine military saints bear arms or have armour. Instead, we only see their heads and headdresses. In the background, one can

Figure 4.2 Relief of Salavat Scherbakov behind the monument to St. Vladimir in the Kremlin (2016). Courtesy of Nina Arkhipova (2020).

see Hagia Sophia with a visible Christian cross on the top, while in the foreground one of the attendants is holding a double-headed eagle. No spear or dagger is present, thus highlighting the peaceful nature of the Byzantines.

The relief introduces a nuanced, complex image of Byzantium in Russian discourse. On the one hand, the Byzantines are depicted as cultural people who provide the Prince of Rus with the baptismal font and the very possibility of baptism. They also provide a connection with the tradition of Christian education (depicted by a book) and a connection with the imperial tradition (symbolized by the double-headed eagle). Putting the cross upon Hagia Sophia, the sculptors fulfilled the dream of some Russian Imperial politicians to install a cross on the dome of this cathedral, if only in relief in front of the Kremlin Gate. At the same time, the presence of armed Russians on the other side of the baptismal font on the background of conquered Cherson in some way separated St. Vladimir from Byzantium, and reminded the viewer of the more recent successes of another Vladimir. Very much like in the textbook, Byzantium here plays the role of the old culture broker, one that is not able to defend itself or influence events. The relief repeats the message of the textbook about cultured and rich, yet unwarlike and feminine, Byzantines who once assisted the mighty and masculine Russians. The highlighted masculinity and more visible military might differentiate the 2016 monument from the image in textbook. This message of military might is vividly present and enhanced in the most recent monument that celebrates St. Vladimir and the Greeks, namely the Cathedral of the Armed forces recently inaugurated in Kubinka, in the Moscow region.

The prince in the new space: Church of Vladimir in the Cathedral in Kubinka

The third decade of the twenty-first century saw an emergence of the new politics of memory in Russian Federation. As in the previous era, Byzantium was absent from the official rhetoric of the president, being mentioned only in the context of the distant past. At the same time, it saw a blending of the story of St. Vladimir with the story of the Second World War, labelled in the national narrative as the Great Patriotic War. At the beginning of the century, the war became a foundation of national self-identification (Perrier-Morenkova 2019). In 2020, the 75th anniversary of the end of the Second World War was expected to become a massive memory feast that coincided with the referendum on the changes to the constitution that allowed Vladimir Putin to stay in his post for some years. Coronavirus spoiled many, but not all, of these events.

In 2020, like six years previously, Prince Vladimir and the Greeks had their place in the celebrations, this time as a part of the wider landscape of memory. On 22 June 2020, the anniversary of the day Nazi Germany attacked the Soviet Union, the president of Russia inaugurated the Cathedral of Russian Armed Forces which is located in the grounds of 'Patriot Park' in Kubinka. As the official statement goes, the park is the 'Russian Defense Ministry's main exhibition venue' (Anonymous 2019: para 4). According to the open-source information, the park holds many exhibitions dedicated to past and present activities of the Russian military, including materiel from Syria and re-enactments of Second World War battles that happened nearby. 'Patriot Park is a recreation area where everyone will find something interesting!' says the official webpage of the venue (Park Patriot n.d.).

The cathedral, standing at a massive height of 95 metres from the ground level to the top of the cross, is the highest church in the Moscow region. The steps of the church were cast from metal scrapped from German guns, while the diameter of the main dome (19.45 m) and height of the bell tower (75 m) connect the cathedral with the numerical symbolism of the anniversary. The cathedral was constructed using donations from different parties: the president of Russia himself sponsored the construction of the most important relic, the complex image of Christ the Saviour, from his private funds and donated it to the cathedral, while the other money came from popular donations and regional authorities. According to media leaks, the creators of the cathedral planned to position images of Vladimir Putin, Russian Minister of Defence Sergey Shoygu and Joseph Stalin in the cathedral, but after some debate, the images were removed and are currently absent from the cathedral (Roth 2020).

The resulting cathedral stands on the ground separate from the main park. It is surrounded by the gallery that demonstrates the heroic feats of Russian people during the Second World War. From the two sides (north and south), the cathedral is surrounded by a small river, and reconstructed earthworks that illustrate one of the battles between the Red Army and Nazi forces in Kubinka in 1941. Thus, the cathedral remains an early modern fortress, with its bastions, ditches and many towers in the centre. A prominent architect historian Sergey Kavtaradze called this style 'Byzantine', but neither the plan nor the general order of the cathedral hints at Hagia Sophia or Pantokrator (Kavtaradze 2020: para 5). Instead, the reminiscences come from St. Petersburg, Moscow and possibly (again) Kiev.

The lower part of the cathedral is dedicated to St. Vladimir. At first glance, the church of St. Vladimir does not look part of some monumental cathedral, but reminds one of the crypt, into which one had to descend. Upon the entrance to the exonarthex of the church of St. Vladimir, one can see a foundation stone laid by Vladimir Putin, as the viewer then passes to the stairs leading downwards. The mosaics of the exonarthex depict the procession of military saints that pass from the City of Sin (depicted with recognizable visual clues from the Tower of Babel and from Westernized castle gates) to the city of heaven. In their procession, the saints, who move both on foot and on horseback, accompany the rider in shining armour with a flag that (rather accurately) depicts a Christogram in its fourth-century form. Angels descend on the procession and bring them the martyrs' heavenly crowns. Above the procession, one finds the image of Archangel Michael depicted on horseback, and the image of a crowned person with a cross in hand. The prototype here is located not in Kiev, but in Moscow. The rows of anonymous martyrs, with Archangel Michael as their leader, as well as the presence of St. Vladimir on horseback, all remind one of the sixteenth-century icon 'Blessed is the Host of the King of Heaven', created either at the behest of Ivan IV in 1552 or at the behest of his father Vasily III in the 1540s (Tychinskaya 2014). Another way to read this is to associate the multitude of the anonymous saints with the many 'unknown soldiers' of the Second World War, to whose memory the cathedral of the all-armed forces is dedicated.

From the stairs flanked by the mosaics the visitors enter the narthex of the church where there is a chance to leave their coats. Contrary to expectations, the space of this lower church is far from monumental. The height of the ceiling is hardly more than three metres. Blurred windows make the space dark and the only sources of light are the high-powered lamps, in chandeliers over the space. In this setting, the traditional warm light of candles is hardly noticeable. The chandeliers are present, but the candles on them are lost in the glowing reflections of electric light and in the many reflections that fill the room. Byzantine motives play an important role in this ensemble of micro-symbols. The Christograms, in diluted and changed forms, are located on every column. St. Vladimir is present on the main icon in the centre of this vaulted space.

The main mosaic on the left wall depicts the baptism of Vladimir (Figure 4.3). The mosaic on the right wall depicts John the Baptist and the descending of the Holy Ghost upon Jesus Christ. This parallelism is not only logical but also inspired by the previous example. In Vasnetsov's first sketch (see Figure 4.1), the scene of the baptism of Vladimir happens in a baptismal font hidden under an arcade – in the dome of which one can see the scene of the baptism of Christ. The modern composition of mosaics in the horizontal space of the lower church imitated the vertical composition of the original sketch in Vasnetsov's work. At the same time, the network of parallels allows the artists to create chronological sequence. The holy martyrs depicted in the

Figure 4.3 The cathedral in Kubinka, lower church, the baptism of Vladimir Mosaic. Author's photo (2020).

exonarthex of the lower church come from the sixteenth century; Vasnetsov's allusions and ornamental Christograms bring in the nineteenth century and Neo-Byzantine architecture, while the foundation stone and the main icon bring in the twenty-first century, the era of another Vladimir.

The question remains: where are the Byzantines in this new landscape of the imperial sainthood? It would not be a mistake to say that the Byzantines are present in the lower church, but their presence has a limit. With the exception of a rider with Christogram, the martyrs from the exonarthex are not explicitly Byzantine. Inside, the icons depict mostly Russian saints, including St. Seraphim of Sarov and St. German of Balaam. In the scene that depicts the baptism of Vladimir (based yet again on Vasnetsov's fresco in Kiev) the artist does not accentuate the Byzantines, but focuses on the image of the prince with his naked upper torso and the comrades-in-arms by his side. The place of Byzantines in this composition is even more limited than it was in the supplementary relief in front of the Kremlin gates.

The upper church, with its many monumental features, has one important feature that connects it with the lower one: the doors of the cathedral, facing west, depict Boris and Gleb, Russian martyr-saints who were present in many icons alongside St. Vladimir. One can read it as a spatial icon that connects the cathedral not only to the Russian Imperial tradition but also to the Grand Duchy of Moscow. However, the main motifs and methods of the upper church are Russian Imperial and Soviet in style. Many mosaics and glass panels unite Soviet warriors and soldiers of the Russian Empire who fought in various wars. The focus of the upper church is the Second World War, and the victories of the Soviet Army, which are combined with Christian symbols. A special mosaic allows visitors to remember the victims of many recent conflicts, including, here, those in Chechnya and the former Yugoslavia. The mosaic of Our Lady above the main entrance (and not in the apse) contradicts the usual Byzantine paradigm. Thus, the upper church is in some sense non-Byzantine, if not *anti*-Byzantine. The only thing that remains are the Christograms, including one above the altar and the Image of Pantokrator in the main cupola.

The cathedral in Kubinka depicts yet another stage in the development of the image of the prince and the Greeks in Russian artistic discourse of the twenty-first century. The main inspiration for this discourse lies not so much in the medieval past, but in the times of Russian Empire. Both the monument to St. Vladimir in Kiev and the frescoes of Vasnetsov played major roles in the new works of art dedicated to St. Vladimir produced during several presidential terms of Vladimir Putin. The artists of the twenty-first century used motifs and compositions created in the time of Russian Empire to produce new images of St. Vladimir and his Greeks. With the passage of time, these images became more and more Vladimir-centred, highlighting not only the baptism but also the prince himself. Some details of his figure likewise passed through this transformation. While the fresco of Vasnetsov Vladimir is mostly in water, in the relief near the Kremlin the upper part of princes's body is above the baptismal font. In the mosaic in Kubinka, this part is even bigger, hinting at possible inspirations in modern media connected with another Vladimir. One can call it a 'masculinization' of the image of the prince.

The image of the Greeks and the people who surround the prince also passed through significant alterations. In the late nineteenth and early twenty-first century, artists developed new images of the Byzantines who participated in the story of St. Vladimir: first with Vasnetsov, and then with the producer of *Prince Vladimir*, the animated movie, both of which created complex images of educated (if effeminate) Byzantines. New Russian textbooks of 2014 supported this narrative. The proliferation of these images coincided with the eras of the active collaboration between the Russian state and international organizations, including European neighbours. On the contrary, the growing autonomy of Russian state in 2014–20 led to a gradual *decrease* in the role that the Byzantine characters play in the depiction of the baptism of St. Vladimir, and to a growing militarization of the image of the prince. In 2016, Salavat Scherbakov designed a monument to Prince Vladimir in Moscow with obvious references to Kiev, using its monument of Vladimir as the inspiration for the main statue, and the frescoes of Vasnetsov as the inspiration for three bas-reliefs surrounding it. The sculptor added many new heroes, highlighting and amplifying the image of pagan Rus as a masculine power, in contrapuntal imagery to the effeminately depicted Byzantines. While the protagonist remained the same, the number and quality of the supportive characters in bas-relief is significantly different. One can say that the role of the Greeks in these compositions gradually diminishes over time.

In the cathedral in Kubinka, Russian artists blended the narrative of St. Vladimir with the narrative of the Great Patriotic War. The creators of the Cathedral of Armed Forces consciously distanced themselves from direct references to Byzantium. Instead of competing with Constantinople or Kiev, they used motifs and methods present in the churches of both cities, aiming to create something new and original. The creators of the cathedral in Kubinka dedicated a lower church to St. Vladimir and incorporated into it a mosaic of the prince during his baptism by the Greeks, transforming both Vladimir and the Greeks into a foundation stone of both Russian old-time glory and present-day glory. Surrounded by metal galleries and waterworks, the cathedral stands alone in the newly created landscape of memory, emanating a feeling of loneliness and isolation as well as the idea of a besieged fortress, contemporaneous with Russian political rhetoric of the day. One wonders whether the change in political rhetoric will, in the future, stimulate the emergence of different versions of the prince and the Greeks.

***

Note: The article was written in 2021 after a field trip to Kubinka. Despite many things changing since then, the principal argument of the article remains valid in the present form. The only addition is the recent investment of Russian power in the cult of St. Vladimir. This time it is not a statue, mosaic or icon, but a patriotic ethno-opera. The opera "Prince Vladimir" will be based on historical sources, including the travelogue of Ibn Fadlan and other recent monographs and scholarly articles. In 2023-2024 the state will participate in the project with a lump sum of 29 mln roubles (roughly 358.000 euros). Singers Yaroslav Dronov (better known under his alias Shaman) and Anton Adasinsky will demonstrate to the audience the importance of Christian values in the person of prince Vladimir.

Note

1   The article will use term 'the Greeks' which was used to denote the Byzantines both in medieval Russian chronicles and remains in use now. The name 'Vladimir' is used in this article in Russian transcription, with the exception of cases when the object of description is in Ukrainian capital. In this article, I use the traditional English spelling of the name of this capital, 'Kiev'.

Bibliography

Anonymous (2019), 'Got it covered: 34-ton titanium-decorated dome placed on top of Russia's grand Military Cathedral', *Russia Today*, 8 November. Available online: https://www.rt.com/russia/472948-russian-military-temple-dome/ (accessed 17 September 2020).

Anonymous (2020), 'Kassovize Sbory Otechestvennih Filmov v Otechestvennom Prokate' [Box office and visits to Russian films in cinemas], *Karmen Media*, 27 December. Available online: https://web.archive.org/web/20080213063846/http://carmen-media.ru/index.cgi/sc2 (accessed 28 September 2020).

Arsentyev, N., A. Danilov, P. Stefanovich and A. Tokareva (2016), *Istoriza Rossii. Uchebnik dlya 6 klassa. Chast Pervaya* [History of Russia. Textbook for the 6 grade. Part 1], Moscow: Prosvechenie.

Artamonov, Y. (2019), 'Krescheniye Rusi' [Baptism of Rus], in *Pravoslavnaya Encyclopedia* [Orthodox encyclopedia], Moscow. Available online: https://www.pravenc.ru/text/159104.html (accessed 21 September 2020).

Beskov, A. (2016), 'Reministsentsii Slavyanskogo Yazichestva v Sovremennoz Rossizskoy Kulture' [Reminiscences of Slavic Paganism in modern Russian culture], in *Colloquium Heptaplomeres*, 10–47, Nizhny Novgorod: Minin University.

Butler, F. (2002), *Enlightener of Rus: The image of Vladimir Sviatoslavich*, Bloomington, IN: Slavica Publishers.

Cherepnin, L. (1960), 'Zaveschaniye knyazya Vasiliya Dmitrievicha' [The will of Prince Vasiliy Dmitrievich], in L. Cherepnin (ed.), *Dukhovniye I dogovorniye gramoty velikih I udelnih knyazey XIV–XVI вв.* [Last wills and deeds of great and local princes of Russia in the 15th–16th centuries], 60–62, Moscow: Russian Academy of Sciences.

Danilov, A. (2012), 'Urok yescho ne okonchen. Intervyu s Tihonom Shevkunovim' [The lesson is not over yet. Interview with Tikhon Shevkunov], *Pravoslavie.Ru*, 13 December. Available online: https://www.pravoslavie.ru/58016.html (accessed 27 September 2020).

Grabar, I. (1926), 'V. M. Vasnetsov. Ocherk' [V. M. Vasnetsov. An essay], *Vasnecov.Ru*. Available online: http://www.vasnecov.ru/?page=0dd38cfc-46e4-4f9b-bd69-f4ae6ceb9098&item=46653ee7-abbb-4e9f-8f52-fd144f12a135&type=page (accessed 29 October 2020).

Griffin, S. (2019), *The Liturgical Past in Byzantium and Early Rus*, Cambridge, MA: Cambridge University Press.

Kavtaradze, S. (2020), 'Lyudi sprashivayut ne Marsu li Bogu voyni on posvyaschen? Chem Horosh I chem Ploh Hram Voorugennih Sil Otkritiy v Podmoskovye' [People ask whether this cathedral is dedicated to Mars. What is good and what is bad in the new cathedral of Armed Forces that was recently opened in Moscow region],

Meduza, 20 Septmeber. Available online: https://meduza.io/feature/2020/06/20/lyudi-sprashivayut-ne-marsu-li-bogu-voyny-on-posvyaschen (accessed 29 September 2020).

Malinova, O. (2019), 'Constructing the Usable Past: The Evolution of the Official Historical Narrative in post-Soviet Russia', in N. Bernsand and B. Törnquist-Plewa (eds.), *Cultural and Political Imaginaries in Putin's Russia*, 85–105, London: Brill.

Park Patriot (n.d.), Information page. https://en.patriotp.ru/about/ (accessed 27 October 2020).

Perrier-Morenkova, E. (2019), 'Memory Watchdogs: Online and Offline Mobilizations Around Controversial Historical Issues in Russia', in N. Bernsand and B. Törnquist-Plewa (eds.), *Cultural and Political Imaginaries in Putin's Russia*, 140–67, London: Brill.

Preobrazhensky, A. (2007), 'Vladimir (Vasiliy) Svyatoslavich', in *Pravoslavnaya Encyclopedia* [Orthodox encyclopedia], Moscow. Available online: https://www.pravenc.ru/text/159104.html (accessed 21 September 2020).

Roth, A. (2020), 'Mosaic glorifying Crimea annexation ditched from new Russian cathedral', *Guardian*, 1 May. Available online: https://www.theguardian.com/world/2020/may/01/mosaic-glorifying-crimea-annexation-ditched-from-new-russian-cathedral-putin (accessed 22 October 2020).

Rus Primary Chronicle (1997), ed. and transl. V. Tvorogov, Saint Petersburg: Nauka. Available online: http://lib.pushkinskijdom.ru/Default.aspx?tabid=4869 (accessed 21 September 2020).

Tychniskaya, P. (2014), 'Konniy Archangel v iskusstve Moskovskoy Rusi Shestnadzatogo Veka. Velikiy Styag tsarya Ivana Groznogo i formirovanie ikonografii archangel Michaila Groznih sil voevody' [Archangel on a horseback in the sixteenth century. Great banner of Ivan the Terrible and formation of iconography of Archangel Michael as the leader of the Heavenly Host], in *Mosckovskiy Kreml' XVI stoletiya. Drevniye Svyatini I istoricheskie pamyatniki* [Moscow Kremlin in the 16th century], 316–18, Moscow: Bookwork.

Vasnetsov, V. (1894) 'Pismo A.V. Vasntesovoy ot 22 Maya' [The letter to A.V. Vasnetsova at 22.05], *Vasnecov.Ru*. Available online: http://www.vasnecov.ru/?type=page&page=63c3a9c4-7e3e-44f8-80e7-bbb33e2305b8&item=4d9eb913-0ffe-4846-b231-0c70db76aff0 (accessed 29 October 2020).

5

Museum Interpretations of Byzantium

Sofia Mali

This chapter examines the interplay between contemporary interpretations of Byzantium and national identity politics in the exhibition constructions of two European national museums: the British Museum, London, UK and the Byzantine and Christian Museum, Athens, Greece. Within the context of each museum's different national, cultural and political framework, this chapter analyses and explains the contemporary interpretation or constructed notion of Byzantine culture as a product of the interaction between the cultural knowledge of Byzantium and national museum curatorial practices and discourse. Its special focus is on issues of identity-making and nation-building. It examines and understands two different, contemporary interpretations of Byzantium as effected through the narratives of each exhibition under study. Most importantly, as well as surprisingly, through each museum exhibition, it identifies and explains the function and significance of each interpretation in the construction of the national identity of the dominant culture or 'imagined community'[1] each museum is part of. By understanding the relation of cultural ideas, beliefs and values to the exhibitionary meaning-making processes, and by analysing and explaining the meanings of Byzantium as presented within each 'exhibitionary complex'[2] under study, this chapter argues that in both museums, Byzantine history, culture and art are used for the explanation of the identity of the 'nation' and the (dominant) 'culture' of the country to which each museum belongs (i.e. Britain, Greece), and for the promotion of the desired image of the corresponding 'nation' (i.e. British, Greek). This meaning is presented as 'natural' and hence as the only 'truth'.[3] In other words, it gives insight into the 'myth'[4] of Byzantium, as seen and (re)presented within the different ideologies of each 'national' and 'cultural' context.

Particularly, this chapter demonstrates that the exhibitions have the effect of (re)constructing a narrative of national identity, a narrative of 'same' and 'other' through Byzantium, within a notion of Europe. Drawing on Derrida's (1992) account of identity/difference, it could be said that the question of who, or what represents 'otherness', or the rationale of the same, is complicated, as each is necessarily tangled up with the other. But then, it could also be said that the question is not what we are, or what we were, but rather what we will become. This is answered by analysing the museums' interpretations, which use national historical narratives attempting to explain the identity of the imagined community of each country, based on who the imagined community were, and who they are (by separating 'themselves' from the 'others') – thus contributing to a future imagined community through the (re)production/(re)construction of the ideology of a national identity. In other words, by analysing an imagined/constructed past and the (re)construction of an imagined/constructed present through the exhibitionary complexes, this chapter also provides insights into the conditions of the possibility of an imagined/constructed future – or, to put it better, of a (re)imagined/(re)constructed future.

Following the 1992 Maastricht treaty, European social/political identity aimed to become unified, and one might expect that European national museums would, therefore, present a 'unified' narrative of European identity. More particularly, this is a reference to the establishment of social/political unity: the 1992 Maastricht treaty did not only aim to increase the social dimension of the union. As Griveaoud (2011) explains, it also aimed at developing 'a new political comprehensiveness because the EU was now acknowledging the fact that it was one entity, which was formed by and worked for the citizens, rather than a body composed of different states, driven by their national interests' – their different, and in some cases conflicting, national interests. Educational exchanges have been encouraged, aiming to overcome cultural differences through mutual respect for diversity, for example. As will be shown in the different exhibitionary complexes under study, the different European cultures are presenting their national identities within a notion of Europe, but also, they resist 'unification' (another illustration of such resistance in the present could be the rise of populism/populist and nationalistic political 'parties' across the EU). The contemporary European identity actually consists of different European/national identities resisting 'unification'. Post-Maastricht Europe, as Lützeler (1994: 9) explains, is a highly contradictory (but dynamic) postmodern structure. Social and cultural change in the EU today might be (and, in fact, is) accelerated, but identity has been disrupted by unemployment, violence, migration and nationalism (Lützeler 1994); in the global present of the current political, financial and Covid-19 crises, even more severely than in the past. What has been intended as (the development of a) European identity in 1992, is today European identities, and hence the use of 'identity(ies)' here. This is the reason why the interpretation of Byzantium/European identity(ies) as effected in the exhibitionary complexes of European national museums is of special interest in the present.

What makes the British Museum particularly important to this study, apart from its dominant academic and intellectual role in museum and curatorial studies, is that it dedicated a separate space of its permanent display to the Byzantine Empire only recently, in 2014. However, as shown in its archives (particularly, its *Trustees Minutes*), the main volume of the collection as we know it today was formulated mainly in the 1980s. Hence, exhibition and curatorial practices around Byzantium in the British Museum were formulated in the 1980s but only revised in 2014. This indicates a change in the current understanding of Byzantium and gives the present study the opportunity to analyse and explain the current interpretations ideas and beliefs on Byzantine history, culture and art as communicated through the British Museum's exhibitionary complex. Similarly, the museum in Athens re-exhibited its permanent early Christian and Byzantine collections in 2004, and its permanent post-Byzantine collections in 2010 (Konstantios 2008). The museum's permanent exhibitions had remained unchanged since its establishment in 1914, with only minor amendments in 2000 (Konstantios 2008). The 2010 museum exhibition was neither aiming at the (re)presentation of a 'unified national narrative' nor would it try to 'present the entire [Byzantine] age with [Greek] national time and its continuity in mind' (Konstantios 2008: 19). This was the aim of the museum when it was first established. Hence, the recent reinterpretation of the collection marks a shift in the understanding of Byzantium. This exhibitionary complex is, therefore, also a valuable source for the understanding of current interpretations, ideas and beliefs on Byzantine history, culture and art (as communicated through it). In this sense, these exhibitionary complexes are closely related and can be considered contemporaneous for the purposes of the present research. In addition, the chosen exhibitionary complexes may be seen as illustrative of the current political and cultural transformations in Europe, as they are part of the structure(s) within which they operate (e.g. the withdrawal of the United Kingdom from the European Union; the rise of populism/nationalism).

Museum interpretations

The representation of past cultures in national museums is a complex subject, constantly changing, combining intellectual and curatorial fashions, cultural presuppositions,[5] national and global politics, while making an effort to maintain a grasp on historical 'truth'. The museums under study are no exception; they construct meaning based on cultural knowledge and understanding. Briefly, cultural knowledge interacts with the exhibitionary meaning-making process, and as a result, the values, ideas and beliefs of each imagined community are (re)produced/(re)constructed in each exhibitionary complex. This will be demonstrated below in the narratives of each exhibitionary complex under study by analysing and explaining selected examples, illustrative of the chapter's argument. Particularly, visual and textual analysis, which involves critical engagement with the notion of visual culture, will help to identify and explain the different museum interpretations of Byzantium. It will help understand the ways in which cultural and social subjectivities are either pictured or made invisible. For the interpretation of the visual images and texts of the exhibitionary complexes under study, semiotic methods are essentially used. Within this framework, the present chapter provides new understandings, new interpretations and new critical perspectives on the constructive notion of the past culture of Byzantium as shaped through the curatorial practices of European national museums at the moment.

British Museum Byzantine exhibitionary complex: Rooms 41 (*Sutton Hoo and Europe AD 300–1100*) and 40 (*Medieval Europe AD 1050–1500*)

According to the titles given to each room, the core idea that binds them together is the narration of the history of Europe from 300 CE to 1500 CE. At first sight, the involvement of Byzantine culture within these two rooms which, according to their titles, narrate the history of Europe, seems awkward. The themes in these rooms refer to the history of the formation of Britain, e.g. *The Sutton-Hoo Ship burial: An Anglo-Saxon royal grave?*; *Anglo-Saxon England AD 450–650* (British Museum: Room 41, 2020); *Celtic Britain and Ireland AD 300–1100* (British Museum: Room 41, 2020), *The Wars of the Roses* (British Museum: Room 40, 2020); also, to the history of Britain in relation to the history of Europe, e.g. *Anglo-Saxon England and the Continent AD 650–1100* (British Museum: Room 41, 2020).

It will be demonstrated that these interpretations are the result of the (re)presentation/(re)production of the cultural ideas, values and beliefs of the British imagined community on its own identity and on Byzantium.

(a) Byzantium: a Roman continuity in the East

Byzantium in the British Museum is presented as a leading influence in the medieval world but is also presented as essentially Roman: as a Roman continuity with only Roman elements composing its history, culture and arts. By looking at Byzantine influences on the cultures (re)presented in Room 41, it will be explained that those influences are (re)presented as Roman influences, and thus, Byzantium is (re)presented as Roman.

One such illustrative example is the Byzantine influence on the Ostrogoths. In Room 41, under the theme *Great Migrations AD 400–750*, in the sub-theme entitled *Ostrogothic Italy*, the museum text reads:

> In the AD 490s, the Ostrogoths established a kingdom in Italy where they were influenced by Roman traditions. Their first king, Theoderic, made consul by the Byzantine Emperor, is named on the Byzantine-style square weight. The coins of King Baduila are also Byzantine in style and show the bust of Emperor Anastasius I. Despite these influences, Ostrogothic women still wore Germanic-style dress on arrival in Italy, like these radiate-headed (Knobbed) and birds' head brooches.
> (British Museum: Room 41, *Great Migrations: Gothic Peoples, 1. Ostrogothic Italy*, accompanying text, 2020)

It refers to Roman influences on Ostrogoth people. According to the text, the Ostrogoths (who established their kingdom in Italy) were influenced by Roman traditions. However, an example of such influences is illustrated here by the Byzantine-style square weight, which bears Theoderic's name, and by the Byzantine-style coins of King Baduila, which are exhibited in this sub-theme.

The ways in which the exhibition elements (objects, texts) relate to each other in sequence (the Byzantine-influenced objects mentioned above and the phrase 'Roman traditions') provide a structure or context within which signs make sense. In other words, they provide the structural forms through which signs are organized into codes or conventions for communication (Jakobson 1971). The text refers to Roman traditions and explicitly links them to the Byzantine-style square weight and King Baduila's coins depicting Emperor Anastasius I (who was a Byzantine emperor). Hence, Byzantium in this framework serves as evidence of Roman influence and is thus (re)presented as Roman. Arnold, Bjornlie and Sessa (2016: 8) explain that matters of cultural influence(s) on Ostrogoth people as well as Ostrogoth identity (i.e. whether Ostrogoth were Goth and/or Roman, or something else) is an extraordinarily complex matter 'that continues to provoke heated debate among modern scholars'. The accompanying text implies that the Byzantine-influenced Ostrogoth objects are products of Roman influence since Byzantine influences are presented as Roman. Byzantium, here, is interpreted and communicated as a continuation of the Roman Empire. Furthermore, in the following sub-theme entitled *The Domagnano Treasure*, the text reads:

> These spectacular items are from a hoard of Ostrogothic jewellery suitable for an aristocratic woman. Made from gold and shimmering with garnets, their style reflects Byzantine influence on the Ostrogothic court.
> (British Museum: Room 41, *Great Migrations: Gothic Peoples, 2. The Domagnano Treasure*, accompanying text, 2020)

Again, here, through these selections and their assembly, i.e. the combination of this text and these objects (the items from a hoard of Ostrogothic jewellery) and the corresponding accompanying text, it is suggested that the Byzantine influences in Ostrogoth jewellery-making are Roman.

The sub-themes *Domagnano Treasure* and *Ostrogothic Italy* are both parts of the syntagm of the theme *Great Migrations: Gothic peoples*. Therefore, the paradigmatic relations in the sub-theme *Domagnano Treasure* involve the same functional contrast with the sub-theme *Ostrogothic Italy*. The cultural knowledge that Byzantium is Roman is taken for granted and hence, Byzantine influences are interpreted as Roman influences; by saying Byzantine influences here, the text suggests Roman influences. These turns of phrase are not there by chance. They have been specifically selected and combined in a particular way; their selection (over others) and combination are a product of the interaction of cultural presuppositions with curatorial practices.

To sum up, the above examples, where Byzantine influence is interpreted as Roman influence, reveal that the exhibitionary complex is mythologically constructed ('myth' as used by Barthes 1972) and that exhibition meaning-making is based on British cultural ideas values and beliefs on Byzantium as a continuation of the Roman Empire in the East.

(b) The Western kingdoms as Roman continuities in the West

An illustrative example of the British Museum's understanding and use of the Western kingdoms as being responsible for the formation of Europe and European identity, as well as the formation of Britain, British identity and, finally, English identity, is the representation of Theoderic's Ostrogoth kingdom as a Roman continuity in the West. As will be explained below, the interpretation of Theoderic's kingdom within the exhibitionary complex is based on the British cultural perception according to which Theoderic's kingdom is explained as 'a continuation of the Roman Empire' (Catholic Encyclopaedia 1912, cited in Mark 2014; also, Arnold 2014). The text of the sub-theme *Ostrogothic Italy* (as above, British Museum: Room 41, *Great Migrations: Gothic peoples, 1. Ostrogothic Italy*, accompanying text, 2020), offers valuable evidence for this. The phrases (a) 'the Ostrogoths established a kingdom in Italy, where they were influenced by Roman traditions' and (b) 'Their first king Theoderic [was] made consul by the Byzantine Emperor' suggest first that the Ostrogoth kingdom is the continuation of the Roman Empire in the West (through the use of the words 'Italy' and 'Roman traditions') and second, that both Byzantium and Theoderic's kingdom are direct Roman continuities, which shared the same Roman traditions. Through the latter, it is suggested that not only did they have common Roman origins but also common ideas and beliefs (the phrase 'made consul by the Byzantine Emperor' suggests these common ideas and beliefs). The use of these words (instead of others) is where 'decisions' in relation to meaning-making are accomplished and revealed. A consul in Byzantium was the highest-ranking member of the judiciary and a member of the Byzantine Senate. The sequence in which this information is provided, i.e. immediately after explaining that 'the Ostrogoths established a kingdom in Italy where they were influenced by Roman traditions' functions as a trigger for the interpretation of the Ostrogoth kingdom as the continuation of the Roman Empire in the West. The 'underlying' thematic paradigm here implies that Theoderic had power and authority in Byzantium, i.e. it implies that Theoderic played an important part in the strategic map and decisions of Byzantium, which was the continuation of the Roman Empire in the East. However, the text does not explain why the Byzantine emperor made him consul. The presentation of this information would have shown that Theoderic and Byzantium did not share the same ideas and beliefs. It is known that Theoderic grew up as a hostage in Constantinople (Burns 1991: 53). After spending ten years of his boyhood in Constantinople (Norwich 1998), it is believed that he had received an education that allowed him to have a 'functional literacy of Latin with reading skills in Latin capitals, including numbers and acronyms', and he 'understood the concept of separate writing systems, such as Greek and Latin' as well as 'the difference between Catholicism, Arianism, and paganism' (Fischer 2013: 99). It is believed that the above knowledge stood him in good stead (Norwich 1998) when he became the Gothic ruler of 'a mixed but largely Romanised barbarian people' (Mark 2014). However, Fischer (2013: 99) argues that the society in which Theoderic lived and acted during his years as a ruler was a 'kleptocracy'.[6] Fischer (2013: 99) explains that 'a major factor for a rule to be termed a kleptocracy is the a priori existence of an imperialist power', and he supports the idea that Italy 'provided that backdrop for Theoderic'. For Fischer (2013), a kleptocracy can only exist as a subsidiary development to an empire. This can explain why Theoderic sought an alliance with the Byzantines, but it does not explain why he would be treated with favour by the Byzantine emperors Zeno, Anastasius and Justin I, and why Zeno would make him consul under the guise of a reward 'for his service to the empire in keeping at bay another Ostrogothic leader named Theodoric Strabo, who harassed the empire, when he was not fighting for its cause' (Mark 2014). Making Theoderic consul is a demonstration of Byzantine diplomatic tactics and not a demonstration of Theoderic's importance for Byzantium. Byzantium's strategy was to maintain an alliance with Theoderic, in order to manipulate him, by giving him a sense of power and authority. Theoderic would rule post-imperial Italy through the reign of the above consecutive Byzantine emperors (Fischer 2013). However, Theoderic's kingdom and Byzantium did not share a common ideology (e.g. Moorhead 1983). Theoderic's kingdom could be said to be autonomous, and not even a continuity of the Roman ideas. Nevertheless, the interpretation of this part of the exhibitionary complex is that Theoderic's kingdom is a continuation of the Roman Empire in the West and that it shared the same Roman traditions, values, ideas and beliefs with Byzantium, which is the continuation of the Roman Empire in the East. Again, these 'facts' are not there by accident; they have been selected and combined in a particular way. The selection of those meanings (instead of others) is the outcome of curatorial work and a result of the interaction of cultural knowledge with curatorial practices. To sum up, Byzantium and Theoderic's kingdom are presented as sharing the same Roman traditions; Byzantium is in the East and the Ostrogoth kingdom is in the West. Hence, what is finally suggested here is that the Roman Empire continued as the Ostrogoth kingdom in the West and as Byzantium in the East.

Another such example is the representation of the Frankish kingdom as a Roman continuity in the West. Under the theme *Great Migrations*, in the sub-theme entitled *Roman Continuities: Signet rings and brooch*, the Franks are presented as the ones who 'wanted to promote themselves as the rightful successors to Rome in the West'. This constitutes part of the interpretation of the Frankish kingdom as a Roman continuity in the West. The museum text reads:

> These signet rings were used for sealing documents in Roman custom, showing that a level of literacy was kept alive by court and religious schools. Although the Franks originally spoke a Germanic language, official documents were written in Latin. The disc brooch, based on a Late Roman medallion, shows Rome enthroned, reflecting the Franks' desire to promote themselves as the rightful successors to Rome in the West.
>
> AD 500–600s Bequeathed by Sir Augustus Wollaston Franks, Compiegne, France (British Museum: Room 41, *Great Migrations AD 400-750. The Franks, 3. Roman Continuities: Signet Rings and Brooch*, accompanying text, 2020)

Here, it is suggested that the Franks were the continuity of the Roman Empire in the West from as early as the 500–600s CE and the signet rings and brooch dated between 500–600s CE are (used as) evidence of this continuity. According to the text, the Franks wanted to promote themselves as the rightful successors to Rome in the West. This indicates that it was their desire, but it also leaves space for ambiguity; they wanted to be so, therefore, they were not – or they wanted to be so and hence they were? Here, it seems that the museum did not want to impose a specific idea upon its interpretation. However, this has not been successful, as the narrative would not be expected to have an effect of confusing or 'mystifying' the visitor – mystification (as used by Barthes 1972) would not be the expected outcome.

Nevertheless, the question is answered by the presentation of evidence that the Franks had been following the Roman customs from as early as the 500s CE, e.g. sealing documents in the Roman custom; showing that a level of literacy was kept alive by court and religious schools; official documents being written in Latin. Through presenting these factors as evidence the text actually suggests that they were already a continuity of the Roman Empire, in the sense of customs, education and language. Hence, here, it is revealed that the museum interprets the Frankish kingdom as a continuity of the Roman Empire in the West. Therefore, the Ostrogoth kingdom and the Frankish kingdom are also placed in a sequence of continuity. The exhibitionary complex implies that the Franks were the successors to Rome in the West after the Ostrogoths, as this text follows the text examined above in sequence.

In the museum exhibitionary complex, all who today would be called Western Europeans are presented as having had distinctive identities, e.g. *The Vandals, Gothic peoples: Ostrogoth, Visigoths, The Franks, The Lombards*. However, it has been explained that the exhibitionary complex demonstrates that the Ostrogoths and Franks had in common their Roman origin and, for this, the Ostrogoths and Franks are placed in sequential order.

(c) The Germanist theme: British identity as Anglo-Saxon and, therefore, English

The interpretation of the Frankish kingdom as the continuity of the Roman Empire after the decline of the Ostrogoth kingdom is used for the (re)construction of the continuity of the Roman Empire in the timeline of Europe. This suggests that people who lived in Britain (i.e. the geographical area inhabited by Romans, Celts, Romano-Celts and later Anglo-Saxons) related to the Romans and the Roman-influenced/Celtic-speaking culture of those peoples of Britain were later appropriated as British; below, it will be demonstrated that the Roman-influenced Anglo-Saxons were later appropriated as English. The most unexpected and surprising theme related to *The Byzantine Empire* theme in sequence, and the representation of the British identity as English, is the centrepiece of Room 41, the *Anglo-Saxon ship Burial* found at Sutton Hoo, Suffolk. The Anglo-Saxon ship burial dates from the early 600s and is 'one of the most spectacular and important discoveries in British archaeology' (*British Museum exhibition catalogue* 2020). As explained in the accompanying text, the burial was arranged inside a wooden chamber built in the middle of a 27-metre-long ship covered by a high earth mound. It is by far the richest grave yet discovered from early medieval Europe and is thought to have commemorated a leading figure, perhaps a king of the Anglo-Saxon kingdom of East Anglia, 'whose true identity remains an unsolvable mystery' (*British Museum exhibition catalogue* 2020). In the text, it is also noted that 'The form of the long carved whetstone and glittering shoulder-clasps evoke Roman symbols of authority, perhaps, in a deliberate attempt to associate their Anglo-Saxon owner with the might of the old Roman Empire' (British museum: Room 41, *Anglo-Saxon ship Burial: Power and authority*, accompanying text, 2020). The above reveals the portrayal of a prominent Anglo-Saxon person as being associated with the Romans. According to the British culturally accepted conception, the Anglo-Saxon period, which lasted from approximately 450 CE to 1066 CE, includes the notion of the creation of *the* 'English' nation, although it has been argued that it was not until the late Anglo-Saxon period that England could be described as a nation-state (Campbell 2000: 19) and that the concept of 'Englishness' developed very slowly (Perkins 2000; Kumar 2003). In the theme *Anglo-Saxon England AD 450–650*, Anglo-Saxon culture and language are presented as something 'new', and dominant. Based on the idea that the Anglo-Saxon period includes the notion of the creation of the English nation, here, it is argued that by presenting the Anglo-Saxon ship burial as one of the most spectacular and important discoveries in British archaeology, the idea that Anglo-Saxons had an important role to play in the formation of the English nation (which, however, in modern British culture is seen as different from the British, a broader term, which is used to refer to the identity of someone who is from England, Scotland, Wales or Northern Ireland, while 'English' is used to refer only to the identity of people from England) is actually supported. Here, it is demonstrated that the museum negotiates matters of the English identity and 'Englishness'.

By the phrase 'the deliberate attempt to associate their Anglo-Saxon owner with the might of the old Roman Empire', it is being suggested that the Anglo-Saxons are associated with the 'old' Romans and not with the Byzantines; Byzantium here is ignored despite the burial ship being dated from the early 600s. The use of the phrase 'old Romans' connotes the Romans of the Western Roman Empire. The text in effect transmits the message of a relation between Anglo-Saxons and (those) Romans, but also between English and (those) Romans. The implication here is that Anglo-Saxons, who are responsible for the formation of the English cultural identity, relate to the Romans and hence, the English nation traces its roots back to Roman times (not the Byzantine). Although the Anglo-Saxon culture and language are presented as something 'new' that replaced the Romano-British culture and language, here, the underlying belief complies with the idea according to which those people relate to the 'old Romans'. This might seem complicated, but it actually isn't. It reflects the idea that the English (of the nineteenth century) often identified themselves with the classical Romans (Hingley, cited in Bell 2007: 208).

The ship burial contained sixteen pieces of silver tableware and a set of ten silver bowls made in the Eastern Mediterranean, 'possibly for religious use' (British museum: Room 41, *Anglo-Saxon ship Burial: Mediterranean silver*, 2020), a large Byzantine silver platter stamped on the back with the control marks of Emperor Anastasius I (r. 491–518 CE), two silver spoons from the Byzantine Empire with Greek inscriptions on their handles, a ladle and cup (not typically Byzantine) as well as a copper basin with animal motifs made in the Eastern Mediterranean. The text reads:

> The silverware probably reached Sutton Hoo through a network of gift exchanges between rulers across Europe, bringing Byzantine luxuries to the Frankish realm (centring on present-day France, Belgium, and Western Germany) and onwards to Anglo-Saxon England. Early Anglo-Saxons did not produce silver dining sets, they typically used wood and horns instead. The silverware may have been used for dining or perhaps, as a display of 'royal treasure'. Exotic and costly, it would have demonstrated its owner's status, wealth, and connections.
> (British museum: Room 41, *Anglo-Saxon ship Burial: Mediterranean Silver*, accompanying text, 2020)

Here, it is suggested that Byzantine craftsmanship was more advanced than Anglo-Saxon craftsmanship and that in the Anglo-Saxon cultural context, Byzantine objects were perceived as 'exotic'. Also, it is suggested that in the 600s, Byzantine objects were brought to Anglo-Saxon England as gift exchanges. Hence, the text implies that the Anglo-Saxons did not have direct relations with the Byzantines, as the gifts were brought to them 'through a network of gift exchange between rulers across Europe', and exclusively not between rulers of the Frankish realm. Through this 'account', it is being suggested that the Anglo-Saxons had relations with the Franks, who had relations with the Byzantines, and by implication, that the Anglo-Saxons did not have relations with the Byzantines. However, as Campbell explains, 'recent work has suggested considerable Byzantine influence on late 6th century Gaul, in particular on fashions' and 'there are indications that such influences appear in England also' (2000: 78). Although Carver (1989, cited in Campbell 2000: 78) explains that the range of contacts indicated by the finds at Sutton Hoo does not imply that seventh-century East Anglian merchants were in direct contact with Syria or Byzantium, and Campbell (2000) further explains that the density and nature of relations between England and Byzantium has a special interest in relation to the Gregorian mission; as he points out, 'if we knew what Gregory the Great thought when dispatching Augustine, we might find that realpolitik had played a part beside pastoral zeal' (2000: 79). The construction of this part of the exhibitionary complex is based on the commonly shared knowledge that the Gregorian mission, headed by Augustine of Canterbury, was sent by Pope Gregory the Great in 596 CE to convert Britain's Anglo-Saxons, resulting in the establishment of Christianity in southern Britain by the death of the last missionary in 635 CE (Mayr and Harting 2010: 50).

The underlying ideology in this part of the complex is that Anglo-Saxons who are responsible for the formation of the English nation relate to the Romans and that in the 600s, they had active relationships with the Franks, but not with the Byzantines, who are (considered) 'other'. Also, that the Anglo-Saxon's conversion to Christianity is linked to Western Christianity (hence, not to Byzantium). Byzantium here is presented as the different, 'other'. However, Anglo-Saxons possess Byzantine objects; they use them as symbols of wealth and power. Hence it could be said that there are Byzantine elements in Anglo-Saxon culture.

For Derrida (1992), no identity is closed and pure; it is always affected by what it excludes and hence identity is in part constituted by what it opposes – the 'different'. The above is an illustration of Derrida's (1992) account: the (re)construction of national identity within the British Museum institutional framework is based on ideas of 'same' and 'other', on the ideas, values and beliefs of the British imagined community on its 'own' identity: on who it thinks it is, i.e. Anglo-Saxons, and hence, English – and who it thinks it is not, i.e. Byzantium.

The above examples show that the significance of the choices in exhibitionary content is based on the interaction of a set of cultural ideas, values and beliefs of the British imagined community on its own identity and on Byzantium with curatorial practices. The product of this interaction is the (re)presentation/(re)production of a particular British identity. The British identity is (re)presented/(re)produced as European, but also as primarily Anglo-Saxon and hence, English – through the use of Byzantium as the 'different', the 'other' to European and to British, and thus, to English. The identity of different 'others' that constitute a particular English identity being offered here is Byzantium and the Continent (i.e. Europe, without the British

Isles). Byzantium at the British Museum Byzantine exhibitionary complex functions to explain the contemporary cultural identity of the British imagined community; however, it is not Britishness, in fact, that is being explained – which would be more inclusive – but rather 'Englishness'; Englishness, as a shared sense of self, as the 'same'. It is a cultural identity constructed by the dominant cultural group, which sees itself as a group bound together by the culture and the history that makes this Englishness.

The Byzantine and Christian Museum

The exhibitionary complex in the Byzantine and Christian Museum of Athens consists of the permanent museum display, which is divided into four parts. Each part is divided into several themes and sub-themes, spread across the museum rooms. The themes and sub-themes are articulated in a 'sequential thematic structure' (Nicks 2002: 361) based on chronology, and carry the following titles: I. *From the Ancient World to Byzantium*; II. *The Byzantine World*; III. *Intellectual and Artistic Activity in the 15th century*; IV. *From Byzantium to the Modern Era*.

In the themes I. *From the Ancient World to Byzantium* and II. *The Byzantine World*, Byzantium is (re)presented through the art, architecture, everyday utensils, burial customs and coins dating from the very first CE centuries to the decline of the Byzantine Empire in 1453. Within these themes, the following interpretations will be identified and explained: (a) the Greek identity of Byzantium and (b) the Greek identity of lands once comprising the Greek territory, which have now been incorporated into modern Turkey after conflicts and events during the post-Byzantine period, i.e. East Trace, the Asia Minor coastline, including Pontus in its northern part. The following interpretations will also be identified and explained in themes III. *Intellectual and Artistic Activity in the 15th century* and IV. *From Byzantium to the Modern Era*, through characteristic pieces of post-Byzantine art, architecture, garments, printed books and ecclesiastical and everyday utensils dating from the fifteenth century to the mid-nineteenth century: (c) the continuation of Greek-Byzantine ideas after the fall of Byzantium and (d) the contribution of the *Greek* Byzantium to the Renaissance. The latter serves the explanation of the European nature of the modern Greek identity.

The above interpretations enable the (re)construction of the identity of *the* 'nation' and *the* 'culture' of the country to which the exhibitionary complex belongs, i.e. the identity of *the* Greek nation and culture. Byzantium here is presented as the continuation of Greek classical antiquity and is placed within the narrative of Greek history. However, what the museum essentially presents is actually 'a' Greek history/identity, being presented as 'the' Greek history/identity. The next section will illustrate these issues and arguments.

(a) The Greek identity of Byzantium

The idea of the continuity of the ancient Greek world to the Byzantine world, and hence the Greek identity of Byzantium, is introduced in various parts of the exhibitionary complex. The most striking illustration of this idea is the interpretation of Byzantium as a Greek Empire demonstrated through the selection of the following object right next to the introductory text and before the entrance to the first museum room. This object is the copy of the mosaic of the Chapel in San Vitale in Ravenna, where Emperor Justinian I is represented. It is through the position of this object within the syntagm of the exhibitionary complex that continuity is suggested. This image functions as a visual statement, which suggests that Byzantium after Justinian became a different, new state, which has its cultural roots back in ancient Greek culture and which was a Greek Empire.

The last lawful Roman emperor could be said to have been Romulus Augustus (e.g. Edwell et al. 2015: 216). However, Emperor Justinian is thought to have been 'the last Roman emperor to speak Latin as a first language' (Wickham 2009: 90), and his reign is thought to have been marked by the restoration of the empire (Haldon 1999: 17–19). Because of his restoration activities, which include his administration system and laws (Watson 1985), Emperor Justinian has also been called the last Roman (e.g. Baker 2002). According to this interpretation, Justinian's successors should not be counted as Roman, but as something else. The introduction of the exhibitionary complex by this mosaic (re)produces this idea, suggesting that Byzantium, or the Byzantine Empire, which is presented within the rooms that follow, is not a continuation of the Roman Empire. Particularly, this places the beginning of this new Empire after the reign of Justinian. It could be said that this beginning is marked by the change of the official language of the empire from Latin to Greek by Emperor Heraclius I in 620 CE (Davis 1990). Hence, it is being suggested that this new empire is a continuation of Greek antiquity and a Greek Empire. The position of this mosaic at the beginning of the exhibitionary complex demonstrates that the exhibitionary complex, which unfolds within the following museum rooms, will (re)present this empire. The idea that Byzantium becomes a Greek Empire after Justinian's reign is also (re)produced/(re)constructed in the following parts of the exhibitionary complex. Initially, the introductory text of theme I. *From the Ancient World to Byzantium* reads: 'The transition from the ancient world to the Byzantine was gradual [...] A milestone in this transition was the legalization of the Christian religion in 313 by the emperor Constantine the Great' [...] (Byzantine and Christian Museum: I. *From the Ancient World to Byzantium*, introductory text, 2020). The key message here is that Byzantium's difference from the ancient world is Christianity. The text further reads:

> In parallel, the transfer of the capital of the Roman Empire from Rome to Constantinople in 330 represented a decisive shift in the empire's centre of gravity from the Latin West to the Hellenized East. The division into a Western and Eastern empire in 395 and the dissolution of the Western half in 476 were significant stages along the way to the end of antiquity, which can be said to have breathed its last with the closure of the philosophical schools in 529, the onset of the barbarian invasions, and the decline of the great urban centres after the sixth century.
> (Byzantine and Christian Museum: I. *From the Ancient World to Byzantium*, introductory text, 2020)

The key message here is that Byzantium is Greek. The West is characterized as Latin, but the East as Hellenized. The end of antiquity is placed between 529 CE when Justinian closed down the Academy of Athens and the Arab invasions along with the decline of the great urban centres after the sixth century. In this way, it is suggested that the actual birth of Byzantium is between the sixth and seventh centuries. It is then, when the Greek language becomes the Empire's official language (e.g. Ostrogorsky 1969; Ahrweiler, cited in Bakounakis 2010). In the introductory text examined above, the beginning of Byzantium is placed in the fourth century. The debate of Byzantium as a name-construct comes into play. The information on the name-construct suggests that at the beginning, i.e. the fourth century, there are several parallel ideas, before the actual formation of Byzantium, and that the actual birth of Byzantium is between the sixth and seventh centuries when Greek becomes Byzantium's official language. As explained above, the parallel ideas are referred to [in] the museum text, but the images of the exhibitionary complex (re)construct the idea that Greek influence was prominent. Ahrweiler's (cited in Bakounakis 2010) interpretation expresses precisely the ideology on Byzantium as presented within the exhibitionary complex:

> Byzantium is the Greek language and orthodoxy, the two main components of Hellenism. Certainly, Byzantium was a multinational empire, but it was a Greek-speaking Empire. The fact that Byzantium was Greek-speaking saved across the Greek culture. When the great French historian Fernand Braudel wrote that there are no French, there are only francophones, and anyone who speaks French is French, he meant that the French language is the amalgamation of the entire civilization and traditions. And Byzantium is Greek-speaking from the 7th century.
> (Ahrweiler, cited in Bakounakis 2010)

Just as Braudel (1990) explained that the French language is the amalgamation of the entire civilization and traditions, so is the Greek language for Byzantium. Hence, the underlying idea in this part of the exhibitionary complex is that since Greek is Byzantium's official language, Byzantium is a continuity of Greek antiquity, and also a Greek Empire.

In conclusion, Byzantium here is interpreted as a continuation of Greek antiquity. The fourth-century Byzantium is interpreted as a different Empire from the Roman, which is significantly Hellenized. Subsequently, the actual birth of Byzantium is placed in the seventh century when Greek becomes its official language. The seventh-century Byzantium is interpreted as a Greek Empire.

(b) The Greek identity of lands once comprising the Greek territory

The introductory text of the exhibitionary complex presents information concerning the Hellenic territories included in Byzantium's territory: the Aegean, Asia Minor, Bithynia (Nicaea), Epirus and Pontus (Trebizond). The text reads:

> In the sixth century, it [Byzantium] was a vast, multinational and still multireligious state. In the eleventh and twelfth centuries, still multinational, it extended over the Hellenic, Aegean, and Asia Minor territories. In the thirteenth century, in 1204,

it ceased to exist, after being abolished by the Crusaders of the Fourth Crusade, and was substituted by small states, in Bithynia (Nicaea), Epirus, and Pontus (Trebizond).

(Byzantine and Christian Museum: museum entrance hall, introductory text, 2020)

The reference to these territories triggers the commonly shared (among modern Greeks) background belief foundational to Greek identity in relation to these territories and consequently to Byzantium, and it is in this way that it is being suggested that Byzantium is a continuity of Greek antiquity. In Greek literature, these territories are referred to as the lost territories (the once Greek territories gradually annexed to the Ottoman Empire after the battle of Manzikert in 1071, and after the fall of the Byzantine Empire in 1453) and are among the claims necessary to the political construct of the 'Great Idea'.[7] It could be said that, in addition to suggesting the Greek identity of Byzantium, and continuity with Greek antiquity, this reference is also suggesting these claims.

(c) The continuation of Greek-Byzantine ideas after the fall of Byzantium

The text that follows introduces the interpretation of the continuation of Greek culture and identity during the several transformations of the Empire after the Fourth Crusade, but also after the fall of the Byzantine Empire, by simultaneously showing to the rest of the medieval world the (still) dominant role of Greek Byzantium. The text reads:

The sack of Constantinople by the Frankish and Latin crusaders in 1204 delivered a crippling blow to the Empire, but also led to new relations and channels of contact.
(Byzantine and Christian Museum: II. *The Byzantine World*, introductory text, 2020)

The Fourth Crusade which took place in 1204 is an event that divides modern historians; to some, it signifies the beginning of the Latin restructuring of the Roman Empire (e.g. Tricht 2011), while to others it is the point in history when Byzantine-Greek identity resisted change, and remains intact despite the transformations (e.g. Bartusis 1997). In other words, this point in history is used by some as proof of the continuity of Greek-Byzantine identity, despite the several changes that took place when Latins and Franks sacked the city and established their kingdoms in Byzantium (the continuation of what Paparrigopoulos called Hellenism). In other words, they use it to establish the formation of modern Greece and modern Greek identity, through a break in continuity which, however, is bridged by the interpretation of Byzantium's (a) resistance to change and (b) revival.

This second interpretation is (re)constructed within the museum exhibitionary complex, through the above-quoted phrase. The way that information is combined in this phrase silences the decisive effect that the crusade had on Byzantium; the city was completely destroyed, and along with the city, the thousand years Empire of Byzantium (e.g. Phillips 2005). It immediately balances the 'crippling blow', by referring to the positive aspects of new relations and contacts. The reference to the relations and contacts triggers the following background knowledge: the accumulation of capital in the West, which allowed the development of industrial capitalism some centuries later, was opened by the first modern colonial empire, Venice, which was created after plundering the Greek territories following the sack of Constantinople. The most important centres of this colonial empire were in the Ionian, the Peloponnese, Crete, Euboea, Cyprus, the Cyclades, Thessaloniki and Aegina. These centres remained parts of this West colonial formation for many years or even centuries after 1204. At the same time, the Byzantine Empire shrank into the Greek successor states of Nicaea, Epirus and Trebizond. The triggering of this knowledge actually functions to establish the continuity of the Greek-Byzantine identity through a break in what could be counted as continuity. This actually suggests that the first 'nation-state', or states of modern Greece, were established in the late Byzantine era, through the formation of the first colonial empire, Venice. In addition to this, the exhibitionary complex attempts to show that what had remained from the Byzantine Empire was still dominating the Eastern and Western world. This makes itself apparent in the text that follows the sentence analysed above:

> Despite their persistent efforts, the Palaiologan emperors could do nothing to halt the political decline of the Empire following their restoration to the Byzantine throne in Constantinople in 1261. Nonetheless, the Palaiologan revival in the arts and letters was a vitally important cultural event that was to have a stimulating effect on both East and West.
> (Byzantine and Christian Museum: II. *The Byzantine World*, the museum, introductory text, 2020)

The text explains that the efforts of the Palaiologan emperors were ineffective, but presents the history of the late Byzantium, from 1261 to 1453, as a rather gloomy story, which is exactly what modern Greek historians do (e.g. Bartusis 1997). The text highlights the Palaiologan revival in the arts and letters, which it regards as a 'vitally important cultural event that was to have a stimulating effect on both East and West'. Through this contention, it is being suggested that Byzantium, despite the political instability, and despite its shrinkage, was still dominant because Greek ideas and values were still prevailing and influencing the then-known world. By saying that the Palaiologan revival in the arts and letters had a stimulating effect on both East and West, the text actually suggests the contribution of Byzantium, of the Greek Empire, to the Renaissance. With regards to Byzantium's last period, in the exhibitionary complex, it is also explained that Byzantium

> reaches its artistic zenith, especially in painting. Saturated in the classical tradition, this great artistic culmination went on to serve as the foundation for yet another glorious phase, in post-Byzantine painting.
> (Byzantine and Christian Museum of Athens II.8. *The Palaiologan Period, the Final Flowering of Byzantium*, introductory text, 2020)

Through this formulation, the text suggests that the Palaiologan period has contributed not only to the preservation of the classical tradition but also to the period after the fall of Constantinople. Icons that are representative of the Palaiologan period such as the icon of the Virgin Mary Hodegetria, which was an especially popular icon in late Byzantium, are used as proof of this. Such icons have been reproduced in the post-Byzantine period, slightly modified, and are still used in the present day as a prototype for the making of icons. In agreement with the above, the following text says that after Constantinople fell in 1453

> Byzantine civilization adapted to its new circumstances and continued to thrive. Rallying around the Orthodox Church, it remained the focal point of the Orthodox world and saw the Greeks and their culture through to the establishment of the modern Greek state.
> (Byzantine and Christian Museum: II.9. *The Fall of Constantinople*, introductory text, 2020)

This text reproduces the Greek cultural beliefs, ideas and values on the formation of modern Greek identity by suggesting that although Byzantium fell in 1453, its culture survived and continued throughout history due to the Orthodox Church. Paparrigopoulos (1871), whose work forms part of and has influenced the Greek culturally accepted literature on Byzantium,[8] explained this under his term 'Hellenic Christianism'. This term signifies the interconnection of the ancient Greek world with Byzantium, the 'Greek ethnicity' of Byzantium, and the Greek-Byzantine foundations of the modern Greek nation, essentially seeing Byzantium as a direct continuity of ancient Greek ideas, values and beliefs, with a substitution of the ancient Greek religion with Christian religion.

These beliefs, ideas and values are also reproduced in theme IV. *From Byzantium to the Modern Era*, which (re)presents the contribution of the Orthodox Church as crucial to the preservation of Byzantine culture and to its continuation through the so-called age of 'darkness' (the period of Turkish sovereignty in Greece after the fall of Constantinople and for the following four hundred years). The church is explained 'as a point of reference for the Christians: a nexus preserving Byzantine tradition, Greek Orthodox instruction, and the Greek language, which would go on to contribute to the creation of a Greek national identity' (Byzantine and Christian Museum: IV. *From Byzantium to the Modern Era*, introductory text, 2020). This summarizes the main points of the interpretation of modern Greek identity as a continuation of Byzantium. Previously, Byzantium was (re)presented as the continuation of Greek antiquity and Byzantium itself as a Greek Empire. This part of the complex serves as proof of the continuity of Byzantine culture (and hence, Greek culture) throughout the years of Turkish sovereignty and hence, of the continuity of Greek identity from the ancient past to the present through Byzantium. Therefore, the exhibitionary complex actually represents the idea of the 'united and continuous Hellenism', which, as the former museum director explained, was not the museum's objective (Konstantios 2008: 19). Although this was not the museum's objective, it has been shown here that these ideas, values and beliefs make themselves apparent within the exhibitionary complex.

(d) The contribution of the Greek Byzantium to the Renaissance

The Palaiologan period in the museum narrative is frequently referred to as the 'Palaiologan Renaissance' and is linked to the migration of Byzantine scholars and artists to the West, who are thought to have triggered the Italian Renaissance (also in Geanakoplos 1958). The following examples are illustrative of the museum's account of the contribution of the *Greek* Byzantium to the Renaissance and, therefore, of the European nature of the modern Greek identity. Through the exhibitionary complex, it is suggested that Byzantium contributed to the Renaissance. This idea is (re)constructed here and functions as another proof of the continuation of Greek-Byzantine ideas, values and beliefs after the fall of Byzantium. Specifically, here it is suggested that before the fall of Constantinople, Byzantine ideas travelled across the West through scholarly clerics and laymen who immigrated to the West. The museum text reads:

> From as early as the 14th c. and above all in the 15th c., just when everything seemed to be leading to the collapse of the Byzantine Empire and the Fall of Constantinople, there was a remarkable upsurge in activity in intellectual and artistic circles. Scholarly clerics and laymen, chiefly pursuing the theological questions of the age, produced noteworthy philosophical and theological treatises. Many of them become extremely active in the West. They familiarize the Western world with basic works of classical and Byzantine literature, thus contributing to the European Renaissance.
>
> (Byzantine and Christian Museum: III. *Intellectual and Artistic Activity in the 15th Century*, introductory text, 2020)

By this formulation, the text suggests that Renaissance humanism, i.e. the study of classical antiquity, was triggered by Byzantine clerics and laymen who spread the basic works of classical (and Byzantine) literature to the West. The underlying idea here is that in Byzantium the study of classical texts never actually stopped and that the classical texts were saved by the Byzantines. This is indicative of both the museum's interpretation of Byzantium's Greek identity, and of the continuity of Greek identity (Hellenism) after the fall of Byzantium, and consequently, and perhaps most importantly, of the European identity of the modern Greeks. Vasiliev (1952: 713) explains that in the nineteenth century, it was thought that the Italian Renaissance was called forth by the Greeks who fled from Byzantium to Italy before the Turkish danger, especially at the fall of Constantinople in 1453. For example, he says that a Russian Slavophile of the first half of the nineteenth century, J. V. Kireyevsky, wrote 'When after the capture of Constantinople, the fresh and pure air of Hellenic thought blew from the East to the West, and the thinking man in the West breathed more easily and freely, the whole structure of scholasticism collapsed at once' (Kireyevsky, cited in Vasiliev 1952: 713–14). This idea is reproduced in the last quoted text, in support of the Greek continuity in Europe and hence, the European element of the modern Greek identity.

Byzantium in the Byzantine and Christian Museum exhibitionary complex is interpreted as a continuity of Greek antiquity, a Greek Empire and responsible for the continuation of Greek culture and identity (Hellenism) from antiquity to the establishment of the modern Greek state. Continuity with Greek antiquity is suggested in terms of language, artistic and architectural traditions, ideas and beliefs, and for the same reasons, Byzantium is seen as a Greek Empire. It is also suggested that these elements were strong enough to survive throughout history. The church is seen as key to the continuity of the Greek language and Orthodox traditions during the years of the Ottoman conquest. In addition, the Greek-Byzantine influences on the Renaissance are interpreted as part of the idea of continuity, but also of the modern Greek identity's European-ness. Through the above, it has been demonstrated that the exhibitionary complex (re)presents/(re)produces the Greek cultural ideas, values and beliefs on Greek-Byzantine identity. More specifically, it has been demonstrated that this particular representation and interpretation of Byzantium stems from the cultural knowledge of Greeks on their 'own' national identity: the Greek, the Byzantine, the Orthodox and the European elements, all of which make up the modern Greek national identity.

Conclusions

This chapter has provided a cross-cultural perspective of the current understandings of the past culture of Byzantium. Throughout this research, it has been argued that the representation of Byzantine culture in each case study is a cultural-ideological or 'mythical' construct – a product of the ideological nature and cultural functions of the presuppositions involved in each museum's curatorial practices. It has been demonstrated that the representation of Byzantium in each museum is actually the (re)construction and (re)production of each imagined community's identity/ Byzantium. As there are different elements combined within an identity, that identity is a combination of identity and difference characterized by concurrent repeatability and differentiality – hence the use of the prefix (re) as in (re)presentation, as well as (re)construction/(re)production – the imagined community in each country (re)constructs/(re)produces its identity, through the combination of the different elements combined within its identity, in relation to the different, the 'other'. The identities communicated through the two exhibitionary complexes are established in relation to Byzantium, i.e. in relation to that which the imagined communities are: either Byzantium the different, invited in identity, invited in the 'same' as in the British Museum or Byzantium the identity, the 'same' as in the Greek museums.

Specifically, this chapter analysed and explained that the (re)presentation of Byzantium in the British Museum is a product of the interaction of the ideas, values and beliefs of the British imagined community on 'same' and 'other' with curatorial practices: Byzantium is (re)presented as the continuation of the Roman Empire in the East, as the other to British identity (invited in the British identity, and hence, the constitutive part of the British identity). British identity is (re)presented as a continuation of the Roman Empire in the West, and hence, European, and primarily Anglo-Saxon – thus, English. Byzantium serves the exhibitionary complex's narrative as the other to the British national identity: the other to the European-English national identity. The choices in images and texts negotiate and document the development of the English identity through the ages, from Roman Britain to the Middle Ages. Simply, British history is narrated in relation to European history, and more particularly, in relation to the history of the formation of Europe and, in relation to Byzantium, in order to explain the English history. The British nation is presented as primarily emerging from the Anglo-Saxons and secondarily from the Franks, who converted to Western Christianity. Europe emerges from all the kingdoms that are presented as continuations of the Roman Empire in the West. Byzantium is the continuation of the Roman Empire in the East, but it is also explained as different, other. Within the exhibitionary complex, no reference is made to the contribution of Byzantium to the formation of Europe, as it is thought of and seen by contemporary scholars (e.g. Ahrweiler 2012; Hughes 2014; James 2014 and so on). However, the beliefs, ideas and values reflected in the above explanations are compatible with the British imagined community's interpretation of Byzantium as different, other, and of the British nation as European, but predominantly, English.

The (re)presentation of Byzantium in the Greek museum is also a product of the interaction of the ideas, values and beliefs of the Greek imagined community on identity and other with curatorial practices: Byzantium is (re)presented as a continuation of the Greek antiquity, as a Greek Empire, and as responsible for the continuation of Greek culture and identity (Hellenism) from antiquity to the establishment of the modern Greek state. Byzantium serves the exhibitionary complexes' narratives as the same; the same to the modern Greek national identity, as opposed to the other, the non-Byzantine, the non-Christian, the non-Orthodox, the non-Greek (invited in the Greek identity and hence, a constitutive part of the Greek identity). Continuity with Greek antiquity is suggested in terms of language, artistic and architectural traditions, ideas and beliefs, and for the same reasons, Byzantium is seen as a Greek Empire. It is also suggested that these elements were strong enough to survive throughout history. The church is seen as key to the continuity of the Greek language and Orthodox traditions during the years of the Ottoman conquest. In addition, the Greek-Byzantine influences on the Renaissance are interpreted as part of the idea of continuity, but also of the modern Greek identity's European-ness. Through the above, it has been demonstrated that the exhibitionary complex (re)presents/(re)produces the Greek cultural ideas, values and beliefs on Greek-Byzantine identity. More specifically, it has been demonstrated that this particular representation and interpretation of Byzantium stems from the cultural knowledge of Greeks on their 'own' national identity: the Greek, the Byzantine, the Orthodox and the European elements, all of which make the modern Greek national identity.

By analysing the above exhibitionary complexes, this chapter was allowed to account for the different interpretations of Byzantium as effected through the two European national museums. However, it was also able to account for the cultural and political implications of the presuppositions in the exhibitionary meaning-making process. On the one hand, the national museums are 'naturalizing' their imagined community, i.e. their 'nation' through their exhibitionary complexes (this is a cultural implication of the presuppositions involved in curatorial practices). On the other hand, the presented ideology within their exhibitionary complexes is entangled with the image of the imagined community that each country in effect promotes (this is the political implication of the presuppositions involved in curatorial practices).

The exhibitionary complexes may also be seen as offering an illustrative account of the cultural implications of the current political transformations in Europe. The exhibition constructions, although 'revised' and contemporaneous, do not reflect the current understandings of Byzantium as found in the literature. They reflect practices of (national) identity-making and nation-building instead. The exhibition constructions can be seen as examples that may demonstrate some aspects of what is at stake in re-viewing 'new' forms of nationhood as well as of current citizenship and civic participation in Europe. In a Europe that has been driven by nationalistic ideologies of the past, informed by the neo-liberal agenda of the present. What is depicted here, could also explain what should be avoided in the reconfiguration of the notion of nationhood as well as citizenship, an act(ion) that has been deemed necessary by most European governments at present.

Acknowledgements

I would like to thank Dr Malcolm Barnard for contributing with valuable advice and suggestions – I am very grateful to him, as well as the editors of this volume, Przemysław T. Marciniak and Markéta Kulhánková for their improving suggestions.

Notes

1   The 'imagined community' following Anderson's (1991) concept of 'nation' is a group of people who perceive and construct themselves as part of that group, which would form the 'culture' and the 'nation' in each country. In other words, given that each country contains many different cultures, including a 'national' culture, 'imagined community' here refers to a socially constructed community, imagined or constructed by those people who claim to represent the 'correct' national culture in each country. More strongly, it refers to 'an imagined political community – and imagined as both inherently limited and sovereign' (Anderson 1991: 6), which constructs its identity, its 'national' identity, based on ideas, values and beliefs of who they think they are (i.e. a unitary or dominant 'self' which in this case would mean the 'same') and, consequently, of who they think they are not (thereby implicitly creating and excluding the 'different', which in this case would also mean the 'other').

2   The term 'exhibitionary complex' is borrowed from Tony Bennett (1995) in order to define the particular things this chapter is interested in looking at in the museum exhibitions. Briefly, the 'exhibitionary complex' contains the objects on display and the exhibition narratives as they are constructed by the museum through texts in the object labels and introductory panels of the exhibition. However, the term 'exhibitionary complex', apart from signifying the visual elements of the display, is also indicative of museum power relations and incorporates the notion of 'exhibition as a practice' (Kirshenblatt-Gimblett 2006: 37). Exhibition as a practice, with all its cultural and political extensions, power relations, as well as communication and interpreting agents. As will be shown here, the exhibitionary complexes are complex political and cultural constructions, which result in the presentation of 'mythological' constructs of Byzantium as the only 'truth' to their audiences, and consequently,

of 'national' identity and dominant cultural values of the country to which each museum belongs.

3   'Truth', as Foucault (1976: 14) has it, is 'a system of ordered procedures for the production, regulation, distribution, circulation, and functioning of statements' linked 'by a circular relation to systems of power which produce it and sustain it, and to effects of power which it induces and which redirect it' (Rabinow 1984: 74). As Foucault further explains, the 'regimes of truth' are the result of scientific discourse and institutions, and are reinforced, but also redefined constantly and can 'in fact be integrated into any function (education, medical treatment, production, punishment)' (1977: 206). It is in this sense that the dominant culture's knowledge(s), regimes of truth and general politics can be integrated into museum curation and 'naturalize' ideological constructions (i.e. dress them up as 'objective' and make them count as the only 'truth').

4   'Myth' is used here in the sense of the Barthesian 'myth', which is another term for ideology. Barthes (1972: 128) explains that the very principle of 'myth' is to turn history into nature. By this, he draws on the concept of Marxist ideology aiming to reveal the ways in which the results of people's actions in history are turned into what appears to be the result of laws of nature. According to Marx and Engels (1970: 47), ideology works like a 'camera obscura', which inverts the image of social reality, presenting itself as objective and universal; also, it not only represents but also is [in] the interests of the ruling class (64–68). Ideology, 'myth' according to Barthes (1972), is a set of values, rules and agreements through which certain historical meanings, which operate in the interests of one particular dominant social or cultural group, are constructed and presented as natural and universal and given to an entire society. The 'myth' of Byzantine culture in the framework of the Byzantine exhibitionary complexes under study is perceived as a cultural reality concerning Byzantine culture among the layers of signification within the constructed images and texts of each Byzantine exhibitionary complex. The functions of ideological narratives concerning Byzantine culture manifest themselves in the sense of the Barthesian 'myth' within the constructed images and texts of the museums' current Byzantine exhibitionary complexes. For Barthes (1972), these choices on exhibitionary meaning depend on the set of ideas, values and beliefs through which one particular dominant social or cultural group constructs a 'reality' and presents it as universal and 'given' to an entire society.

5   Presuppositions are highly influential in the process of meaning-making; they are the basis for interpreting and constructing meaning. Presuppositions, here, refer to the set of cultural ideas, beliefs and values concerning the interpretation of Byzantine culture and art that are fixed in the minds of the dominant cultural group, or better, the imagined community of each country, and also concern the identity and nature of the imagined community of each country to which the museums/museum curators belong.

6   A 'kleptocracy' is a society whose leaders make themselves rich and powerful by stealing from the rest of the people (*Cambridge Dictionary* 2020).

7   The term 'Great Idea' refers to political and nationalistic ideals popularized in the Greek world from the second half of the nineteenth century. The Great Idea is a diverse concept, deriving from the political and nationalist contexts of this period, 'making it problematic for historical research' (Margaritis 1999: 203). The emergence of this idea in the collective consciousness of the modern Greek state is not self-existent or instantaneous, but 'it seems to come as a result of

the emergence of the phenomenon of the conscious nationalist movements in Europe in the 19th century employing the particular elements of Greek society' (Hobsbawm 2000: 192).

The 'Great Idea' was the axis of the internal and foreign policy of Greece until the third decade of the twentieth century. The onset of the Great Idea was to broaden the Greek borders to include areas with Greek populations that were under foreign domination. More particularly, the Great Idea, the ideological expression of Greek nationalism, had as its goal 'the liberation of all Greeks who were under Turkish sovereignty and their integration into a nation-state with its capital in Constantinople' (Veremis 1999: 31). Also, the Great Idea was inspired as a term for demagogic reasons, by the first Constitutional Prime Minister of Greece, John Koletis, in the mid-nineteenth century and particularly in 1844 (Vlachodimou 2008). It is worth mentioning that Koletis based his entire policy on the Great Idea. The Great Idea endeavours to regain the lost territories of the Byzantine Empire and it remained the aim of all Greek governments until August 1922, when it was finally abandoned after the catastrophe of Asia Minor (Skopetea 1988).

8   Culturally accepted literature in each country is formed by culturally accepted publications on Byzantium (academic and non-academic) such as, for example, the first volumes of the *History of the Greek Nation* produced after the establishment of the modern Greek state in 1830 (particularly the work of Paparrigopoulos) and literature about and around them, the national curriculum of each country and available history schoolbooks, with particular emphasis on the 1950s and 1960s when Byzantium was (re)invented, or the decade of 1980s, where historical revisionism practices were put into action, and in the last decade, when Byzantium is being retheorized. The history and art history literature proposed by the museums under study, through their own publications, or by books on Byzantium sold in their shops and history schoolbooks, is also included in the culturally accepted history literature explored in this context.

Bibliography

Ahrweiler, G. H. (2012), *Giati to Vyzantio*, Athens: Metaichmio.
Anderson, B. ([1983] 1991), *Imagined Communities: Reflections on the Origin and Spread of Nationalism*, London: Verso.
Arnold, J. J. (2014), *Theoderic and the Roman Imperial Restoration*, New York: Cambridge University Press.
Arnold, J., S. M. Bjornlie and K. Sessa, eds. (2016), *A Companion to Ostrogothic Italy*, Leiden and Boston: Brill.
Baker, G. P. (2002), *Justinian: The Last Roman Emperor*, New York: Cooper Square Press.
Bakounakis, N. (2010), 'Sinentefxi me tin Heleni Glykatzi Ahrweiler: Eimaste oloi Vyzantinoi', *To Vima: Politismos*, 3 April. Available online: http://www.tovima.gr/culture/article/?aid=324009 (accesed 13 April 2020).
Barthes, R. (1972), *Mythologies*, New York: The Noonday Press.
Bartusis, M. ([1992] 1997), *The Late Byzantine Army: Arms and Society, 1204–1453*, Philadelphia: University of Pennsylvania Press.
Bell, D. (2007), *The Idea of Greater Britain: Empire and the Future of World Order, 1860–1900*, Princeton, NJ: Princeton University Press.

Bennett, T. (1995), *The Birth of the Museum: History, Theory, Politics*, London: Routledge.
Braudel, F. (1990), *Ecrits sur l'histoire II.*, Paris: Flammarion.
British Museum (2020), Room 41, *Anglo-Saxon ship Burial: Mediterranean Silver*, accompanying text.
British Museum (2020), Room 41, *Anglo-Saxon ship Burial: Power and Authority*, accompanying text.
British Museum (2020), Room 41, *Great Migrations: Gothic Peoples, 1. Ostrogothic Italy*, accompanying text.
British Museum (2020), Room 41, *Great Migrations: Gothic Peoples, 2. The Domagnano Treasure*, accompanying text.
British Museum (2020), Room 41, *Great Migrations AD 400–750. The Franks, 3. Roman Continuities: Signet Rings and Brooch*, accompanying text, 2020.
British Museum Exhibition Catalogue (2020), Sutton Hoo and Europe, in Room 41, London: British Museum.
Burns, T. S. (1991), *A History of the Ostrogoths*, Bloomington and Indianapolis: Indiana University Press.
Byzantine and Christian Museum (2020), I. *From the Ancient World to Byzantium*, introductory text.
Byzantine and Christian Museum (2020), II. *The Byzantine World*, the museum, introductory text.
Byzantine and Christian Museum (2020), III. *Intellectual and Artistic Activity in the 15th century*, introductory text.
Byzantine and Christian Museum (2020), museum entrance hall, introductory text.
Byzantine and Christian Museum of Athens (2020), IV. *From Byzantium to the Modern Era*, introductory text.
Byzantine and Christian Museum of Athens (2020), II.8. *The Palaiologan Period, the Final Flowering of Byzantium*, introductory text.
Byzantine and Christian Museum of Athens (2020), II.9. *The Fall of Constantinople*, introductory text.
Cambridge Dictionary (2020), 'Kleptocracy'. Available online: http://dictionary.cambridge.org/dictionary/english/kleptocracy (accessed 15 November 2016).
Campbell, J. (2000), *The Anglo-Saxon State*, London: Cambridge University Press.
Davis, L. D. (1990), *The First Seven Ecumenical Councils (325–787): Their History and Theology*, Collegeville, MN: Liturgical Press.
Derrida, J. (1992), *The Other Heading*, Bloomington and Indianapolis: Indiana University Press.
Edwell, P., G. Fisher, G. Greatrex, C. Whately and P. Wood (2015), 'Arabs in the Conflict between Rome and Persia AD 491–630', in G. Fisher (ed.), *Arabs and Empires before Islam*, 214–75, Oxford: Oxford University Press.
Fisher, S. (2013), 'Literacy and Text Production in the Age of Germanic Kleptocracy – The Elusive Case of Theoderic', in A. Kaliff and L. Munkhammar (eds.), *Wulfila 311–2011 International Symposium. Uppsala Universitet June 15–18*, 97–114, Uppsala: Edita Västra Aros.
Foucault, M. (1976), 'La fonction politique de l'intellectuel', *Politique Hebdo* 247 (29 November): 31–33.
Foucault, M. ([1977] 1979), *Discipline and Punish: The Birth of the Prison*, New York: Vintage Books.

Geanakoplos, D. J. (1958), 'A Byzantine Looks at the Renaissance: The Attitude of Michael Apostolis towards the Rise of Italy: To Cultural Eminence', *Greek, Roman and Byzantine Studies* 1 (2): 157–62.
Griveaoud, M. (2011), 'Why is the Maastricht Treaty Considered to be so Significant?', in *E-International Relations Students*. Available online: http://www.e-ir.info/2011/05/29/why-is-the-maastricht-treaty-considered-to-be-so-significant-2/ (accessed 19 May 2017).
Haldon, J. F. (1999), *Warfare, State and Society in the Byzantine World, 565–1204*, London: University College London Press.
Hobsbawm, E. J. (2000), *E epochi ton epanastaseon, 1789–1848*, Athens: M.I.E.T.
Hughes, B. (2014), [Radio] *Byzantium Unearthed*. Episode 1. BBC Radio 4 Extra. 2 December. 02:30.
Jakobson, R. (1971), 'Language in Relation to Other Communication Systems', in R. Jakobson, *Selected Writings*, vol. 2, 570–79, Mouton: The Hague.
James, L. (2014), 'A Short History of Byzantium'. *History Today*, 64 (3). Available online: https://www.historytoday.com/archive/short-history-byzantium (accessed 8 February 2023).
Kirshenblatt-Gimblett, B. (2006), 'Exhibitionary Complexes', in I. Karp, C. A. Kratz, L. Szwaja and T. Ybarra-Frausto (eds.), *Museum Frictions: Public Cultures/Global Transformations*, 35–45, Durham, NC: Duke University Press.
Konstantios, D. (2008), 'I mouseiologiki mas protasi', in *Byzantine Collections*, 14–27, Athens: Greek Ministry of Culture.
Kumar, K. (2003), *The Making of English National Identity*, Cambridge: Cambridge University Press.
Lützeler, P. M. (1994), *Europe after Maastricht: American and European Perspectives*. Oxford: Berghahn Books.
Margaritis, G. (1999), *Elliniki istoria: Tomos C*, Patras: E.A.P.
Mark, J. J. (2014), 'Theodoric the Great', in *Ancient History Encyclopedia*, 9 October. Available online: http://www.ancient.eu/Theodoric_the_Great/ (accessed 19 November 2020).
Maroević, I. (1998), *Introduction to Museology: The European Approach*, Munich: CIP.
Marx, K. and F. Engels (1970), *The German Ideology: Part One*. New York: International Publishers.
Mayr-Harting, H. (2010), *The Coming of Christianity in Anglo-Saxon England*, Philadelphia: Pennsylvania State University Press.
Moorhead, J. (1983), 'The Last Years of Theoderic', *Historia: Zeitschrift Für Alte Geschichte*. 32 (1): 106–20.
Nicks, J. (2002), 'Curatorship in the Exhibition Planning Process', in B. Lord and G. D. Lord (eds.), *The Manual of Museum Exhibitions*, 345–72, Lanham: Altamira Press.
Norwich, J. J. (1998), *A Short History of Byzantium*, London: Penguin.
Ostrogorsky, G. (1969), *History of the Byzantine State*, New Brunswick, NJ: Rutgers University Press.
Paparrigopoulos, C. (1871), *I Istoria tou Ellinikou Ethnous* I, vol. a–d., Athens: Eleftheroudakis.
Perkins, B. W. (2000), 'Why Did the Anglo-Saxons Not Become More British?', *English Historical Review*, 115 (462): 513–33.
Phillips, J. (2005), *The Fourth Crusade and the Sack of Constantinople*, London: Pimlico.
Rabinow, P., ed. ([1984] 1991), *The Foucault Reader: An Introduction to Foucault's Thought*, New York: Pantheon Books.

Skopetea, H. (1988), *To protypo vasilio kai i megali idea: Opseis tou ethnikou provlimatos stin Ellada (1830–1880)*, Athens: Polytypo.
Tricht, F. V. (2011), *The Latin 'Renovatio' of Byzantium: The Empire of Constantinople, 1204–1228*, Leiden and Boston: Brill.
Vasiliev, A. A. (1952), *History of the Byzantine Empire*, vol. 1, 2nd edn., Madison: University of Wisconsin Press.
Veremis, T. (1999), *Elliniki tafthotita kai ethnikismos sti neoteri Ellada*, Athens: M.I.E.T.
Vlachodimou, G. (2008), 'Apo ton Polyzoidi ston Paparrigopoulo', MA diss., University of Thessaloniki, Thessaloniki.
Voegelin, E. (1952), *The New Science of Politics: An Introduction*, Chicago and London: University of Chicago Press.
Watson, A., ed. (1985), *The Digest of Justinian*, vol. 1, Philadelphia: Pennsylvania University Press.
Wickham, C. (2009), *The Inheritance of Rome: A History of Europe from 400–1000*, London and New York: Allen Lane Penguin Books.

Part Two

Byzantium and Modern Media

6

Byzantium in Comics

Lilia Diamantopoulou

Several graphic novels and webcomics have recently turned to themes from Byzantine history, with one of the most original projects being the adaptation of *Digenis Akritas* as a wuxia – a Chinese storytelling form for martial arts adventures.[1]

These comic adaptations offer new ways of looking back to Byzantine history and literature, providing useful insights into their contemporary reception and adaptation. Of course, such comic adaptations are not a new phenomenon. Back in the 1950s, two publishing houses elaborated Byzantine themes on a large scale: *Mosaik* by Hannes Hegen in the German Democratic Republic (GDR/DDR), and the Atlantis editions in Athens with the Greek version of the magazine *Classics Illustrated* published by the Pechlivanidis brothers.[2]

Both periodicals aspired to offer a new alternative to American comics using illustrated narrations as an innovative medium with the twofold goal of, on the one hand, introducing young and reluctant readers to history and so-called high literature (or the classics), and, on the other, shaping ethical and political convictions. Both series were notably popular and have been reprinted several times, especially in the 1970s. In researching the two magazines, one notices an imbalance in the quantity of research; while *Mosaik* by Hannes Hegen has received numerous significant studies, the exploration of the Greek *Classics Illustrated* is still in its early stages.[3]

The comparison of the two periodicals permits us to take several questions into consideration: what was the perceived readership of the two periodicals and what was their thematic scope? Which strategies were used to present the Byzantine world or to adapt Byzantine literature to the medium of the comic (e.g. the necessary abridgement and linguistic adaptation of the original)? Did the periodicals represent American, anti-American or pro-Soviet alignments and what is the role of Byzantine themes in this respect?

These are some of the questions which come to mind while researching these comics. For some of these questions, the following observations may provide an answer, for others less so. Either way, these questions aspire to reveal the relevance of the two periodicals as an object of further research.

'Soft power' in *Classics Illustrated*

Recent research has read America's mass media and pop culture through the lens of 'soft power', especially as regards those behind the Iron Curtain (Nye 2004; Fraser 2014). Different cultural media, such as film, music and cartoon, were used as a way of promoting and building a narrative about the American lifestyle and world politics. The term 'soft power' was first coined by American political scientist Joseph Nye, who also served as an official in both the state and defence departments. According to Nye, the United States won the Cold War with a combination of soft and hard power – institutions and ideas mattered as much as military power. In his 1990 book, *Bound to Lead: The Changing Nature of American Power*, Nye described soft power as the co-optive power of the US culture; communications could influence or direct the decisions and behaviour of others without the need for military force intervention. Soft power means getting others to want what you want, via the intangible resources of culture, ideology and institutional norms. The lifestyle promoted by the American media helped undermine the Soviet Union, along with the hard power of military force and nuclear weapons. In the Cold War victory, Mickey Mouse, Hollywood and Coca-Cola marched with the marines.

Mickey Mouse, the world's most famous mouse, premiered as part of an animation film in the cinemas of New York in November 1928. Walt Disney's creation was an immediate success. The adventures of the Disney hero were translated into German in 1953 (Dolle-Weinkauff 1990: 63, 89). In Greece, Mickey appeared a year later in the magazine *Gelio kai Chara* [Laughter and joy] published by the Pechlivanidis brothers' Atlantis editions.[4]

A similar successful product imported from the USA by the Pechlivanidis brothers was the magazine *Classics Illustrated*, which they discovered during a business travel in 1950 and for which they secured the translation and printing rights for the Greek market.[5] The Pechlivanidis brothers could thus rely on a proven and successful American magazine.[6] With the motto 'Education comes with entertainment',[7] *Classics Illustrated* used a combination of text and pictures to make works of classic literature accessible to the wide public.

In March 1951, Pechlivanidis printed the first translated issue: *Les Misérables* by Victor Hugo.[8] People were magnetized by the magazine, which was printed in colour throughout. *Klassika Eikonografimena* as well as *Gelio kai Chara* were entirely printed in four-colour offset, at a time when colour was rare in the press. This triggered a real 'revolution' in children's comic books. *Classics Illustrated* was among the first books for children and adolescents that did not merely depict texts; instead, they combined texts with pictures, transferring dialogue into 'bubbles'. 'At that time, the market was leaving behind the dull black-and-white journal, customarily decorated with a tacky jacket, asking for something livelier, happier, more vivid', recalls Pantelis Pechlivanidis (2012: 42). The pictures *and* the language used made an impression on the Greek audience; this was not the official 'purified' (but still simple) *katharevousa*, into which 'classic literature' was usually translated (had it been translated into Greek at all), nor the written erudite modern language, *dimotiki*, which was usually used in children's magazines, such as *Diaplasis ton paidon* or *I zoi tou paidiou*, but the simple *dimotiki* which was used in direct speech.[9] The introduction of this novelty was certainly related to the new medium of comics, where direct speech inserted in 'bubbles' dominated.[10]

Notwithstanding the positive reception of Greek *Classics Illustrated*, criticism appeared almost immediately: 'The "Americanized" form of Victor Hugo's heroes and of other famous characters of world literature surprised, irritated, disturbed and angered as much as the publisher's intention to "release classic literature on the sidewalk"' (Tsaousis 1996).

As a reaction to these critical anti-American voices, the editors began to produce their own, genuine Greek titles, first with *Perseus and Andromeda* (No. 43, ~Oct. 1952) and then with *Kolokotronis* (No. 55, ~Feb. 1953).[11] Vassilis Rotas (1889–1977), a man of the theatre with substantial experience in the adaptation of literary works for children, was responsible for the intellectual quality of the magazine. Rotas had fought in the Balkan Wars, the First and the Second World Wars as well as the Greco-Turkish War of 1919–22. During the Axis occupation of Greece in the Second World War he joined the National Liberation Front (EAM), whose main driving force was the Communist Party of Greece (KKE). While fighting for the Greek Resistance he did not forget the theatre: 'Rotas had organized one of the small mobile troupes of the Theatre of the Mountains, consisting of both guerrilla soldiers and recruits from the sympathetic local population' (Van Steen 2000: 127). Rotas wrote or adapted several of the Greek-themed issues, while also translating most of the American issues.[12] Already the third Greek issue was inspired by a Byzantine emperor: *Konstantinos Paleologos* (No. 60). The following Greek issues, *Thiseas and Minotauros, Iraklis, Kanaris o pyrpolitis, To chani tis Gravias, Alexandros o Megas, Rigas Feraios, Vasilios Voulgaroktonos*, etc., clearly show a preference for heroic figures and a selection of themes that range from antiquity and the Greek Middle Ages to modern times. Through his choices Rotas helped shape the Greek canon of 'classics'. While the American *Classics Illustrated* are based on an already recognized canon of classics in world literature, the Greek *Klassika Eikonografimena* created their own canon. This newly created canon focused on heroic figures as moralistic role models. Rotas focused on ancient mythology and theatre, medieval literature and history as well as the stories and heroes of the Greek War of Independence (1821–30). Karagiannis estimates that at least thirty-four Greek-themed issues featured Vassilis Rotas's adaptations (Karagiannis 2007: 85). Within the Greek series of *Classics Illustrated* over ten issues dealt with clearly Byzantine themes. They are mainly divided into male (*Konstantinos Palaiologos, Vasilios Voulgaroktonos, Constantine the Great, Julian the Apostate, Justinian, Heraclius*, the *Byzantine Akritai* as well as *Digenis Akritas*) or female (*Athinais/Eudokia, Eirene the Athenian, Theodora, Kassiani, Anna Comnena*) characters.[13] Important topics of Byzantine history such as iconoclasm, the Nika Revolt, the fall of Constantinople, etc., are taught through the illustrated magazine. The visual models mostly come from the world of theatre or film.

While *Vasilios Voulgaroktonos* (No. 115) concerned the rise of the Byzantine Empire, its fall was represented by *Konstantinos Palaiologos* (No. 60), illustrated by the famous artist Mentis Mpostantzoglou. The issue was published to mark the 500th anniversary of the fall of Constantinople on 20 May 1953.[14] The texts were written by Eirini Foteinou, which was the pseudonym of Sophia Mavroeidi-Papadaki, one of the most important figures of modern Greek children's literature.[15] Sophia Mavroeidi-Papadaki is well known as an educator and writer but also for her engagement in the Greek Resistance against the Nazis in the Second World War. She wrote the lyrics of the Hymn of ELAS, the Greek People's Liberation Army, the military arm of the left-wing National Liberation Front (EAM). Within the series of Greek *Classics Illustrated*, Mavroeidi-Papadaki wrote several issues[16] and several books for children published by Atlantis editions.[17] Among them was also a three-volume work, *Stories from Byzantium*, published by Pechlivanidis in 1969–70.[18]

The appearance of Byzantium in the magazine and in the editor's programme is clearly connected with the scholarly developments and a surging public interest in artistic (visual arts, theatre, literature) adaptations of Byzantine personalities and their cultural legacy. The rediscovery of Byzantium in the first half of the twentieth century and especially in the 1930s is mainly connected with the construction of a Greek identity in the context of the *Megali Idea* and the Balkan Wars; Byzantium was perceived as a binding element between antiquity and modernity following Paparrigopoulos's model from his *History of the Greek Nation* (1853).[19]

Theodoros Grammatas discusses the turn of literature and theatre towards history, especially the 1821 War of Independence, in connection with 'their need to regain contact with antiquity and the glorious ancestral past, the making of national consciousness and identity, and finally the development of a national theatre' (Grammatas 2002: 97). It has to be noted that, after 1964, additional leaflets promoting royalist ideas were inserted in the magazine.[20] As Elias Kanellis points out, *Classics Illustrated* carried a nationalistic, or rather populist, ideological identity full of stereotypes, which had been adopted and aestheticized by both political camps, the Right and the Left (2011: 59–61).

The issues of *Classics Illustrated* transmit an American as well as a Greek literary and cultural canon, consciously or unconsciously communicating clashing ideologies and using the comics as a medium of 'soft power'. *Classics Illustrated* is an example that clearly shows the evolution of the comic book genre as it was adapted to new national audiences. Creative practices as a form of moral setting, which promoted and built a narrative of Greek historical identity in the aftermath of the Second World War and during the Greek Civil War were of crucial importance in the highly polarized struggle between the left and right ideologies that started in 1943 and set the tone for the Cold War period.

The 'Hardliners' in *Mosaik* by Hannes Hegen

In the German Democratic Republic (GDR/DDR), the attempt to instil political education through children's literature is much more visible. Especially after the 30th meeting of the SED's Central Committee on 31 January 1957, the SED's children's and young people's literature was particularly closely monitored. Initially, even the reading of comics was punished (Knigge 1996: 222). In addition, supplemental leaflets with propagandistic material were placed into the magazines.[21] The SED's attempt to influence and pressurize the artists can be seen in one of the most popular comic series of the GDR: *Mosaik* published by the draughtsman Hannes Hegen (Johannes

Hagenbarth, 1925–2014), the cartoonist who was the creator and the editor of the adventure stories of characters such as Dig, Dag, Digedag and Knight Runkel.[22]

In early March 1955, the twenty-nine-year-old graphic artist Hannes Hegen was looking for a new job in the German publishing house Neues Leben. It was a fortunate coincidence that the director of Neues Leben had just been assigned by the Central Council of the FDJ (Free German Youth) to design an independent and socialist response to Western comics.[23] Since 90 per cent of the profit (an estimated 1.5 million marks) went to the FDJ, the *Mosaik* team economically supported the communist political youth work (Grünberg and Hebestreit 2014: 12; also Grünbart 2017: 151). However, Hegen quickly came into conflict with the FDJ for ideological reasons. The first conflicts can be traced back to the beginning of the employment of the editor-in-chief Ernst Dornhof in May 1958; his main function was to control and censor each issue and attend to party line fidelity in the magazine (Friske 2010: 39). The stories developed in the magazine should also convey socialist history and the history of the German Democratic Republic. These clearly propagandistic themes finally appeared in the form of additional independent stories ('Klaus und Hein erzählen aus dem Pionierleben', 'Steinchen an Steinchen') because Hannes Hegen was unwilling to cooperate.

Like *Classics Illustrated*, *Mosaik* featured the character of a novum. When Hegen started writing stories about the adventures of the Digedags, similar concepts had already been tried out internationally. But in the socialist bloc, this form of illustrated narration seems to be unprecedented. This also made the magazine very vulnerable to criticism, due to the hostility towards the new medium, as had been the case with the Greek *Classics Illustrated*.

Criticisms of Western comics in the GDR, and especially of the *Mosaik* were repeating themselves. Over the years, various campaigns against 'trash literature' were led, whether from the side of leading functionaries of the SED, FDJ or the pioneer organization, or by way of worried teachers and parents. To distinguish themselves from the American term 'comic', *Mosaik* used the term 'Bildergeschichten/illustrated stories'. The magazine also changed its style from images with bubbles, to subtitled pictures (Friske 2010: 62). Hegen recalls: 'I never intended to call the *Mosaic* magazines a comic. I have always understood myself as a draftsman of 'Bildergeschichten' [illustrated stories]. That is something different! They are not these short, only a few pages long, series of images squeezed into a book without any relation to each other. I wanted to tell more comprehensive, broad-based and historically funded stories in pictures; in one or more issues' (Hannes Hegen in Lindner 2017: 111).

The main plot of the Byzantine-themed issues is the quest of Dig and Dag to find Digedag who got lost in one of the previous issues. The plot starts to develop with 'The border strategist' ['Der Grenzstratege'] (No. 109, Dec. 1965), following several adventures in the 'Castle Peripheria' (No. 110–112, Jan.–Mar. 1966), the 'Chariot racing' ['Das Wagenrennen'] (No. 113, Apr. 1966) in Constantinople, the 'Astrologist of the court' ['Die Hofastrologen'] (No. 116, Jul. 1966), the 'Marriage with Eirene' ['Hochzeit mit Eirene'] (No. 119, Oct. 1966), finally concluding with 'The escape through the Dardanelles' ['Flucht durch die Dardanellen'] (No. 126, May 1967).

The way the *Mosaik* team worked was similar to their colleagues at *Classics Illustrated*. Hegen sent his team to the archives, the museums and to theatres and cinemas, always with a sketchbook and/or a camera in their pockets, collecting ideas and potential models.[24] The in-depth research of the team is evident above all in the representation of the mechanical automata in the palace of the Byzantine Emperor Andronikos II of Constantinople. These include trees with singing birds, roaring lions and moving beasts which are woven into the narrative (No. 115 and 116, Jun. 1966, 78, 132f.), well known from the report of Luitprand of Cremona (*c.* 920–927).[25]

According to Kramer's (2018: 136–39) study, the main literary source of the Byzantine adventures is Joseph Victor Scheffel's novel *Ekkehard* (1855). The text was adapted for *Mosaik* by Lothar Dräger. Burg Rübenstein (No. 97, 20–21) may be inspired by Joseph Victor von Scheffel's castle Runkelstein (Kramer 2018: 129–32) but it also looks a lot like Meteora. In the city views of Constantinople, especially in the views of the Imperial Palace, the perspective is always kept realistic.[26] The depiction of the harbour of Constantinople on the Bosphorus, the Golden Gate (No. 112), or the palace of Konstantinos Porphyrogennetus, are correctly transferred.[27] It is even possible to recognize the visual and literary sources used for the panels. Other visual inspiration came from contemporary films, e.g. *Ben Hur* for the Roman series or the movie *Theodora, Imperatrice di Bisanzio* from 1954 (Kramer 2018: 135) for the scenery in Constantinople. The Italian history movie, as well as the Greek film *Kassiani* (1960), were significant sources for the 'Theodora' issue of *Classics Illustrated* (No. 298).

Researchers have asked themselves why, of all places, Byzantium was chosen as a historical backdrop. Kramer (2002: 353) explains the choice by the fact that declining Byzantine conditions were used as a parody of contemporary history in the GDR. Grünbart (2017: 163) remarks: 'Byzantium was suitable as a layer: in an orientalizing, fairy-tale-like manner, a cosmos was created that could subtly reflect elements of everyday life in the GDR. Connections between communist states and possible Byzantine roots were made several times during the Cold War period.'[28]

The imaginary trips to the Far East countries serve the curiosity and nostalgia for the exotic Orient and wanderlust, especially after the construction of the Berlin Wall in 1961. Alongside this dreamful wanderlust they try to teach the young readers history. The Greek-themed stories testify to a profound knowledge, an understanding of Greek words, which plays in the naming of places and names, and a good knowledge of the Eastern Mediterranean.[29] But the knowledge goes far beyond that: *Mosaik* magazine also testifies to a good knowledge of primary sources and secondary bibliography.

In the 1950s and especially in the 1960s, Byzantine Studies developed as an independent subject in the GDR and established itself at the universities of Berlin, Leipzig and Halle. However, Michael Grünbart, who has examined in detail the development of the subject regarding the *Mosaik* magazines, concludes: 'So far it has not been possible to establish whether the staff of the MOSAIK of Hannes Hegen had contacts with the research units mentioned' (2018: 46).

Who was behind the Greek-themed stories? It is worth taking a closer look at the team around Hannes Hegen. To ensure the monthly publication of the magazine, Hegen hired a group of graphic artists in March 1957. One of the newcomers in the team was the German-Greek illustrator Nikol[as] Dimitriadis (1909–77).[30] Dimitriadis was born in Chania/Crete in 1909 but inherited German citizenship from his grandfather, who had studied in Leipzig in the nineteenth century. Until 1939 he worked in Greece (probably Athens) as an illustrator and designer, until in 1940 he was drafted into the German military by the German embassy in Athens. In September 1940 he worked for Otto Bayer editions in Leipzig, where a brother of his father was living. This is where he met his wife Elfriede; they married in July 1943. Dimitriadis was first in French, then in American captivity and in 1947 the family met again in Munich and decided to return to Greece. In Greece, Dimitriadis worked 'as a draughtsman for a Greek magazine, also freelance for book publishers and children's magazines etc.', his wife Elfriede recollects.[31] Were the Greek *Classics Illustrated* among these magazines? Unfortunately, too little is known about his drawing style at this time, so no clear statements can be made, but it is highly probable that he worked as an illustrator for Atlantis editions in the years 1947–55, since there wasn't much choice of experienced graphic artists in Athens at the time. However, Kostas Pechlivanidis had studied printing techniques in Leipzig and the editors had inherited the printing press of Bavarian lithographer Grundman (Margomenou 1996; Tsaousis 1996).

The Dimitriadis family, consisting of six members, returned to Germany in 1955 and initially resided with their parents-in-law who owned a small hotel in Hainichen. Later, they moved to Dessau where Dimitriadis secured a job at DEWAG, a German advertising agency. Upon obtaining a new job at *Mosaik*, the family relocated to Berlin-Schöneweide. Within the 'Römer' and 'Neos' series, Dimitriadis was regarded as one of the most significant draughtsmen, alongside Horst Boche. He also designed his own supporting character, Zenzi, who was the girlfriend of Teutobold. This was a unique occurrence within *Mosaik* by Hannes Hegen.

No. 18 'The Attack from the Air' may have been influenced by Nikol Dimitriadis and his Cretan background. The plot is about the conquest of Rome by a new 'wonder weapon', namely special force 'Icarus'. The soldiers of this troop are equipped with parachutes and are catapulted into the city in two waves of attack with huge catapults. The Digedags are informed by spies, so Dig invents a defensive device (a saw propeller) with which the parachutists can be overcome. This explains why the paratroopers are given the name of the young Cretan Icarus who fell from the sky. The manoeuvre is strongly reminiscent of the 'Air battle of Crete', also known as 'Operation Merkur'. The comparison with the air battle is underlined by the cover picture: in the initially submitted sketches the parachutes are eagle shaped. They were rejected by editor-in-chief Ernst Dornhof, because they were reminiscent of the German Federal Eagle, but the connection to the eagle of the Fallschirmjäger (Paratroopers) seems more probable. In the inner part of the magazine there is also an allusion to the attacking eagle, which is the symbol of the Fallschirmjäger, by the aerodynamic posture of the legionaries in their flight pose ('heels together, knees bent, chest out, arms stretched out, fingers long'). Since Dimitriadis was born in Chania, Crete, the destruction of the island must have particularly affected him. The role and function of Dimitriadis during the Second World War remains to be examined.

Significantly one of the three characters, namely Digedag, becomes 'invisible' during the Roman series.[32] Dig and Dag find traces of their disappeared friend in the archive of a mosaic workshop in Constantinople, where sketches with numerous inscriptions are made by Digedag.

Various anecdotes about 'Dimi' circulated in the *Mosaik* team; thus, his statement 'Is not to be seen!' (δεν φαίνεται!), with which he justified carelessly drawn details, became a winged word. He was also said to be afraid of the tax office (Lettkemann 1997: 9; 2022b: 18). In winter 1960, before the construction of the Berlin Wall, Dimitriadis's family fled to Western Germany, passing through several refugee camps and finally settling in Munich in 1961. Nikol spent some months drawing for Rolf Kauka's comic magazine 'Fix and Foxi' and 'Mischa'. Although Nikol Dimitriadis was now working in Munich, his contact with Hegen and his team remained, first through visits, then through letters. Could the cooperation with *Mosaik* magazine continue from a distance?

In Munich, Dimitriadis worked in secondary acting roles for television and film productions (for example, in *To katharma* [*Das Mädchen von Piräus*], 1963). Later he pursued this activity as a hobby and worked as an extra at the Bavarian State Theatre. He was also employed again as a cartoonist and designed, among others, the children's comic *Felix der Kater* of the Bastei editions, whilst from 1964 on he was involved in the children's comic *Max & Molly* (Lettkemann 1997; Von Knorre 2002).

The Digedags of the *Mosaik* editions are currently experiencing a revival with several reprints. Perhaps this can be explained as part of the phenomenon of 'Ostalgie' (nostalgia for the former GDR). Indicatively, a board game, based on the chariot race on the hippodrome, has been recently developed. Byzantium remains a popular theme.

But when the young readers of today take these reprinted magazines of *Classics Illustrated* and the Digedags in their hands, are they really aware of the political conjunctions of Greece and Germany in the 1950s and 1960s? And in what way does the reception and 'soft power' change when time has passed, and the socio-political frame has changed? These are some questions for further discussion and research.

Notes

1 See, for example: *1453*, 2008; *The Hounds of Hell*, 2011; for *Digenes*, see https://www.digenes.com (accessed 5 September 2020).

2 For the history of the publishing house Atlantis and the magazine *Classics Illustrated*, see the instructive account by Pantelis Pechlivanidis (2012: 37–56) regarding his father's library. The Pechlivanidis family library, but not the Atlantis publishing archive, was donated to the University of Crete (closed collections ΠΕΧ). I have extensively studied this collection for the purpose of another article discussing the issues; see *Erotokritos*, *Erofili* and the *Sacrifice of Abraham* (Diamantopoulou 2017).

3 Most of the articles about *Classics Illustrated* were published in newspapers. Studies in greater extent provide Feggerou (2012), Skarpelos (2000) and Zoiopoulos (2000). For a good insight into *Mosaik* by Hannes Hegen, I recommend, as a start, Lindner (2017) and Friske (2010).

4 The magazine was weekly, had twenty-eight pages and was first published in 1954. With three pauses, the first from 1958 to 1960, the second from 1961 to 1962, and the third from 1965 to 1966, the magazine continued its circulation until 1970 and published a total of 603 issues. The series presented Walt Disney's heroes (Donald Duck, Mickey Mouse, Uncle Scrooge, Pluto, Goofy, Chip and Dale, the Werewolf,

etc.) as well as other competing companies such as Warner Bros. (Bugs Bunny, Tweety and Sylvester, Duffy Duck, etc.), MGM (Tom and Jerry) and the publishing house 'Western Printing' (Little Loulou, Uncle Viglis) to the young readers. The publication of *Gelio kai Chara* was stopped when the Greek publisher started using the title 'Mickey', which provoked the legal intervention of the American company who owned the intellectual rights. *Mickey* reappeared in Greece in 1966 after the printing permission had been obtained by editor Evangelos Terzopoulos, famous for editing the magazine *Gynaika* [Woman]. See Kassis (1998); Tarlanezos (2006); Koskinas (2008).

5 Pechlivanidis was excited and immediately asked to meet with the publisher Albert Lewis Kanter in his office in New York. His nephew recalls: 'My uncle rushed to meet him immediately and without hesitation he asked [for] the publishing rights for the Greek language. The Jewish-American Kanter felt specially honoured and granted rights, even with a special price, because this way they were spreading in a country with a long historical tradition, making a further step towards globalization' (Pechlivanidis 2012: 48).

6 For American *Classics Illustrated* see the voluminous work of William B. Jones (2011). For the detailed history of the editor, see the chapter 'Albert Kanter's Dream' (Jones 2011: 9–16). *Classics Illustrated* has been published in several countries, such as Brazil, England, Belgium, Netherlands and Germany, but these countries did not proceed to create their own issues to the extent that the Greek *Classic Illustrated* did. Recently some English translations of the Greek *Classics Illustrated* were published by Classic Comic Store Ltd. (No. 1 *Theseus and the Minotaur*, No. 2 *Jason and the Argonauts*, No. 3 *The battle of Marathon*, No. 4 *Achilles*, No. 5 *The battle of Thermopylae*, No. 6 *Alexander the Great of Macedonia*, No. 7 *Daedalus and Icarus*, No. 8 *Prometheus*, No. 9 *Orpheus and Eurydice*, No. 10 *Oedipus Rex*).

7 This was the motto of *Classics Illustrated*, see for example the back cover of *Digenis Akritas*, No. 1035.

8 Aris Malandrakis (2001) describes the appearance of the issue as follows: 'That icy morning of March 1, 1951 an unexpected event shook the smuggle-readers of the Newsstands. Next to the hanging headlines announcing "communist hideouts" and deportations of "lousy traitors", the colorful covers of a magazine showed some other … misérables, who were praised by Victor Hugo, in the form of comics'. *Les Misérables* was a spectacular success. The issue immediately sold out and had to be reprinted twice in a short time, selling a total amount of over one million copies, while the average edition of issues never fell below 200,000–300,000 copies.

9 Pantelis Pechlivanidis recalls: 'With a rich, colourful and vivid illustration, translated in a simple, understandable and enjoyable language, which at the same time accurately reproduced the original, the *Classics Illustrated* sensitised, touched and brought the audience—large and small—close to all this treasure of world literature. A treasure, which until then was buried in lengthy translations into katharevousa, without vivid pictures and in a less affordable price' (2012: 50).

10 Therefore, it was necessary to explain to the readers this new way of reading in the very first issue: 'The images have to be read from left to right in the order 1, 2, 3, 4, etc. This sign shows a person talking. These bubbles show that the person from whom they appear, is not saying the words in the caption, but thinking them' (Malandrakis 2001: 10; image in Zoiopoulos 2000: 126).

11 *Kolokotronis* (No. 55/235/1049/2039, Illustrations: K. Grammatikopoulos) was developed by Rotas into the near homonymous theatrical play *Kolokotronis or the*

disaster of Dramalis, a heroic drama in three acts (written in 1954, first edited in 1955). The play was based on the *Memoirs of Kolokotronis* and *The Old Man of Morea* (1931) by Spyros Melas. The dating of the issues is not clear and can only be given approximately and in relation to the issues of the American series. The short pause in publication in early 1954 (after No. 88) also must be taken into consideration. This was due to the currency reform which is also obvious in the pricing of the volumes (from previously 4,000 to 5 drachmas; see Zoiopoulos 2000, 138–39).

12 The Pechlivanidis brothers gave Rotas a free hand. Rotas was almost exclusively responsible for the selection of the Greek literary works to be adapted and published: 'The themes for the "Classics" were chosen almost exclusively by Rotas. He would propose them to Pechlivanidis who would always approve them' (Margomenou 1996: C111).

13 The individual issues are not discussed in detail here. For information on the contents of the Byzantine-themed issues, see Nikolaou (2017).

14 See the announcement in No. 59, *Western Stories (Istories Dyseos)*.

15 See the special issue 1772 (2004) of *Nea Hestia* dedicated to Sophia Mavroeidi-Papadaki.

16 For example, *Alexander the Great* (No. 1011), *Pandora* (No. 1087), *Daidalos and Ikaros* (No. 1216), *Athinais – The empress of Byzantium Eudokia* (No. 1219), *Anna Komnene: 'Alexias'* (No. 1222), *Perikles* (No. 1223), *Jason* (No. 1237).

17 For example, *Atalanti* (1957) and *Alexander and the Mermaid* (1959).

18 Second edition in 2003 by Patakis.

19 For this argument, see also Tziovas (2014: 123–24).

20 Theodoros Karagiannis (2007: 541) refers to supplemental leaflets of a royalist character, as for example in *Constantine the Great* where, in a genealogy of kings with the same name, King Constantine II of Greece is praised. This addition must have been inserted in a reissue after 1964 and was not included in the previous issues.

21 For such examples, see Friske (2010: 43–45).

22 For biographical information, see Kramer (2002: 84–88) and Lindner (2017).

23 Hannes Hegen was given the task to deliver, until mid-June 1955, a print-ready picture story of thirty-two pages, so that the first issue could go over the counters in December 1955. 'That was less because of a Christmas surprise but had more to do with the Young Pioneers. They were founded on December 13th (1948). So *Mosaik* was some kind of a gift from the publishing house for the birthday party of the pioneers', recalls Hegen in Lindner (2017: 111).

24 See for example the pictures of the 3D models of Rome, dated around 1957–58 in Lindner (2017: 132–34).

25 For the sources of the automata and their function see Berger (2006). The main source for the comic may have been Brett's article on the automata published in 1954.

26 Research has already dealt in detail with the analysis of the original templates and the comic illustrations. See Friske (2010: 75–81) and Grünbart (2018: 49–62).

27 If somebody is familiar with the nineteenth-century engravings of the English graphic artist Thomas Allom it is possible to recognize them immediately as a model (Friske 2010: 75–76). Allom's illustrations were first published in 1841. They have been used since in numerous editions dealing with Istanbul, the Holy Land and the Far East, and were extremely well received by the contemporary public. 'Of course, the minarets of Allom's 19th century Istanbul had to disappear, because in 1228 there were no mosques in Constantinople' (Friske 2010: 76).

28 Grünbart also makes a reference to Hunger (1984: 32–33) who compared the communist party conference speeches in the GDR with Byzantine rhetoric and the personality cult.
29 The speaking names and the language games in *Mosaik* play an important role (Fiedler 2003; on the names, see Wagner (2017).
30 For a first approach to the work and life of the illustrator Dimitriadis, see Lettkemann (1997) and Von Knorre (2002). Some of the Nikol Dimitriadis application documents are preserved in the *Mosaik* archive (see Lindner 2017: 119). From this point I have to express my special thanks to Alexander von Knorre for giving access to the letter written by Elfriede Dimitriadis in 2002. I also have to thank Philipp Zölls (Stadtarchiv Munich), Angela Brehm (Stadtarchiv Hainichen) and Olaf Hillert (Stadtarchiv Leipzig) for helping me find information about Dimitriadis's biography. While working on the present article I exchanged ideas with Gerd Lettkemann whose extended research on Nikol Dimitriadis is published in *Mosaiker 47* and *48* (Lettkemann 2022a, 2022b) with a reference to our discussion. In this frame it is not possible to present my research results about Nikol Dimitriadis's biography, but I will publish them separate and in more detail in another context.
31 Handwritten letter from Elfriede Dimitriadis to Alexander von Knorre, 21 March 2002.
32 Digedag travels to Rome and disappears or becomes 'invisible' (No. 20, Jul. 1958; not present as a figure from No. 21 to 140). Digedag's itinerary leads from Rome through the Byzantine Empire, and only then does he continue his journey eastwards to China. Digedag had learned to make himself invisible from an Indian fakir, but he did not manage to make himself visible again (No. 39, Feb. 1960).

Bibliography

Berger, A. (2006), 'Die akustische Dimension des Kaiserzeremoniells: Gesang, Orgelspiel und Automaten', in F. A. Bauer (ed.), *Visualisierungen von Herrschaft. Frühmittelalterliche Residenzen – Gestalt und Zeremoniell*, 63–77, Istanbul: Ege Yayınlar.

Brett, G. (1954), 'The Automata in the Byzantine "Throne of Solomon"', *Speculum*, 29: 477–87.

Diamantopoulou, L. (2017), 'Intermedial Translation: Erofili, Erotokritos and The Sacrifice of Abraham in the Greek Classics Illustrated', in L. Giannakopoulou and K. Skordyles (eds.), *Culture and Society in Crete: From Kornaros to Kazantzakis*, 259–84, Cambridge: Cambridge University Press.

Dolle-Weinkauff, B. (1990), *Comics: Geschichte einer populären Literaturform in Deutschland seit 1945*, Weinheim and Basel: Beltz.

Feggerou, P. (2012), 'Ta "Klassika Eikonografimena" kai to istoriko mythistorima gia paidia: mythos kai pragmatikotita', PhD diss., National and Kapodistrian University, Athens.

Fiedler, S. (2003), *Sprachspiele im Comic: Das Profil der deutschen Comic-Zeitschrift Mosaik*, Leipzig: Leipziger Universitätsverlag.

Fraser, M. (2014), *Weapons of Mass Distraction: Soft Power and American Empire*, New York: St. Martin's Press.

Friske, M. (2010), *Die Geschichte des Mosaik von Hannes Hegen*, Berlin: Lukas Verlag.

Giddins, G. (2004), 'Seduced by Classics Illustrated', in S. Howe (ed.), *Give Our Regards to Atomsmashers! Writers on Comics*, 78–94, Toronto: Pantheon.

Grammatas, T. (2002), *To elliniko theatro ston 20o aiona*, Athens: Exantas.

Grünbart, M. (2017), 'Griechisches Feuer von links, hinten und vorne: Mit Ritter Runkel von Rübenstein auf Abenteuer in Byzanz', in T. Enseleit and Ch. Peters (eds.), *Bilder vom Mittelalter Vorstellungen von einer vergangenen Epoche und ihre Inszenierung in modernen Medien*, 147–70, Münster: Readbox Unipress.

Grünbart, M. (2018), 'Reisen bildet und verbildet. Mit den Digedags ans Goldene Horn', in W. Wagner (ed.), *Ritter Runkel in seiner Zeit. Mittelalter und Zeitgeschichte im Spiegel eines Geschichtscomics*, 45–66, Berlin: Be.bra Wissenschaft Verlag.

Grünberg, R. and M. Hebestreit (2014), *Mosaik-Handbuch – Die Welt der Digedags*, Leipzig: Lehmstedt.

Hunger, H. (1984), *Byzanz: Eine Gesellschaft mit zwei Gesichtern*, Kopenhagen: Munksgaard.

Jones, W. B. (2011), *Classics Illustrated: A Cultural History*, Jefferson, NC: McFarland.

Kanellis, I. (2011), 'Tou Leonida to spathi Kolokotronis to forei', *The Books' Journal*, 6, April: 59–61.

Karagiannis, A. (2007), *O Vasilis Rotas kai to ergo tou gia paidia kai efivous. Theatro. Poiisi. Pezografia, Klassika eikonografimena*, Athens: Synchroni epochi.

Kassis, K. (1998), *Elliniki Paralogotechnia kai Komiks*, Athens: Alfeios.

Knigge, A. C. (1996), *Comics: Vom Massenblatt ins multimediale Abenteuer*, Reinbek bei Hamburg: Rowohlt.

Konstantinou, E. (1998), *Byzantinische Stoffe und Motive in der europäischen Literatur des 19. und 20. Jahrhunderts*, Frankfurt a. M.: Peter Lang.

Koskinas, E. (2008), *Chartionoi Iroes. Aspromavra Oneira*, Athens: Plessasbook.

Koukoulas, G. (2006), *Gynaikes sta komiks: Iroides gia kathe chrisi*, Athens: Futura 2006.

Koukoulas, G. (2008), 'Epanastatika eikonografimena', *Kyriakatiki Eleftherotypia*, 7, 23 March.

Kounelaki, P. (2003), '"Klassika" me tous iroes tou Omirou. Ta mythika prosopa tis Iliadas kai tis Odysseias sti nea seira ton "Klassikon Eikonografimenon" tis "K" se diaskevi Vas. Rota', *Kathimerini*, February.

Kourtovik, D. (1989), 'Klassika eikonografimena kai klassikes prokatalypseis', *Eleftherotypia*, 19 April.

Kramer, T. (2002), *Micky, Marx und Manitu: Zeit- und Kulturgeschichte im Spiegel eines DDR-Comics 1955–1990: "Mosaik" als Fokus von Medienerlebnissen im NS und in der DDR*, Berlin: Weidler.

Kramer, T. (2018), 'Bild- und Textquellen der Runkelserie als Stilensemble', in W. Wagner (ed.), *Ritter Runkel in seiner Zeit. Mittelalter und Zeitgeschichte im Spiegel eines Geschichtscomics*, 117–36, Berlin: Bebra Wissenschaft Verlag.

Lettkemann, G. (1997), 'Der Zeichner Nikol Dimitriadis', *Digefax*, 14: 9–12.

Lettkemann, G. (2022a), 'Auf der Spur Dimis. Der Zeichner Nikol Dimitriadis. Erster Teil: Dimi und die alten Römer', *Mosaiker*, 47, 5–24.

Lettkemann, G. (2022b), 'Auf der Spur Dimis. Der Zeichner Nikol Dimitriadis. Zweiter Teil: Vom Neos nach Kaukasien', *Mosaiker*, 48, 5–27.

Lindner, B. (2017), *Die drei Leben des Zeichners Johannes Hegenbarth*, Nürnberg: Junge Welt.

Malandrakis, A. (2001), 'Oi aristokrates ton komiks', *Eleftherotypia*, 9, 36: 10–13.

Marciniak, P. and D. C. Smythe, eds. (2016), *The Reception of Byzantium in European Culture since 1500*, Farnham: Routledge.

Margomenou, M. (1996), 'Ta eikonografimena trion geneon Ellinon', *To Vima*, 25 November: C111.
Nikolaou, K. (2017), 'Byzantium and its Perception in the Mid-Twentieth Century 'Classics Illustrated' Comic Books', *Balkan Studies*, 52: 61–84.
Nye, J. (1990), *Bound to Lead: The Changing Nature of American Power*, New York: Basic Books.
Nye, J. S. (2004), *Soft Power: The Means to Success in World Politics*, New York: Public Affairs.
Pechlivanidis, P. (2012), 'Antifonisi: I mikri istoria tis vivliothikis tou patera mou kai tis oikogeneias Pechlivanidi', in *Vivliothiki tou Panepistimiou Kritis: Ta vivlia pou agapisan oi adelfoi Pechlivanidi kai dorithikan sti vivliothiki tou Panepistimiou Kritis*, 37–56, Rethymno: Syllogos Filon tis Vivliothikis tou Panepistimiou Kritis.
Pouliasis, E. (2016), 'Oi piges sta istorika tefchi ton Klassikon Eikonografinemon: "To Chani tis Gravias"', *Nea Paidia*, 160, October–December: 98–112.
Skarpelos, G. (2000), *Istoriki mnimi kai ellinikotita sta komiks*, Athens: Kritiki.
Soloup [Antonis Nikolopoulos] (2012), *Ta ellinika comics*, Athens: Topos.
Tarlantezos, L. (2006), *Istoria ton komiks*, Athens: Aigokeros.
Tsaousis, K. (1996), 'Ta eikonografimena trion geneon Ellinon', *To Vima*, 28 August.
Tziovas, D. (2014), *Re-imagining the Past: Antiquity and Modern Greek Culture*, Oxford: Oxford University Press.
Van Steen, G. A. H. (2000), *Venom in Verse: Aristophanes in Modern Greece*, Princeton, NJ: Princeton University Press.
Vatopoulos, N. (2002), 'Ta "Klassika" ton paidikon mas chronon, *Kathimerini*, 8 June.
Von Knorre, A. (2002), 'Ein Wanderer zwischen den Welten', *Digefax* 30.
Wagner, W. E (2017), *Ritter Runkel in seiner Zeit. Mittelalter und Zeitgeschichte im Spiegel eines Geschichtscomics*, Berlin: be.bra Verlag.
Zoiopoulos, N. (2000), *Ta chartina oneira ton paidikon mas chronon*, Athens: Technikes ekdoseis.

7

Games of Byzantium: The Image of the Empire in Three Strategy Videogames

Marco Fasolio

The Middle Ages and Byzantium in popular culture, and their impact on videogames: some remarks

Our knowledge of the Middle Ages made significant progress after the seventeenth century (Occhipinti 2004: 207–28), but their understanding in non-academic culture is still anchored to several predominant clichés, which were developed from the late fourteenth until the mid-twentieth century (Sergi 2002: 89–98; 2005: 9 ff.; 2016: 197–205). Humanists and Renaissance scholars, who pretended to draw their inspiration directly from classical antiquity, tried to trace a clear line between themselves and medieval men. However, what most of them had in mind while envisioning the Middle Ages[1] – the fourteenth century – was chronologically closer to their own time, but had arguably been one of the most challenging eras in Euro-Mediterranean history. These scholars almost unconsciously assigned the fourteenth-century's notorious 'unpleasant features' to all the centuries that had preceded it since the collapse of the Western Roman Empire (Sergi 2005: 99–100); thus, they introduced the 'black legend', or rather the 'Gothic myth' of the Middle Ages, to borrow the words coined to describe late medieval architecture and book scripts (Binding 1989: 1575–6; Petrucci 1992: 162–63; Panofsky 1969: 137–87). Nevertheless, although some aspects of the medieval centuries' negative reputation were already established during the early modern era, Enlightenment thinkers are primarily responsible for the negative connotations with the term 'medieval' among non-specialists. According to these theories, medieval societies were to blame for many of the most obnoxious practices and institutions that had tormented humanity in the past, or that were still active during their own lifetimes. However, like their predecessors, they were committing an error of historical perspective, tending to backdate to the Middle Ages the hardships that Europeans had suffered during the so-called Iron century (Kamen 1971).[2] Effectively, they invented the concept of the 'Dark Ages' as a sort of counter-model to their self-representation. Yet, the 'darkest side' of their Middle Ages image[3] was to a large extent *not* medieval, but rather a consequence of the developments that occurred in the early modern period (Raedts 2002: 1–20; Sergi 2005: 39 ff.; Münster 2010, I: 468–88).

Reception studies make it clear that the allegedly positive clichés related to the Middle Ages were mainly an outcome of nineteenth-century Romantic culture, nationalist ideologies and their later offshoots in the first decades of the twentieth century. Historicism, especially in its 'quest for the origins' version (Hobsbawm 1983: 263–307; Geary 2002: 15 ff.), along with a new exotic taste for the 'obscurity' of the Middle Ages, gave a substantial boost to medieval studies. It has also encouraged the emergence of 'Medievalism', namely the rediscovery and the reconstruction of the Middle Ages through literary works, re-enactments and the imitation of artistic and architectural styles (Porciani 2004: 253–79; Ortenberg 2007: 51 ff.; di Carpegna Falconieri 2011: 106–20). However, Romantic and post-Romantic intellectuals were captivated by just a few elements of medieval civilization that were mainly related to the later period,[4] producing a fragmented image of the Middle Ages. Nonetheless, it was a rather influential one since, from the second half of the nineteenth century, many European towns were reshaped according to this neo-medieval or Neo-Gothic taste (Chavarría Arnau and Zucconi 2016), forging the common sense of how the medieval style should look,[5] a style even more pronounced after those trends were imported to the US (Bordone 1993: 199–210).

Consequently, stereotypes concerning the Middle Ages have survived to the present day. However, whereas the ideas of early modern thinkers are now chiefly expressed in the linguistic field,[6] 'enlightened' prejudices are still alive, almost in the same way they were centuries ago. Indeed, the misconceptions related to the 'Dark Ages' have been seamlessly conveyed through several non-academic outlets, including school history textbooks (Albertoni 2010: 128–34; Ciccopiedi 2010: 142–48; Gamberini 2010: 120–27; Gandino 2010: 101–06; Garofani 2010: 149–55; Milani 2010: 113–19; Musci 2010: 182–91; Pohl 2010: 94–100; Provero 2010: 107–12; Rao 2010: 135–41; Sergi 2010: 92–93). The adjective 'medieval' itself became employed as a synonym of barbaric, backward, unhuman, superstitious, with no relevant difference in the word's usage among educated and non-educated speakers (di Carpegna Falconieri 2011: 22 ff.). Instead, Romantic views of the medieval era continue to exert their influence primarily through their visual impact,[7] either with historical re-enactments[8] or Neo-Gothic monuments,[9] which would later become the iconographic basis of the fantasy genre in novels, comics (Bordone 2004: 711–35; Musci 2010: 183–90) and films (Gandino 2004: 737–55). It is nearly self-evident that this complex amalgam of non-scholarly outlooks concerning the Middle Ages represents an appealing background for any videogame creator, since both its 'dark' and 'bright' sides can attract a large audience, which is not necessarily restricted to history enthusiasts. In addition, provided that a minimum degree of graphic design technology is available, medieval scenarios are no less suitable for a wide range of applications, including action, role-play and countless real-time and turn-based strategy videogames.[10] Therefore, just considering the entertaining and lucrative potential of this combination of the exotic and obscure fascination with the Middle Ages and their recreational implementations, it is unsurprising that the videogame industry has widely exploited medieval subjects since the early 1980s, and that approach has not gone out of style (Cuenca López 2011: 257–63; Jiménez Alcázar 2009: 311–65; 2011: 299–340). In this context, Byzantium has played a secondary role as a driving force in developing new games.

Although Byzantinism, understood as a rediscovery and reinterpretation of some aspects of Byzantine culture, was in many respects the 'Eastern relative' of Medievalism, as they had common points of origin, or at least comparable, roots – i.e. the fascination with something that was perceived as exotic, mysterious and, in the case of Byzantium, lavishly decadent – and a similar chronology, in terms of their emergence; it was a niche phenomenon in the Western hemisphere, having only a minor impact on non-academic culture (Angelov 2003: 3–23; Auzépy 2003; Marciniak 2018: 47–53). Since the late eighteenth century, the Neo-Byzantine or Byzantine Revival style became relatively widespread as an aesthetic taste in fine arts and architecture in Orthodox countries,[11] but had considerably less diffusion in the former Latino-Germanic world.[12] Given that the videogame industry is a predominantly American, Japanese and (to some extent) Western European affair, whereas Greece and the Slavic countries have never retained a leading role in the industry, it is difficult to imagine a large audience for a Byzantine-based product that lacks a solid cultural and iconographic background, like those provided by Neo-Gothic and fantasy portrayals of the Western Middle Ages. And it is even harder to imagine a game developer who would use Byzantine motifs as a source of inspiration, without being an expert on the topic. To understand the distinction, think of how many Westerners have even heard of Victorien Sardou's drama *Theodora*, or have seen Alexander Nevskij's Cathedral in Sofia, compared to those who have seen films like *The Lord of the Rings*, Disney's *Robin Hood* or a photo of the British Parliament. Also, consider the fact that in the US and Western Europe,[13] the average citizen's knowledge of Byzantine civilization is often limited to a few facts concerning mosaics, Justinian and Theodora – if those citizens have any knowledge of Byzantium at all. Even the anti-Byzantine clichés,[14] which had been conceived during the Enlightenment and perpetuated by nineteenth-century historiography (Guillou 1966: 27–39; Ronchey 2002: 154–59; Gallina 2010: 156–58), are known only by a small minority of well-educated people. The usage, deriving itself from enlightened scholars of the words 'Byzantine' and 'Byzantinism' are often employed as synonyms for something pedantic, uselessly complicated, and subtle in most non-Greek and non-Slavic European languages; they are likewise perceived as lofty when appearing in writing, and are seldom heard at all in speech, contrary to the term 'medieval'.

Consequently, unlike medieval or medieval-like settings, which are relatively standard for several videogame genres, purely Byzantine or predominantly Byzantine games are almost entirely absent; the only (partial) exceptions to this general rule are *Assassin's Creed: Revelation*, set in early Ottoman Constantinople (and the only non-strategic game that partly exploits post-Byzantine settings), and, to a lesser degree, *Rise of the Tomb Raider*, whose plot is chiefly inspired by a fanta-Byzantine fictional story. Nonetheless, Byzantine history covered the entire medieval chronology, and the empire undeniably played a leading role in the period, despite its current lack of popularity. Hence, Byzantium could not be excluded from strategic videogames set in a medieval Euro-Mediterranean scenario, if they would make some claim to historical plausibility. This chapter analyses the image of Byzantium in three of these videogames, namely *Age of Empires II: The Age of Kings*, *Medieval II: Total War* and *Europa Universalis IV*, all of which date from the late 1990s until the present day. We discuss how Byzantium is related to, and is influenced by, gameplay, learned and popular clichés, and scholarship.

Yet, before addressing the 'Byzantine issue' in this survey of case studies, we make some essential introductory remarks concerning the early history of video gaming, the first occurrences of the strategic genre and its (more or less) medieval subjects.

The Byzantine Empire in strategy videogames, with a historical introduction

If the word 'videogame' indicates a sort of game that is played by pressing buttons or by using any kind of joystick to control and move images on a screen, then the first ever designed videogame was the *Cathode-ray tube amusement device*, whose prototype dates back to 1947; due to its high manufacturing cost, however, this game was never released on the market. Although a few others were developed during the 1950s, it was not until the following decade that the 'history of videogames' became relevant, since none of the previous iterations had been designed to be played by users, but were meant to be scientific experiments or *mirabilia*, to be displayed in fairs and exhibitions. One of the last versions of these early videogames was *Tennis for Two* (1958), the ancestor on the oscilloscope of the later and world-famous *Pong*. Accordingly, what is probably the first fully-fledged videogame was *Spacewar!*, a two-player game set in space where users try to destroy each other's spaceship by shooting missiles. *Spacewar!* was developed by Steve Russell, then an MIT researcher, between 1961 and 1962, and was designed to be played on a PDP-1 minicomputer.[15] Even though the original version was never commercialized, given that a PDP-1 cost approximately $120,000[16] at the time, *Spacewar!*, unlike its predecessors, somehow went beyond the prototype stage and was initially circulated among the small community of academics and programmers who had access to computers at the time. The codes were public domain and requests could be made to Russell to reproduce the game on other PDP-1s. But *Spacewar!*'s most significant growth in popularity occurred during the final years of the decade, when its later versions were adapted to other platforms, making it almost omnipresent in computer science's departments ('The Great Videogame Swindle?' 1996: 64–68, 211–29; Accordi Rickards 2014: 13–17).

History made an appearance in these early game design phases, as the first strategic videogame, i.e. *The Sumer Game* – best known with its later title *Hamurabi* – featured a historical setting. Originally designed with the FOCAL programming language, and developed by David Dyment in 1968, *The Sumer Game* is a purely textual TBS videogame, which was adjusted for the BASIC programming language by David H. Ahl in 1971. The player manages an ancient Sumerian town as King Hammurabi, buying grain and crop fields to feed his subjects. As a result of the limits imposed by early programming languages, *The Sumer Game* had a rather elementary format, but was a forerunner in its genre, since it already possessed most of the basic features of later textual videogames and the ideas behind it were the core of those that would inspire every strategy videogame in the following decades. The FOCAL version ran on a PDP-8, thus having the same initial problems related to the cost of its platform[17] that had affected *Spacewar!* Nevertheless, after it was converted into BASIC to work with early PCs and eventually renamed *Hamurabi*,[18] the game quickly became a classic of its kind, in particular since 1973, when Ahl listed it in his popular type-in compilation of computer games, *101 BASIC Computer Games* (Ahl 1973: 128–29; Accordi Rickards 2014: 18).[19]

Although history made its entrance into videogames in the late 1960s, it was not until the early 1980s that some medieval elements were introduced in videogames, through the 'backdoor' of fantasy quests. Beginning in 1981 with the half-graphic and half-textual *Ultima I: The Age of Darkness* for the Apple II, the open-world role-play series *Ultima* by Richard Garriott, and its 1979 predecessor, *Akalabeth: World of Doom*, by the same author, became arguably the forerunner of fantasy videogames. During his childhood, Garriott was a fan of the tabletop game *Dungeons & Dragons*, and a keen reader of Tolkien's trilogy *The Lord of the Rings*, whose fantasy subjects naturally turned into the primary source of inspiration for *Ultima*. Split into three different trilogies, with its last title released in 1999 for Microsoft, the main series of *Ultima* essentially founded the role-playing genre as we know it today. Being one of the most significant and imitated role-playing games in history (Accordi Rickards 2014: 64–67), its extensive use of a medieval-like ambience might be credited for establishing the first bond between the latter and videogames. In this framework, the Nintendo action-adventure saga *The Legend of Zelda*, created by Shigeru Miyamoto and Takashi Tezuka, possibly the most famous of its kind, deserves mention here. The first instalment of the game was released in 1986 with the title *The Legend of Zelda*, and – as had been the case with *Ultima* – all the vicissitudes of the player's avatar,[20] in his quests to save princess Zelda, take place in a fictional universe called Hyrule. This world is aesthetically based primarily on elements supposedly taken from medieval Western Europe, albeit influenced by fantasy imagery (Accordi Rickards 2014: 88–89, 107–09, 121). Many changes in graphics and gameplay occurred between the mid-1980s and 2019, when *The Legend of Zelda: Link's Awakening*, the last title of the Zelda series at the time, was put on the market – but nothing relevant had changed in terms of the game's structure and setting, which remained almost untouched over nearly three and a half decades. Together with its great commercial success, the 'longevity' of *The Legend of Zelda* has decisively contributed to strengthening the already existing link between medieval/fantasy atmospheres and videogames, making the latter the most interesting media to study for an overview of the contemporary image of the Middle Ages outside academia.

During the 1990s, when political strategy had already existed for more than twenty years, and – thanks to series like *Ultima*, *The Legend of Zelda* and others akin to them – some kind of medieval iconography was introduced in videogames, the time was ripe for the Middle Ages to become the subject of a strategic title, which meant that Byzantium was going to make its debut on the scene. *Age of Empires* (hereafter *AoE*) is a series of RTS videogames, with some features of the so-called God games,[21] wherein the player manages a civilization through different periods of a historical epoch. Its first title, eponymous of the series, was released for Microsoft PCs in 1997 by the Ensemble Studios and was dedicated to antiquity, from the Stone to the Iron Ages. An expansion, *The Rise of Rome* (1998), added the Romans to a player's options. After Sid Meier's *Civilization* (1991), which cannot be considered a fully-fledged historical videogame,[22] *AoE* was one of the first (perhaps even *the* first) non-textual strategic title based entirely on historical events. Its considerable commercial success made it a type of touchstone in the following years. With significant improvements in graphics and the game engine – yet maintaining nearly unaltered the game mechanics from the previous episode – the second instalment of the series, namely *Age of Empires II: The Age of Kings* (1999), along with its expansion *The Conquerors* (2000), was set during the medieval period (Jiménez Alcázar 2009: 341–45; Cuenca López 2011: 261–62). The game's historical context was vast: spanning from the 'Dark Age', across the 'Feudal Age' and the 'Castle Age', and into the 'Imperial Age' – which may roughly correspond to late antiquity, early, high and late Middle Ages. In *AoE II*, the Byzantines were one of the possible choices for the player, and their presentation in the game reads as follows:

> While the Western Roman Empire decayed and collapsed, its eastern half in Byzantium remained an imperial titan for centuries to come. Repulse countless invasions with imposing fortifications, command vast and versatile armies amassed from within and outside your borders, and immolate enemy fleets with siphons of Greek Fire. Your heavily-armored Cataphracts inspire fear from the Danube to the Euphrates while your scholars propel you into a new age of technology and learning!

Despite its brevity, this introduction effectively summarizes the image of the empire that the authors had in mind when they shaped the profile of Byzantine civilization, as well as the kind of experience a player could try by choosing it. The 'original Byzantines' would have certainly approved of the description's first sentence, since they used to describe themselves as 'Ρωμαίοι', *scilicet* 'Romans' and to call their realm the 'βασιλεία τῶν Ῥωμαίων', namely 'empire of the Romans'. Nonetheless, the game designers went a little bit too far with Roman continuity, since, whenever selected, Byzantine characters would speak Latin, saying words like 'ago', 'condo', 'impero', 'pugno' or 'porro', rather than Greek, which would have indeed been more accurate. In *AoE II*, all civilizations were divided into four categories, according to the architecture of their buildings: Western European, Central European, Middle Eastern and East Asian. The Byzantines were put into the third category, side by side with Turks, Saracens and Persians. Even though such company may seem unusual, this choice was understandable from a geographical perspective. Either the graphic engine did not allow different architectural styles for each civilization, or it would have been unwise to categorise those described as 'Eastern Romans' among Central or Western Europeans. Yet, despite its seeming consistency, this decision produced a bizarre outcome concerning the game's Byzantine temples/churches, which looked identical to a mosque with two minarets. In contrast, their wonder[23] resembled the basilica of Hagia Sophia in Constantinople, with a consequently blatant – although presumably unintentional – historical and visual contradiction.

Setting aside these inconsistencies for a moment, if we analyse the second and the third sentence of the presentation, we will notice that they are even more revealing about what was taken into account when Byzantium was designed, particularly when it comes to their application in the game's dynamics The Byzantines are labelled a 'defensive civilization', and this is undoubtedly true when some of their unique features are examined, since all their buildings have gradually increased resistance bonuses to enemy attacks once the player advances through the ages, and their counter units[24] are consistently cheaper to recruit. In contrast, their siege weapons have severe development limitations, compared to most of the other civilizations. As far as the military is concerned, *AoE II* Byzantines could be counted among the best choices for a player, given that, apart from their deficits in terms of catapults, trebuchets and, with a glaring historical mistake, cavalry archers (McGeer 1991a, I: 393–94), they have access to nearly all the relevant technological advancements, which gives their armies and navies one of the most balanced structures of the entire game. However, what makes the Byzantines 'truly Byzantine' in this field are the consistent benefits their fire ships have been awarded – perhaps as a tribute to the mysterious Greek fire – and their unique military unit:[25] the cataphract. The latter is the most effective cavalry unit against infantry in *AoE II*, and the only one, except for Persian war elephants, that can cause 'trample damage' to enemy soldiers just by approaching them. Outside the military sphere, which is the most important in *AoE II*, as well as in most strategic, historical videogames, Byzantium also possesses an excellent technological tree, merely lacking a single advancement in the economic sector, in addition to a cost reduction of 33 per cent to progress towards the Imperial Age.

It is apparent to a Byzantinist's eye that the empire which *AoE II*'s creators portrayed was much more similar to Anastasius I's or Justinian I's, rather than to Basil II Boulgaroktonos's, Alexios I Komnenos's or Michael VIII Palaiologos's. There is no doubt that the leitmotif underlying most of the distinctive qualities assigned to the Byzantines was the continuity with Rome. This continuity is well exemplified by an otherwise incomprehensible artistic licence, such as the use of Latin, by the cataphract, which was already available to the Romans in *The Rise of Rome*, and also by the combination of a simpler achievement of the Imperial Age, with the ample opportunities of technological growth, which presumably represented an attempt to reproduce the Byzantine political, cultural and, to some extent, military primacy during late antiquity and the early Middle Ages. That being said, when one considers the blatant inaccuracies such as the temple, the lack of powerful mounted archers and, once again, the language spoken by Byzantine characters, the feeling remains that everything has been extracted from a few pages of a mediocre Western European school textbook, discussing the aftermath of Romulus Augustulus's abdication and Justinian I's *renovatio imperii* (Albrecht 2007: 11–40). It seems that even the most common stereotypes concerning the empire – apart from its quasi-proverbial wealth – did not have much visible influence on the game's authors. Additionally, the label 'defensive civilization' – which may look like a veiled accusation of unmanliness, or perhaps a distant offshoot of the debate regarding 'Byzantine pacifism' (Gallina 2016: 72–78) – is most likely the result of a short passage about the walls of Constantinople that was included in the aforementioned school textbook.

Creative Assembly's ongoing videogame series *Total War* (hereafter *TW*) began in 2000 with *Shogun: Total War*, and is entirely dedicated to PC TBS videogames, set mostly in historical contexts. *TW* instalments focus heavily on war – as one can easily guess from the title – but also have engaging, albeit less immersive, scenarios dealing with religion, diplomacy, trade, economy and administration. Because MicroProse had already pioneered the genre of TBS historical videogames in the early 1990s with

Civilization, the innovative aspect of the *TW* series lies neither in the topic it addresses nor in how it is addressed, but rather in the double interface that characterizes each of its titles. The player manages the government of his/her principality, which includes overseeing diplomatic interactions, city improvements, recruitment, army movements, religious policies, economic activities, espionage and so forth, from a sort of interactive map, wherein it is possible to visualize the whole of the selected realm and to concentrate on the provinces, agents and military forces. This makes the relevant moves accessible within a turn, while battles and sieges take place 'on the field', as every single unit is controlled in real-time. Released in 2002 and supplemented with an expansion named *Viking Invasion* the following year, *Medieval: Total War* was the first chapter of the series set in the Middle Ages, with a chronology ranging from 1087 until the fall of Constantinople in 1453. This time frame included Byzantium among the 'factions' players could select for their campaigns (Jiménez Alcázar 2009: 353–54; Cuenca López 2011: 261). Both *Shogun: TW* and *Medieval: TW* had their fair amount of success, but it was *Rome: Total War* (2004) and its expansions *Alexander* (2006) and *Barbarian Invasion* (2005) – the latter of which also displayed the Eastern Roman Empire during its very first century of life, from the late fourth century to 476 CE – that brought the series to the fore, as the games sold nearly four times the number of copies than the previous *TW* titles (Edge Staff 2006). The same popularity was enjoyed in 2006 by the sequel of *Medieval: TW* and by its expansion: *Medieval II: Total War* and *Kingdoms*. Both remained faithful to the system of the double interface and kept a similar chronology (1080–1530) to their medieval-set predecessor, but implemented several improvements in the graphics and the game engine that had made *Rome: TW* so popular, therefore exploiting the 'long wave' of the latter's fortune with the public (Jiménez Alcázar 2009: 356–59).

Our analysis of Byzantium's portrayal takes only *Medieval II: TW* into consideration, not only for self-evident brevity, because of its more significant popularity compared to *Medieval: TW*, and due to the remarkable similarities between the two, but also since, unlike the first title, the updated versions of the sequel can still be downloaded and played on contemporary platforms, thus making it easier to check the following remarks. In the author's own experience, *Medieval II: TW* is a delightful and entertaining product, as it features a well-balanced game experience between grand strategy and military tactics, posing a real challenge to the players' abilities. Nevertheless, except for remarkable attention to detail regarding military units, the design of the Byzantine faction is full of avoidable historical inaccuracies whose roots are hard to explain, even accepting a few artistic licences, and considering the necessary compromises between historical veracity and gaming requirements. The presentation of Byzantium itself contains several of the tritest anti-Byzantine commonplaces, and is quoted in full below. The introductory sentences alone indicate the creators' flawed approach to Byzantium:

> Byzantium is the shadow that remains of the old Roman Empire. Despite retaining the civilized ways of the Roman legacy, the Byzantines have done little to further it. In fact, it is their reverence of the old ways that have brought the empire to a point of stagnation, in a world that has gradually kept moving on. The differences

between the thinking in Byzantium and the West were most profoundly highlighted with the Great Schism, the division of Christendom. Despite boasting the world's trade capital and home of Orthodox Christianity in Constantinople, the Byzantine Empire is well past its zenith and is now in steady decline. The outer regions of the empire have been slipping from the Emperor's grasp for decades now. To the West, the Normans have taken southern Italy, and in the east the Turks have moved into Asia Minor after their decisive and terrible victory at Manzikert. The latter of these two losses was the worst defeat the empire had suffered in its entire history. To make matters worse, general corruption, chaos, and dissent has led to some of the other provinces closer to home to rebel. Arguably, the greatest threat to Byzantium lies in its independence from Rome. There is significant risk that the lords of the West will consider the lands of Orthodox Christianity to be fair game unless the Pope decrees otherwise. It is a true irony that Constantinople may now have to appease Rome after becoming the new capital of the Roman Empire centuries ago. If the Byzantine Empire is to once again become the dominant power of the East, then it will first need to reclaim its heartlands wholly before encroaching upon the borders of another power. The Byzantine legacy is long and predominantly proud, but unless the Emperor can turn things around in a hurry, it is a legacy that will soon end.

The reader is presented with a poor – and probably accidental – paraphrase of Edward Gibbon's famous rant against the Byzantine Empire and its subjects in the 48th chapter of *The History of the Decline and Fall of the Roman Empire* (Gibbon 1788: 1–4), mixed with a touch of Montesquieu's harsh anti-Byzantine judgements in *Considérations sur les causes de la grandeur des Romains et de leur decadence* (Montesquieu [1734] 1960: 180–81), as it is filled with 'enlightened' prejudices and outdated historiographical concepts. It must be underscored that these games are not scholarly works – yet, as a historian, it is quite discouraging to see that even in 2006, the distorted echo of Gibbon's ideas was still 'in the air', as if more than two centuries of Byzantine studies had passed without leaving a trace outside academia. Although there is no doubt that certain die-hard misconceptions indirectly influenced such words, their choice was not simply a passive reception of some historiographical stereotypes: they were purportedly also meant to stimulate the players' decision to choose the Byzantines by leveraging their eagerness to turn the tide of history, and to 'reclaim the Roman legacy' against all odds. However, this is merely the surface of the issue, since one might be inclined to virtually lead the empire without reading a single line of the description, hence, it is perhaps more helpful to concentrate on how the Byzantines look during the campaign.

Since *Medieval II: TW* starts in 1080, scholars would expect that the *basileus* in charge would have been Nikephoros III Botaneiates (Angold [1984] 1997: 124–26) instead of a fictional forty-five-year-old Alexios I Komnenos, Latinized as Alexius in the game, who was then actually twenty-three, and still held the rank of *megas domestikos* (Varzos 1984, I: 87–113). Moreover, *Medieval II: TW*'s Alexius has four sons, i.e. his heir Prince John, who is twenty-two, Princess Anna, who is twenty, Andronicus, who is two, and Isaac, who is one, despite the fact that none of them existed before the year 1083.[26] In *Medieval II: TW*, succession to the throne works within a purely dynastic framework and does not assume the possibility of a usurpation, so it might be concluded that the chronological inaccuracies were made on purpose, since the Komnenoi are far more 'famous' and easily recognizable as an imperial lineage than the Botaneiatai, at least among educated non-specialists, while the presence of an adult heir apparent and a princess is common to all factions in the game's starting date, given that the absence of an heir, combined with the sudden death of the ruler, would have meant a very early 'game over'. Yet the authors deviated most from historical reality in regards to the geography of the empire. In 1080, nearly ten years after the battle of Manzikert (1071), the Turks had occupied almost the entire Anatolia, except for Trebizond, Cilicia and Northern Syria, which were in the hands of independent dynasts like Theodore Gabras and Philaretos Brachamios. Still, at the same time, the empire continued to exert its authority over most of the Balkans – save for Northern Illyria – in addition to Cyprus and the Aegean Islands (Angold [1984] 1997: 117 ff.). Instead, according to *Medieval II: TW*'s strategic map, in 1080, Byzantium controlled Peloponnese, Macedonia, Thrace, Cyprus, Rhodes and the region around Nicaea, whereas Epirus and Bulgaria were under the rule of rebels, and, with a striking anachronism, Crete was (already) Venetian. Surprisingly, Cilicia, Edessa, Antioch and the Pontic district were appropriately allotted to the rebels. Still, it is hard to assume that this specific historical accuracy was a consequence of being familiar with the writings of Yarnley (1972: 331–53) or Bryer (1970: 175), but was more likely somewhat incidental. The authors made no single claim to produce an accurate historical reconstruction; therefore, they should not be blamed too much for their flaws. Nonetheless, even granting them this 'extenuation', there are no visible grounds related either to the game mechanics, the graphic engine's limitations or the power balance among the factions during the campaign,[27] to explain such fanciful geography without assuming some laziness.

There is little to remark on regarding the buildings – which are similar in each faction[28] – except for the fact that, maybe as a reminder of its trumpeted 'Roman legacy', Byzantium is the only one with access to baths and aqueducts. The empire is correctly placed with Russia among the Orthodox countries, and hence is excluded from the unique mechanics of the Papacy, which are, of course, reserved for Catholics. Conversely, in the light of the chronological and geographical inaccuracies stressed previously, it is a small wonder to see how much effort the game designers put into reproducing the Byzantine army's array. The preliminary information before the campaign's start clearly warns the player that the greatest weakness of the Byzantine armies is their lack of gunpowder units during the late phases of the game. Although this is not entirely true, because it is known that, in 1453, the defenders of Constantinople had some light cannons at their disposal, they did not use them, as their firing would have damaged the walls (McGeer 1991b, II: 786; Heath and McBride 1995: 18–19). It must also be noted that during their last decades, the Byzantines were no longer in a position to besiege a walled fortress, and the last remnants of their world had fallen long before the game's end date (1530), whereas massive exploitation of firearms on battlefields occurred only after the second half of the fifteenth century. According to the same pre-start disclaimer, Byzantium's strength lies in heavy cavalry and archers, mounted and dismounted likewise, which is noticeable throughout the game's progress. The empire may indeed recruit three types of powerful heavily armoured knights, such as cataphracts, Latinkon cavalry – surely a spelling mistake for 'Latinikon' – and 'Byzantine lancers'; three different mounted archers, namely the Skythikon, the Vardariotai and the 'Byzantine cavalry'; two advanced units of foot archers, such as the 'Trebizond archers' and the 'Byzantine guard archers'; a very effective heavy infantry, which includes the foot Latinkon and lancers, the Varangian guard, as well as the standard units available to most factions.[29]

An expert of Byzantine military issues could undoubtedly point out that the use of cataphracts was in steady decline after the battle of Manzikert (Soria Molina 2013: 93), or that Varangians gradually became a ceremonial palatine unit, ceasing to be used on the battlefield after the thirteenth century (Dawkins 1947: 39–46; Blöndal 1978: 167–76; D'Amato 2010: 10–12). We should consider, however, that the mechanics of the game make it almost impossible to provide an accurate evolution of one country's army, because there are no explicit technological advancements like those in the *AoE* series, and everything in this field depends on the player's skills in relation to the construction of the relevant buildings. The game's mechanics make these kinds of inaccuracies almost structural and de facto they are non-correctable. Meanwhile, it is surely noteworthy that significant effort has been made to represent the multinational nature of the Byzantine army, with the Skythikon, the misspelled Latinikon (Bartusis 1992: 139 ff.; Heath and McBride 1995: 22–23), and even the obscure Vardariotai, which were Turkic tribes settled in a theme located in Northern Bulgaria (Janin 1930: 437–49). In addition, the standard imperial cavalry and infantry – 'Byzantine cavalry' and 'Byzantine guard archers', respectively, in *Medieval II: TW* – which were historically efficient both as archers and in close combat, are adequately depicted as such, while the presence of the 'Byzantine lancers' was probably meant to recall the *pronoiarioi* (Bartusis 1992: 157 ff.; Heath and McBride 1995: 11–12; Bartusis 2012: 32 ff.), as the unit is almost identical to one named 'Pronoia cavalry' in *Medieval: TW*.

After this short comparison between the 'real Byzantium' and the one portrayed in *Medieval II: TW*, it seems clear enough that, as the focus and the title of the series did not leave the designers much choice, they gave priority to the military aspects of the game, leading them – perhaps not deliberately – to overlook other, equally important elements. Bearing in mind the restrictions owed to the gameplay, the authors' attempt to somehow reproduce a standalone Byzantine army evidently implied some up-to-date readings about the topic, and this must undoubtedly be praised. However, their significant commitment to recreating the elements of the warfare's sphere as plausibly as possible clashes even more sharply with their carelessness in other essential areas of the game. Except for the issues concerning the Komnenian genealogy and chronology, which can be partly ascribed to playability, it is hard to determine why the strategic map was so erroneous, inasmuch as it was not by any means beneficial to the potential enjoyment of the product,[30] nor was it caused by technical constraints. Repetition of clichés about the weakness and the unending decline of the empire appear to be somewhat functional for the rhetorical call to arms addressed to the player. Although such clichés are often the only 'notions' that non-insiders have about late medieval Byzantium (Gallina 2010: 156–61), a little effort to avoid such passive assimilation of those concepts would have enhanced the quality of the game, without compromising the 'decadent charm' of the Byzantine faction. In short, the image of the Byzantine

Empire in *Medieval II: TW* may be described as a sort of Ianus Bifrons, since, to satisfy the primary audience of the *TW* series – i.e. strategic wargame fans – the developers' thoroughness was encouraged only insofar as the military side of their product was concerned. This enabled the players to lead fairly realistic imperial armies, but, on the other hand, the same players would have ruled over a fictional *basileia*, whose portrait was still regrettably fashioned out of a rough version of some 'enlightened' historians' ideas, a concept which had surely not passed through the filter of Byzantinism's most refined cultural modes.

The final case study concerns the series *Europa Universalis* (hereafter *EU*) by the Swedish videogame publisher Paradox Interactive, which began in 2000 and was based on the homonymous board game released in 1993, whose inventor, Philippe Thibaut, also adapted it to PC gameplay. All the series instalments are historically set RTS videogames, in which the player can manage any state that existed in the world during the modern era, with chronologies varying from 1492–1789 for the first title, 1419–1820 for the second, 1453–1792 for the third,[31] until 1444–1821 for the fourth and current iteration. In contrast with the *AoE* and *TW* games, which are heavily focused on war and military issues, *EU* ones decidedly privilege political, religious, diplomatic and economic elements in the country's management, as battles and sieges are always resolved automatically by the AI.[32] At the same time, the type of army is restricted to a single kind of infantry, cavalry and, after a specific date, artillery unit, which the player can improve upon by achieving the relevant technological advances during the campaign. Among the games discussed here, titles of *EU* are by far the best in terms of historical accuracy. Their almost impeccable reproduction of the political geography, the rulers' succession over time, the plausibility of international relationships and so forth, reveal an attention to detail in every country's profile, and it would be nearly impossible to see significant discrepancies between the game's progress and the actual history, with the only variable in the outcomes being the abilities or inabilities of the player. To put it more succinctly, Castile/Spain, Portugal and England/Great Britain would almost invariably build great colonial empires, France and the Ottomans would nearly always be the mightiest nations in the Euro-Mediterranean scenario, Muscovy would often crush its neighbours, form Russia, and colonize Siberia and North-Eastern Asia. On the other hand, countries such as the Kingdom of Cyprus, the Duchy of the Archipelago or the Emirate of Granada rarely survive longer than a few decades, and even more rarely do they become significant powers. Still, the depth and the complexity of *EU*'s mechanics – which had been improved and modified in each chapter, but without revolutionizing the core of the game – provide a steep learning curve, which may discourage those who are not so strongly motivated, and may sometimes even frustrate the (virtual) ambitions of the most experienced players.

As with *TW*, we discuss here the image of Byzantium in *EU* only as presented within the last title of the series, namely *Europa Universalis IV* (2013). Beginning precisely the day after the battle of Varna, on 11 November 1444, with only nine years left before the collapse of the historical Byzantium, the game puts the player who accepts the challenge of choosing the empire in a precarious position. Ruled by a thirty-seven year old, John VIII Palaiologos (1425–48), the *basileia* exerts its authority over the city of Constantinople – one of the most lucrative European trade hubs in *EU IV* – its immediate territories and the Peloponnese. The player is the suzerain lord of the Duchy of Athens, has claims over most of the Greek mainland, has the government rank of an empire within the system of a feudal monarchy, is Greek by culture, Orthodox by religion and has been placed in the Eastern European 'technology group'.[33] The empire has a relatively small army and navy, but this would not have necessarily been a significant disadvantage, in and of itself, unless its territory was almost entirely encircled by the Ottomans. They are already one of the most powerful countries from the start of the game and were 'designed to desire' imperial provinces, making even bare survival impossible if Byzantium is controlled by either the AI or by an unskilled player. Based on the author's significant experience as a player, the Byzantines have yet to last more than twenty to twenty-five years during the campaign, and the only exception occurs when the player is controlling Byzantium or is deliberately taking action as a foreign ally to help the empire – though not always successfully – against its Turkish foe. It must also be said that, although this evaluation's focus will be on the Palaiologan State, the *basileia* is not the only Byzantine realm displayed in *EU IV*. Players may also select the Empire of Trebizond, culturally Pontic and ruled by the Komnenoi; the Despotate of Epirus, Greek and under despot Charles II Tocco (1429–48); and the Gothic principality of Theodoro-Mangup, all of which, with the partial exception of Epirus, have their own unique features. Furthermore, because it is possible to start the game at any point from 1444 to 1821, after Constantinople's fall, the hopeless Despotate of Morea is also available, for those audacious players who think that playing Byzantium is too easy and would like to try to restore it from the ashes; a task that may also be accomplished with Trebizond and Epirus once the empire itself has fallen.

Apart from a few minor deviations from historical truth, including the incorrect age of John VIII, who was born in December 1392 and was hence fifty-one in 1444 (Papadopoulos [1938] 1962: n. 90; Nicol [1972] 1992: 339 ff.; Djurić [1989] 1995)[34] – a Byzantinist might have little to complain about the portrait of Byzantium in *EU IV*. The 'geopolitics' of the empire is substantially correct, since by 1444, Athens had been subdued to Byzantine suzerainty by despot Constantine Palaiologos (Nicol 1992: 28–29) and, even though Morea was then autonomous from Constantinople (Zakythinos [1932] 1975, I: 94 ff.), the fact that the *basileia* is considered a 'feudal monarchy' partly mitigates this minor flaw, while the absence of the Venetian strongholds of Corone and Modone from the game is due to their nature as micro-enclaves, which is quite difficult to represent on the strategic map. The only significant deviation regarding Byzantium, along with Trebizond, Epirus and Theodoro-Mangup, concerns the appearance of their towns and the units they can recruit in later phases of the game. The former recalls Russian architecture, while the latter was chiefly modelled on Polish and Russian armies during the modern age. This is a consequence of the 'Eastern European technology group', in which all Byzantine principalities were included; nevertheless, although none of them would have probably ever employed winged hussars in case they would have survived to the fifteenth century, none of them existed after 1479, hence, there is no historically based understanding of what could have happened to their armies afterward. To number Byzantine principalities among the 'Anatolian' countries, like the Ottomans and the other minor Turkish emirates, would have produced equally awkward outcomes over time. Moreover, it would have been a futile effort to create a specifically dedicated 'technology group' for the Byzantines and, perhaps, their fellow Balkan lordships,[35] because all sixteenth-, seventeenth- and eighteenth-century developments would have required inventing them from scratch.

These elements show that the game's designers consulted at least some Wikipedia pages about the empire, and had referenced a historical atlas. However, it is possibly easier to guess where they want to lead the player who chooses Byzantium and reconstruct their image of the empire by observing its unique 'missions tree'[36] and, to a lesser degree, its 'national ideas'.[37] Nonetheless, it must be said that in *EU* games there are no conditions under which one may be declared the 'winner', since everyone sets their target according to the potential of the country that they have selected and their abilities. Therefore, the authors may only encourage some moves by giving temporary or permanent bonuses, upon the player completing some specific goals. Still, nothing compels the player to reach them if they wish to follow different paths. Byzantine 'national ideas' do not offer much help, since they are rather generic regarding the name and their effects,[38] and they might be historically suitable to most countries in the game. The only concepts that look somewhat 'more Byzantine' than the others are perhaps 'regulation of mercenaries', which is presumably based upon the extensive presence of the latter in late medieval Byzantine armies (Bartusis 1992: 139 ff.), and gives a -15 per cent cost in their maintenance, and 'restore the ecumenical patriarch'. In this regard, Theodoro and, to a greater extent, Trebizond seem to have been more customized than their Constantinopolitan counterparts. It is enough to list a few Tebizondian 'national ideas' to see their difference from the Byzantine ones listed in footnote 38. Trebizond has 'Komnenoi princesses', which is reminiscent of the exploitation of matrimonial alliances with the neighbouring Turkic chiefs by the Pontic *basileis* (Zachariadou 1979: 333–58), and provides diplomatic bonuses; 'terminus of the silk road', that reproduces the crucial intermediary role in the Western trade with Armenia, Persia and Central Asia of the tiny empire's capital (Karpov [1981] 1986); 'Komnenoi in exile', which is probably an attempt to symbolize the emperors' pride for their ancestry and their self-bestowed title of 'Mega-Komnenoi' (Lampsides 1967: 114–25; Macrides 1979: 238–45); 'Greek scholars abroad', which presumably recalls important scholars of Trebizondian descent, like Bessarion or George of Trebizond (Savvides 2009: 183–207).[39]

As far as the missions are concerned, the 'customization balance' is wholly overturned, favouring the Palaiologoi, since the *basileia* is the only country within the Byzantine culture's group with its own special 'missions tree'. Byzantine missions are mainly centred around the gradual restoration of the power, prestige and influence of the old empire: first, as it was during its medieval apogee and then – if the player manages to achieve that already challenging task – as it existed under Justinian I. Initial goals are about the reconquest of Balkan, Anatolian and Southern Italian provinces, and the re-evangelization of former Turkish lands, in order to reconstruct something similar to what the empire was under the Macedonian dynasty, at least in terms of its territorial extension. Since even the most talented player will not be able to accomplish such results until the second half of the sixteenth century, the effect would be bewildering, even more so after completing the mission 're-establish the theme system', which restores former Greek names to Anatolian provinces and gives a substantial manpower bonus to the empire for the remainder of the campaign. If a player decides to follow this 'restoration plan' until the end, they will be busy for the rest of the game trying to take back Syria, Egypt, Northern Africa, Italy and Southern Spain; and converting Antioch, Jerusalem, Alexandria and Rome to Orthodoxy as a means to 'restore the pentarchy' of the five original patriarchates under imperial rule. The 'time machine' sensation is guaranteed in each step of the process, as the anachronism becomes more striking while the game progresses. However, this approach reveals much of the developer's strategy to focus the attention of the players on Byzantium – which is, in fact, one of the most popular, if not *the* most popular, countries among the *EU* community, since it is self-evident that designers tried to stimulate players' eagerness to prove themselves capable of making the 'purple phoenix' rise again. Despite the greater sophistication in implementing their intentions, in such terms, the approach of *EU IV* creators does not seem to be too much different from those we have underlined in *Medieval II: TW* and, to a lesser degree, in *AoE II*. It is Roman heritage and Orthodoxy, and their 'practical reification', that developers had in mind when they imagined the potential projections of all Byzantine realms. This goal is demonstrated by the fact that only the Palaiologoi have a unique 'missions tree', whereas Epirus, Trebizond and Morea are first charged with restoring the *basileia* on their own to enjoy their Ῥωμαιοσύνη fully. In *EU IV*, the Byzantines are Ῥωμαῖοι until their final days – and even afterwards, they never lose grasp of their imperial past, as one can immediately find out by reading the description of the 'restore the Byzantine Empire' option: 'The glorious Byzantine Empire is gone, but as long as there are Greeks in Constantinople, there is the hope of resurrection. We can take its place in spirit, but we cannot take its name unless we prove worthy ...'

In conclusion, we cannot draw an image of Byzantium in strategy videogames that would suit all the products considered, since each of the games' mechanics, gameplay and time period differs, and these factors significantly affect the final results. The author first hypothesized that *AoE II*'s Byzantines were influenced by a few notions about the late antique empire that were likely taken from school textbooks. This resulted in a significant emphasis on Roman continuity – though maybe exaggerated, given that Byzantine characters speak Latin – and its purported advantage, compared to other medieval civilizations, but produced an incongruous non-sequitur with the 'Islamic appearance' of imperial temples. The author then detailed *Medieval II: TW*'s incongruity between the appreciably plausible and detailed representation of Byzantine armies and the empire's several, mostly inexplicable geo-chronological inadvertences. These elements were placed within a framework greatly influenced by a popular version of the Enlightenment's historiography about Byzantium. Still, the developers made solid reference to the Roman legacy of the Eastern Empire, even though the campaign starts in the year 1080. Lastly, save for a few minor inaccuracies, *EU IV*'s Eastern Roman world looks relatively more realistic than *AoE II*'s and *Medieval II: TW*'s and, although the game begins at the very twilight of the Byzantine civilization, the authors manifestly encouraged the player to gradually restore the empire's former glory, as it was during Justinian I's or Constantine the Great's reigns. Notwithstanding the discrepancies that were listed above, a few common elements may still be pointed out. Regardless of how it is portrayed, Roman heritage is always presented as a critical aspect of the *basileia*. It is also used as bait to attract players towards choosing the Empire, either to live that heritage during the Middle Ages or to restore it thoroughly by military conquest and prestige. Albeit up-to-date scholarly literature did not inform the games' Byzantine imagery, neither did 'enlightened' and later prejudices about the empire, except in the cases of the *TW* titles. The same fate befell Byzantinism, which seems not to have touched the virtual Byzantine Empires of our videogames, whilst exoticism and decadence – which is somewhat evoked in *Medieval II: TW*, but does not seem to be related to the late nineteenth-/early twentieth-century cultural trend – could have been excellent ways to attract a more sophisticated, romantic or culturally oriented audience, even in a context where statesmanship and warfare rule the roost.

Ludography

Age of Empires (1997–2020, series), dev.: Ensemble Studios, Big Huge Games, Robot Entertainment, Relic Entertainment, Hidden Path Entertainment, Forgotten Empires, World's Edge, Tantalus Media, pub.: Microsoft, Xbox Game Studios, plat.: Microsoft Windows, Classic Mac OS, Windows Mobile, PlayStation 2, OS X, N-Gage, Nintendo DS, Windows Phone, iOS, Android.
Age of Empires (1997), dev.: Ensemble Studios, pub.: Microsoft, plat.: Microsoft Windows.
Age of Empires II: The Age of Kings (1999), dev.: Ensemble Studios, pub.: Microsoft, plat.: Microsoft Windows.
Akalabeth: World of Doom (1979–1981), dev.: Richard Garriott, pub.: California Pacific Computer Co., plat.: Apple II, DOS.
Alexander (2006, expansion of *Rome: Total War*), dev.: The Creative Assembly, pub.: Sega, plat.: Microsoft Windows.
Assassin's Creed: Revelation (2011), dev.: Ubisoft Montreal, pub.: Ubisoft, plat.: PlayStation 3, Xbox 360, Microsoft Windows.
Barbarian Invasion (2005, expansion of *Rome: Total War*), dev.: The Creative Assembly, pub.: Sega, plat.: Microsoft Windows.
Civilization (1991), dev.: MicroProse, pub.: MicroProse, plat.: MS-DOS.
Europa Universalis (2000), dev.: Paradox Development Studio, pub.: Strategy First, plat.: Microsoft Windows.
Europa Universalis II (2001), dev.: Paradox Development Studio, pub.: Strategy First, plat.: Microsoft Windows.
Europa Universalis III (2007), dev.: Paradox Development Studio, pub.: Paradox Interactive, plat.: Microsoft Windows, OS X.
Europa Universalis IV (2013), dev.: Paradox Development Studio, pub.: Paradox Interactive, plat.: Microsoft Windows, OS X, Linux.
Hamurabi (1973), des.: Doug Dyment, plat.: PC.
In Nomine (2008, expansion of *Europa Universalis III*), dev.: Paradox Development Studio, pub.: Paradox Interactive, plat.: Microsoft Windows.
Kingdoms (2007, expansion of *Medieval II: Total War*), dev.: The Creative Assembly, pub.: Sega, plat.: Microsoft Windows.
Medieval: Total War (2002), dev.: The Creative Assembly, pub.: Activision, plat.: Microsoft Windows.
Medieval II: Total War (2006), dev.: The Creative Assembly, pub.: Sega, plat.: Microsoft Windows.
Napoleon's Ambition (2008, expansion of *Europa Universalis III*), dev.: Paradox Development Studio, pub.: Paradox Interactive, plat.: Microsoft Windows.

Pong (1972), dev.: Atari, pub.: Atari, plat.: arcade, several consoles.
Rise of the Tomb Raider (2015), dev.: Crystal Dynamics, pub.: Square Enix, Microsoft Studios, plat.: Xbox 360, Xbox One, Microsoft Windows, PlayStation 4, macOS, Linux, Stadia.
Rome: Total War (2004), dev.: Creative Assembly, pub.: Activision, plat.: Microsoft Windows.
Shogun: Total War (2000), dev.: The Creative Assembly, pub.: Electronic Arts, plat.: Microsoft Windows.
Spacewar! (1962), des.: Steve Russell, plat.: PDP-1.
Tennis for Two (1958), des.: William Higinbotham, plat.: Analog computer.
The Conquerors (2000, expansion of *Age of Empires II: The Age of Kings*), dev.: Ensemble Studios, pub.: Microsoft, plat.: Microsoft Windows.
The Legend of Zelda (1986–2019, series), dev.: Nintendo EAD, Capcom, Grezzo, Nintendo EPD, pub.: Nintendo, plat.: Nintendo Entertainment System, Super Nintendo Entertainment System, Game Boy, Nintendo 64, Game Boy Color, Game Boy Advance, GameCube, Wii, Nintendo DS, Nintendo 3DS, Wii U, Nintendo Switch.
The Legend of Zelda: Link's Awakening (2019), dev.: Grezzo, pub.: Nintendo, plat.: Nintendo Switch.
The Rise of Rome (1998, expansion of *Age of Empires*), dev.: Ensemble Studios, pub.: Microsoft, plat.: Microsoft Windows.
The Sumer Game (1968), des.: Doug Dyment, plat.: PDP-8.
Total War (2000–19, series), dev.: The Creative Assembly, pub.: Electronic Arts, Activision, Sega, plat.: Microsoft Windows, OS X, Linus, iOS, Play Store.
Ultima (1981–99, series), dev.: Origin Systems, Blue Sky Productions, Looking Glass Studios, Electronic Arts, Bioware Mythic, pub.: Origin Systems, Electronic Arts, plat.: Apple II, Atari 8-bit, VIC-20, C64, DOS, MSX, FM Towns, NEC PC-9801, Atari ST, Mac OS, Amiga, Atari 800, NES, Master System, C128, SNES, X68000, PlayStation, Microsoft Windows.
Ultima I: The Age of Darkness (1981), dev.: Richard Garriott, Origin Systems, pub.: California Pacific, Origin Systems, Sierra On-line, plat.: Apple II, Atari 8-bit.
Viking Invasion (2003, expansion of *Medieval: Total War*), dev.: The Creative Assembly, pub.: Activision, plat.: Microsoft Windows.

Notes

1   They had named this time the 'Dark Ages', as such, exactly to indicate the millennium that stood in the middle (*medium aevum, aetas media*) between them, the supposed 'moderns', and the 'ancients' (McLaughlin 1988: 131–42).
2   Namely from the last quarter of the sixteenth century until the final decades of the seventeenth century.
3   The term often brought into play the appalling practices of the Inquisition, witch-hunting or the post-medieval degeneration of the feudal system (Sergi 2005: 43–51).
4   For example, court culture, knighthood (Girouard 1981; Bologna 2004: 327–87; Domenichelli 2004: 293–325), communal society (Vallerani 2004: 187–206), crenellated castles and Gothic churches (Clark 1962; Bordone 1993: 173–85; Marconi 2004: 491–94).
5   Indeed, the Neo-Gothic style gained such an aesthetic strength that some architects even dared to add some alleged quasi-medieval features, such as mullioned windows

or flying buttresses, to genuine medieval buildings, which did not look 'medieval enough' (Bordone 1993: 177–80).
6   For example, words like 'medieval' and 'Gothic' were created during those years, as we have seen above.
7   Notwithstanding the relevance of prose literature and poetry, particularly until the mid-twentieth century.
8   Like the flamboyantly dressed flag-wavers and trumpeters in Italian towns (di Carpegna Falconieri 2011: 106–20).
9   The evocative and whimsical charm of the British Parliament in Westminster, the national assembly in Budapest, the castle of the Valentino Park in Turin (Marconi 2004: 507–20), the walls of Carcassonne (Poisson 2004: 537–45) or the entire old town of San Marino (di Carpegna Falconieri 2017: 191–98), just to mention some of the best known among them, is nowadays still indisputably active.
10 Henceforth RTS and TBS respectively.
11 This style is especially prevalent in Russia (Savelyev 2005).
12 As far as the Neo-Byzantine style in France is concerned, see Kampouri-Vamvoukou (2003: 87–100).
13 Neither is Byzantine culture widely known in Japan.
14 Such clichés depicted an Empire as ruled by effeminate eunuchs, political intrigues and pointless religious discussions, and its history as an endlessly prolonged decadence.
15 The PDP-1 was one of the oldest mini-computers, whose production started in 1959.
16 Equivalent to more than $1,000,000 today.
17 A PDP-8 cost more than $18,000 (Schein 2004: 271), equivalent to about $150,000 today.
18 In 1971, a programme's file name could contain at most eight characters, and since the word 'Hammurabi' has nine characters, it was shortened to 'Hamurabi'.
19 Basically, a list of codes that had to be typed manually, and then possibly saved on floppy discs in order to run programmes on early PCs.
20 Zelda's avatar was named Link.
21 A God game can be considered as a subgenre of the management and strategic videogames as casts the player the player in the position to control the game on a considerably large scale, as if he was a sort of divinity or a leader with supernatural powers.
22 For example, the game starts in 4000 BCE and the player can choose between many civilizations, almost none of which existed at the time, while the leader of the selected one remains 'in charge' from the beginning until the end, which is set in 2100 CE, for a total of 6,100 years.
23 In *AoE II*, the wonder is a special building that allows players to win the game in some circumstances if they are able to preserve it for a given period of time. The wonder is the only building that is different for each of the game's civilizations.
24 Namely pikemen, skirmishers and camel warriors.
25 Each civilization has its own unique military unit, which is different from all others.
26 Anna was born in 1083, John in 1087, Andronikos in 1091 and Isaac in 1093 (Varzos 1984, I: 176–97, 203–54).
27 In fact, the Byzantines would have been equally powerful with a more realistic map.
28 There are actually some small differences between Islamic, Eastern European and Western European buildings, but, apart from the minarets and domes of Islamic towns, all cities and castles in the game have a rather standardized appearance.

29 Town militias, catapults, trebuchets and ballistas along with the fleet, which does not display significant differences from one faction to another.
30 Either making it easier to learn its mechanics or introducing a better gameplay balance.
31 Expanded to 1399–1820 with the expansions *Napoleon's Ambition* (2007) and *In Nomine* (2008).
32 I.e. artificial intelligence.
33 Technology groups affect the appearance of the cities and the military units, as well as those units' names and features as the game progresses.
34 The age of his heir and brother Constantine, who would have become emperor after his sibling's death as Constantine XI, is correctly thirty-nine (Papadopoulos [1938] 1962: n. 95; Nicol [1972] 1992: 369 ff.; Nicol 1992).
35 *Scilicet* Serbia, Albania, Bosnia, Montenegro, etc.
36 Missions can be completed by reaching pre-determined goals in territorial expansion, religion, economy and so forth, giving temporary or, more rarely, permanent bonuses to the country, once the player achieves them.
37 In the *EU* series, 'ideas' represent specific bonuses regarding any aspect of the game that are permanently awarded to the country once it complies with certain conditions. In *EU IV*, 'national ideas' pertain only to a single realm or group of realms with similar features (culture, government type, religion, etc.), and may be unlocked by achieving a certain number of simple 'ideas' that can be obtained by every country in the game.
38 Here is their list: 'regulation of mercenaries', 'repopulation of the countryside', 'State administrative reform', 'Byzantine merchant class', 'the new imperial army' and 'restore the ecumenical patriarch'.
39 There are also 'Pontic mountains', 'legacy of the Alexiad' and 'the lessons of the fourth Crusade'.

Bibliography

Accordi Rickards, M. (2014), *Storia del videogioco. Dagli anni Cinquanta a oggi*, Roma: Carocci.

Ahl, D. H. (1973), *101 BASIC Computer Games*, Maynard, MA: Digital Equipment Corporation.

Albertoni, G. (2010), 'Campagne curtensi senza economia chiusa', *Mundus. Rivista di didattica della storia*, 5–6: 128–34.

Albrecht, S. (2007), 'Byzanz in deutschen, französischen und englischen Schulbüchern' in A. Helmedach (ed.), *Pulverfass, Powder Keg, Baril de Poudre? Südosteuropa im europäischen Geschichtsschulbuch. South Eastern Europe in European History Textbooks*, 11–40, Hannover: Hahn.

Angelov, D. G. (2003), 'Byzantinism: The Imaginary and Real Heritage of Byzantium in Southeastern Europe', in D. Keridis, E. Elias-Bursac and N. Yatromanolakis (eds.), *New approaches to Balkan Studies*, 3–23, Dulles, VA: Brassey's (IFPA-Kokkalis Series on Southeast European Policy, 2).

Angold, M. ([1984] 1997), *The Byzantine Empire, 1025–1204: A Political History*, London and New York: Longman.

Auzépy, M. F., ed. (2003), *Byzance en Europe*, Paris: Presses Universitaires de Vincennes.

Bartusis, M. C. (1992), *The Late Byzantine Army: Arms and Society, 1204–1453*, Philadelphia: University of Pennsylvania Press.
Bartusis, M. C. (2012), *Land and Privilege in Byzantium: The Institution of Pronoia*, Cambridge: Cambridge University Press.
Binding, G. (1989), 'Gotik', in *Lexikon des Mittelalters*, IV, 1575–76, München and Zürich: Artemis.
Blöndal, S. (1978), *The Varangians of Byzantium*, Cambridge: Cambridge University Press.
Bologna, C. (2004), 'Miti di una letteratura medievale. Il Sud', in E. Castelnuovo and G. Sergi (eds.), *Arti e storia nel Medioevo*, IV, *Il Medioevo al passato e al presente*, 327–87, Torino: Einaudi.
Bonini, G., A. Brusa, R. Cervi and E. Garimberti, eds. (2011), *Il paesaggio agrario italiano medievale. Storia e didattica. Summer school Emilio Sereni, 2ª edizione 24–29 agosto 2010*, Gattatico: Istituto Alcide Cervi.
Bordone, R. (1993), *Lo specchio di Shalott. L'invenzione del medioevo nella cultura dell'Ottocento*, Napoli: Liguori.
Bordone, R. (2004), 'Editoria tra Ottocento e Novecento. Fumetto', in E. Castelnuovo and G. Sergi (eds.), *Arti e storia nel Medioevo*, IV, *Il Medioevo al passato e al presente*, 711–35, Torino: Einaudi.
Bryer, A. A. M. (1970), 'A Byzantine Family: The Gabrades, c. 979–c. 1653', *University of Birmingham Historical Journal*, 12: 164–87.
Chavarría Arnau, A. and G. Zucconi, eds. (2016), *L'invenzione di uno stile nell'architettura tra fine '800 e inizio '900*, Firenze: all'Insegna del Giglio.
Ciccopiedi, C. (2010), 'Chiese plurali e centralizzazione della riforma', *Mundus. Rivista di didattica della storia*, 5–6: 142–48.
Clark, K. (1962), *The Gothic Revival: An Essay in the History of Taste*, London: J. Murray.
Cuenca López, J. M. (2011), 'La storia e il paesaggio medievale nei videogiochi', in G. Bonini A. Brusa, R. Cervi and E. Garimberti (eds.), *Il paesaggio agrario italiano medievale. Storia e didattica. Summer school Emilio Sereni, 2ª edizione 24–29 agosto 2010*, 257–63, Gattatico: Istituto Alcide Cervi.
D'Amato, R. (2010), *The Varangian Guard: 988–1453*, Oxford: Osprey Publishing.
Dawkins, R. M. (1947), 'The Later History of the Varangian Guard: Some Notes', *The Journal of Roman Studies*, 37: 39–46.
di Carpegna Falconieri, T. (2011), *Medioevo militante: La politica di oggi alle prese con barbari e crociati*, Torino: Einaudi.
di Carpegna Falconieri, T. (2017), 'San Marino neomedievale', in G. Allegretti (ed.), *Città di San Marino*, 191–98, San Marino: Ente Cassa di Faetano (Storia dei Castelli della Repubblica di San Marino, 9).
Djurić, I. ([1989] 1995), *Il Crepuscolo di Bisanzio. I tempi di Giovanni VIII Paleologo*, transl. S. Vacca, Roma: Donzelli.
Domenichelli, M. (2004), 'Miti di una letteratura medievale. Il Nord', in E. Castelnuovo and G. Sergi (eds.), *Arti e storia nel Medioevo*, IV, *Il Medioevo al passato e al presente*, 293–325, Torino: Einaudi.
Edge Staff (2006), 'The Top 100 PC Games of the 21st Century' (2006), *Edge*, 25 August. Available online: https://web.archive.org/web/20121019052748/http://www.edge-online.com/features/top-100-pc-games-21st-century (accessed 8 February 2020).
Gallina, M. (2010), 'Bisanzio senza bizantinismi', *Mundus. Rivista di didattica della storia*, 5–6: 156–61.

Gallina, M. (2016), *Incoronati da Dio. Per una storia del pensiero politico bizantino*, Roma: Viella.
Gamberini, A. (2010), 'Processi di ricomposizione politica alla fine del Medioevo e avvento degli stati regionali', *Mundus. Rivista di didattica della storia*, 5-6: 120-27.
Gandino, G. (2004), 'Il cinema', in E. Castelnuovo and G. Sergi (eds.), *Arti e storia nel Medioevo*, IV, *Il Medioevo al passato e al presente*, 737-55, Torino: Einaudi.
Gandino, G. (2010), 'Dai Longobardi ai Carolingi', *Mundus. Rivista di didattica della storia*, 5-6: 101-06.
Garofani, B. (2010), 'Diverse ortodossie, non eresie', *Mundus. Rivista di didattica della storia*, 5-6: 149-55.
Geary, P. J. (2002), *The Myth of Nations: The Medieval Origins of Europe*, Princeton, NJ: Princeton University Press.
Gibbon, E. (1788), *The History of the Decline and Fall of the Roman Empire*, vol. 5, London: A. Strahan and T. Cadell.
Girouard, M. (1981), *The Return to Camelot: Chivalry and the English Gentleman*, London: Yale University Press.
Guillou, A. (1966), 'Le monde de Byzance dans la pensée historique de l'Europe: le siècle des lumières', *Jahrbuch der österreichischen Byzantinistik*, XV: 27-39.
Heath, I. and A. McBride (1995), *Byzantine Armies: 1118-1461 AD*, London: Osprey Publishing.
Hobsbawm, E. (1983), 'Mass-Producing Traditions: Europe, 1870-1914', in E. Hobsbawm and T. Ranger, *The Invention of Tradition*, 263-307, Cambridge: Cambridge University Press.
Janin, R. (1930), 'Les Turcs Vardariotes', *Échos d'Orient*, 29: 437-49.
Jiménez Alcázar, J. F. (2009), 'Videogames and the Middle Ages', *Imago temporis. Medium aevum*, 3: 311-65.
Jiménez Alcázar, J. F. (2011), 'The Other Possible Past: Simulation of the Middle Ages in Videogames', *Imago temporis. Medium aevum*, 5: 299-340.
Kamen, H. (1971), *The Iron Century: Social Change in Europe, 1550-1660*, London: Weidenfeld & Nicolson.
Kampouri-Vamvoukou, M. (2003), 'L'Architecture de styl néo-byzantin en France', in M. F. Auzépy (ed.), *Byzance en Europe*, 87-100, Paris: Presses Universitaires de Vincennes.
Karpov, S. P. ([1981] 1986), *L'Impero di Trebisonda, Venezia, Genova e Roma, 1204-1461: rapporti politici, diplomatici e commerciali*, transl. E. Zambelli, Roma: Il Veltro.
Lampsides, O. (1967), 'Le titre "Megas Komnenos" (Grand Comnène)', *Byzantion*, 37: 114-25.
Macrides, R. (1979), 'What's in the Name «Megas Komnenos»', *Ἀρχεῖον Πόντου*, 35: 238-45.
Marciniak, P. (2018), 'Oriental like Byzantium: Some Remarks on Similarities between Byzantinism and Orientalism', in A. Alshanskaya, A. Gietzen and C. Hadjiafxenti (eds.), *Imagining Byzantium: Perceptions, Patterns, Problems*, 47-53, Mainz: Verlag des Römisch-Germanischen Zentralmuseums.
Marconi, P. (2004), 'Il borgo medievale di Torino. Alfredo d'Andrade e il borgo medievale in Italia', in E. Castelnuovo and G. Sergi (eds.), *Arti e storia nel Medioevo*, IV, *Il Medioevo al passato e al presente*, 491-520, Torino: Einaudi.
McGeer, E. (1991a), 'Cavalry', in A. Kazhdan (ed.), *The Oxford Dictionary of Byzantium*, 3 vols, vol. 1, 393-94, Oxford: Oxford University Press.

McGeer, E. (1991b), 'Firearms', in A. Kazhdan (ed.), *The Oxford Dictionary of Byzantium*, 3 vols, vol. 2, 786, Oxford: Oxford University Press.
McLaughlin, M. L. (1988), 'Humanist Concepts of Renaissance and Middle Ages in the Tre- and Quattrocento', *Renaissance Studies*, 2 (2): 131–42.
Milani, G. (2010), 'Comuni borghesi e comuni aristocratici', *Mundus. Rivista di didattica della storia*, 5–6: 113–19.
Montesquieu, Charles-Louis de Secondat, Baron de La Brède et de ([1734] 1960), *Considerazioni sulle cause della grandezza e decadenza dei Romani*, transl. G. Pasquinelli, Torino: Boringhieri.
Münster, R. (2010), 'Enlightenment Perspective on the Middle Ages', in A. Classen (ed.), *Handbook of Medieval Studies: Terms – Methods – Trends*, I 3 vols, vol.1 468–88, Berlin: De Gruyter.
Musci, E. (2010), 'Il Medioevo disegnato. La comunicazione storica fra stereotipi ed esempi virtuosi', *Mundus. Rivista di didattica della storia*, 5–6: 182–91.
Nicol, D. M. ([1972] 1992), *The Last centuries of Byzantium 1261–1453*, Cambridge: Cambridge University Press.
Nicol, D. M. (1992), *The Immortal Emperor: The Life and the Legend of Constantine Palaiologos, Last Emperor of the Romans*, Cambridge: Cambridge University.
Occhipinti, E. (2004), 'Gli storici e il medioevo. Da Muratori a Duby', in E. Castelnuovo and G. Sergi (eds.), *Arti e storia nel Medioevo*, IV, *Il Medioevo al passato e al presente*, 207–28, Torino: Einaudi.
Ortenberg, V. (2007), *In Search of the Holy Grail: The Quest for the Middle Ages*, New York: Hambledon Continuum.
Panofsky, E. (1969), *L'œuvre d'art et ses significations*, Paris: Gallimard.
Papadopoulos, A. T. ([1938] 1962), *Versuch einer Genealogie der Palaiologen, 1259–1453*, Amsterdam: A. M. Hakkert.
Petrucci, A. (1992), *Breve storia della scrittura latina*, Roma: Bagatto Libri.
Pohl, W (2010), 'Popolazioni, etnie, popoli', *Mundus. Rivista di didattica della storia*, 5–6: 94–100.
Poisson, O. (2004), 'La cittadella di Carcassonne e il suo restauro nel XIX secolo', in E. Castelnuovo and G. Sergi (eds.), *Arti e storia nel Medioevo*, IV, *Il Medioevo al passato e al presente*, 537–45, Torino: Einaudi.
Porciani, I. (2004), 'L'invenzione del Medioevo', in E. Castelnuovo and G. Sergi (eds.), *Arti e storia nel Medioevo*, IV, *Il Medioevo al passato e al presente*, 253–79, Torino: Einaudi.
Provero, L. (2010), 'Un potere senza delega', *Mundus. Rivista di didattica della storia*, 5–6: 107–12.
Raedts, P. (2002), 'Representations of the Middle Ages in Enlightenment Historiography', *The Medieval History Journal*, 5: 1–20.
Rao, R. (2010), 'Le comunità rurali fra mito e realtà', *Mundus. Rivista di didattica della storia*, 5–6: 135–41.
Ronchey, S. (2002), *Lo Stato bizantino*, Torino: Einaudi.
Savelyev, Y. R. (2005), «*Византийский стиль» в архитектуре России. Вторая половина XIX — начало XX века*, Санкт-Петербург: Лики России, Проект-2003.
Savvides, A. G. K. (2009), *Ιστορία της αυτοκρατορίας των μεγάλων Κομνηνών της Τραπεζούντας (1204–1461)*, Θεσσαλονίκη: Αδελφών Κυριακίδη.
Schein, E. H. (2004), *DEC is Dead, Long Live DEC: The Lasting Legacy of Digital Equipment Corporation*, San Francisco, CA: Berrett-Koehler Publishers.

Sergi, G. (2002), 'La rilettura odierna della società medievale: i miti sopravvissuti', in *Medioevo reale Medioevo immaginario. Confronti e percorsi culturali tra regioni d'Europa*, 89–98, Torino: Città di Torino (Atti del convegno, Torino, 26 e 27 maggio 2000).

Sergi, G. (2005), *L'idea di medioevo: fra storia e senso comune*, Roma: Donzelli.

Sergi, G. (2010), 'Il Medioevo: un introduzione', *Mundus. Rivista di didattica della storia*, 5–6: 92–93.

Sergi, G. (2016), *Soglie del medioevo. Le grandi questioni, i grandi maestri*, Roma: Donzelli.

Soria Molina, D. (2013), 'Cataphracti y clibanarii (y III). La caballería pesada del ejército romano-bizantino, de Justiniano a Alejo Comneno', *Aquila Legionis*, 16: 75–123.

'The Great Videogame Swindle?' (1996), *Next Generation*, 23: 64–68, 211–29.

Vallerani, M. (2004), 'Il comune come mito politico. Immagini e modelli tra Otto e Novecento', in E. Castelnuovo and G. Sergi (eds.), *Arti e storia nel Medioevo*, IV, *Il Medioevo al passato e al presente*, 187–206, Torino: Einaudi.

Varzos, K. (1984), *Η γενεαλογία των Κωμνηνών*, 2 vols, Θεσσαλονίκη: Κέντρον Βυζαντινών Ερευνών (Βυζαντινά κείμενα και μελέται, 20/α-β).

Yarnley, C. J. (1972), 'Philaretos: Armenian Bandit or Byzantine General', *Revue des études arméniennes*, 9: 331–53.

Zachariadou, E. A. (1979), 'Trebizond and the Turks (1352–1402)', *Αρχείον Πόντου*, 35: 333–58.

Zakythinos, D. A. ([1932] 1975), *Le despotat grec de la Morée*, 2 vols, London: Variorum.

8

From History to Propaganda and Back: Byzantium in the Romanian Historical Cinema

Florin Leonte

For nearly two decades, from the mid-1960s until the early 1980s, Romanian cinema produced over a dozen movies that treated historical events occurring in the distant past, either in antiquity or in the Middle Ages.[1] These events centred on local rulers and characters and reflected what the official ideology of Romania's socialist regime (1947–89) perceived as key elements of its statehood. In particular, during these decades, the idea of a nation born in a hostile environment dominated by political superpowers like the Romans,[2] the Ottomans or the Russians captured the imagination of historians and artists alike.[2]

One historical period that drew the attention of film producers was the time spanning the fifteenth and the sixteenth centuries when the two medieval Romanian principalities of Moldavia and Wallachia attempted to oppose the growing influence of the Ottoman Empire in the Balkans with varying degrees of success (Housley 2013: 30–42). While for several decades, the two provinces sporadically attained political autonomy, for most of the time they remained in a state of vassalage to the Ottomans. The foreign kingdoms of Hungary or Poland also intervened in local politics by supporting those leaders who answered their regional commercial or military interests (Cristea and Pilat 2017: 71, 222). Yet, since during this period a series of documented successful military campaigns temporarily kept the Ottomans at bay, south of Danube, the political events of this time remained in popular culture a crucial period in the formation of the Romanian ethnic identity. Subsequently, from the second half of the nineteenth century and during the twentieth century (Boia 2001: 113–52), several rulers of the two principalities who led the anti-Ottoman campaigns began to be portrayed as national heroes who shaped decisively the Romanian ethnic identity (Eagles 2014).

Two personalities of the Romanian Middle Ages received particular attention in Romanian historiography as well as in many forms of popular culture like cinema: Stephen III of Moldavia (ruler of Moldavia between 1457–1504), also known as Stephen the Great (Ștefan cel Mare) and Vlad III Drăculea (1456–62, ruler of Wallachia) also known as Vlad the Impaler (Vlad Țepeș) (Papacostea 1990). The former, Stephen, proved successful in juggling the regional interests of the kingdoms of Hungary and Poland and in preventing the Ottoman Empire's expansion in the region in a series of armed conflicts (Pilat 2013: 171–79). The latter, Vlad, followed a similar pattern of diplomatic action combined with successful military action (Cazacu 2017: 79–134). Although eventually the two principalities lost their autonomy, both princes remained in the collective memory in the two principalities as defenders of their provinces' independence and strategists who, despite the lack of resources, were able to outperform large armies (Cazacu 2017: 135–63). Information on the rule of these two princes comes from Western sources (especially diplomatic documents), several later local chronicles and also the fifteenth-century Byzantine chronicles of Doukas, Kritoboulos of Imbros, and Laonikos Chalkokondyles who provide lengthy accounts of the situation in the Danubian principalities and of their relations with the Ottomans. Recent research has corroborated these sources with other textual evidence and progress has been made in discerning facts and legendary accounts as, for instance, in the accounts of Vlad's rule. If Chalkokondyles provided a balanced account of the Wallachian-Ottoman relations under Vlad's rule (especially the feud with his brother, Radu the Fair), several later German chronicles featured the image of a prince with ruthless methods of fighting (among which the most famous was impalement) against both his internal and the external enemies.[3] Regardless of the legends concerning their feats of arms or their cruelty, both princes' activities indicate the tendency to strengthen the principalities' statehood, a process perceivable in the later Middle Ages in other geographical areas as well (Gorovei 1997).

Such events and personalities have provided material not only for scientific research but also for popular literature and representations. Two movies titled after the two rulers were produced in the 1970s: *Ștefan cel Mare: Vaslui 1475* (Stephen the Great, 1975, directed by Mircea Drăgan) and *Vlad Țepeș* (Vlad the Impaler, 1979, directed by Doru Năstase) (Colăcel 2018: 99–109). A third movie produced in the same decade, *Frații Jderi* (The Jder Brothers, 1974, directed by Mircea Drăgan), dealt with the same period and historical characters (Colăcel 2018: 110–12). It was inspired by a long novel published in the 1930s by the prolific Romanian writer Mihail Sadoveanu (1880–1961) (Sadoveanu 2003). In contrast with the screenplay of the two other movies, the novel's plot had more depth and complexity as it explored the intricate biographies of the members of a Moldavian family loyal to Stephen the Great. All three movies included clear ideological markers especially in the long speeches delivered by the characters who, unsurprisingly, addressed issues that were also pressing at the time of the movies' production, in particular independence from foreign influence and intervention.[4]

In this way, the three movies can be connected with a set of cultural-ideological principles implemented in Romania in the 1970s (Deletant 1995: 72–103). This contrasted with the situation in the late 1960s when the communist regime practised a rather loose form of censorship and even allowed for certain levels of social criticism, as reflected in the movies with historical characters which also focused on the activities of legendary national heroes: *Haiducii* (1966), *Neamul Șoimăreștilor* (1965) and *Tudor* (1963) (Colăcel 2018: 32–50). In the ensuing decade, which coincided with an increase of authoritarianism, popular artistic representations became heavily geared towards the official state ideology. Recent historiography has argued that the so-called *Tezele din iulie* (July Theses), a programme intended to reinforce the socialist regime's ideology, radically changed the artistic and intellectual landscape (Deletant 1995: 82). One of the outcomes of this programme was that the state propaganda began to produce a variety of artistic materials (literature, cinema, music, exhibitions, song competitions and public celebrations) that were intended to generate a narrative of continuity between the first peoples inhabiting the provinces north of Danube and the ideological principles of the socialist regime. During the 1970s, school textbooks and other public representations carefully pictured the two above-mentioned rulers, Stephen and Vlad, as visionaries who foresaw a glorious national future which was to be fulfilled later (Boia 2001: 219). In addition to the theme of independence, the key element of this narrative was the idea of an ethnically homogeneous state. This ideology, dubbed national-communism, became visible in most areas of intellectual life as well as for much of the historiography produced in this decade which involved research into matters pertaining to the formation of Romanian identity (Boia 2001: 221).

Because of the potential large audiences, these movies were supervised at the highest political level and were designed in accordance with the officially accepted aesthetics and contents. Censorship committees were in constant alert to track down all public manifestations contrary to the agenda of the political regime. As a result, all aspects of the filmmaking (plot, characters, dialogues, setting) were carefully scrutinized. Among these, references to Byzantine history, closely related to the time and place of the movies, also found a place. In this chapter, I will look at these three movies' content and context in order to understand how they treated Byzantine realities and how they approached events occurring in the post-Byzantine world.

The movies

In line with their ideological commitments, all three movies show linearity of plot and schematism that avoids in-depth insights, ambiguities or character development.[5] In *Ştefan cel Mare* the initial focus is on Moldavia's archenemy, Mehmed II, the conqueror of Byzantine Constantinople, whose plans for the full conquest of the Balkans and Southern Europe are unveiled. Because of the Ottomans' plans to advance in Europe, Mehmed decides to subdue Moldavia for good. Yet, Stephen refuses to pay the heavy tribute to the sultan who gathers a huge army and crosses the Danube. In preparation for the confrontation with the Ottomans, Stephen attempts to forge an alliance with the Western kingdoms but fails, a situation which avails him the opportunity to present himself as a lonely David against Goliath. The movie repeatedly makes this representation clear. Despite his scarcity of resources, Stephen resorts to various military stratagems like poisoning the wells, looting the villages or skirmishes; eventually, he draws the Ottoman armies into a swamp where he easily defeats them, since they became unable to make use of their famous cannons. Mehmed, the once-mighty conqueror of Constantinople, concedes defeat and accepts the prince's superior military capacity. In the epilogue, the Moldavian voivode addresses the armies at the commemoration of the battle in a heavily patriotic speech that prophesizes the future glory of the locals.

The second movie, *Vlad Țepeș*, has several interweaving storylines: one about Vlad's fight against the Ottomans, one about relations with the Western states and another about internal conflicts with the boyars (the local landowners). It debuted with Vlad III's first day of rule in 1456 and continued with several successful attempts to stop the interference of the neighbouring kingdom of Hungary which had just repelled the Ottomans in the Balkans. Having returned to his homeland, Wallachia, and having been enthroned as the successor of Vlad Dracul, Vlad III chastises the old boyars for their previous acts of treason and corruption and makes bold promises for complete justice. He also promises the independence of the province from both the Hungarian kingdom and the Ottoman Empire. Vlad accuses the boyars gathered at his court of treason and eventually impales them mercilessly with the aim of providing a model of good behaviour. The movie continues with Vlad's last three years of rule during which he succeeds in his efforts to discipline the population and to bring justice in the country. However, after he punishes the Ottoman delegates asking for the yearly tribute, he triggers Mehmed's wrath, who then decides to invade the principality. Having defeated the Ottomans, he is nevertheless betrayed by the boyars allied with the Hungarian king, Matthias Corvinus, and spends his final years in prison in Budapest.

The third movie, *Frații Jderi*, remains focused on a similar idea of the enlightened ruler who rises to political power. The main character is a young man, Ionuț Jder, who helps Stephen III to oppose a plot against his family which eventually leads to the formation of a substantial local army that could confront the Ottomans. Although the movie also includes a romance involving the youth, it is predicated upon similar conflicts between, on the one hand, the ruler supported by the lower classes of free peasants and, on the other, the Ottomans and the treacherous boyars.

Cinematic Byzantium

Despite the linearity of their plots, the movies strive to provide a realistic picture of the historical events they reference. The influence of contemporary historical movies is easy to detect in techniques like long wide-angle shots already in use in other movies with historical themes. Judging by the technical standards of 1970s Romanian cinema, it appears that the producers put considerable effort into accurately representing many of the details used in the construction of their overt ideological message. Such attempts to ensure historical accuracy is reflected, inter alia, in the multiple references to Byzantium as an inherited set of cultural, social and political practices.

In all three movies, these references surface with a high frequency. This should not come as a surprise, especially due to the fact that historically, after the fall of Constantinople in 1453, the rulers of the Romanian principalities sought to fashion themselves as legitimate continuators of the Byzantine political and spiritual traditions. Evidence for this strategy is abundant: lavish donations to Athonite monasteries, works of art and architecture as well as the appropriation of Byzantine court traditions (in terms of hierarchy, legal terminology or dressing) indicated the rulers' adherence to Byzantine practices and ideological framework (Negrău 2011; Pippidi 2001). This process was conceptualized in the notion of *Byzance après Byzance* (Byzantium after Byzantium), introduced by the Romanian historian Nicolae Iorga in a monograph published in the beginning of the twentieth century (Iorga 1935).[6] He was the first to systematically analyse how Byzantine political ideology survived in the actions of the Moldavian and Wallachian rulers. Iorga argued in favour of the deep and long-lasting Byzantine influence on the political, cultural and religious development of the two Romanian principalities, Moldavia and Wallachia. His research covered the period between the years after the fall of Constantinople, when many Byzantines took refuge in the Balkans, and the nineteenth century. The permanence of Byzantine forms, in Iorga's view, helped to formulate a framework for the study of the history of the Balkans in general and of the Romanian principalities in particular (Georgescu 1980: 7–29). Indeed, his perspective modelled a number of later studies concerned with the idea of national identity which tended to incorporate Byzantine political ideas into the regional aspirations of autonomy (Negrău 2011).

The movies embed several kinds of references to Byzantium. In most cases, they represent a little more than mere allusions. Mehmed's own enumeration of personal titles (*Ştefan cel Mare*) reflects the Byzantine imperial rhetoric, as he proclaims his universal hegemony exerted from Constantinople, the city which he presents as standing in between East and West. The sultan often presents himself as the Conqueror of Constantinople and, conversely, the Moldavians and Wallachians are fighting to restore the former glory of Byzantium and eventually Constantinople. Yet, apart from such occasional allusions, the three movies included more systematic references in three key areas: the chronology of events, the setting of many episodes and the construction of characters.

First, the movies hold a marked chronological link with Byzantine history. Their events occurred in the immediate aftermath of the fall of Constantinople in 1453, an event with which they were tightly connected. The memory of Byzantium's final demise is frequently evoked as a key event in the development of the plot and it becomes the canvas upon which the rulers' actions unfold. In all three movies, the fall of Constantinople triggers the advancement of Mehmed's forces north of Danube and the Ottoman conquests. Echoes of this event surface in the Ottoman court debates. According to the narrative developed, the defeat of Byzantium was connected with the military campaigns in the Balkans and both actions constituted necessary steps in fulfilling the grand plan of controlling the entire Christendom in East and West. Mehmed, the conqueror of Constantinople, thus appears in all the movies to develop a full-fledged discourse of *translatio imperii*.

The second category of Byzantine references pertains to the physical setting of the cinematic representations. Most conspicuously, when shifting focus towards the Ottoman camp, the movies provide glimpses into the cityscape of Constantinople in the first years after 1453. Thereby they establish a connection between the dominant space of the movie (the Danubian principalities) and the Byzantine space, and between the Byzantine past and the present. Thus, although under complete Ottoman control, the image of Byzantine Constantinople still lurks in the background of several events. *Vlad Țepeș* echoes the Wallachian ruler's imprisonment in Constantinople by Mehmed, who had supported his brother, Radu cel Frumos (Radu the Fair, 1437–75), for the throne of Wallachia (Cazacu 2017: 156–60).[7] In *Ștefan cel Mare* the sultan's palace in Constantinople appears in the very beginning and features several lavishly decorated halls.

Furthermore, despite the movies' focus on military campaigns, many locations are set indoors within the precincts of the princely courts of Stephen (Suceava), Vlad (Târgoviște) and Mehmet II (Constantinople). In these instances, Byzantine court customs and practices find constant evocation: the rulers appear surrounded by high-ranking courtiers while in the dialogues the emphasis is on their titles and positions inspired by the Byzantine fashion, e.g. *logofăt* (equivalent to the Byzantine *logothetes*) or *spătar* (equivalent to the Byzantine spatharios) (Gorovei 2005: 41–49). The movies often zoom into the court life and present a picture of feeble corrupt courtiers and, with rare exceptions, of loyal boyars.

By contrast, both Stephen and Vlad embody the ideal of the powerful and virtuous ruler which resembled the model of the Byzantine *basileus*. All three movies draw extensively on the relations between ruler and courtiers as they open with court scenes during which the former make important decisions. In *Frații Jderi*, Stephen appears in the first year of his rule presiding over one of the first councils taking place at Neamț Monastery. In *Ștefan cel Mare*, the same Stephen vigorously objects to the Ottoman ambassadors' requests in front of the approving courtiers. In a similar vein, *Vlad Țepeș* begins with a scene in the court hall during the very first day of Vlad's reign when he announces his intentions of establishing justice. He uses the boyars' titles and also appoints other boyars in administrative positions which echo the Byzantine hierarchy.[8] Later on, in a show of authority, he dismisses his courtiers and promises revenge.

The Byzantine court milieu is also reproduced in the representation of Mehmed's retinue. In *Ștefan cel Mare*, the sultan is portrayed surrounded by his courtiers in his Constantinopolitan palace. Mehmed debates with his close advisors the necessity to initiate the construction of a new court residence that would better reflect the sultan's ambitions. The change clearly points to the attempts of delimiting himself from the previous Byzantine customs. The image of the Byzantine court is also reinforced by the presence of several Italian personalities: Constanzo da Ferrara, the artist, who offers Mehmed the gift of a medallion from the King of Naples; Girolama Zorzi, the Venetian ambassador in Constantinople; and Benedetto Dei, the Florentine chronicler and traveller into the Middle East.[9] In their speeches, the Italian guests echo the Byzantine legacy and the connections between Western and Eastern Christianity.

The portrayal of Stephen and Vlad as rulers with Byzantine traits can further be detected in their relations with the common people and the church. The narratives repeatedly indicate that it was the local peasants who supported both Stephen and

Vlad. Stephen (*Frații Jderi*) offers to the locals who participated in military campaigns a *chrysobull* (i.e. *hrisov*, Romanian) of land property, an echo of the Byzantine institution of *pronoia*.[10] On the other hand, the church largely held a low position in these movies. In this case, the suggestion was that rulers had conflicts with the provinces' metropolitans who instead supported the boyars (mainly local landowners). Once again, the parallel with the late Byzantine conflicts between emperors and church becomes clear in the direct dialogues between metropolitans and rulers which also echo the concerns of the time vis-à-vis decision-making processes.

However, the three movies also add spiritual and political nuances predicated on Byzantine models. Both Stephen and Vlad emerge as protectors of Christianity whose demands for help are rejected by the Western courts from Poland to Italy. The presentation of Stephen the Great holds prophetic tones. In *Frații Jderi*, right in front of him, monk Nicodim quotes a prophecy from the book of the Revelation:

Apoi am văzut cerul deschis și iată că s-a arătat un cal alb! Cel ce sta pe el se cheamă „Cel credincios" și „Cel adevărat" și El judecă și Se luptă cu dreptate. Ochii Lui erau ca para focului; capul îl avea încununat cu multe cununi împărătești.

[I saw heaven standing open and there before me was a white horse, whose rider is called Faithful and True. With justice he judges and wages war. His eyes are like blazing fire, and on his head are many crowns. He has a name written on him that no one knows but he himself.]

(Revelation 19:11–12)

Nicodim then proceeds to explain to Stephen that the time has arrived for him to impersonate the rider on the white horse, the rider who will destroy the Beast, that is, the Ottomans.

A similar instance with apocalyptic undertones surfaces in *Vlad Țepeș* as the ruler tries to convince a priest, who defended the boyars, of the necessity to take harsh measures against them:

Dacă nici după aceasta nu Mă veți asculta și veți păși împotriva Mea. Atunci și Eu cu mânie voi veni asupra voastră și vă voi pedepsi înșeptit pentru păcatele voastre.

[If in spite of this you still do not listen to me but continue to be hostile toward me, then in my anger I will be hostile toward you, and I myself will punish you for your sins seven times over.]

(Leviticus 26:27–28)

Not only do the rulers encapsulate Byzantine traits but also several other characters maintain connections with the Byzantine world. In *Ștefan cel Mare*, Mara Branković, the daughter of Eirene Kantakouzene and mother of Mehmed II, suggests to her son her willingness to mediate an agreement between the Christians and Muslims.[11] Many of the sultan's ambassadors and counsellors featuring in the movies are of Byzantine Greek origin. Even if several of them converted to Islam, the sultan often reminds them of their Byzantine and Christian origin which might have posed a threat to his plans (*Ștefan cel Mare*). Most prominently, the former Byzantine official George Amiroutzes plays the part of the sultan's close counsellor and teacher of history (*Ștefan cel Mare*).[12] He is portrayed as a skilled Greek scholar from Trebizond, mentor of David Komnenos, the last Trapezuntine emperor, and interested in history and natural sciences. However, his personality held a certain ambiguity in tune with the Byzantine and post-Byzantine sources which evaluated his actions as a betrayal of the Byzantine cause. In a long dialogue with the sultan, Amiroutzes presents to the sultan the plans of the citadel of Suceava, the voivode's residence. Then he gives further history lessons in which he outlines the Moldavian past, as if from a Byzantine perspective.

Another prominent character with Byzantine origins, Thomas Katavolinos, features in *Vlad Țepeș*. As late medieval sources suggest, Katavolinos was the sultan's secretary and a member of a wealthy Byzantine family.[13] In the movie, he plays the part of an Ottoman legate with the task of collecting information on the Wallachians' strategies. When Vlad confronts him with regard to his allegiance for the Ottomans, Katavolinos admits that he has Byzantine Greek origins to which he was still attached. Thus, the presence of both Amiroutzes and Katavolinos indicate that the movies adopted an ambiguous portrayal of the Byzantine individuals portrayed as easily shifting their allegiances but also as powerful, influential and potentially helpful.

The sources of Byzantine references

All these references pertaining to the chronology of events, setting and characters reveal that even if not a central feature in the two movies, the appeal to Byzantine realities emerges as a means of emphasizing the movies' reality effects. Arguably, Byzantinism helped to frame a worldview in tune with the official ideology of the time. Particularly attractive was the idea of state sovereignty which pointed to Romania's situation in the 1970s when isolationist policies had grown strong. One can also identify the theme of the popular political leader, another attempt to justify the authoritarian tendencies of that period; the same leader is presented as an influential power broker not only in home affairs but also abroad where he tries to find diplomatic solutions. Doubtless, this image reflected other ambitions of the regime during the complicated political games of the last decades of the Cold War. Thus, within this ideological framework, Byzantium is represented as a distant political entity whose features and history are subtly integrated at most levels of the movies (gestures, setting, language, official titles, plot) in order to give birth to a realistic message with nationalistic undertones.

Nevertheless, even if a plethora of studies focusing on the Romanian cinema during the socialist regime emphasized the connection between filmmakers and the political apparatus, one should resist the temptation of overestimating contemporary political influences. The origins of these forms of Byzantinism in the historical movies of the 1970s can also be identified elsewhere in previous sources. First and foremost, arguably, the films were aligned with a mythology that began to take shape in the nineteenth century during the initial stages of the process of nation-building (Boia 2001: 30-72). We can also notice that in contrast to the nineteenth-century patriotic narrative that romanticized certain national heroes, the movies produced by socialist propaganda attempted to reach a higher level of historical accuracy and made better use of the available historical information. If Byzantine representations remained scarce in the nineteenth century, when Iorga's monograph was published in 1935 Byzantium gained a firm place in Romanian historiography as well as in popular culture. Sadoveanu's novel *Frații Jderi*, which inspired the movie, was published immediately after *Byzance après Byzance*, and is a witness to the phenomenon of the growing interest in the Byzantine world as it includes similar Byzantine references to events, setting and characters.

Furthermore, there is continuity not only with the uses of Byzantine realities and representations developed in the interwar period (1919-39) but also with renewed interest in the late Byzantine history in the decades preceding the production of movies. In the late 1950s and 1960s the fifteenth-century Byzantine chronicles of Georgios Sphrantzes, Doukas, Kritoboulos of Imbros and Laonikos Chalkokondyles were translated into Romanian.[14] The translator of the four Byzantine narratives, Vasile Grecu, a Byzantinist with a long career that had begun before the instauration of the communist regime, added introductory studies in which he argued for the importance of Byzantine textual sources in the study of Romanian history. The four translations inaugurated the new series, *Scriptores Byzantini* of the Academy of the People's Republic of Romania, by that time a highly politicized institution that backed the ideological commitments of the new regime (Vasile 2011). While maintaining academic standards, the introductory studies and the structuring of these translations insisted on the information relevant to the local history of the fifteenth century. Especially in the translation of Laonikos Chalkokondyles's *Histories*, the most detailed Byzantine account of the Romanian principalities in the fifteenth century, Grecu underlines the evidence connected to the narrative of the Wallachian and Moldavian princes (Grecu, 'Introduction', *Laonikos Chalkokondyles* 1958: 19-22). The link between the translations and the movies is striking especially in terms of the emphasis on the foreign relations of Moldavia and Wallachia with the Ottomans and the Byzantines, as well as in terms of the archaizing language preferred by the translators.

Thus, to conclude, the representation of Byzantine realities in Romanian historical cinema suggests that filmmakers used Byzantium not only as a canvas for ideological messages but also as a means to capitalize on previous perspectives of the Byzantine world. The movies display continuity between interwar approaches to Byzantium and the later representations typical for the Cold War regime and ideology. Iorga's appealing concept of *Byzance après Byzance* proved that it had a long-lasting influence in both the study of Romanian medieval history as well as in the popular imagination about the Romanian Middle Ages. In this way, for the film producers, cinematic Byzantium served as a symbolic bridge connecting the distant past, present and future as envisaged in the political climate of the mid-1970s.

Notes

1. In the recent decades, the growing interest in the art and propaganda of the socialist regimes during the Cold War has produced a number of substantial monographs. See Colăcel (2018) and Imre (2012).
2. A chronological and also thematic analysis of all the uses of history in the propaganda of Romania's communist regime can be found in Boia (2001). Cf. Eagles (2014).
3. On the development of late medieval and early modern German and Hungarian legends about Vlad in the light of historical facts, see Cazacu (2017: 164–247).
4. As a matter of fact, the opening credits of the movie *Ștefan cel Mare* include a quote from the then president Nicolae Ceaușescu's political writing that points precisely to such matters.
5. Even contemporary film criticism has remarked on the rather poor construction of the movies' plots and characters. See Căliman (2017: 200–04).
6. Although his theory was met with some criticisms, Iorga's merit in recognizing the Byzantium's dynamic role in forging the political identity of the Danubian principalities can hardly be overestimated.
7. Cf. Laonikos Chalkokondyles, *Histories*, 2.9.82–2.9.108 (transl. A. Kaldellis).
8. For the Byzantine influence on the court titles in the Romanian principalities, see Gorovei (2005: 41–60).
9. This representation of Mehmed as a patron of arts and admirer of Italian Renaissance art echoed certainly the reality. See Raby (1982).
10. Indeed practices resembling the Byzantine *pronoia* were widespread in Moldavia and Wallachia; Georgescu (1980: 67).
11. On Mara Branković and her political involvement in the post-Byzantine world, see Popović (2010).
12. On George Amiroutzes in general, see *PLP* 784. On his political career in Mehmed's service, see Greene (2015: 28–29).
13. On Thomas Katavolinos as the sultan's secretary, see Greene (2015: 35–41).
14. All four of these translations were published within a short space of time: Laonikos Chalkokondyles (1958, tranls. V. Grecu), Michael Kritoboulos (1963, tranls. V. Grecu), Georgios Sphrantzes (1966, tranls. V. Grecu) and Ducas (1958, tranls. V. Grecu).

Bibliography

Boia, L. (2001), *History and Myth in Romanian Consciousness*, Budapest: CEU Press.
Căliman, C. (2017), *Istoria filmului românesc: (1897–2017)*, Bucharest: Contemporanul.
Cazacu, M. (2017), *Dracula*, Leiden: Brill.
Colăcel, O. (2018), *The Romanian Cinema of Nationalism: Historical Films as Propaganda and Spectacle*, Jefferson, NC: McFarland.
Cristea, O. and L. Pilat, (2017), *The Ottoman Threat and Crusading on the Eastern Border of Christendom during the 15th Century*, Leiden: Brill.
Deletant, D. (1995), *Ceaușescu and the Securitate: Coercion and Dissent in Romania, 1965–1989*, London: M.E. Sharpe.
Ducas (1958), *Istoria Turco-Bizantina (1341–1462)*, transl. Vasile Grecu, Bucharest: Editura Academiei Republicii Populare Române.

Eagles, J. (2014), *Stephen the Great and Balkan Nationalism: Moldova and Eastern European History*, London: I.B. Tauris.
Frații Jderi (1974), [Film] Dir. Mircea Drăgan, Romania.
Georgescu, V. (1980), *Bizanțul și instituțiile românești pînă la mijlocul secolului al XVIII-lea*, Bucharest: Editura Academiei Republicii Socialiste România.
Georgios Sphrantzes (1966), *Memorii*, ed. and transl. Vasile Grecu, Bucharest: Editura Academiei Republicii Socialiste România.
Gorovei, Ș. (1997), *Întemeierea Moldovei. Probleme controversate*, Iași: Editura Universității Al. I. Cuza.
Gorovei, Ș. (2005), 'Titlurile lui Ștefan cel Mare. Tradiție diplomatică și vocabular politic,' *Studii și Materiale de Istorie Medie*, 23: 41–78.
Greene, M. (2015), *Edinburgh History of the Greeks, 1453 to 1768: The Ottoman Empire*, Edinburgh: Edinburgh University Press.
Housley, N. (2013), *Crusading and the Ottoman Threat, 1453–1505*, Oxford: Oxford University Press.
Imre, A. (2012), 'The Socialist Historical Film', in S. Ponzanesi and M. Waller (eds.), *Postcolonial Cinema Studies*, 78–95, New York: Routledge.
Iorga, N. (1935), *Byzance après Byzance*, Bucharest: Institut d'études byzantines.
Kritoboulos (1963), *Critobul din Imbros: Din domnia lui Mahomed al II-lea, anni 1451–1467*, transl. Vasile Grecu, Bucharest: Editura Academiei Republicii Populare Romîne.
Laonikos Chalcocondyles (1958), *Expuneri istorice*, transl. Vasile Grecu, Bucharest: Editura Academiei Republicii Populare Române.
Laonikos Chalkokondyles (2014), *The Histories*, ed. and transl. Anthony Kaldellis, Cambridge, MA: Harvard University Press.
Negrău, E. (2011), *Cultul suveranului sud-est european șI cazul Țării Românești: o perspectivă artistică*, Iași: Lumen.
Papacostea, Ș. (1990), *Ștefan cel Mare domn al Moldovei (1457–1504)*, Bucharest: Editura Enciclopedică.
Pilat, L. (2013), 'Between Ottoman Empire and Latin Christendom: Moldavia as Frontier Society in the Late Middle Ages', in G. Karman and Radu G. Păun (eds.), *Europe and the 'Ottoman World': Exchanges and Conflicts (Sixteenth to Seventeenth)*, 171–93, Istanbul: The Isis Press.
Pippidi, A. (2001), *Tradiția politică bizantină în Țările Române în secolele XVI–XVIII*, Bucharest: Editura Academiei Române.
Popović, M. (2010), *Mara Branković: eine Frau zwischen dem christlichen und dem islamischen Kulturkreis im 15. Jahrhundert*, Wiesbaden: Harrassowitz.
Raby, J. (1982), 'A Sultan of Paradox: Mehmet the Conqueror as a Patron of Arts,' *Oxford Art Journal*, 5: 3–8.
Sadoveanu, M. (2003), *Frații Jderi*, București: Gramar.
Ștefan cel Mare: Vaslui 1475 (1975), [Film] Dir. Mircea Drăgan, Romania.
Trapp, E., ed. (1976–2001), *Prosopographisches Lexikon Der Palaiologenzeit*, Vienna: Verlag der Österreichischen Akademie der Wissenschaften.
Vasile, C. (2011), *Politicile culturale comuniste in timpul regimului Gheorghiu-Dej*, Bucharest: Humanitas.
Vlad Țepeș (1979), [Film] Dir. Doru Năstase, Romania.

9

Imagination of Byzantium and the Byzantines in Modern Turkish Popular Literature and Cinema

Buket Kitapçı Bayrı

Books always speak of other books, and every story tells a story that has already been told.

(Umberto Eco 1983: xxiv)

Byzantium emerged as a central theme in the political discourse on Turkey in the 2000s. On 14 November 2004, French president Jacques Chirac, in support of Turkey's accession to the European Union, said, 'Nous sommes tous des enfants de Byzance' (We are all the children of Byzantium). His comment was not well received in certain French and Turkish media at the time (Atal 2004; *Spiritualité chrétienne* 2004). The negotiations for full Turkish membership in the European Union started in 2005, but internal opposition to Turkey's full membership in the EU, coupled with the slow accession process, stalled accession negotiations in 2016. Interestingly, as Turkey moved away from the European Union, there were more and more negative references to Byzantium in Turkish political discourse, including in the media close to Turkey's ruling party.

On 26 February 2014, newspapers and social media in Turkey circulated an image of a student from Middle Eastern Technical University wearing a 'Byzantine costume' while protesting the construction of a boulevard, Malazgirt 1071 (Manzikert 1071), being built through a wooded area of the campus (*En Son Haber* 2014). Some in the media called the student a 'leftover Byzantine'. The 'costume' in question was a helmet identical to the ones worn by the Byzantine characters in Turkish superhero films of the 1970s. The same media connected this incident to a message graffitied on a wall in Kadıköy during the Gezi protests in September 2013 (Yanık 2015; Dağtaş 2016), which became the subject of heated debate. It read 'Zulüm 1453'te başladı' (Oppression started in 1453) (*En Son Haber* 2013).

The battle of Manzikert occurred in year 1071, fought between Byzantine and Seljukid forces, and in 1453 the Ottomans conquered Byzantine Constantinople – two events of particular significance in recent Turkish public memory. What do these two acts – the graffiti and the Byzantine helmet – signify? What is the source of these historical imaginations? Why and how did Byzantium become a topic in political debate in Turkey in recent years?

160   *Byzantium in the Popular Imagination*

Figure 9.1 Cover photo of Abdullah Ziya Kozanoğlu, *Battal Gazi Destanı* (1946). Public domain.

Film, television and literature as cultural forms of history and memory are influential in creating and sustaining historical imaginations (De Groot 2008, 2010). As scholars on the reception of Byzantium in Europe have stated, however, the important work of the Byzantinists, the true battle for Byzantium, has not been fought in university classrooms, but in popular works, such as the novels and plays influencing popular imagination about the event (Marciniak and Smythe 2016: 5–6). In Turkey, the historical imagination surrounding Byzantium and the Byzantines has been shaped through popular 'historical' novels, comic series and superhero films, but there have been very few studies analysing these sources with respect to Byzantine representation in popular culture (Özcan 2011; Bayrı 2013a, 2013b, 2013c; Canko 2019a, 2019b). This chapter aims to fill that gap, dealing thoroughly with the popular historical novels from the early republican era and the 1970s-era Turkish movies, connected by the names of Ahmet Ziya Kozanoğlu and Battal Ghazi, while giving a short prospect of the forthcoming years.

Novels and films featuring Battal Ghazi as a protagonist have been selected to narrow the scope of analysis, given the substantial amount of source material available. In addition, the existence of a fifteenth-century medieval epic on Battal Ghazi, the *Battalname*, provides the perfect starting point (Grégoire 1936; Canard 1937; Dedes 1996; Yürekli 2012; Bayrı 2019a, 2020). Analysing variations of stories featuring the same hero, but written in different historical periods, helps illustrate how and why the content of the hero's character and its meaning change over time, in relation to shifting political, social and ideological contexts. Such stories also create a sense of 'consciousness and being', perceived as being consistent over time (Köksal 1984).

This chapter[1] examines the representation of Byzantium and the Byzantines in Abdullah Kozanoğlu's novels in general, and in his *Battal Gazi Destanı* (The Legend of Battal Ghazi) in particular. It concludes with an examination of movies on Battal Ghazi produced in the 1970s, and of films making social commentary on the legend in the 1980s. Through these stories, one discerns how Byzantium and the Byzantines are defined, as the political, ideological, social and cultural contexts change – and how, by the 1990s, in the modern Turkish popular imagination, the terms 'Byzantium' and 'Byzantines' had come to be metonymies for 'Westernized cosmopolitan', i.e. 'rich, urban and degenerate' Istanbul, and of Istanbouliotes with Westernized lifestyles. 'Western', in this respect, also connotes Christian or non-Muslim.

The Byzantines in popular historical novels of the early Turkish Republic: Kozanoğlu's *Battal Gazi Destanı* as a case study

The oral roots of the *Battalname* may be traced as far back as the arrival of the Danishmendid Turks in Malatya (Melitene) in the twelfth century (Dedes 1996, 1: 1–3). The Turkish newcomers, especially the leaders of the Danishmendid dynasty that controlled Malatya for the better part of the twelfth century, took an interest in local Muslim legends and associated themselves with local heroes, thus creating continuity with the Muslim Arab past (Dedes 1996, 1: 9–10). In the fifteenth century, the stories of Battal Ghazi/Seyyid Battal, the pseudo-historical Arab Muslim warrior within the historical context of the Arab confrontation with Byzantium during the ninth and tenth centuries, were recorded in written form, under the patronage of the Ottoman frontier lords (Yürekli 2012: 77–78).

In the *Battalname*, Battal Ghazi is an Arab warrior who serves the emir of Malatya/Melitene. He is an urban-based (Malatya) peripatetic warrior in the epic, who belongs to a group variously described as soldiers of Islam, Muslims, Mohammedans and as ghazis, soldiers taking part in raids against the infidels. The Battal Ghazi of the late medieval epic remains contextualized largely within the Abbasid-Byzantine frontier zone of the ninth and tenth centuries. His forays into Rum/Romanland (i.e. Byzantium) are extremely limited, because Byzantium's strong defences make it difficult to enter. His activities, apart from his incursions at Amorion and Constantinople, take place around the frontier zone, not far from Malatya – or, usually, in places fantastically far afield. In the Ottoman Empire, the janissaries and the frontier lords especially cherished the memory of Battal Ghazi and his medieval epic.

Historical novels have played an important role in the formation of national historical conscious (Wesseling 1991; Price 1999; Slotkin 2005; Eriksonas 2008: 117–32; Rigney 2008). One can perceive a similar process during the transmission of the stories of Battal Ghazi into the popular historical novels and films of the twentieth century. While the stories and the hero changed character and content in relation with the historiography and discourse surrounding the prevailing national narratives, they simultaneously shaped the national conscious, especially among the young male population.

Byzantium and its history entered into the Ottoman non-Muslim and Muslim master narratives, which centre on questions related to imperial and national identities, especially after the Ottoman Noble Edict of the Rose Chamber in 1838/39 (Eksertzoglou 2004; Kılıç-Yıldız 2013, 2014; Çelik 2016).[2] Late Ottoman Muslim historians incorporated Byzantine history into their general histories, particularly comparing the Byzantine Empire with the Ottoman Empire in order to reveal the successes of the latter (Ursinus 1986, 1988). In relation to this growing interest in the Byzantine Empire, as early as 1918/1919, courses on Byzantine history were offered in the Darülfünûn Faculty of Literature in Istanbul (Yusuf Behçet 1920). Within this political and ideological environment, Turkish popular history books on Byzantium were written, and as early as 1912, historical novels were translated into Turkish by Ottoman Muslim intellectuals (Altınay [1912] 1328; Lombard 1913).

In 1926, the Turkish republican regime, set on elevating the Turkish element of nationalism, deemphasized the country's Islamic character to embrace an outwardly secularist ideology, and to demonstrate its commitment to modernity, in an attempt to break away from the image of the disastrous years of the late Ottoman Empire. History and archaeology played an important role in the creation of the Turkish nation-state. A radical process of rewriting history to position the Turkish nation at the centre of civilization got under way in the 1930s, largely as an attempt to create a rich, ancient and historically legitimated origin for the Turkish nation. Earlier Anatolian civilizations were embraced and the recent Ottoman and Islamic past were downplayed in the official historical narratives (Ersanlı 2006).

The same period also witnessed a boom in the production of historical novels (Sertelli 1930, 1930a; Sam 1946; Sertoğlu 1950, 1955, 1956, 1960, 1967, 1968, 1970, 1971). Abdullah Ziya Kozanoğlu (1906–66) emerged as one of the most popular historical novelists of the period, producing books that would be reprinted many times until the 1970s and revived in the 2000s (Kozanoğlu 1929, 1944a, 1944b, 1946, 1952, 1964, 1965; Demiray 1954; Özcan 2013) (Figure 9.1). His *Battal Gazi Destanı* (1929, rep. 1946, rep. 1965) closely relates to the radical process of rewriting history to position the Turkish nation at the centre of civilization, especially after the 1930s, when popular history books and historical novels were perceived as utilitarian tools for social engineering and the education of young (and particularly the male) generations, in accordance with the ideologies of the newly founded nation-state (Hutcheon 1989; Çeri 2000; Türkeş 2001/2002, 2002; Argunşah 2002; Parla 2006; Uygun 2014). Eighteenth- and nineteenth-century Western scholars' harsh judgement of Byzantine civilization prevail in Kozanoğlu's novels (Ursinus 1986; Millas 2000, 2006; Belge 2008; Kılıç-Yıldız 2014). According to this judgement, Byzantium had an authoritarian political system and a culture permeated by blind religious belief. Presenting the Ottoman Empire as the continuation of the Byzantine Empire, a theory introduced by 'orientalist' Western scholars such as Gibbon and Diehl, found acceptance in Kozanoğlu's historical novels as a useful way to downgrade the Ottoman and Islamic past, and to break from it.

The early republican historical novels, including those by Kozanoğlu, targeted young male readers. Such novels are characterized by adventure, heroism and the construction of masculinity within a relatively conservative nationalistic narrative (De Groot 2010: 78–88). Byzantium and the Byzantines exist to edify the heroic adventures of the 'Turkish' heroes. For instance, Kozanoğlu's *Arena Kraliçesi* (The Queen of the Hippodrome) is about the adventures of a Uyghur Turk, Caberhan, who comes to Constantinople in 532, before the Nika Revolt, and has an affair with Theodora (d. 548), the wife of the Byzantine emperor, Justinian the Great (527–565). Caberhan successfully ends the rebellion, and while doing so makes every effort not to hurt the common Byzantines (Kozanoğlu 1964).

The stories in *Savcı Bey* (Savcı Beg) also take place in Byzantine Constantinople. The novel centres on the adventures of the Ottoman prince Savcı Bey (d. 1385?), eldest son of the Ottoman sultan Murad I (1362–89) and his friendship with the Byzantine prince John V Palaiologos (1341–76; 1379–90; 1390–91), son of the Byzantine Emperor Andronikos IV (1376–79). Savcı Bey dies at the hands of the cruel Ottoman sultan, Bayezid I (1389–1402) (Kozanoğlu 1944a). The action of *Sarı Benizli Adam* (Yellow-Complexioned Man) is set amid the Ottoman Interregnum Period (1402–13) in Byzantine Constantinople, and concerns the adventures of one of the sons of Bayezid I, Prince Mustafa (1421–22), who is wrongly accused of being a false prince, Düzme Mustafa (Kozanoğlu 1944b). *Fatih Feneri* (Lantern of the Conqueror) is about Orhan, the so-called son of Düzme Mustafa, who lives in Byzantine Constantinople and helps Mehmed II (1451–81) conquer Constantinople (Kozanoğlu 1952).

The Battal Ghazi of Kozanoğlu's *Battal Gazi Destanı* is no longer an Arab warrior, as in the medieval *Battalname*, but a Turkish hero from Malatya (Kozanoğlu 1929, 1946, 1965). His adventures now take place only in Constantinople, and not along the Abbasid-Byzantine frontier of the ninth and tenth centuries, nor in Malatya. He arrives in Constantinople during the reign of Byzantine Emperor Leo V, the Armenian (813–820), to rescue his fellow townsman, the Amir of Malatya, from the Byzantine dungeons. While in Constantinople, he leads the people in a rebellion against the cruel Byzantine emperor and helps Mişel Löpeg (Michael II, 820–829) seize the throne. In this novel, Battal Ghazi is the charming Turkish hero of the Turkish people, who had been living in Anatolia even during the Byzantine Empire. He is courageous, righteous, revolutionary and anti-monarchical. He defends not only the poor, oppressed Turks in Anatolia but also the Byzantines against their cruel rulers. He is also quite secular.

Byzantium

Kozanoğlu reveals what he understands about the Byzantine Empire in *Battal Gazi Destanı*. Although it has been argued by some scholars that what distinguishes history writing from historical novel is the referential aspect of the former genre (Rigney 2001), Kozanoğlu uses his referential technique and authority to give an air of truth to his stories, citing various primary and secondary historical sources. At the beginning of his novels, for example, he cites each of the following: a nineteenth-century lithographic print of the *Battalname*, Arseven's *Eski İstanbul* (Arseven ([1912] 1328), Vasiliev's *Histoire de l'empire byzantine* (Vasiliev 1932), Rambaud's *Études sur l'histoire byzantine* (Rambaud 1912) and finally, Diehl's *Figures byzantines* (Diehl 1906/08), *Histoire de l' empire byzantine* (Diehl 1919), *Byzance: grandeur et décadence* (Diehl 1919; Kozanoğlu 1965: 4).

Kozanoğlu's novels are constructed around the idea that the Ottoman Empire was the continuation of the Byzantine Empire, and hence should be deemed unworthy, except for certain of its glorious periods, which remained exempt from Byzantine influence. Kozanoğlu states that the Ottoman Empire was the 'New Byzantium'. He develops this idea, drawing a general outline of how he perceives the two empires. For Kozanoğlu, the Ottoman sultans, whom he had seen, by nature, as good, just and pure, were sullied by Byzantine traditions, and by the city of Constantinople – or by Byzantine women (Kozanoğlu 1964: 36–37; 1965: 8–9, my translation):

> The Byzantine Empire, which was founded in 300, included many ethnic groups, such as Rums, Armenians, Latins and Turks. In 1453 when Mehmed II conquered Constantinople, the only change that occurred was the Turkish dynasty replacing the Byzantine one. The same Byzantine spirit of enslaving others, and of worshipping a single man, continued to live in the Ottoman Empire. The new Byzantine rulers, the rulers of Rum (i.e. the Ottoman rulers) spoke Turkish, prayed in Arabic, wrote poetry in Persian, made love in the Rum language and swore in Armenian. The Rum, Armenian, Persian and Albanian slaves bowed before the sultan as if he were God, and kissed the floor. The Turkish nation, which did not bow before the sultan, retreated to Anatolia.

Within the context of the new Turkish nation-state ideology, Kozanoğlu finds the most obvious faults in both the Byzantine and Ottoman Empires in the forms of their multiethnic character, their multilingualism and their method of governance: absolute monarchy. Similar disapproving attitudes toward the multiethnicism, multilingualism and cosmopolitism of the Byzantine Empire are easily perceived in Kozanoğlu's other novels related to Byzantium. In *Arena Kıraliçesi*, the Byzantine empress is depicted as a dancer; the Byzantine emperor is an Armenian peasant; the organizer of games at the hippodrome is an Athenian beggar and a champion of the games is a Venetian porter from Galata; and finally, the patriarch is an apprentice butcher (Kozanoğlu 1944a: 71–72; 1964: 82–83). After learning all this, the protagonist, the Turkish Caberhan, 'becomes disgusted by the immoral and disrespectful Byzantium' (Kozanoğlu 1964: 84).

Kozanoğlu also introduces a new, secular understanding of religion, and shares his wish for a new faith that unifies all religions. In this belief system, there would be no priests, imams or rabbis, and no churches, monasteries, mosques, lodges or synagogues. Faith and belief in God would be a private and individual affair. Praying five times a day and fasting would not be necessary, as reciting God's name and feeling his presence in one's heart would be enough to be considered a good Muslim. The consumption of wine 'in moderation' would be permissible. Byzantium was evil because, according to Kozanoğlu, it represented the Dark Ages, when the Byzantine church and the Byzantine emperors exploited religion (Kozanoğlu 1965: 80).

Constantinople

All of Kozanoğlu's novels related to Byzantium are set in Istanbul (i.e. Constantinople), and the city is painted as perfidious (*kahpe*). This negative impression was already visible in some of the late nineteenth-century Ottoman historiography, as was the idea of the corruption of the Ottomans by Byzantine immorality, institutions and practices – all of which eventually led to the collapse of the Ottoman Empire (Mehmed Murad 1325–32 [1909–16]; Celal Nuri [1912–13] 1331; Ursinus 1988: 312–13; Kılıç-Yıldız 2014: 1–2). In addition, this narrative can be read alongside the 'downgraded' status of Istanbul with the founding of the republic, and in conjunction with the elevation of Ankara, which became the capital and the symbol of the new, modernizing regime. Hence, Istanbul/Constantinople, the capital of the decadent Byzantine and Ottoman Empires, is personified in the novels as perfidious at every turn, including its characterization of Byzantine women. In the novels, the names of residential areas of Istanbul are given in Turkish and in Greek, possible reminders of the city's tainted Byzantine and Ottoman pasts. Istanbul is depicted as a city in which water has no colour, the roads are slippery and strangers mate on every corner. It is a city populated by people from some seventy-two nations. Laskaridis (Lascarid), Düzme Mustafa's friend, and the guardian of the Anemas dungeons, prophesized that 'the Turks, by conquering Istanbul, would mix with the Byzantines and get used to the Byzantine slavishness, perfidy and treachery and that they would become as lazy, lame, foul, sycophantic and ostentatious as the Byzantines. To turn Turks into Byzantines would be Byzantines' most delicious revenge against the Turks' (Kozanoğlu 1965: 163–64).

Byzantine women

In Kozanoğlu's novels, one of the central themes is the Turkish quest for women. The Rum women of Byzantium are the objects of the Turkish heroes' desire, and they partner in love affairs with many: Battal Ghazi with Elenora, the daughter of the true Byzantine emperor, Mişel Löpeg; Caberhan with Theodora, soon to become empress; Savcı Bey with İrini Kantakuzinos (Eirene Kantakouzene? (d. 1457)), the granddaughter of Vasileas Kantakuzinos (John VI Kantakouzenos? (1347–54); and Düzme Mustafa with Aleksandra, a Rum servant in the Byzantine palace. Most of these affairs end in marriage, but Turkish flings with other Rum women, who frequently owned taverns in

Galata, are also recounted, with rather titillating descriptions (Kozanoğlu 1944b: 14, 45, 76; 1964: 23–25, 41–43).

The Rum women are always passionate about the Turkish men, and the Turkish men likewise passionate about Rum women (Kozanoğlu 1944b: 76); yet passion is not a good thing, according to Kozanoğlu. Hence, one should be wary of the climate and the women of Istanbul (Kozanoğlu 1964: 41–43). Although in the medieval *Battalname*, Battal Ghazi is polygamous and most of the time marries Byzantine women (the emperor's daughters), the protagonist's tone is not demeaning toward his female conquests. In Kozanoğlu's novels, however, while the male heroes are monogamous, the book's tone is misogynistic in its descriptions of women, as are the heroes' approaches to those women. Like the city of Istanbul, symbolizing Byzantium, the Byzantine women are presented as perfidious, unstable and moody.

Superhero films of the 1970s, Byzantium and the Byzantines

After the death of Mustafa Kemal Atatürk in 1938, and especially during the 1950s, Islam began to re-enter mainstream culture, and during this time the Democrat Party (DP) endeavoured to promote Islam as a way to siphon political support away from the Republican People's Party (CHP). The reincorporation of Islam into the national identity accompanied Turkey's integration into the Western world, economic liberalization and urbanization. The secularist policies of previous decades were relaxed, and Islam became more prominent in the everyday life of cities, in part due to the import of culture from the countryside, which accompanied large-scale migration from rural areas. Although the DP promoted Islam to gain political support against the CHP, the dominant ideology of the early Turkish Republic was not overthrown, but rather competed with – and sometimes pragmatically overlapped with – the re-introduction of Islam into the national identity. The DP promoted Islam to gain political support in the country, but it also led a pro-Western policy at the beginning of its rule. Turkey joined NATO in 1952. Upon Turkey's alliance with NATO, relations with Greece began to improve.

In this decade, the Ottomans and their 470-year-old capital became central to the state's politics of culture and identity (Altınyıldız 2007: 295–305). Kozanoğlu's *Fatih Feneri* was published in 1951, in the wake of the celebrations for the 500th anniversary of the conquest of Constantinople; Aydın Arakon's *İstanbul'un Fethi*, the first Turkish film related to Byzantium, was shot and produced in 1951, as part of the same preparations. Byzantium remained part of the political and cultural narratives, due to their emphasis placed on Istanbul and its conquest – and also due to the country's improving relations with the West, and especially with Greece. In 1953, with the selection of Istanbul as the venue of the Xth International Congress of Byzantine Studies (occurring in 1955), the prospect of the arrival of many international scholars to Istanbul (and from their wider travels in Turkey), acted as a powerful impetus for the restoration and repair of Byzantine monuments in Istanbul (Bayrı 2019b).

The 1960s were a period of change worldwide, including in Turkey, with leftist ideologies and youth movements gaining momentum. One finds traces of all these phenomena in the 1970s superhero movies, which borrowed most of their heroes from the popular historical novels of the late Ottoman Empire and the early republican period (Scognamillo 1998a, 1998b; Scognamillo and Demirhan 1999; Ginsberg and Lippard 2010: 518–23; Arslan 2011). Turkish films related to Byzantium from the 1950s into the 2000s can be grouped into three categories: 1) 'historical' films and TV series, which claim to be historically accurate, and were sometimes produced with the input of a historian such as *İstanbul'un Fethi* (1951); 2) superhero films of the 1960s and 1970s; and 3) parodies of these same superhero movies in 2000s.

The 1960s and 1970s were crisis years for Turkish cinema, in terms of quality. Out of 1,100 movies produced between 1970 and 1975, fifteen of them were low-budget superhero/fantasy films with a Byzantine theme (Scognamillo 1998b). In superhero films of the 1960s and 1970s, in addition to Battal Ghazi, other heroes were based on historical figures, including Malkoçoğlu, and new heroes emerged, such as Kara Murat (*Fatih'in Fedaisi Kara Murat* 1972) and Tarkan (*Tarkan* 1969; Tellan 2016: 243–58).[3] With the exception of Tarkan, all of them were played by the same actor, Cüneyt Arkın (d. 2022). In fact, except for their names, all the heroes resemble each other, in terms of props, settings and values, which the filmmakers try to pass on to their audience.

Battal Gazi Destanı (1971), directed by Atıf Yılmaz, contains elements from both the medieval epic *Battalname* and one of Kozanoğlu's novels, *Battal Gazi Destanı*. The opening scene of the film is similar to the *Battalname*. The Byzantines refuse to pay tribute to the Amir of Malatya, and kill Hüseyin Ghazi, Battal's father, prompting the son to seek vengeance against the fourteen Byzantine lords responsible for his father's death. However, the story diverges from the *Battalname*, with Battal meeting the Byzantine princess Elenora, with whom he falls in love. One day Elenora, disguised as a warrior, sets out to visit Battal in the forest, but is waylaid by henchmen of the Byzantine emperor on her way to meet him.

Battal flees from the Byzantine soldiers and hides out at the Monastery of the Forty Virgins, which actually turns out to be a brothel. There Battal meets Hammer (Ahmer of the *Battalname*), who is with Faustina, the most famous harlot of Anatolia. Hammer and Battal decide to wrestle in front of Faustina, to show her which one of them is stronger. Whoever loses must convert to the religion of the other. Hammer loses, converts to Islam, and the two bestow nicknames on each other. The wrestling scene and the loser's conversion originate in the *Battalname*. Battal and Hammer become brothers in arms, and together set off for Istanbul, disguised as monks, to rescue Elenora.

In Istanbul, the Byzantines catch Battal and torture him. A group of beggars living underground in the cisterns rescues him. It so happens that their leader is in fact the legitimate Byzantine emperor, and Elenora's father. Doctors at the underground palace of the beggar king help Battal recover from his torture wounds. Battal then rescues Elenora from the clutches of the wicked, imposter Byzantine emperor, toppling him and handing the crown to the beggar king, the legitimate emperor. The hero marries Elenora, who converts to Islam and becomes Ayşe Sultan.

Portions of the film about the beggar king, and its depictions of Byzantine women as harlots, are borrowed from Kozanoğlu, as is the setting of Istanbul. Scenes were filmed on location at the Rumeli fortress, the Church of Myrelaion Monastery, Chora

Church, the underground cisterns, the aqueducts and at the kiosk in the garden of the Istanbul Archaeological Museums. In these films, one can discern from the crosses on the Byzantine clothes and palaces that they are Christians. They are also rich and cruel, not only to the Muslim Turks, but to their fellow Christians as well. While the Byzantines come across as perfidious, cowardly and treacherous, Battal Ghazi – similar to Kozanoğlu's depiction in the novel – is the Turkish hero, the champion and saviour of the poor, the honest and the oppressed: Muslim Turks and Byzantines alike. All of the Turks in the film have rural backgrounds, either as peasants or as nomads. The Battal of the film is monogamous, like Kozanoğlu's character, but unlike his portrayal in the *Battalname*.

The other three movies on Battal Ghazi – *Battal Gazi'nin İntikamı* (1972) (The revenge of Battal Ghazi), *Savulun Battal Gazi Geliyor* (1973) (Get out of the way! Battal Ghazi is coming) and *Battal Gazi'nin Oğlu* (1974) (The son of Battal Ghazi) – have little to do with the medieval *Battalname* or with Kozanoğlu's novels. Rather, they have similarities with Murat Sertoğlu's historical novels on Battal Ghazi (Sertoğlu 1967, 1968, 1970). In Sertoğlu's novels, especially *Battal Gazi*, Islam and Islamic history are more pertinent than in Kozanoğlu's works. In these movies, a militaristic, Byzantine order of Black Knights seeks to conquer Anatolia and to convert its people to Christianity. References to the motherland, the flag and 'martyrs dying in the name of the motherland' are tossed around. Battal Ghazi, the hero of the oppressed, rural poor in Kozanoğlu's novel and Atıf Yılmaz's film, here becomes a national hero who defends the motherland against the Christian knights. The films have an odd mix of episodes, borrowing from the such stories as the infant Moses being hidden in his Nile basket, and from the Arthurian legend of Excalibur. Fantastic figures, such as pirates, also make appearances.

The common theme in all of these films is the confrontation between poor, rural and nomadic Turkish Muslim Battal and the urban, rich Christian Byzantines. The conflict between Rums and Muslims in the *Battalname* is taken from its original frontier environment and transported to the historic city of Istanbul. The shifting loyalties and mutual influences between the Byzantines and the Muslims, such as in *Battalname*, are left out of the films. The Roman identity of the Byzantines is disregarded, in favour of their depiction as oppressive occupiers of historic Istanbul, with Battal Ghazi appearing as a Turkish version of Robin Hood.

In the 1970s, few Turkish films addressed the country's social and economic problems. In the 1980s, however, more such movies were made, typically looking at the social, cultural and economic problems of provincial migrants into the cities. Of interest here, Istanbul stood in for 'the city', and is painted in the vein of Byzantium in the films from the 1960s and 1970s. To the protagonists, arriving from their Anatolian villages and towns in search of jobs and a better life, Istanbul is the city of their fantasies, with streets paved with gold (*taşı toprağı altın İstanbul*), but it is also cruel, Westernized, and immoral compared to the conservative values widely held in the provinces (Güçhan 1992: 112–14, 128).

In 1980s films, the newcomers to the city appear to identify with Battal Ghazi, and with the other superheroes of those 1970s films, as well as with the rural Turks. As soon as the provincials arrive in the city, they challenge its cultural fabric, similar to

Battal Ghazi confronting the Byzantines. They proclaim that they will conquer this cruel, rich city, *kahpe* Istanbul, and become its ruler ('Allah'ın izniyle şah olacağız İstanbul'a şah!'). The representation of Istanbul as rich, cruel and immoral, a place to be 'conquered' by the provincials, has led to the term *Byzantium* taking on new, symbolic, social and economic meanings today. The city of Istanbul is associated with a contrived, 'historical' Byzantium, and its 'wealthy, Westernized, immoral, cruel, and snobbish inhabitants' are conflated with the similarly characterized Byzantines.

Byzantium in the popular imagination, 1990s and 2000s

Beginning in the 1980s, neo-nationalism gained momentum in Europe, in the face of fears of a European super-state transcending the nation-state. During this same period, Eastern European countries, where the Byzantine legacy has left a huge footprint, began emerging from the ideological grip of the defunct Soviet Union, leading to the revival of national narratives (Jenkins and Sofos 1996; Angelov 2003: 3–23). Similar trends can be traced in the Turkish history of the period. Turkish governments from the 1980s onward developed close relations with the West, and a liberalized economy, while accelerating the pace of neo-nationalist Islamic movements in the country (Çakır 1990). Close relations with the West, and the concurrent rise in Islamic sensibility in politics, are reminiscent of the Turkish situation in 1950s. By the end of 1990s, Turkey had experienced the rise of political Islam, and with it, the introduction of neo-Ottomanism and an 'Islamist' politics of culture. This development set the stage for a battle between Islamists and Kemalist secularists for control of the national narrative.

There was a general interest in history during the 1980s, and the Ottoman archives were opened to the public. In Turkish academia, Byzantine studies continued to gain ground in 1990s (Necipoğlu 1999, 2013). Along with a general interest in history, a new boom in historical novels set in a 'Byzantine' storyworld took hold (Gürsel 1995; Coral 1998; Çıracıoğlu 1999; İleri 2007; Altun 2011; Uğur 2013; Ergin and Karakaya 2017). Starting from the late 1990s, historical films and TV series became quite popular, some of them featuring Byzantium. In the 2000s, this trend accelerated (*Kuşatma Altında Aşk* 1997; *Hacivat Karagöz Neden Öldürüldü?* 2006; *Fetih 1453* 2012; *Fatih'in Fedaisi Kara Murat* 2015; *Diriliş: Ertuğrul* 2014–19; *Kuruluş Osman* 2019–21). Select historical events, among them the conquest of Constantinople, were re-edified in populist political discourses and in popular culture (Kara 2007, 2012; Brockett 2014). TV series and movies, some of them financially supported and promoted by the ruling Justice and Development Party (AKP), were embraced as alternatives to the 'morally degenerate cultural products' of the 'Westernist/Kemalist' cultural elites (Özçetin 2019).

The assertion that 'oppression started in 1453', mentioned at the beginning of this chapter, challenges a master national narrative shared by most of the political and ideological stances in Turkey, and is traceable to the late Ottoman Empire. As shown here, the narrative has been used as a trope in popular works, including historical novels and films, asserting that the 'Turks' brought justice, equality and prosperity to the Byzantine territories and people, saving them from the oppressive emperors in Constantinople. In the 2010s, the popularity of these films – featuring the Turkish heroes fighting against the Byzantines – reflected in the aforementioned 'Byzantine helmet' worn by the student from Middle Eastern Technical University. These 1970s films borrowed most of their heroes from the early republican-era historical novels, which in return were popular among youth of the era. As noted, these novels were republished many times.

Although the superhero films were not intended to be funny, they evolved into 'cult comedies' by the end of 1990s, due to such production errors (goofs) as actors wearing wristwatches or planes flying in the background. Such lines and catchphrases as 'kahpe Bizans' ('perfidious Byzantium') and 'savulun, Battal Ghazi geliyor' ('get out of the way, Battal Ghazi is coming') as well as the kitschy costumes, were appropriated as comic elements in contemporary caricatures, social media and graffiti in the 1990s and 2000s. In addition, at least two parodies were filmed satirizing the superhero genre and its atmosphere (*Kahpe Bizans* 1999; *Bizans Oyunları: Geym of Bizans* 2016).

Conclusion

In the medieval epic *Battalname*, Byzantium is defined as the Rum (Romanland, Land of Rome), which is under the direct control of the Byzantine emperor who ruled at Constantinople. It came to symbolize twentieth-century Istanbul in the historical novels of the early republican era, as well as in superhero films of the 1960s and 1970s. Friendly but infidel Rums (Romans) in the medieval *Battalname* become perfidious, cruel, rich and immoral multiethnic people in the early Turkish republican novels; in the film adaptations, the Byzantines are the urban Istanbouliotes depicted as perfidious, snobbish, rich and Westernized. The Arab, urban Muslims of the *Battalname* become peasant or nomadic Turks from Anatolia, and Battal Ghazi himself, the Arab warrior of the ninth and tenth centuries, emerges as a Turkish hero in the early republican novels, battling decadent empires. In the films, the poor, rural Turks – as well as the Byzantines – are oppressed by the cruel, rich and Christian Istanbouliote Byzantines. In 1980s films dealing with the social and economic problems of provincial migrants moving into urban areas, Istanbul epitomizes the big city, which is portrayed in the same vein as Byzantium in the superhero movies of the 1970s.

During the campaign for municipal elections in Istanbul held in March 1994, Recep Tayyip Erdoğan, the candidate of the Refah Partisi (RP or Welfare Party, AKP's precursor), declared that the one who 'catches' Istanbul would rule the whole of Turkey, and would be able to 'catch up' with the dynamism of the world powers. The RP compared the elections to the second conquest of Istanbul (Constantinople). They claimed that by reconquering Istanbul (i.e. by winning elections), they would dispatch the ones who had been willing to re-Byzantinize the city (Çakır 1994: 188–89). The politicians' language was reminiscent of the 1980s movies, in which the protagonists from rural backgrounds take on Istanbul, with the aim of 'conquering' the city.

The symbolic importance of the 'conquest of Constantinople' for the followers of RP in the 1990s can also be glimpsed in an incident from 1997. RP leader Necmettin Erbakan, after being forced to step down as prime minister in February due to pressure from the secular establishment, commemorated the 1453 conquest of Constantinople by Ottoman Sultan Mehmed II on 29 May 1997, touching down inside Istanbul's İnönü Stadium in a helicopter to meet his supporters. According to news reports, Erbakan, dressed in white, demanded that Hagia Sophia be restored to a mosque, and reminded his audience of none other than Mehmed II (*Milliyet* 1997: 1). Thus, to Erbakan's conqueror, the secular establishment and its supporters played the Byzantines.

Recep Tayyip Erdoğan, RP mayor of Istanbul from 1994 to 1998, went on to lead the AKP, founded in 2001, ruling Turkey as prime minister from 2003 to 2014, and again reigning over it as president since 2014. Of note, the second generation of provincial migrants to the cities has been an important part of the AKP's base, including in Istanbul, bringing to life the narrative of challenging Byzantium and the Byzantines, conquering their city and its Westernized, secular, urban and cruel inhabitants. RP, and later AKP, wove the reconquest of Constantinople into the narrative of their victories against political and cultural opponents. As Turkey moved away from the European Union – and with the Gezi event in 2013 – a narrative of symbolic conquest emerged, representing AKP as the party of the victorious 'Muslim Turks' against the 'Christian West', and as a powerful government within Turkey, arrayed against its political and cultural opponents. Afterwards, the injection of Byzantines and Byzantium as foils in the political discourse, on social media, and in TV series, films, cartoons and literature, became increasingly acute.

In this context, one incident of youthful graffiti during the Gezi protests, invoking 1453 as the beginning of twenty-first-century oppression, along with the incident of the student wearing a Byzantine helmet in 2014, can be considered as performative, postmodernist vehicles – challenging the homogenizing and 'othering' narratives. Any opposition to the government was represented as an enemy of the nation, and personified as 'Byzantine' in contemporary political discourse. The helmeted youth made fun of this representation by identifying himself as a so-called 'Byzantine'. These two acts, the graffiti and the Byzantine helmet, can be viewed as parodic aphorisms of 'historiographic metafiction', poking fun at the authority of mainstream political discourse, and at the dominant, national narratives.

Notes

1 For some of the subjects treated in this chapter, see also Bayrı (2013a, 2013b, 2013c).
2 Noble Edict of the Rose Chamber (Hatt-ı Şerif of Gülhane) called for the establishment of new institutions that would guarantee security of life, property and honour to all subjects of the empire regardless of their religion or race. The edict set forth many key provisions for the future reforms (1839–76), which were intended to effectuate a fundamental change of the empire from the old system to that of a modern state.

3   Tarkan is a fictive Central Asian Turkish hero who, along with his wolf, fights against Chinese and 'barbarian' rulers. The Kara Murat character was created by Rahmi Turan and drawn by Abdullah Turan. The newspaper *Günaydın* began carrying the Kara Murat comic strip in 1971, and for the ensuing eighteen years, from 1974 to 1992, it was published independently.

Bibliography

Altınay, A. R. ([1912] 1328), *Bizans İmparatoriçeleri*, Istanbul: Teshil-i Tıbahat Matbaası.
Altınyıldız, N. (2007), 'The Architectural Heritage of Istanbul and the Ideology of Preservation', *Muqarnas*, 24: 281–305.
Altun, S. (2011), *Bizans Sultanı*, Istanbul: Sel Yayıncılık.
Angelov, D. G. (2003), 'Byzantinism: The Imaginary and Real Heritage of Byzantium in Southeastern Europe', in D. Keridis, E. Elias-Bursac and N. Yatromanolakis (eds.), *New Approaches to Balkan Studies*, 3–23, Dulles, VA: Brassey's.
Argunşah, H. (2002), 'Tarihi Romanın Yükselişi', *Hece (Türk Romanı Özel Sayısı)*, 66–67 (July): 440–49.
Arseven, C. E. ([1912] 1328), *Eski İstanbul âbidat ve mebanisi. 1.cilt. Şehrin tesisinden Osmanlıların fethine kadar*, Istanbul: Matbaa-i Hayriye.
Arslan, S. (2011), *Cinema in Turkey: A New Critical History*, New York: Oxford University Press.
Atal, N. (2004), 'Bizans'ın içinden misiniz?', *Sabah*, 17 November. Available online: http://arsiv.sabah.com.tr/2004/11/17/siy102.html (accessed 19 January 2020).
Battal Gazi Destanı (1971), [Film] Dir. Atıf Yılmaz, TR: Uğur Film.
Battal Gazi'nin İntikamı (1972), [Film] Dir. Natuk Baytan, TR: Uğur Film.
Battal Gazi'nin Oğlu (1974), [Film] Dir. Natuk Baytan, TR: Uğur Film.
Bayrı, B. K (2013a), 'Contemporary Perception of Byzantium in Turkish Cinema: The Cross-examination of Battal Gazi Films with the *Battalname*', *Byzantine and Modern Greek Studies*, 37 (1): 81–91.
Bayrı, B. K. (2013b), 'Türkiye'de Popüler Kültürde Bizans Metaforu', *Toplumsal Tarih*, 232 (April): 77–83.
Bayrı, B. K. (2013c), 'Bizans Tahayyülünün Şekillenmesinde Abdullah Ziya Kozanoğlu Etkisi, Büyük Türk Romanları ve Bizans', *Toplumsal Tarih*, 229 (January): 91–93.
Bayrı, B. K. (2019a), '"Homo Byzantinus" in the Late Medieval Turkish Muslim Warrior Epics', *REB*, 77: 117–47.
Bayrı, B. K. (2019b), '10th International Congress of Byzantine Studies, Istanbul September 15–211955', *YILLIK: Annual of Istanbul Studies*, 1: 123–44.
Bayrı, B. K. (2020), *Warriors, Martyrs and Dervishes: Moving Frontiers, Shifting Identities in The Land of Rome (13th and 15th Centuries)*, Leiden: Brill.
Belge, M. (2008), *Genesis: 'Büyük Ulusal Anlatı' ve Türklerin Kökeni*, Istanbul: İletişim.
Bizans Oyunları: Geym of Bizans (2016), [Film] Dir. Gani Müjde, TR: Avşar Film, Tükenmez Kalem Film.
Brockett, G. D. (2014), 'When Ottomans Become Turks: Commemorating the Conquest of Constantinople and Its Contribution to World History', *American Historical Review*, 119 (2) (April): 399–433.
Canard, M. (1937), 'Delhemma, Sayyid Battal et Omar al-Noman', *Byzantion*, 12: 183–88.

Canko, D. Y. M. (2019a), 'Türk Edebiyatında Bizans İmparatoriçeleri ve Selim İleri'nin Hepsi Alev' Romanı', *RumeliDE Dil ve Edebiyat Araştırmaları Dergisi*, 16: 308–18.
Canko, D. Y. M. (2019b), 'Abdullah Ziya Kozanoğlu ve Murat Sertoğlu'nun Romanlarında Bizans Kadın Algısı', *International Journal of Interdisciplinary and Intercultural Art*, 4 (8) (September/October): 45–56.
Celal Nuri ([1912–13] 1331), *Tarihi-Tedenniyat-ı Osmaniye, Mukadderat-ı Tarihiye*, Istanbul: Yeni Osmanlı Matbaa ve Kütüphanesi.
Coral, M. (1998), *Bizans'ta Kayıp Zaman*, Istanbul: Milliyet Yayınları.
Çakır, R. (1990), *Ayet ve Slogan. Türkiye'de İslami Oluşumlar*, Istanbul: Metis.
Çakır, R. (1994), *Ne Şeriat, Ne Demokrasi: Refah Partisini Anlamak*, Istanbul: Metis.
Çelik, Z. (2016), *About Antiquities: Politics of Archaeology in the Ottoman Empire*, Austin: University of Texas Press.
Çeri, B. (2000), 'Cumhuriyet Romanında Osmanlı Tarihinin Kurgulanışı', *Tarih ve Toplum*, 198: 19–26.
Çıracıoğlu, V. (1999), *Kara Büyülü Uyku*, Istanbul: Can Yayınları.
Dağtaş, M. H. (2016), '"Down with Some Things!" The Politics of Humour and Humour as Politics in Turkey's Gezi Protests', *Etnofoor/Humour*, 28 (1): 11–34.
De Groot, J. (2008), *Consuming History*, London: Routledge.
De Groot, J. (2010), *The Historical Novel*, London and New York: Routledge.
Dedes, Y. (1996), *Battalname*, 2 vols, Cambridge, MA: Harvard University.
Demiray, K. (1954), *Türkçe Çocuk Edebiyatı*, Istanbul: MEB Yayınları.
Diehl, C. (1906/08), *Figures byzantines*, 2 vols, Paris: Armand Colin.
Diehl, C. (1919), *Histoire de l'empire byzantin*, Paris: Auguste Picard.
Diehl, C. (1919), *Byzance: grandeur et décadence*, Paris: E. Flammarion.
Diriliş: Ertuğrul (2014–19), [TV Series] Dir. Metin Günay, Akif Özkan, Hakan Arslan, TR: Tekden Film.
Eco, U. (1983), *Postscript to the Name of the Rose*, transl. W. Weaver, New York: Harcourt Brace Jovanovich.
Eksertzoglou, H. (2004), *Osmanlı'da Cemiyetler ve Rum Cemaati. Dersaadet Rum Cemiyet-i Edebiyesi*, transl. F. Benlisoy and S. Benlisoy, Istanbul: Tarih Vakfı Yurt Yayınları.
Ergin M. and Y. Karakaya (2017), 'Between Neo-Ottomanism and Ottomania: Navigating State-led and Popular Cultural Representations of the Past', *New Perspectives on Turkey*, 56: 33–59.
Eriksonas, L. (2008), 'Towards the Genre of Popular National History: Walter Scott after Waterloo', in S. Berger, L. Eriksonas, and A. Mycock (eds.), *Narrating the Nation: Representations in History, Media and the Arts*, 117–32, Oxford: Berghahn Books.
Ersanlı, B. (2006), *İktidar ve Tarih: Türkiye'de Resmi Tarih Tezinin Oluşumu, 1929–1937*, Istanbul: İletişim.
Fatih'in Fedaisi Kara Murat (1972), [Film] Dir. Natuk Baytan, TR: Erler Film.
Fatih'in Fedaisi Kara Murat (2015), [Film] Dir. Aytekin Birkon, TR: Es Yapım.
Fetih 1453 (2012), [Film] Dir. Faruk Aksoy, TR: Aksoy Film, Med Yapım.
Ginsberg, T. and C. Lippard, eds. (2010), *Historical Dictionary of Middle Eastern Cinema*, Toronto: Scarecrow Press.
Grégoire, H. (1936), 'Comment Sayyid Battal, martyr musulman du VIIIe siècle, est-il devenu, dans la légende, le contemporain d'Amer (d. 863)?', *Byzantion*, 11 (2): 571–75.
Güçhan, G. (1992), *Toplumsal Değişme ve Türk Sineması: Kente Göç Eden İnsanın Türk Sinemasında Değişen Profili*, Ankara: İmge Kitapevi.
Gürsel, N. (1995), *Boğazkesen/Fatih'in Romanı*, Istanbul: Can Yayınları.

Hacivat Karagöz neden öldürüldü? (2006), [Film] Dir. Ezel Akay, TR: İstisnai Filmler ve Reklamlar (IFR).
Hutcheon, L. (1989), 'Historiographic Metafiction: Parody and Intertextuality of History', in P. O'Donnell and R. C. Davis (eds.), *Intertextuality and Contemporary American Fiction*, 3–32, Baltimore, MD: Johns Hopkins University Press.
İleri, S. (2007), *Hepsi Alev*, Istanbul: Doğan Kitap.
İstanbul'un Fethi (1951), [Film] Dir. Aydın Arakon, TR: Atlas Film.
Jenkins, B. and S. A. Sofos, eds. (1996), *Nation and Identity in Contemporary Europe*, London: Routledge.
Kahpe Bizans (1999), [Film] Dir. Gani Müjde, TR: Arzu Film, Tükenmez Kalem Film, Özen Film.
Kara, H. (2007), 'The Literary Portrayal of Mehmed II in Turkish Historical Fiction', *New Perspectives on Turkey*, 36: 71–95.
Kara, H. (2012), *Osmanlı'nın Edebi Temsili: Tarihsel Romanda Fatih*, Istanbul: Hat.
Kılıç-Yıldız, Ş. (2013), 'Byzantium between "East" and "West": Perceptions and Architectural Historiography of the Byzantine Heritage', Ph.D. diss., Middle Eastern Technical University, Ankara.
Kılıç-Yıldız, Ş. (2014), 'Osmanlı'dan Cumhuriyet'e Entelektüellerin Gözüyle Bizans İstanbul'u', *Doğu Batı Dergisi*, 68: 103–26.
Korat, G. (2010), *Rüya Körü*, Istanbul: Yapı Kredi Yayınları.
Kozanoğlu, A. Z. (1929), *Seyyid Battal*, Istanbul: Türk Neşriyat Yurdu.
Kozanoğlu, A. Z. (1944a), *Bizans'ta Türk Şehzadeleri: Savcı Bey*, Istanbul: Türkiye Yayınevi.
Kozanoğlu, A. Z. (1944b), *Bizans'ta Türk Şehzadeleri: Sarı Benizli Adam*, Istanbul: Türkiye Yayınevi.
Kozanoğlu, A. Z. (1946), *Battal Gazi Destanı*, Istanbul: Türkiye Yayınevi.
Kozanoğlu, A. Z. (1952), *Fatih Feneri*, Istanbul: Türkiye Yayınevi.
Kozanoğlu, A. Z. (1964), *Arena Kraliçesi*, Istanbul: Atlas Kitabevi.
Kozanoğlu, A. Z. (1965), *Battal Gazi Destanı*, Istanbul: Atlas Kitabevi.
Köksal, H. (1984), *Battalnamelerde Tip ve Motif Yapısı*, Ankara: Kültür Bakanlığı.
Köprülü, M. F. (1931), 'Bizans Müesseselerinin Osmanlı Müesseselerine Tesiri Hakkında Bazı Mülahazalar', *Türk Hukuk ve İktisat Tarihi Mecmuası*, 1: 165–313.
Kuruluş Osman (2019–21), [TV Series] Dir. Fethi Bayram, Metin Günay, Ahmed Yılmaz, TR: Bozdağ Film, Tekden Film.
Kuşatma Altında Aşk (1997), [e] [Film] Dir. Ersin Pertan, TR: Sarmal A.Ş.
Lombard, J. (1913), *Bizans: Bizans İmparatorluğunun tarihine müstenid, Bizansın seyyiatını, safhat-ı ahlâkiye ve ruhiyesini hâki musavver romandır*, transl. Hasan Bedreddin, Istanbul: Mihran Matbaası.
Marciniak, P. and D. C. Smythe (2016), *The Reception of Byzantium in European Culture since 1500*, Farnham: Routledge.
Mehmed Murad ([1909–16] 1325–32), *Tarih-i Ebu'l Faruk*, 7 vols, Istanbul: Amedi Matbaası.
Milliyet (1997), May 30: 1.
Millas, H. (2000), *Türk Romanı ve 'Öteki': Ulusal Kimlikte Yunan İmajı*, Istanbul: Sabancı Üniversitesi.
Millas, H. (2006), 'The Image of the Greek Minority of Istanbul in Turkish Literature: Past and Recent Tendencies', in M. Kappler (ed.), *Intercultural Aspects in and around Turkic Literatures*, 69–82, Wiesbaden: Harrassowitz Verlag.

Necipoğlu, N. (1999), 'The Current State and Future Direction of Byzantine History in Turkey', in Ç. Kafescioğlu and L. Thys-Şenocak (eds.), *Aptullah Kuran İçin Yazılar/ Essays in Honour of Aptullah Kuran*, 37-41, Istanbul: Yapı Kredi Yayınları.
Necipoğlu, N. (2013), 'Türkiye'de Bizans Tarihi Çalışmalarına Dair Gözlemler', *Toplumsal Tarih*, 229 (January): 76-77.
Özcan, A. (2011), *Türkiye'de Popüler Tarihçilik (1908-1960)*, Ankara: Türk Tarih Kurumu.
Özcan, A. (2013), 'Abdullah Ziya Kozanoğlu'nun İlk Eserleri ve Yayımlanış Tarihleriyle İlgili Yanlışlar', *Kurgan* 3 (13) (May-June): 67-71.
Özçetin, B. (2019), '"The Show of the People" against the Cultural Elites: Populism, Media and Popular Culture in Turkey', *European Journal of Cultural Studies*, 22 (1): 1-16.
Parla, J. (2006), 'Türk Romanında Tarih ve Üstkurmaca', *Virgül*, 100 (October): 6-10.
Price, D. W. (1999), *History Made, History Imagined: Contemporary Literature, Poiesis and the Past*, Urbana and Chicago: University of Illinois Press.
Rambaud, A. (1912), *Études sur l'histoire byzantine. Préface et notes de Ch. Diehl*, Paris: Armand Colin.
Rigney, A. (2001), *Imperfect Histories: The Elusive Past and the Legacy of the Romantic Historicism*, Ithaca: Cornell University Press.
Rigney, A. (2008), 'Fiction as a Mediator in National Remembrance', in S. Berger, L. Eriksonas, and A. Mycock (eds.), *Narrating the Nation: Representations in History, Media and the Arts*, 79-96, Oxford: Berghahn Books.
Sam, K. (1946), *İmparatoriçe İren*, Istanbul: Gün Basımevi.
Savulun Battal Gazi Geliyor (1973), [Film] Dir. Natuk Baytan, TR: Uğur Film.
Scognamillo, G. (1998a), *Türk Sinema Tarihi, 1896-1997*, Istanbul: Kabalcı Yayınevi.
Scognamillo, G. (1998b), 'Türk Sinemasında Bizans Oyunları', *Sanat Dünyamız: Özel Bizans Sayısı*: 155-63.
Scognamillo G. and M. Demirhan (1999), *Fantastik Türk Sineması*, Istanbul: Kabalcı Yayınevi.
Sertelli, İ. F. (1930), *Bizansın Son Günleri*, Istanbul: Muallim Halit.
Sertelli, İ. F. (1930a), *İstanbul'u Nasıl Aldık*, Istanbul: Muallim Halit.
Sertoğlu, M. (1950), *Teodora'nın Ölümü*, Istanbul: Güven Yayınevi.
Sertoğlu, M. (1955), *Bizansın Aşk İlahesi İmparatoriçe Teodora*, Istanbul: Güven Yayınevi.
Sertoğlu, M. (1956), *Bizans Alevler İçinde*, Istanbul: Güven Yayınevi.
Sertoğlu, M. (1960), *Bizanslı Aspasya*, Istanbul: Aydın Yayınevi.
Sertoğlu, M. (1967), *Battal Gazi*, Istanbul: İtimat Kitabevi.
Sertoğlu, M. (1968), *Battal Gazi'nin Oğlu*, Istanbul: İtimat Kitabevi.
Sertoğlu, M. (1970), *Battal Gazi'nin Oğlu: Kanlı Takip*, Istanbul: İtimat Kitabevi.
Sertoğlu, M. (1971), *Battal Gazi'nin Torunu*, Istanbul: İtimat Kitabevi.
Slotkin, R. (2005), 'Fiction for the Purpose of History', *Rethinking History*, 9 (2): 221-36.
Tagmat, Ç. (2014), 'Fetih Derneği ve İstanbul'un Fethi'nin 500. Yılı', *Tarih, Kültür ve Sanat Araştırmaları Dergisi*, 3 (4) (December): 46-60.
Tarkan (1969), [Film] Dir. Tunç Başaran, TR: Arzu Film.
Tellan, B. (2016), 'Kara Murat: Çizgi Romandan Beyazperdeye bir Akıncının Sergüzeştleri', in H. Çolak, Z. Kocabıyıkoğlu Çeçen, and N. I. Demirakın (eds.), *Ayşegül Keskin Çolak'a Armağan: Tarih ve Edebiyat Yazıları*, 243-58, Ankara: Kebikeç.
Türkeş, Ö. (2001/02), 'Romana Yazılan Tarih', *Toplum ve Bilim*, 91: 166-212.
Türkeş, Ö. (2002), 'Güdük Bir Edebiyat Kanonu', in T. Bora and M. Gültegingil (eds.), *Modern Türkiye'de Siyasal Düşünce: Kemalizm*, vol. 2, 442-44, Istanbul: İletişim.
Uğur, V. (2013), *1980 Sonrası Türkiye'de Popüler Tarihi Roman*, Istanbul: Koç Üniversitesi Yayınları.

Ursinus, M. (1986), 'Byzantine History in Late Ottoman Turkish Historiography', *Byzantine and Modern Greek Studiesi*, 10 (1): 211–22.

Ursinus, M. (1988), 'From Süleyman Pasha to Mehmet Fuat Köprülü: Roman and Byzantine History in Late Ottoman Historiography', *Byzantine and Modern Greek Studies*, 12 (1): 305–14.

Uygun, İ. (2014), 'Cumhuriyet Dönemi Tarihi Romanları, 1923–1946: Eski Kahramanların Yeni Söylemleri', MA diss., Bilkent University, Ankara.

Vasiliev, A. A. (1932), *Histoire de l'Empire byzantin*, 2 vols, transl. P. Brodin and A. Bourguina, Paris: Auguste Picard.

Wesseling, E. (1991), *Writing History as a Prophet: Postmodernist Innovations of the Historical Novel*, Amsterdam: John Benjamins.

Yanık, L. K. (2015), 'Humour as Resistance? A Brief Analysis of the Gezi Park Protest Graffiti', in Isabel David and Kumru F. Toktamış (eds.), *Everywhere Taksim: Sowing the Seeds for a New Turkey at Gezi*, 153–83, Amsterdam: Amsterdam University Press.

Yeşim, R. Ş. (1964), *Bizanslı Beyaz Güvercin*, Istanbul: Türkiye Yayınevi.

Yusuf Behçet (1920), *Kurûn-ı Vustada Şark Akvâmı Tarihi. 1335–1336 Sene-i Tedrisiye Bizans Tarihi*, Istanbul: Darülfünûn Matbaası.

Yusuf Behçet (1925), *Kurûn-ı Vusta. Bizans Tarihi, 330–1056. 1341–1342 Senesi*, Istanbul: Edebiyat Fakültesi Tarih Zümresi Neşriyatı.

Yürekli, Z. (2012), *Architecture and Hagiography in the Ottoman Empire: The Politics of the Bektashi Shrines in the Classical Age*, Farnham: Ashgate.

Spiritualité chrétienne (2004), 'A propos de l'entrée de la Turquie dans l'Union Européenne', November. Available online: http://www.spiritualite-chretienne.com/actualite/turquie.html (accessed 19 January 2020).

En Son Haber (2014), 'ODTÜ'de yol protestosuna Bizans kıyafetiyle katıldı', 26 February. Available online: https://www.ensonhaber.com/odtude-yol-protestosuna-bizans-kiyafetiylekatildi-2014-02-26.html (accessed 22 March 2021).

En Son Haber (2013) 'Kadıköy'de Zulüm 1453'te başladı yazılaması', 15 September. Available online: https://www.ensonhaber.com/kadikoyde-zulum-1453te-basladi-yazilamasi-2013-09-15.html (accessed 22 March 2021).

10

Byzantium in Greek Cinema and Television

Konstantinos Chryssogelos

Greek cinema and television in context

Any study that attempts to outline the reception of Byzantium in Greek filmography, for both the big screen and television, including television series, should first take into consideration the development of Greek cinema over the years. As is the case with the filmic production of other countries, such as Germany and Brazil, scholars and film critics argue that there is a line separating post-war Old Greek Cinema (hereafter OGC) from New Greek Cinema (hereafter NGC), the latter emerging in 1970, with Theo Angelopoulos's *Reconstruction* (*Αναπαράσταση*) (Rafaïlidis 1970: 16; Karalis 2012: 143–45; Stassinopoulou 2015: 832) but also comprising a few earlier films from the 1950s and 1960s (Bakogiannopoulos 1999: 37–55; Kolovos 2002: 132, 142–45; Valoukos 2011: 37–42). Other scholars stress the artificiality of such a distinction, contending that continuity, rather than rupture, is the key to approaching Greek cinema as a whole (Chalkou 2008: 1–9; Stassinopoulou 2012: 139–40; Poupou 2013: 164). Be that as it may, the juxtaposition of OGC and NGC is a convenient methodological tool, especially for the synoptic character of the present survey, that allows us to put in order the multifaceted history of Greek post-war cinema, provided it does not lead us to downplay the undisputed artistic value of many pre-1970 films, or to overestimate any film that is thought to belong to NGC.

Within this framework, it is important to note that the existence of the so-called OGC did not cease after 1970, although many directors and actors associated with it were gradually absorbed by the rising power of a new medium that competed with the big screen throughout the 1970s, and ultimately won – namely, television (Bakogiannopoulos 1999: 38; Soldatos 2020a: 279, 299). Thus, the 1970s were by and large dominated by films of NGC which, more often than not, failed to achieve the commercial performance of earlier cinema (Karalis 2012: 181–82; Soldatos 2020a: 312). As for television, after the fall of the dictatorship in 1974, a significant number of filmmakers and actors within the NGC, some of whom had suffered considerable hardship in the previous years (prosecutions, exile, etc.), found a place in the new medium (see the third section of this chapter).

At first, the co-existence of what came to be called the OGC and NGC was anything but peaceful. As the former was gradually deteriorating (Soldatos 2020a: 286), making a transition to television, advocates of NGC emphasized the qualitative difference between the 'old' and the 'new'. According to them – and this attitude is shared by several film critics to this day – OGC's sole purpose was to make a profit, therefore its poor-quality production comprised mainly either melodramatic or overblown films, with directors consciously avoiding tackling the country's social and political issues (Kolovos 2002: 130–34; Soldatos 2020a: 332). Conversely, the work of the NGC, so the same critics argue(d), was to provide social commentary and the reconsideration of Greek history, and this in an innovating and ground-breaking way, namely by employing new techniques or conversing with past masterpieces of world cinema – something that, in their opinion, OGC had failed to do (Karalis 2012: 148; Soldatos 2020a: 278). It should be stressed here that the quest for a new cinematic language, both in terms of content and form, resulted in divergent artistic approaches. This shows that the directors associated with the beginnings of NGC could hardly be viewed as members of a homogeneous group of filmmakers (Valoukos 2011: 41–42; Stassinopoulou 2015: 847), although as regards content a left-wing, or anti-right-wing, reading of current socio-political aspects of Greece was more or less the norm (Valoukos 2011: 41).

Inevitably, this preoccupation with society and current politics left little room for period dramas, except those that dealt with the Greek Civil War (1946–49) or the events leading up to it. Such films were part of the left-wing environment that had already taken over the Thessaloniki Film Festival before the fall of the dictatorship (Soldatos 2020a: 294) and could be regarded as a response to OGC films from around the same period, which were filled with right-wing and/or nationalistic rhetoric, akin to that employed by the fascist regime but also not completely alien to future right-wing governments (Soldatos 2020a: 172). Despite the lack of period dramas in NGC, it is logical to assume that, if such films were produced, they would express the same 'iconoclastic' attitude. On the other hand, films of this genre, especially those glorifying different events from the Greek War of Independence (1821–30/32), were not uncommon in OGC, especially in the second half of the 1960s and the first years of the 1970s (Stassinopoulou 2015: 841–42; Soldatos 2020a: 170–78).

Even if OGC was receptive to period dramas, some historical eras were naturally more difficult to recreate, due to budget restrictions and the relative absence of reliable sources on several aspects of everyday life and culture. In this way, Byzantium's long history, as well as the first centuries of Ottoman rule (fifteenth–seventeenth centuries), are mostly, albeit not completely, absent both from OGC and NGC. Focusing on Byzantium, Greek cinematic production includes, to my knowledge, six feature films, three TV series and one TV movie, over the period from 1960, with *Kassiani Hymnographer* (Κασσιανή υμνογράφος), to 2003 with *The Stage Actresses* (Οι θεατρίνες). Their artistic merits notwithstanding, all these productions are closely related to the historical and cultural context at the time of their making. Thus, for them to be properly construed, the status of Greek cinema at a given historical moment and its interaction with contemporary cinematic trends in Greece and abroad – although the latter will be discussed only briefly in this chapter – should be taken into consideration. Moreover, as we shall see, the dichotomy between OGC and NGC, both aesthetically and in terms of evolution in time, is also pertinent to this discussion since it allows us to highlight several aspects of the films and series in question. It should be noted, however, that of the three TV series, two seem to have been erased or simply lost, whilst one is only available in a private collection (Agathos and Papadopoulos 2016: 252, n. 24). It is self-evident that in such cases we must rely exclusively on secondary sources.

Days of love, mystery and glory (1960–71)

The first Byzantine-themed film of Greek cinema was *Kassiani Hymnographer* (1960), directed by Ilias Paraskevas and written by 'Kostas Papageorgiou, the Athenian', as stated in the opening credits. The screenplay is reportedly based on a theatrical work written by the latter (Agathos and Papadopoulos 2016: 252), although I have not been able to confirm this. The film is set in the ninth century, and it relates the story of Kassiani, the famous ecclesiastical and secular poetess. The plot includes the famous bride-show in the imperial palace, in which she was rejected by future Emperor Theophilos in favour of Theodora, due to the bold and intelligent answer she gave to his misogynistic remark, and her subsequent decision to lead a monastic life (Silvas 2006).

For anyone familiar with the historical facts, it is obvious that Papageorgiou took many liberties. For instance, in the film, the bride-show takes place in the year 800, during the reign of Michael II, although it was actually held in 830, shortly after Michael's passing (Garland 1999: 96). The basic premise of the plot, namely the secret love affair between Kassiani and Theophilos, also defies historical truth, as does the marriage between Kassiani and the fictional character Aquila, a Byzantine general. Moreover, the film suggests that it was Theophilos who put an end to the second iconoclast era, allegedly awe-struck by Kassiani's piety after she received the monastic tonsure, although it is well known that the veneration of the icons was restored by Theodora after her husband's death. On the other hand, certain subtle details, such as the mention of the rebel Euphemios, who revolted in Sicily during Michael's reign (Bekker 1838: 81–83; Treadgold 1997: 436), or the presence of a court jester by the name of Denderis (Bekker 1838: 91; Garland 1999: 99), suggest that the said changes were made by the screenwriter intentionally, probably in an attempt to make the scenario more intriguing or simply because they were more attuned to the kind of story he wanted to tell.

Interestingly, as far as genre is concerned, *Kassiani* seems to be a Greek appropriation of the 'sword-and-sandal' movies, that is, Hollywood epics about the Roman Empire set in the time of early Christianity, which were in vogue during the late 1950s and the early 1960s (Detweiler 2009: 110; Reinhartz 2009: 420–21). Although with a considerably lower budget and many technical limitations, *Kassiani* follows the pattern of these films, such as *Ben Hur* (1959), where the adventure and the romance of the first part progressively give place to the utter triumph of the Christian faith. In the same way, *Kassiani* sees its protagonist entangled in a passionate affair, which eventually costs her husband his life during an impressive sword-fight with her lover. After all this commotion, Kassiani repents and decides to dedicate herself to God. The last part of the film, which is mostly made up of long sequences inside the convent, is essentially a glorification of Greek Orthodox monasticism. In the American counterpart, the part which concerns Christian devotion is traditionally accompanied by ethereal music; in the case of *Kassiani*, this is replaced by Greek Orthodox chants. It is also worth noting that, in the Greek film, the Byzantine setting has been somewhat 'Romanized', as attested by the clean-shaven male cast, although in the ninth century many more beards would be expected (*ODB* 1: 274).

Aesthetically and semantically, *Kassiani*, with its mixture of romance and adventure, and the absence of any social or political commentary, is a typical example of what exponents of NGC would regard as OGC. Yet, it could also be considered as exceptional due to its subject, as well as for Paraskevas's attempt to direct the Greek version of a Hollywood Roman epic. Nonetheless, the film's commercial performance was anything but spectacular (Soldatos 2002: 194) and its impact extremely limited; neither Soldatos nor Karalis includes it in their respective *Histories of Greek Cinema*. In any case, *Kassiani* bears witness to the fact that the so-called OGC of the 1960s was perfectly capable of experimenting creatively with formulas and motifs that came from abroad, something the proponents of NGC have been reluctant to admit.

Unfortunately, the same cannot be said of Giorgos Skalenakis's *Imperiale* (Βυζαντινή ραψωδία, 1968). It is worth noting that the film's Greek title (*Byzantine Rhapsody*) is the same as the working title of Costis Palamas's verse-epic *The King's Flute* (Η φλογέρα του βασιλιά) (Agapitos 1994: 5). It also corresponds with Palamas's own characterization of his poem 'The Widow's Son' ('Ο γυιός της χήρας'), which usually prefixes the said work (Bouboulides 1974: 209). Seemingly driven by the personal ambition of actor Thodoros Roumbanis, who was the producer, composer and protagonist of the project, *Imperiale* relates the tragic passion between an unnamed general and the 'augusta' of Byzantium who, in several summaries of the film, is identified with Zoe (Koliodimos 2001: 85), the niece of Basil II. Astrologers foretell the end of the world, and the empress resolves to spend her last day on earth with her lover, whom she had exiled to a distant fortress some years ago, so as to not jeopardize her position at court. As it turns out, the astrologers' prediction was nothing but a hoax, therefore the empress decides to return to the palace and reclaim her throne. Meanwhile, the emperor, also unnamed, has secretly arrived at the fortress. In one of the last scenes, the empress is made to believe that her husband has proclaimed her dead and so she rushes to ride back to the capital. However, her lover is unwilling to let her go; in the final scene he shoots her with an arrow and kills her.

If the augusta is indeed Zoe and the film is set in the year 1000, as other sources report (Karalis 2012: 125), then the plot is completely fictional. Zoe was first married in 1028 and, by that time, she was fifty years old (Garland 1999: 137). However, we know that she was involved in many affairs throughout her reign and was a self-centred and egotistical woman (Garland 1999: 136–38, 146), all of which correspond to the way the augusta is portrayed in the film. Such a character is in keeping with the film's major theme: how different people react to the imminent end of the world. More specifically, the general is driven exclusively by his unrequited passion for the augusta and wishes to spend his last day with her. At the beginning of the film, he is ready to invade the capital but then aborts this plan when he sees his beloved augusta arriving at the fortress. For her part, Zoe seeks her lover only because she is made to believe the end is nigh, but she has no qualms about leaving him when she realizes that the hoax may cost her the imperial throne.

Fascinating as all this sounds, *Imperiale* comes across as a rather disjointed blend of disparate elements. It is turgid and overdramatic, filled with prolix soliloquies that often make little sense, and includes an unnecessarily lengthy sword-fighting sequence, as well as several scenes of Greek Orthodox liturgy. We may assume that Skalenakis – or Roumbanis – wanted to offer the audience the 'complete Byzantine experience', including religious devotion, court intrigues and impressive duels. However, in the end, the only redeeming factors are the captivating landscape of the medieval fortress and the physical beauty of the two main protagonists, Thodoros Roumbanis and Betty Arvaniti. The audience evidently thought likewise, for the commercial performance of *Imperiale* was moderate at best, although some sources report that the reception abroad, especially in the USA, was more favourable (Karalis 2012: 125; Soldatos 2020a: 261–62). Opinions on the artistic value of the film vary. Mitropoulou (1980: 265) regards it as an unworthy work in the filmography of Skalenakis, whom she praises for his other films. Soldatos laconically notes its peculiar character (2020a: 261–62), whereas Karalis regards it as an underrated masterpiece (2012: 125, 223). For my part, I concur with Mitropoulou and Soldatos.

Three years later, Panagiotis Konstantinou wrote and directed *Iliogenniti* (*Ηλιογέννητη*, 1971), which was brought to my attention by Professor Vrasidas Karalis. A film that has fallen into oblivion, briefly discussed only by Koliodimos (2001: 187), *Iliogenniti* is set in the fourteenth century, in an unspecified province of the empire. Iliogenniti, the daughter of a just landowner by the name of Kallergis is forced into marrying Markos, the son of his greedy opponent, Mavrolikos. Kallergis hopes the union will put an end to the rivalry. However, Iliogenniti falls in love with Stratis Karlas, who is being employed by Kallergis but, in reality, has returned to his hometown to avenge Mavrolikos for the murder of his father, Yorgis, and the confiscation of his land. After the sudden death of Mavrolikos, halfway through the film, Stratis continues to seek justice for his deceased father, whereas Iliogenniti strives to shun the planned wedding. Kallergis's attempt to bring peace to the land is in jeopardy, as the tension between Stratis and Markos builds. The plot culminates in the duel between the two young men, which is stopped thanks to the intervention of Iliogenniti, who accepts marriage to Markos and urges Stratis to back down. However, Markos realizes that she is in love with Stratis and thus agrees to let her marry him instead. In the last scene, presumably just before the wedding ceremony, Kallergis exclaims that 'the age of evil' has given way to 'the age of good'.

A major theme in *Iliogenniti* is the daughter's obligation to her father. The audience witnesses the heroine's struggle as she tries to free herself from these restrictions and follow her own desire, namely her love for Stratis. Bearing in mind the era, a complete emancipation is not to be expected, but it seems that, by the end of the film, Iliogenniti has at least managed to have her voice heard. As regards the other characters, Konstantinou's intention to bring the story to a happy end by any means renders some of their actions less believable. For instance, Markos is depicted alternately as a brute and an upright person, although it could be argued that, to some extent, these nuances constitute the most intriguing aspect of the film. Finally, in relation to the era it purports to portray, *Iliogenniti* takes place in late Byzantium only by name. Except for the fashion – although 1970s haircuts can be seen – evidence of a Byzantine milieu is scarce, not to mention the major historical inaccuracy of rifles being used as weaponry (on Byzantine weapons, see *ODB* 3: 2192; Haldon 2008). References to the central power speak vaguely of 'the governor of the State' or the 'government', and there is also a passing reference to the 'Saracens', with no further elaboration. It should be noted too that many of the characters' names, such as Iliogenniti, Mavrolikos, Stratis and Markos, make the whole story seem more like a modern Greek folk tale than a period drama set in Byzantium.

The three films discussed are related to the poetics of what is now called OGC – at least the lighter side of it, for the 'old (post-war) cinema' produced many daring movies as well. As is the case with Greek blockbusters of the 1960s and early 1970s, these films deal primarily with romance and love, often in an affected way, their main purpose being to captivate, fascinate or move the audience, rather than to make it ponder over the contemporary socio-political problems of Greece. By 1971, when *Iliogenniti* was released, NGC had already made its appearance, whereas the fans and the crew of the 'old cinema' had begun turning their attention to television. Given that the big screen would not show any interest in Byzantium for some years, the next chapter belongs rightfully to the new medium.

Life in the catacombs (1973–76)

According to Agathos and Papadopoulos (2016: 245–50), there are four Byzantine-themed TV series, although one could challenge the inclusion of the adaptation of Alexandros Papadiamantis's third novel, *I gyftopoula* (*Η γυφτοπούλα*, 1974) in their list. The series is set in fifteenth-century Byzantium, but it is best construed as one of the many adaptations of classic Greek novels that appeared on Greek television in the 1970s, by such celebrated authors as Nikos Kazantzakis, Angelos Terzakis, M. Karagatsis and others (Kyriakos 2019: 42, n. 19). In other words, the focus in this case should be more on Papadiamantis, whose second novel had also been adapted for television in 1973 (Agathos and Papadopoulos 2016: 247), or modern Greek prose literature in general, than on Byzantium. On the other hand, two TV 1970s series set in Byzantium, *En Touto Nika* (*Εν τούτω νίκα*, 1973) and *Porphyra and Blood* (*Πορφύρα και αίμα*, 1977), should be seen in the light of their writer Nikos Foskolos's past and future success as a screenwriter, and, to a lesser degree, a director.

Foskolos, a representative of 'commercial cinema' in the 1960s and 1970s, was one of the most prolific and profitable screenwriters of his era (Karalis 2012: 133–34), with successes including the scenarios for *Blood on the Ground* (*Το χώμα βάφτηκε κόκκινο*, 1965), which was nominated for an Academy Award for Best International Feature Film, and the phenomenally successful *Lieutenant Natasha* (*Υπολοχαγός Νατάσα*, 1970). In 1971 he began collaborating on TV projects, and that same year he wrote the screenplay for *Unknown War* (*Άγνωστος πόλεμος*, 1971), which enjoyed unprecedented enthusiasm (Agathos and Papadopoulos 2016: 245). Sadly, both this and his two Byzantine-themed series are unavailable to the public, with *Unknown War* and *Porphyra and Blood* in all probability permanently lost. According to Agathos and Papadopoulos (2016: 246), in *En touto nika*, which is set in the court of Constantine the Great, both he and his mother, Helena, were presented 'in a rather hagiographic way', whereas in *Porphyra and Blood*, which was based on the then recently published award-winning novel *Romanos Diogenis* (1974) by Kostas Kyriazis, Foskolos 'was criticized for using his usual mannerisms and the pompous vocabulary known from his films and TV series' (249). Furthermore, Foskolos's own comment on *En touto nika* (cited in Agathos and Papadopoulos 2016: 246), in which he interprets Byzantium as a Greek Orthodox empire that relates to both the sophisticated and the popular audience, in that the latter has always been fascinated by 'thrones, kings ... love affairs, wars', shows how he approached the era: Byzantium is a spectacle and a space for affirmation, not reconsideration. We may note here that this perception is like what we witness in *Kassiani Hymnographer* and *Iliogenniti – Imperiale* is a different beast.

Since the fourth Byzantine-themed TV series (*Alexios Kallergis/Αλέξιος Καλλέργης*, 1984), which in reality is set in Crete during the Venetian occupation, is probably lost as well (Agathos and Papadopoulos 2016: 252, n. 24), we move on to the TV movie *1000 years ago: The Feast of Calends in 976 AD* (*1.000 χρόνια πριν: Γιορτή Καλενδών 976 μ.Χ.*, 1976), a Greek/French coproduction, which was broadcast on 31 December 1976 on Greek and French television simultaneously (Agathos and Papadopoulos 2016: 250–51). This intriguing film is the first visual work on Byzantium that saw the large-scale collaboration of artists who were associated either with OGC or NGC. The project was developed during Roviros Manthoulis's tenure as art director of the Greek National Television; his 1966 film *Face to Face* (*Πρόσωπο με πρόσωπο*) had been blacklisted by the fascist regime, forcing him to live in exile for some years (Karalis 2012: 120). The screenplay for *1000 Years Ago* was written by the renowned playwright and lyricist Iakovos Kambanellis, brother of Giorgos, who had starred as Aquila in *Kassiani Hymnographer*. It was based on a story by Giorgos Stamboulopoulos, yet another director whose film *Open Letter* (*Ανοικτή επιστολή*, 1968) had been censored by the dictators (Soldatos 2020a: 251–52). The cast of the film included many celebrated actors of OGC, whereas the soundtrack was by the acclaimed composer Stavros Xarhakos.

1000 Years Ago visualizes New Year's Eve in the year 976, i.e. a thousand years before 1976, with the celebration of the Calends, a custom deriving from Roman times. According to primary Byzantine sources, this celebration lasted four days and included the consumption of large amounts of wine and food, as well as merry songs, dances and mimic performances (*ODB* 1: 367–68; Kaldellis 2012). The Calends was a period during which people relaxed, reconciled with their rivals and enjoyed themselves. All the above is included in the film, which is a true feast of joyful entertainment; a carnivalesque ritual in which people make fun of authority, but also of each other and themselves, and this in the complete absence of religion. This was indeed a bold representation of Byzantium, especially in comparison to previous attempts, although it does not go as far as to challenge established notions on power and religion. The TV special focused on the secular, even heathen, aspect of the empire, a loud and frenetic spectacle that was appropriate for New Year's Eve celebrations. The music and the choreography were inspired by modern Greek folk dances, thus stressing the continuity of folk culture throughout the centuries – a similar statement was made in Nikos Koundouros's *Young Aphrodites* (Μικρές Αφροδίτες, 1963; music by Yannis Markopoulos), which is set in ancient Greek times. It is also worth mentioning that the cover of Xarhakos's album of the film's score, *976*, depicts a cupid (or a cupid-like angel) playing the flute – so much for the Christian empire of the Greek Middle Ages!

1000 Years Ago could be regarded as the counterpoint to Foskolos's series about Byzantium, inasmuch as we can judge from secondary sources with regard to the latter; at the same time, it could be viewed as the link that at once connects and juxtaposes the ideology and the aesthetics of OGC and NGC. Most importantly, though, it is the project that brought together the representatives of both sides. Just like the celebration of the Calends, it was an opportunity to reconcile, but as soon as the feast was over, it was time for each party to go its own way. Truly, when Byzantium re-emerged in Greek filmography, towards the end of the 1980s, it was claimed exclusively by NGC.

The era of iconoclasm (1987–2003)

By the second half of the 1980s NGC, which according to some critics had by then changed its character, abandoning overt political criticism in favour of introspective social commentary (Valoukos 2011: 45–48; Karalis 2012: 201, 217–18), had hit a wall. Except for a few films, its cinematic production had never appealed to OGC's audience, and the core of its followers was originally formed by journalists, critics, intellectuals, filmmakers and youngsters, all of whom sought or encouraged new means of expression. However, over the years NGC alienated many of its fans, who felt that the movement was overproducing tedious, pretentious films which no one would watch. In 1987, the time seemed to be ripe for the disgruntled to make a statement, which took the form of constant booing during the screening of films that they thought fitted the said negative bill (Soldatos 2020a: 404). Among them was *Doxobus* (Δοξόμπους), a film about fourteenth-century Byzantium, directed by Fotos Labrinos, an accomplished director in the field of Greek documentaries, and written by Panos Theodoridis, an archaeologist and an intellectual (Chryssogelos 2019: 267).

A difficult and demanding film to watch, but also one of the most intriguing cinematic experiences on Byzantium ever, *Doxobus* is set in the time of the Civil War between the elderly Andronikos II and his grandson and future Emperor Andronikos III. Beautifully shot, albeit too elliptical in its narrative style, the film explores the many faces of power in a district and episcopate of today's Northern Greece, and by extension how life, society, and economy in a nearby small village by the name of Doxobus are affected, and eventually changed, by the war. A close study has revealed that the screenwriter did an impressive job in writing the scenario, by employing a vast array of primary and secondary sources (Chryssogelos 2019: 270–75). For his part, Labrinos undertook the difficult task of recreating an era about which our knowledge is limited, and this by using the documentary style with which he was already familiar (Stefani 2009: 13; Chryssogelos 2019: 267–68). Scholars have argued, although laconically, that Labrinos was particularly influenced by Andrei Tarkovsky's seminal *Andrei Rublev*, released in 1966, the 'abstract-symbolic cinema' of Hungarian filmmaker Miklos Jancso and the films of Armenian director Sergey Parajanov (Kyriakidis 1999: 119; Agathos and Papadopoulos 2016: 253).

Be that as it may, the result is a slow-paced film, dense and rich in historical detail, which needs multiple viewings to be comprehended fully. Apparently, Labrinos's purpose was to demolish the notion of a Greek and solely Christian empire, by counter-suggesting that Byzantium was a nexus of corrupted religious leaders, oppressed multi-ethnic inhabitants and persecuted heretics (Chryssogelos 2019: 278–79). Given that the authoritative voice of modern Greece, namely its official state ideology, regards Byzantium as a Greek Orthodox empire that constitutes an integral component of the current nation's glorious past, we may assume that Labrinos's intention in *Doxobus* was to speak not merely about the Middle Ages but also about the present and future of modern Greece. This assessment urges us to reconsider the film's political aspect and so to challenge the view regarding the emergence of a more reserved and withdrawn cinematic code in the second half of the 1980s (Chryssogelos 2019: 277), at least in some striking cases.

It is certainly interesting to note that *Doxobus* was not the only film at the 28th Thessaloniki Film Festival that tackled Byzantium and its cultural heritage. Dimos Theos's *Captain Meïdanos* (Καπετάν Μεϊντάνος), a cerebral and equally challenging film, dealt with the inadequacy and ultimately the inability of the human mind to recreate the past and thus reconstruct history, especially the images of those who took part in it. The tone is set already in the first scene of the film, in which the protagonist quotes John of Damascus's famous assertion that 'the icon and that which is depicted on the icon are two different things' (ἄλλο γάρ ἐστιν ἡ εἰκὼν καὶ ἄλλο τὸ εἰκονιζόμενον) (Kotter 1975: 125; Kyriakos 2006: 38–40). Therefore, Byzantine theological discourse about the icon was an important aspect of the film's reflections, as confirmed by the director in a contemporary interview (cited in Soldatos 2002: 246–47), even though the plot itself was not set in Byzantium. To these we may add Kostas Sfikas's experimental film *Allegory* (Ἀλληγορία, 1986), a copy of which I have not been able to find. According to its description in a leaflet that was edited for the 27th Thessaloniki Film Festival, the film's topic is 'the spiral development of history', which is represented in the form of two axes, one horizontal and one vertical. In the leaflet it is argued that the horizontal axis is that 'of the cyclical world of the Byzantine mountains, with the lands of the symbols of fallen antiquity and secularized Christianity' (cited in Kyriakidis 1999: 117 and Soldatos 2020a: 398). It is not clear what this means, but it does suggest that Byzantium was an indispensable component of the whole experience. Whatever the case, it seems that for some reason, which needs to be explored further, by the second half of the 1980s, specific aspects of the Greek Middle Ages had become part of the *NGS* and its concerns.

A few years later, Giorgos Stamboulopoulos, whom we have already encountered as the author of the story on which the screenplay for *1000 Years Ago* was based, wrote and directed *Two Suns in the Sky* (Δύο ἥλιοι στον ουρανό, 1991), which is set in the time of Theodosios the Great (379–395), and takes place – although not actually filmed there – in Alexandria (Egypt), Antioch and Thrace. The plot follows a Byzantine commander by the name of Lazarus, who is accompanied by a historian named Athanasios, the 'Two-minded' (δίβουλος), and his efforts to extinguish the remnants of the old religion, along with non-Orthodox heresies; a seemingly easy task which is carried out by means of torture and violence but is eventually hindered by the opposition of the theatre actor Timotheus, formerly a heretic of Alexandria – presumably an Arian, not a Gnostic, as argued by Agathos and Papadopoulos (2016: 254; on Theodosios's anti-Arian policy, see Treadgold 1997: 71–73 and Greatrex 2008: 240) – and later a devotee of Dionysos in Antioch. As Stambouloupoulos himself relates on his website (stambouloupoulos. com/films/two-suns-in-the-sky), the project met with immense difficulties, but was eventually brought to fruition, in this way endowing Greek cinema with yet another quality film about Byzantium. The filmmaker also adds that his motivation was to explore the historical process through which Greeks became Christians, and to present a response to the reinforcement of religion in Eastern Europe, in the aftermath of the fall of communism.

The main theme of *Two Suns* is the juxtaposition between Orthodox Christianity as an oppressive state religion (Karalis 2014) and the ancient Greek spirit, which is characterized by spiritual freedom (Agathos and Papadopoulos 2016: 254). Closely following and creatively appropriating the plot of Euripides's *Bacchae*, from which the title 'two suns in the sky' is taken (v. 918), Stambouloupoulos identifies Lazarus with Pentheus and human justice, and Timotheus with Dionysos, or Dionysios's son, and divine justice. An important aspect of the film's poetics is the metaphor of stage acting, associated not only with Timotheus and his staging of *Bacchae*, but also with Christian preaching in church. The latter appears in two scenes where a bigoted clergyman in Antioch, standing on his 'stage' and addressing his 'audience', condemns theatres and actors, in a passionate hate-speech. Although his name is not mentioned, this cleric could well be John Chrysostom, a deacon and priest in Antioch during Theodosios the Great's reign (*ODB* 2: 1057), as the sermon in the first scene contains direct references to Chrysostom's twelfth homily on the First Epistle to the Corinthians (cf. *PG* 61: 102–25). In other instances, the advocates of Orthodoxy – hermits, stylites – are seen quoting the New Testament, especially those passages that teach the faithful to obey secular power. It is self-evident then that, for Stambouloupoulos, self-repression and conformity are deeply embedded in Orthodox Christian mentality. To the contrary, Timotheus contends in one scene, as he speaks to the audience, that the spectator should make up his/her [*sic*] own mind about the meaning of the plays staged before his eyes.

If *Doxobus* is the meeting point of history and cinematic art, *Two Suns* dramatizes the transfiguration of history into myth. Following a revolt in Antioch incited by Timotheus, Lazarus is desperately and obsessively trying to capture the constantly fleeing stage actor. At one point he succeeds in incarcerating him, but Timotheus manages to miraculously escape in, just as Dionysos did in *Bacchae*. The pursuit starts anew, but now in Thrace, 'the land of the Greeks'. To his amazement, Lazarus discovers that, there, Timotheus is worshipped as a god. As the Christian commander finds himself unable to cope with the otherworldly land, which is inhabited by pagans pretending to be Christians – yet another use of the 'acting-metaphor' in the movie – he gradually falls into madness. In the penultimate evocative scene, Lazarus is drawn, as if by magic, into the Dionysian ritual of the actors, played out in the wilderness. As in *Bacchae*, he is mutilated by the Maenads, while the deified Timotheus, dressed in white, watches from above. Did this really happen? The whole story is narrated by Athanasios, the historian who accompanied Lazarus, but by that point he had deserted his commander. In the final scene – which shows a Christian funeral procession, but most probably not of Lazarus's body, as argued by Agathos and Papadopoulos (2016: 254) – Athanasios assures the audience that he wrote down things as they really happened. But we are left wondering whether the 'two-minded' historian is to be trusted after all.

Within this context, Agathos and Papadopoulos's assertion (2016: 254), that 'Before Alejandro Amenabar's *Agora* (2009), Stamboulopoulos took a position in favor of the last Gentiles who were fighting a losing battle against the Christians', could be discussed further. In my view, *Agora* does not side openly with the Gentiles, whose manners are occasionally depicted as equally savage. It is true that Amenabar lays more emphasis on the Christians, whose religious leader Cyril is instigator of their crimes. However, the film condemns religious obscurantism, whereas it praises humanist atheism, portrayed by the free-thinking philosopher Hypatia. Her stand is the exact opposite of that of the religious mobs roaming around Alexandria and fighting against each other, which behaviour results in the destruction of the city's famous library. For his part, Stamboulopoulos does not seem to condemn religious mysticism, which he traces among both the Gentiles and the Christian heretics, but rather Orthodox Christianity as a *sine qua non* component of state oppression.

In 2003, the world of Byzantine theatre, although now that of the mimes, was revisited by Panagiotis Portokalakis in his film *The Stage Actresses* (*Οι θεατρίνες*), discussed briefly by Agathos and Papadopoulos (2016: 255) and Soldatos (2020b: 88–89). I was only able to find a poor-quality copy of the movie, with badly distorted sound, from which I was able to understand that Portokalakis juxtaposes the carefree world of the mime actresses and the strict environment of a well-respected family. Some of the characters' names, such as Antonina, Valens and Comito, suggest that the plot is set in early Byzantium, perhaps in the time of Justinian – Antonina was the name of Belisarius's wife and Comito that of Theodora's sister; both sisters were female mimes in their youth (Garland 1999: 11). The first scene constitutes a meta-narrative comment on the film's setting, possibly made by a group of red-clothed buffoons, who appear occasionally and lend the story a humorous tone. Portokalakis's take on Byzantium is at first more light-hearted than that of *Doxobus* and *Two Suns in the Sky*, but the story evolves into a tragedy with dark overtones. Without doubt, one can discern similar reflections regarding the establishment on one hand and the alternative universe of theatres and folk and street art on the other. Moreover, it is tempting to assume that in the scenes depicting the Byzantines' entertainment, including mimic performances, Portokalakis harks back to *1000 Years Ago*.

The past and the future

As shown, films and series on Byzantium cover many periods of the empire's long history, although the earlier productions differ in their approach from the later ones. Let us reiterate that the distinction between OGC and NGC is useful, provided it does not impose a fatalistic aesthetic evaluation in favour of the latter. All six films, with their focus either on romance and adventure, or politics and society, have their artistic merits, regardless of the ideological standpoint of each filmmaker and screenwriter.

As regards TV series, the unavailability of those written by Foskolos makes it difficult to draw definite conclusions, although it is reasonably to suppose that they would have been like his overall exuberant style. On the other hand, *1000 Years Ago* is an intriguing TV movie in its own right, which relates both to *Two Suns in the Sky*, due to Stamboulopoulos's involvement, and *The Stage Actresses*, for the snapshots of everyday entertainment. Finally, we saw that 'Byzantium' could also mean more than 'Byzantine-themed period films', namely a space for various reflections and experimentations.

In place of a concluding remark, we may wonder what the future holds. As I began working on this chapter, I received a message from director Konstantinos Antonopoulos. He kindly informed me that he is preparing a short film – already in pre-production – and a feature film on Byzantium, both set in the reign of Justinian II (late seventh/early eighth century). This message is a sharp reminder that there are no boundaries between art and history, and papers on the reception of Byzantium in Greek cinema are merely efforts to assess the past, in anticipation of the future.

Bibliography

Agapitos, P. (1994), 'Byzantium in the Poetry of Kostis Palamas and C. P. Cavafy', *Kampos*, 2: 1–20.

Agathos, T. and Y. C. S. Papadopoulos (2016), 'Imperial Palaces and Village Huts: Byzantium in Greek Cinema and Television', *Mediterranean Chronicle*, 6: 243–59.

Bakogiannopoulos, Y. (1999), 'O Neos Ellinikos Kinimatografos (1967–1999)', in A. Kyriakidis (ed.), *I Elliniki matia. Enas aionas ellinikou kinimatografou*, 37–55, Thessaloniki: Festival kinimatografou Thessalonikis.

Bekker, I. (1838), *Theophanes Continuatus, Ioannes Cameniata, Symeon Magister, Georgius Monachus* (*CSHB* 45), Bonn: E. Weber.

Bouboulides, Ph. (1974), '"O gyios tis chiras" tou K. Palama (filologikes paratiriseis)', *Dodoni: epistimoniki epetiris tis Filosofikis Scholis tou Panepistimiou Ioanninon*, 3 (1974): 205–16.

Chalkou, M. (2008), *Towards the Creation of "Quality" Greek National Cinema in the 1960s*, Glasgow: University of Glasgow.

Chryssogelos, K. (2019), 'The Byzantine Heritage in Greek Cinema: The (Almost) Lone Case of Doxobus (1987)', in D. Slootjes and M. Verhoeven (eds.), *Byzantium in Dialogue with the Mediterranean: History and Heritage*, 267–83, Leiden and Boston: Brill.

Detweiler, C. (2009), 'Christianity', in J. Lyden (ed.), *The Routledge Companion to Religion and Film*, 109–30, London: Routledge.

Garland, L. (1999), *Byzantine Empresses: Women and Power in Byzantium, AD 527–1204*, London and New York: Routledge.

Greatrex, G. (2008), 'Political – Historical Survey, c. 250–518', in E. Jeffreys, J. Haldon and R. Cormack (eds.), *The Oxford Handbook of Byzantine Studies*, 232–48, Oxford: Oxford University Press.

Haldon, J. (2008), 'Military Technology and Warfare', in E. Jeffreys, J. Haldon and R. Cormack (eds.), 473–81, *The Oxford Handbook of Byzantine Studies*, Oxford: Oxford University Press.

Kaldellis, A. (2012), 'The Kalends in Byzantium, 400-1200 AD: A New Interpretation', *Archiv für Religionsgeschichte*, 13 (1): 187-203.
Karalis, V. (2012), *A History of Greek Cinema*, New York and London: Bloomsbury.
Karalis, V. (2014), 'Religion and Greek Cinema', *Filmicon*. Available online: http://filmiconjournal.com/blog/post/35/religion_and_greek_cinema (accessed 29 November 2020).
Koliodimos, D. (2001), *Lexiko ellinikon tainion apo to 1914 mechri to 2000*, Athens: Ekdoseis Genous, Alimos.
Kolovos, N. (2002), *Neoelliniko Theatro (1600-1940) - Kinimatografos, Tomos V': O Ellinikos Kinimatografos*, Patras: Hellenic Open University.
Kotter, P. B. (1975), *Die Schriften des Johannes von Damaskos, III: Contra imaginum calumniatores orationes tres* (*Patristische Texte und Studien 17*), Berlin and New York: De Gruyter.
Kyriakidis, A., ed. (1999), *I elliniki matia. Enas aionas ellinikou kinimatografou*, Thessaloniki: Festival kinimatografou Thessalonikis.
Kyriakos, K. (2006), 'Mythologikes anafores sto kinimatografiko ergo tou Dimou Theou', in S. Kersanidis (Ed.), *Dimos Theos*, 33-41, Athens: Aigokeros.
Kyriakos, K. (2019), Ως ναυάγια αἱ λέξεις … *I proslipsi tou ergou tou Alexandrou Papadiamanti ston kinimatografo, sto theatro kai stin tileorasi*, Athens: Aigokeros.
Mitropoulou, A. (1980), *Ellinikos Kinimatografos*, Athens: Papazisis.
Oxford Dictionary of Byzantine Studies (1991), A. Kazhdan (Ed.), 3 vols, New York and Oxford: Oxford University Press.
Poupou, A. (2013), 'Book Review: New Greek Cinema 1965-1981: History and Politics by Stathis Valoukos, Athens: Egokeros, 2011', *Filmicon*, 1:160-66.
Rafaïlidis, V. (1970), 'Ellinikes tainies megalou mikous: Anaparastasi', *Synchronos Kinimatografos*, 9-10: 13-16.
Reinhartz, A. (2009), 'Jesus and Christ-figures', in J. Lyden (Ed.), *The Routledge Companion to Religion and Film*, 420-39, London: Routledge.
Silvas, A. M. (2006), 'Kassia the Nun c. 810-c. 865: An Appreciation', in L. Garland (Ed.), *Byzantine Women: Varieties of Experience, 800-1200*, 17-39, Aldershot and Burlington, VT: Ashgate Publishing.
Soldatos, Y. (2002), *Ellinikos Kinimatografos. Enas aionas*, Athens: Kochlias.
Soldatos, Y. (2020a), *Istoria tou ellinikou kinimatografou, tomos A'*, Athens: Aigokeros.
Soldatos, Y. (2020b), *Istoria tou ellinikou kinimatografou, tomos B'*, Athens: Aigokeros.
Stassinopoulou, M. A. (2012), 'Definitely Maybe: Possible Narratives of the History of Greek Cinema', in L. Papadimitriou and Y. Tzioumakis (Eds.), *Greek Cinema: Texts, Histories, Identities*, 131-43, Bristol and Chicago: Intellect.
Stassinopoulou, M. A. (2015), 'The "System", "New Greek Cinema", Theo Angelopoulos: a Reconstruction (1970-1972)', in L. Dreidemy, R. Hufschmied, A. Meisinger, B. Molden, E. Pfister, K. Prager, E. Röhrlich, F. Wenninger and M. Wirth (Eds.), *Bananen, Cola, Zeitgeschichte: Oliver Rathkolb und das lange 20. Jahrhundert. Band 1*, 832-47, Vienna: Böhlau Verlag.
Stefani, E. (2009), '19 Questions for Fotos Lamprinos', in *Fotos Lamprinos*, 11-13, Thessaloniki: Festival kinimatografou Thessalonikis.
Treadgold, W. (1997), *A History of the Byzantine State and Society*, Stanford, CA: Stanford University Press.
Valoukos, S. (2011), *Neos Ellinikos Kinimatografos (1965-1981). Istoria kai politiki*, Athens: Aigokeros.

Part Three

Byzantium and Literature

11

'Beware of Greeks Bearing Gifts':
Byzantium in Czech Historical Fiction

Markéta Kulhánková

Contact between the Czech lands and Byzantium during the Middle Ages were rare and mostly marginal. The only case of Byzantium having a strong cultural and religious impact on the development in the region of contemporary Czechia and Slovakia occurred in the second half of the ninth century, with the well-known and well-researched mission of Saints Cyril and Methodius to Great Moravia (Dvorník 1970; Kouřil et al. 2014). Subsequently, contact was limited to sporadic participation by Czechs in crusades (Albrecht 2001; Soukup 2006), with the most famous case being Duke and later King of Bohemia Vladislaus II taking part in the Second Crusade (Dvorník 1928; Soukup 2006: 56–58). Finally, at the twilight of the Byzantine Empire, between 1426 and 1452, a peculiar episode of negotiations occurred between Czech Utraquists (followers of the church reformer Jan Hus) and the Constantinopolitan patriarchate (Paulová 1953; Albrecht 2001: 92, 94–95). The latter two cases are mostly unknown in Czech society, apart from narrow scholarly circles. In contrast, the Moravian mission of Constantine/Cyril and Methodius has a firm place in both the school curriculum and the national narrative, and thus can serve as a helpful introduction before we move to the main topic of this chapter – the use of Byzantium in Czech historical fiction.

It is known among Byzantinists, specialists in the Slavonic Middle Ages, and more broadly among historians that the name Great Moravia (Μεγάλη Μοραβία) was coined by Constantine Porphyrogennetus in *De administrando imperio* (ed. Moravcsik 1967: ch. 13, 38, 40–42). Three explanations of the adjective 'great' were offered: first, it might have been used to indicate the remoteness of this region, from the viewpoint of Byzantine Empire, in comparison to the homonymous area by the Serbian Morava River (Dostálová 1966); second, it could point to the fact that the state did not exist anymore when Constantine wrote his work (Bowlus 1995: 10); or, third, it might suggest that the region had previously been home to migratory peoples (Havlík 1993: 76). Regardless of which of the three meanings above prevailed in the mind of Emperor Constantine when writing the instruction for his son, the adjective did not contain any indication of the importance of the remote region, about which he had only scant information. Moreover, other contemporary documents used only the proper noun Moravia to entitle this polity (Bowlus 2009: 312). The idea that the name suggested great political importance began to be a part of the Czech (and Slovak) national narrative only in the nineteenth century, and was further actively supported in the second half of the twentieth century by communist propaganda (Macháček 2009: 248–49). Although this misinterpretation has already been set straight even in high school textbooks (Antonín et al. 2018: 127), self-deceit about the glorious Great Moravian distant past still has its place in Czech and Slovak (and Moravian) political and societal discourse, and the mission of the two 'Apostles to the Slavs' forms an important part of this myth,[1] with the Byzantine origin and cultural component strongly backgrounded or even completely neglected. A good example of the prevailing narrative is the tenth episode of the popular animated educational TV series *The History of the Brave Czech Peoples* (*Dějiny udatného národa českého* 2010-12), entitled 'Great Moravia', which goes as follows: the ruler Rastislav is endeavouring to consolidate his rule and autonomy, and to stop the expansion of the Franks. He also wants to Christianize his people. The first offer comes from Bavaria, but the priest speaks only Latin and the people do not understand. So, Rastislav says, 'Let's try in Thessaloniki; perhaps the brothers from the East will help'. Therefore, the 'brothers' came, brought the Gospel in Slavic language and also the Glagolitic script, and baptized Rastislav's people. There is not a single mention of Byzantium in the entire episode, yet the idea of Pan-Slavism is strongly emphasized.[2]

Likewise, Czech historical novels dealing with the period of Great Moravia and the mission of Constantine and Methodius set aside the mission's Byzantine background to focus on recreating the Slavonic distant past. An account of these novels has already been given elsewhere (Havlíková 2017: 204–08). This chapter will examine the small group of Czech works of historical fiction, in which Byzantium is not simply a marginal part of the narrative universe, but the actual setting (cf. Ryan 2014: 2.1). The question is simple: how and for what purposes is Byzantium re-imagined in contemporary Czech literature?

'Lines stiff as wires': Karel Čapek

The oldest and shortest work of interest for the present topic was written by one of the most famous Czech writers of the interwar period – Karel Čapek (1890–1938), who became internationally renowned for his visionary dramas and novels such as *R.U.R.*, *The Makropoulos Secret*, *The White Disease* and *The War with the Newts*.[3] Čapek, also known for his essays, children's and travel books, and literary criticism, wrote during the 1920s and 1930s a series of pseudo-historical short stories, most of them as a sort of allegorical response to the internal and external political and cultural issues of his time (Steiner 1990). The stories were originally published in newspapers and were not collected until seven years after Čapek's death, in 1945, in a book entitled *Apocryphal Tales* (*Kniha apokryfů*, Čapek 1992; in English Čapek 1997). Čapek's literary technique in these stories reminds us somewhat of Byzantine *ethopoiia* (definitely an unintentional connection on Čapek's part). In a sort of paraphrase of biblical, mythological and historical events or famous literary themes, written mostly in the form of a dialogue, Čapek creates alternative versions of the 'official' narrative.[4] Among the twenty-nine short stories, most of them drawing their themes from the Bible, ancient history, the Renaissance and beyond, there is also one entitled 'Iconoclasm' ('Obrazoborectví'), which first appeared on Resurrection Sunday in 1936, a year when Catholic and Orthodox Easter coincided.[5]

The story is set during the reign of Constantine V, probably in the early 750s, shortly before the iconoclast synod of Hieria. The laymen Prokopios, characterized as 'a connoisseur and enthusiastic collector of Byzantine art', visits Abbot Nikeforos with the hope that he can win an alliance with the old monk, once an icon painter himself, in the fight against iconoclasm. However, their discussion of art leads to the opposite result: the conservativism, jealousy and small-mindedness of the old man guide him to support iconoclasm – which in his eyes heads towards the elimination of new, bad and heretical art – even if this effort would also mean the destruction of all works of art:

> Prokopios stood up, visibly crushed. 'But Nikeforos,' he pleaded, his words tumbling out in a rush, 'paintings will be destroyed, too! Listen, all works of art will be burned or smashed to pieces!'
>
> 'There, there,' the abbot said soothingly. 'It's a pity, a great pity. But if the world is to be saved from bad art, we mustn't look too harshly on the occasional blunder. Just so long as people don't have to kneel down before lopsided manikins such as the ones done by your – now what was –'
>
> 'Papanastasias.'
>
> 'Yes, that's the man. That Cretan school is an abomination, Prokopios. I'm glad you drew my attention to the Synod. I'll be there, Prokopios. I'll be there, even if they have to carry me. I'd reproach myself to my dying day if I weren't in on it – Providing they tear down that Archangel Gabriel,' Nikeforos laughed, the wrinkles spreading across the whole of his face. 'God be with you, my son,' he said, raising his contorted hand in benediction.
>
> 'God be with you, Nikeforos,' Prokopios sighed despairingly.
>
> Abbot Nikeforos walked away, shaking his head thoughtfully. 'That crude Cretan school,' he muttered. 'Bad drawing. High time somebody put a stop to it … Dear God, it's heresy … that Papanastasias … and Papadianos, too … Those aren't figures, they're idols, accursed idols,' Nikeforos exclaimed, his voice rising and his martyred hands flailing the air. 'Idols … idols … idols …'[6]

Both the characters in the story and the names of the painters are fictive, as is the name of the monastery (Saint Simeon). The term Cretan School, which in fact applies to post-Byzantine painting, is used for the hypothetical new type of art imagery. This kind of apparent anachronism occurs often in the *Apocryphal Tales*, and is to be read not as a sign of the author's lack of knowledge about Byzantium, but as an intentional strategy to distort the illusion of historical authenticity (Otruba 1992: 482).[7]

This story can be read as an allegory of the always-present clash between generations and human narrow-mindedness, but there is an even more concrete parable, one related to developments in art contemporary to Čapek: specifically, to disputes between the avant-garde and the traditional approach to art, which was highly topical in the Czechoslovakia of the 1930s:

> '[…] Lines stiff as wires, and that garish gold! Did you notice that in his latest mosaics the Archangel Gabriel is standing at such a slant he looks like he's falling over? Why, our Cretan can't even draw a figure so it stands up properly!'
> 'It may be,' Prokopios offered hesitantly, 'that he did it intentionally for reasons of composition –'
> 'Rubbish!' the abbot sputtered, and his face swelled with anger. 'For reasons of composition! So one can draw badly for reasons of composition, is that it? […]'[8]

It is noteworthy that, in the 1920s and 1930s, Byzantine studies were flourishing in Czechoslovakia: Kondakov Seminar, the academic organization of art historians specializing in Byzantine art, was founded in 1925, and the first volume of the scholarly journal *Byzantinoslavica*, which focused on the relationships between Byzantium and the Slavs, appeared in 1929. The importance of Byzantium for the Christianization of Slavs, and especially of the Cyrillo-Methodian mission, were emphasized among Czech intellectuals. Moreover, the impetus for promoting the study of Byzanino-Slavic studies came by the first Czechoslovak president, Tomáš Garrique Masaryk (1878–1937), a scholar who was himself interested in Byzantine elements of the Slavic world (Foletti and Palladino 2020: 97–109), and also Čapek's close friend. It might well be that this milieu contributed to Čapek's choice of Byzantium for the setting for his short story.

'Which other city could be compared to Constantinople?': Radovan Šimáček

The second example is a young-adult novel entitled *Cross against Cross* (*Kříž proti kříži*, Šimáček 1980), published amid the period of normalization (1969–87, the period of hard censorship and wide repressions after the suppression of the Prague Spring and the Soviet invasion of Czechoslovakia; see Fawn and Hochman 2010: 173–74). Its author was the prolific journalist and writer Radovan Šimáček (1908–82), whose oeuvre includes, apart from non-fiction works, several historical novels for both young adults and adults, mostly set in the medieval Czech lands. With an effort at historical accuracy, Šimáček narrates the Fourth Crusade from the viewpoint of the young Czech nobleman Vítek z Klokot (1194(?)–1253(?)) – a real historical figure, about whom, however, there is only very scant information available – without any kind of proof that he took part in the crusade (cf. Albrecht 2001: 89). The book was published within the best-known Czech series of adventure fiction for children and young adults, established in 1958 and, with some interruptions, continuing until the present ('Knihy odvahy a dobrodružství' [Books of bravery and adventure]).

The narrative builds mainly on two historical works, memoirs by the Picardian knight Robert de Clari, and of the nobleman and Marshal of Champagne, Geoffrey of Villehardouin. In addition, extracts from the Latin verse chronicle *Historia Constantinopolitana* by Gunther of Paris are incorporated into the work several times. The three historians also act as characters in the novel. The focus is on the inner development of the hero-narrator, who gradually changes from a young, naïve nobleman – eager to fight for a holy purpose and to prove his knightly virtues – to a disillusioned soldier who had come to understand that his own (and many others') enthusiasm for fighting against Muslims and for liberating the Holy Sepulchre had been taken advantage of, in order to serve the greedy interests of a handful of powerful men.

If Vítek's initial naïve ideas about the crusade were subjected to reflection and substantially corrected, the same cannot be said about his biased views of Byzantium and of the Byzantines. On the one hand, he is outraged that, instead of infidels, he is forced to fight against his fellow Christians:

> They invoke our commitment, our honour, to get us to stay. We, however, invoke our conscience. We did not tack the cross to our shoulders to fight cross against cross.[9]

On the other hand, his prejudices against the Byzantines are faithful to the Western sources the author used:

> Even the ancient Romans used to say: Beware of Greeks bearing gifts.[10]

> Vojen wanted us to have our knives sharpened, for you cannot believe those deceitful Greeks and who knows what trap they are going to set for us.[11]

After the hero arrives in Constantinople, these prejudices intermingle with amazement, becoming an ambivalent mixture of disdain and captivation:

> Nor could I resist the enchantment as I walked the streets of Constantinople. The inhabitants of Constantinople themselves proudly call their city the mistress of the world. If they mean the extent and wealth of their metropolis, I think they are right because which other city could be compared to Constantinople? Those who know Rome, Paris, and other big cities, such as those in Champagne, Burgundy, and Flanders, famous for their wealth, agree with me. Constantinople surpasses them all with its extent, but also its sightly architecture, many churches, treasures of art, and wealth [...] After all I have been told and I have learned myself, I would say that this magnificent city, which is the pride of the Greeks, boasts of its wealth and treasures but at the same time is worried about them, for it is a city in itself corrupted, that deceives and disapproves of everyone and so does not trust anyone in fear of being deceived.[12]

In general, the atmosphere of the book, its way of depicting the past, and its narration of the hero's inner development, without being heavily ideologically biased, are to a large extent compatible with the official demands on socialist young-adult literature: being critical of both the feudal system and the church, while subordinating its action and adventure to educational and informative purposes.

Honouring the namesake: Jan Cimický

> When the author, years ago, at a conference in France, introduced himself to a colleague, a psychiatrist from Thessaloniki, this colleague, without forewarning, started talking to him in Greek; supposedly, it was not possible not to speak Greek with such a name ... Therefore, the author started searching for the man whose name is always born by one of the great boulevards in great Greek cities and started slowly unveiling his personality. This novel wants to bring Ioannis Tzimiskis closer to the present, to help readers to understand his actions, and this attempt is undertaken by his namesake, whose ancestors long ago really came from Greece and had their name eventually changed to its present form.[13]

It is clear from the quotation above that the renown Czech psychiatrist and writer of popular (mostly crime) fiction had a peculiar reason for writing his only historical novel.

Cimický's (b. 1948) novelistic biography opens shortly before the death of Constantine Porphyrogennetus and the accession to the throne by his son Romanos (959) – in the novel the best friend of Ioannes – but the book also provides analepsis with Ioanness's childhood and early youth, and it ends with Ioanness's death in 976. Both Ioannes and the two important side characters, Romanos and his wife Theophano, are depicted in an idealistic manner. Ioannes is a brave and honest man and an outstanding military leader, strongly devoted first to Emperor Constantine and then to Romanos; he is deeply loving of his modest and faithful wife, Maria. Romanos is a somewhat weak emperor, but a brave soldier who would prefer battle to a ruler's duties, yet tries hard to maintain them. He falls passionately in love with the tavernkeeper's daughter, Theophano, who reciprocates his feelings frankly, and shows herself to be a worthy empress. After Romanos's strange and unexplained death, Theophano, counselled by good advisors, makes the sacrifice of marrying Nikephoros Phokas in order to secure peace and stability for the empire. Even this anti-hero, Nikephoros Phokas, has more positive than negative characteristics, but after he, because of his lack of monarchical skill and absence of diplomatic craft, appears as a threat to the empire, Theophano, who in the meantime gave vent to her (again, honest and deep) love for Ioannes, does not see any other possibility than politically motivated murder. Ioannes learns about it only after it is accomplished, and so does not have an opportunity to prevent the impious act. Afterwards, both Ioannes and Theophano humbly accept their penalties, imposed by Patriarch Polyeuctus, and Ioannes becomes a good and prudent emperor – although he never stops missing and loving the woman of his life, Theophano, whom he is never to meet again.

In the reconstruction of historical events and reality, the author apparently relies almost exclusively on two basic handbooks available in Czech: he paraphrases, and sometimes copies word for word, passages from the only Czech survey of Byzantine history (Zástěrová et al. 1992).[14] Further, he adopts information about Byzantine writers and quotes translated extracts of their work from Dostálová (2003).[15] It is apparent that Cimický did not advance deeply in his study of Byzantine history and society, and he did not consult any foreign historical surveys, not to mention Byzantine sources.[16] This lack of historical accuracy does not cause any real harm to the plot, since his aim was to provide an idealized, novelistic biography of his hero, based only loosely on historical sources. However, his superficial knowledge of Byzantium also resulted in the book's lack of vividness: the descriptions of the setting, buildings, people's clothing and all other objects are very limited – usually, again, based only on the two aforementioned sources (cf. also Kindlerová 2005). Apart from distorting Byzantine proper names (Porfyrogennes instead of the standard Czech transliteration Porfyrogennetos or Porfyrogennitos, Sklera instead of Skleros, etc.), another striking historical lapsus is Cimický's construction of the intellectual and literary world of Byzantines, which is entirely based on superficial knowledge and the modern reception of ancient literature. The wise emperor and his educated protégé read, love and discuss those ancient authors, both Greek and Latin, who first come to the mind of an average educated contemporary person, but hardly to a Byzantine man of letters, as Presocratic philosophers (p. 15), Virgil, and Ovid. In order to emphasize their outstanding education, the author lets Constantine and Ioannis frequently quote these authors in Latin (p. 17, 73), including, e.g. verses from Euripides (p. 83).

These were only several examples of a largely arbitrary treatment of the narrative world, illustrative for a historical fiction writer for whom the idealized past and the thrilling and/or actualizing story is more important than verisimilitude, and who (by right) expects even more limited knowledge of the chosen historical period from his audience.

'My nose does not err': František Kalenda

The last writer in this short survey is anthropologist, novelist, and journalist František Kalenda (b. 1990). His early debut, the historical crime novel *The Despot*, was published in 2011, and its plot takes place in 1361 on the Peloponnese under the rule of the despot Manuel Kantakouzenos. Despite some of the usual weaknesses of debut novels, *The Despot* shows the literary talent of its author, who afterwards wrote five other historical novels. This book is unique in the context of Czech literature about Byzantium, not only because it is the only crime novel set in the Byzantine environment, but particularly because it combines the author's own experiences within the space of the plot, blending modern Greek culture with historical sources. Sometimes, elements of modern Greek reality infiltrate the historical scenes, such as drinking 'ouzo' and the revelation of the future victim's Greek origins when he screams 'Yiamas!' during a carousal (p. 34). Equally reminiscent are the motifs of abundant bureaucracy (p. 45) and the ever-present network of family relationships (p. 82), which are depicted as 'theatricality intrinsic to (the character's) nation' (p. 92) – all of which can probably be attributed to the (not particularly balanced) image of modern Greece and Greeks in the Czech Republic. This combination, including the anachronisms, is part of the authorial intention to increase the vividness of the distant place and past times through contemporary elements and allusions.

The main character is of Western origin, and the author apparently built his work on Western sources (including the *Chronicle of Morea*). So, once more, similarly to the Šimáček novel discussed above, the Greek-Byzantine environment is presented and commented on from a Western point of view.

A couple of years after his first book, and after a novel set in medieval Transylvania and a series taking place in the Czech lands during the rule of Charles IV, Kalenda returned to a Byzantine setting with the children's novel *Dog, Cat, and an Orphan* (2016), which narrates the mysterious story of a twelve-year-old orphan boy who grew up under the protection of the Order of Saint John. The plot begins around the middle of the twelfth century, in the order's commandery in Mailberg, lower Austria, near the current border between Austria and the Czech Republic. The hero escapes after a mass murder of commandery residents by two mysterious visitors, and he only gradually discovers that he himself was the main target of the attack. Afterwards, the boy, who has the special gift of understanding the speech of animals, sets off on an adventurous and dangerous journey to Constantinople, where he expects to find his only living relative and possible protector, and to reveal the mystery of his origin. On this journey, he and his dog are accompanied by the daughter of a bandit (with her cat), and a mysterious knight. The novel appeared in an attractive style, alluding to medieval manuscripts (with explanatory notes in the margins and comprehensive abstracts of each chapter), and is charmingly illustrated by the renowned artist Renáta Fučíková.

In contrast to the previous works discussed here, the historical circumstances create a stage for the story but do not play a primary role in the narrative: in this case, the journey to Byzantium itself does not take on a hostile character. The strange and exotic city is the hero's goal and his saviour. However, this does not mean the absence of Western prejudices and stereotypes concerning Byzantium, both medieval and modern, as the following extract illustrates (this is one of the aforementioned comprehensive abstracts, with the hero's dog as the narrator):

> Even in the crowded centre of the world, my nose does not err. The age-old rule that Greeks cannot be trusted, just as sweet speeches and smiles, is confirmed.[17]

Eventually, between his first and second Byzantine novel, the author became familiar with the theme of Western prejudices against Byzantium, even those on a scholarly level: in 2012, he defended a bachelor's thesis entitled 'The Byzantine Empire as Reflected in Western Chronicles (1095–1204)', which focused primarily on Western prejudices.[18] Of course, the book's enchanting description of Constantinople and the city's ambivalent impression on the hero cannot be omitted:

He understood that he had never seen a City before. All previous cities were only a kind of smaller village in comparison to this Byzantine Empire metropolis. It was as if he suddenly saw an entire kingdom bent over two shores. He was welcomed by sculptures, walls of palaces with rows of columns, and the imposing dome of the largest Christian church. Maybe of the largest church in the world. From the bay called Golden Horn, Martin had a stunning view of the entire Strait of Bosphorus: to a quarter called Pera dominated by a magnificent tower in the middle of the citadel, from which a chain stretched across the bay, and to the endless city with a magnificent church on the opposite side.

They anchored at one of the countless harbours, where dozens, no, hundreds of ships arrived. And they all shouted – gulls and people. He heard not only Greek, Latin, and French, but perhaps all the languages of the world. It was as if they had arrived at Babylon.

'So, this is the capital of the world,' sounded Leon's wonder-struck voice next to him.[19]

Although Kalenda eventually chose another field for his professional specialization, and another prevailing setting for his subsequent literary works, Byzantium is set to emerge in his novels anew: currently, he is working on a new children's book, set during the period of Emperor Heraclius, with an environment and atmosphere rich with encounters between Christendom, Zoroastrianism and rising Islam – a setting which promises another perspective than one of Western bias.[20]

Conclusion

In the introduction, we saw that Byzantium is generally absent rather than present in the Czech discourse. This fact allowed more freedom for the handful of writers who chose Byzantium as the setting for their novels, instead of historical periods and places more familiar to the average Czech reader. Most of the authors indeed took advantage of the occasion to construct the narrative world, and to fill that environment in agreement with their own, unique imaginations and aims. We have seen examples of various subgenres of Byzantine historical fiction, and the (quite different) functions that world has within these books: a pseudo-historical short story, where an episode of Byzantine history is used as a parable for the author's contemporaneity; an attempted educational reconstruction of historical events, both faithful and attractive to young readers; a novelistic, idealized biography; a crime story which mixes the past with the present; and finally, a mystery story where the historical environment functions more or less as an attractive backdrop.

In the narratives of Čapek and Šimáček, the contemporary cultural and social environment of the period are most perceptible. In the novels of Šimáček and Kalenda, Byzantium is seen through the biased eyes of a medieval Westerner, relying mostly on Western sources and secondary bibliographies – emphasizing the exoticism and otherness of Byzantine culture. Čapek used a well-known historical event to comment on his contemporaneity. Cimický created a peculiar combination, turning a modern non-fictional narrative into a fictional world, filled with his own imagination, and independent of historical reality.

The image of Byzantium in contemporary Czech literature is one more piece of evidence that, although there is a tendency to emphasize the Great Moravian connection to Eastern Christianity and to think about the Czech lands as a bridge connecting the West and the East in the Czech discourse, modern Czech literature is deeply rooted in the Western tradition. Thus, the main characteristic of Byzantium as a story world in Czech literature is its *otherness*, both literally and symbolically.

Notes

1. Another widespread high school textbook (Fronk et al. 2009), without explicitly promoting this myth, by no means tries to reject it.
2. The episode is available online: https://www.ceskatelevize.cz/porady/10177109865-dejiny-udatneho-ceskeho-naroda/208552116230010/. The series is based on an award-winning book (Seifertová 2003). In the seventh chapter on Great Moravia, it is mentioned that both missionaries were Byzantines and that they came from Thessaloniki in Greece. The margins of each page are dedicated to parallel events from world history. In this particular chapter, only the kingdoms of the Franks, the nomadic Magyars and the Norse Vikings are mentioned.
3. For an introduction to his rich literary work, see Bradbrook (1998).
4. For a short sketch of the collection, see Bradbrook (1998: 140–43).
5. Čapek always planned the newspaper publications of his stories so that there is a connection with the current events. A somewhat strange (but almost symptomatic for Čapek) coincidence is that the date of Easter that year, 12 April, was the birthday of Ioannis Metaxas, the Greek Minister of Defence at that time. Only on the following day, 13 April 1936, after the sudden death of his predecessor, was Metaxas appointed prime minister and the way to the 4th of August Regime irreversibly open.
6. Transl. Comrada (Čapek 1997: 110–11). Prokopios povstal, zřejmě zdrcen. 'Nikefore,' vyhrkl, 'ale take jiné obrazy budou zničeny! Slyšíte, všechno umění bude spáleno a rozbito!'

'Ale, ale,' děl opat chlácholivě. 'Je to škoda, veliká škoda. Ale má-li se svět zbavit špatné kresby, nesmíme se dívat příliš přísně na nějaký ten přehmat. Jen když se už lidé nebudou klanět zkresleným panákům, jaké dělá ten váš – nu –'

'Papanastasias.'

'Ano, ten. Pramizerná krétská škola, Prokopie. Jsem rád, že jste mne upozornil na ten synod. Budu tam, Prokopie, budu tam, i kdyby mne tam museli na rukou donést. Do smrti bych si vyčítal, kdybych při tom nebyl. Jen když otlukou toho archanděla Gabriela,' zasmál se Nikeforos scvrklými tvářičkami. 'Bůh s vámi, synu,' řekl zvedaje zkřivlou ruku k požehnání.

'Bůh s vámi, Nikefore,' vzdychl beznadějně Prokopios.

Opat Nikeforos odcházel potřásaje zamyšleně hlavou. 'Špatná krétská škola,' mumlal. 'Nejvyšší čas, aby se jim to zatrhlo … Ach bože, jaký blud … ten Papanastasias … a Papadianos … To nejsou figury, ale modly, zatracené modly,' vykřikoval Nikeforos mávaje svýma zmučenýma rukama. 'Modly ... modly ... modly ...' Čapek (1992: 215–16).

7   Similarly, Thersites calls himself a 'true classical Greek' (pravý řecký antický člověk), Homer is presented as a contemporary of the Trojan War ('Thersites') and, on the eve of Christ's birth, the old wife from Bethlehem reproaches her husband who allowed the Holy Family to bed down in their stable, swearing to 'Dear Christ,' 'sweet Mary and Jesus' and 'holy Mary' (prokristapána, Jezus Maria, panenko Maria – 'Holy Night').

8   Transl. Comrada (Čapek 1997: 106). '[...] Linie jako dráty, a to křiklavé zlato! Všiml jste si, že na jeho poslední mozaice stojí archanděl Gabriel tak šikmo, jako by padal? Vždyť ten váš Kréťan ani neumí nakreslit panáka, aby pořádně stál!'

'Totiž,' namítl váhavě Prokopios, 'náhodou to udělal úmyslně, z kompozičních důvodů –'

'Tak vám uctivě děkuju,' vyhrkl opat a nadul popuzeně tváře. 'Z kompozičních důvodů! Pak tedy se může z kompozičních důvodů špatně kreslit, že? [...]' (Čapek 1992: 220).

9   Šimáček (1980: 201, author's translation): 'Dovolávají se našeho závazku, naší cti, abychom zůstali. My se však dovoláváme svého svědomí. Nepřipjali jsme si kříž na rameno, aby bojoval kříž proti kříži.'

10 Šimáček (1980: 116, author's translation): 'Už staří Římané prý říkali, že se bojí Řeků, i když přinášejí dary.'

11 Šimáček (1980: 155, author's translation): 'Vojen dbal, abychom měli nože nabroušené, neboť těm prolhaným Řekům není co věřit a kdoví, jakou past na nás chystají.'

12 Šimáček (1980: 157, 161, author's translation): 'Ani já jsem se neubránil okouzlení, když jsem procházel cařihradskými ulicemi. Sami obyvatelé Cařihradu nazývají své město hrdě vládkyní světa. Mají-li tím na mysli velikost a bohatství své metropole, myslím, že tak činí právem, neboť které jiné město by se mohlo měřit s Konstantinopolí? Ti, kdo poznali Řím, Paříž či jiná velká města, například v Champagni, Burgundsku nebo ve Flandrech, slynoucí obchodem, mi dávají za pravdu. Cařihrad je všechny předčí svou rozlehlostí, ale i výstavností, počtem svatyní, uměleckými poklady a bohatstvím. (157) ... Po tom všem, co mi bylo řečeno a co jsem sám poznal, řekl bych, že to velkolepé město, které je chloubou Řeků, se sice vynáší svým bohatstvím a poklady, ale zároveň se o ně bojí, neboť je to město v sobě zkažené, které kdekoho klame a zklame, takže pak nikomu nedůvěřuje z obavy, aby nebylo samo oklamáno.'

13 Cimický (2005: the jacket, author's translation): 'Když se autor před lety na jedné konferenci ve Francii představil kolegovi psychiatrovi ze Soluně, ten na něho bez varování spustil řecky: prý s takovým jménem není možné, aby řecky neuměl ... A tak autor začal pátrat po člověku, jehož jméno nese vždy jedna z největších ulic ve velkých řeckých městech, a pozvolna pronikal do jeho osobnosti. Tento román chce přiblížit Ioannise Tzimiskise současnosti, chce vést k porozumění jeho činům, co což se pokouší jeho jmenovec, jehož předkové kdysi skutečně z Řecka přišli a jejichž jméno dostalo nakonec současnou podobu ...' Actually, there is no other big Greek city apart from Thessaloniki, where one of the central boulevards bears Tzimiskis's name. This inaccuracy illuminates very well the entire novel.

14 An illustrative striking parallel standing in for all, for those who are able to read Czech: Zástěrová et al. (1991: 183): 'Poslední z nich [bitev] byla svedena 21. července. V obrovském horku byl boj veden s urputnou zuřivostí do konce sil.' Cimický (2005: 246): '21. července, v obrovském horku, začal boj a na smrt zuřil s urputnou

ničivostí a nepříčetností.' Cf. also Zástěrová et al. (1991: 175) and Cimický (2005: 190); there are many other such passages.

15   Cf., e.g. Dostálová's translations of Kassia and Ioannes Geometres (Dostálová 2003: 154, 180) with Cimický (2005: 197–98, 237).
16   It is fair to mention that both principal sources for Tzimiskis's life and career, the *History* of Leo the Deacon and the *Chronicle* of John Skylitzes were not available even in English translation at the time that Cimický wrote his novel (see the English translations of Talbot and Sullivan 2005 and Wortley 2010).
17   Kalenda (2016: 120, author's translation): 'Dokonce i v zalidněném středu světa se můj čich jako obvykle nemýlí. Potvrdí se letité pravidlo, že Řekům se nedá věřit, stejně jako sladkým řečičkám a úsměvům.'
18   In Czech, available online: https://is.cuni.cz/webapps/zzp/detail/118996/.
19   Kalenda (2016: 118–19, author's translation): 'Uvědomil si, že nikdy předtím neviděl Město. Všechna předešlá byla jen o něco menšími vesnicemi ve srovnání s metropolí Byzantské říše. Jako by před sebou najednou spatřil celé království vměstnané na dva břehy. Vítaly je tu sochy, zdi paláců s řadami sloupů i nepřehlédnutelná kopule největšího křesťanského chrámu. Možná největšího chrámu na světě vůbec. Ze zátoky, které se říkalo Zlatý roh, měl Martin úžasný výhled na celou Bosporskou úžinu: na čtvrť jménem Pera, jíž vévodila velkolepá věž uprostřed citadely, odkud se natahoval řetěz přes zátoku, i na nekonečné město s velkolepým chrámem na straně protější.'

'Zakotvili v jednom z nesčetných přístavů, kam vplouvaly a odkud zase vyplouvaly desítky, ne, stovky lodí. A všichni pokřikovali – racci i lidé. Neslyšel tady jenom řečtinu, latinu nebo francouzštinu, ale snad veškeré jazyky světa. Jako kdyby ve skutečnosti doplули až do Babylonu.'

'*Tak tohle je hlavní město světa*, ozval se udiveně Leon po jeho boku.'
20   I thank František Kalenda for an inspiring discussion about both his view of and approach to Byzantium as an author, and about the reception of Byzantium in literature and modern society.

Bibliography

Albrecht, S. (2001), 'Böhmen und Byzanz und was sie voneinander wußten', in G. Prinzing and M. Salamon (eds.), *Byzantium and East Central Europe*, 81–97, Cracow: Jagiellonian University Press.

Antonín, R. et al. (2018), *Starší dějiny pro střední školy. Část první: Pravěk, starověk, raný středověk*, Brno: Didaktis.

Bowlus, C. R. (1995), *Franks, Moravians, and Magyars: The Struggle for the Middle Danube, 788–907*, Philadelphia: University of Pennsylvania Press.

Bowlus, C. R. (2009), 'Nitra: When Did it Become a Part of the Moravian Realm? Evidence in the Frankish Sources', *Early Medieval Europe*, 17: 311–28.

Bradbrook, B. R. (1998), *Karel Čapek: In Pursuit of Truth, Tolerance and Trust*, Brighton: Sussex Academic Press.

Čapek, K. (1992), *Menší prózy*, Prague: Československý spisovatel.

Čapek, K. (1997), *Apocryphal Tales*, transl. Norma Comrada, North Haven, CT: Catbird Press.

Cimický, J. (2005), *Tzimiskis*, Prague: Baronet.

Dějiny udatného národa českého (2010–12), [TV series] Lucie Seifertová – Pavel Koutský, Czech Republic: Czech Television.
Dostálová, R. (1966), 'Megalé Moravia', *Byzantinoslavica*, 27, 344–49.
Dostálová, R. (2003), *Byzantská vzdělanost*, 2nd edn, Prague: Vyšehrad.
Dvorník, F. (1928), 'Manuel I. Komnenos a Vladislav II., král český', in M. Weingart, J. Dobiáš and M. Paulová (eds.), *Z dějin východní Evropy a Slovanstva*, 58–76, Prague: A. Bečková.
Dvorník, F. (1970), *Byzantine Missions among the Slavs. SS. Constantine-Cyril and Methodius*, New Brunswick, NJ: Rutgers University Press.
Fawn, J. and J. Hochman (2010), *Historical Dictionary of the Czech State*, 2nd edn, Lanham, MD: The Scarecrow Press.
Foletti, I. and A. Palladino (2020), *Byzantium or Democracy*, Rome and Brno: Viella and Masaryk University Press.
Fronk, V. et al. (2009), *Dějepis 7. Středověk a počátky nové doby. Učebnice pro základní školy a víceletá gymnázia*, Pilsen: Fraus.
Havlík, L. (1993), '"Hē megalē Morabia" und "hē chōra Morabia"', *Byzantinoslavica*, 54: 75–82.
Havlíková, L. (2017), 'The Adoption of Byzantine Motifs in Nineteenth- and Twentieth-Century Czech and Moravian Historical Novel Production', in P. Marciniak and D. C. Smythe (eds.), *The Reception of Byzantium in European Culture since 1500*, 203–11, Farnham: Routledge.
Kalenda, F. (2011), *Despota*, Roztoky u Prahy: Signum.
Kalenda, F. (2012), 'Obraz Byzance v západních kronikách (1095–1204)', BA thesis, Charles University in Prague. Available online: https://is.cuni.cz/webapps/zzp/detail/118996/ (accessed 16 March 2021).
Kalenda, F. (2016), *Pes, kocour a sirotek: Putování podivuhodné trojice skoro až na konec světa*, Prague: Meander – Vyšehrad.
Kindlerová, D. (2005), rev. 'Cimický, Jan, Tzimiskis', *iLiteratura.cz*, 31. October. Available online: http://www.iliteratura.cz/Clanek/18067/cimicky-jan-tzimiskis (accessed 16 March 2021).
Kouřil, P. et al. (2014), *The Cyril and Methodius Mission and Europe*, Brno: The Institute of Archaeology of the Czech Academy of Sciences.
Macháček, J. (2009), 'Disputes over Great Moravia: Chiefdom or State? The Morava or the Tisza River?' *Early Medieval Europe*, 17: 248–67.
Moravcsik, G. (1967), *Constantine Porphyrogenitus. De administrando imperio*, 2nd edn, Washington, DC: Dumbarton Oaks Research Library and Collection.
Otruba, M. (1992), 'Žánry Čapkovy drobné žurnalistické beletrie', in K. Čapek, *Menší prózy*: 477–504, Prague: Československý spisovatel.
Paulová, M. (1953), 'L'empire byzantin et les Tchèques avant la chute de Constantinople', *Byzantinoslavica*, 14: 158–225.
Ryan, M.-L. (2014), 'Space', in P. Hühn et al. (eds.), *The Living Handbook of Narratology*, Hamburg: Hamburg University. Available online: https://www-archiv.fdm.uni-hamburg.de/lhn/node/55.html (accessed 20 February20 2023).
Seifertová, L. (2003), *Dějiny udatného českého národa a pár bezvýznamných světových událostí*, Prague: Knižní klub.
Šimáček, R. (1980), *Kříž proti kříži: křižácký rytířský román*, Prague: Albatros.
Soukup, P. (2006), 'Pilgrimage Element in Crusades with Czech Participation in the Twelfth Century', in D. Doležal and H. Kühne (eds.), *Wallfahrten in der europäischen Kultur*, 53–64, Frankfurt a. M.: Peter Lang.

Steiner, P. (1990), 'Opomíjená sbírka: Čapkova kniha apokryfů jako alegorie', *Česká literatura*, 38, 306–20.
Talbot, A.-M. and D. F. Sullivan (2005), *The History of Leo the Deacon: Byzantine Military Expansion in the Tenth Century*, Washington, DC: Dumbarton Oaks Research Library and Collection.
Wortley, J. (2010), *John Skylitzes: A Synopsis of Byzantine History, 811–1057*, Cambridge: Cambridge University Press.
Zástěrová, B. et al. (1992), *Dějiny Byzance*, Praha: Academia.

12

Imagining Action: Explanation in Twentieth-Century Historiographical and Fictional Rewritings of the *Chronicle of Morea*

Matthew Kinloch

The reception of Byzantine historiographical narratives in modernity offers an opportunity to unlearn disciplinary assumptions that have conditioned scholarly understandings of the Byzantine past and its textual traces. Historians of Byzantium, whether they frame their practice in terms of reception or not, are constantly engaged with the reception of medieval narratives, as well as in attempting to identify and explain the reception of other narratives (i.e. potential sources) within them. How modern historical fiction receives Byzantine historiography has yet to be seriously studied; however, it too (like modern historiography) receives, reworks and redeploys earlier historiographical narratives, both medieval and modern. Historians typically claim closer relationships to past reality for their narrative products than historical novelists. However, the analysis of how histories and historical novels actually receive earlier narratives destabilizes and blurs rigid dichotomies separating fact from fiction, history from novel and historian from novelist.

Byzantine historiography, like other historiographies, is not 'motivated by the question of the *reality* of the past. The reality of the past is a given, it is an enabling supposition of historical enquiry' (White 2005: 148). That stuff really happened in the past is not up for debate. The debate revolves instead around what can *truly* be asserted about that stuff 'on the basis of the (professionally determined) admissible evidence' (White 2005: 148). In recent decades (especially since the 1990s), scholars have increasingly reassessed what they believe can be truly asserted about the Byzantine past on the basis of historiography. The complacent equation of historiographical narratives with past reality has given way to the more nuanced evaluations of the referential capacity of Byzantine historiography. The literary, rhetorical and generic qualities of historiography have received increasing attention and primacy to the point where today, even the most theoretically conservative historians acknowledge that history is a form of literature. However, even questions of the literariness of historiography, where arguably the greatest transformation has occurred, have failed to do more than displace the dyad of history versus literature into the realm of practitioner approach. One can approach historiography as a literary critic (understood as 'an end in itself') or as a historian (instrumentalizing literariness to gain true knowledge of the past), but not both (Macrides 2010: xi). Historians are still asking, 'How much history is there in Byzantine historical texts?' (Kaldellis 2016: 293). The principal difference is that today scholars place Byzantine historiography, or more specifically certain elements of it, further towards the literary end of the scale than previous generations. The same is true for a host of other foundational binaries, such as the division between fact and fiction, real and imagined, content and form, true and false, primary and secondary, on which (Byzantine) history as a discipline depends. The project of Byzantine history requires that these binaries be identified, distinguished, separated and the privileged element presented as the product of research in isolation. Scholars may now acknowledge that the literary and rhetorical form of Byzantine historiographical narrative affects its truth value, but there is still no place in modern scholarship for anything that is explicitly imagined, fictitious or false, there is only space for the exclusively and verifiably real, factual and true. In Byzantine studies, the sceptical and deconstructive critiques, seen in some other branches of historical enquiry, as well as the compromises made as a result, have either been ignored (e.g. Jeffreys, Haldon and Cormack 2008: 14–15) or, less often, explicitly rejected (e.g. Haldon 1984; Kaldellis 2010).

Today, knowledge of the Byzantine past remains both the objective and product of *doing* Byzantine history. This requires a single past reality to be retained as accessible, albeit through its reflection in the distorting mirror of historiography (Mango 1975). *Doing* Byzantine history remains a process whereby the careful analysis and decipherment of medieval historiographical narratives (and other 'sources') are used to produce modern historiographical and argumentative narratives. Historical fiction has yet to enter this conversation. However, by thinking about the construction of the thirteenth-century Byzantine past and the reception of medieval historiographical narratives in different types of modern texts, namely the realist novel and realist historiography, the rigid binaries and absolutism of traditional practice can be explicated and disrupted. In contrast to historiographical narrative, historical fiction locates its story-products in time-and-place-specific contexts, but steps beyond what historians would recognize as the truths we know about it and in the process reveals the slippage between historiographical and fictive modes of narration.

This chapter seeks to create openings in the generic and categorical walls constructed to maintain a proper distance between medieval source material, modern historiography and historical fiction, by comparatively examining how action is explained in four narratives about thirteenth-century Byzantine and Frankish Greece. The first is the fourteenth-century *Chronicle of Morea*, the most detailed medieval 'source' for the period. The second is a modern historical novel, Alfred Duggan's *Lord Geoffrey's Fancy* (1962), while the third and fourth are two early twentieth-century histories of the Latin crusader states in southern Greece and the Eastern Mediterranean, Rennell Rodd's *The Princes of Achaia* (1907) and William Miller's *The Latins in the Levant* (1908). I begin by introducing these four narratives and their relationship to each other. I continue by offering three short case studies, each relating to structurally central battle scenes. My focus in these case studies is on how action is explained in each narrative and how explanations change or remain static between earlier and later narratives.

Lord Geoffrey's Fancy

Alfred Duggan's (1903–64) historical novel *Lord Geoffrey's Fancy* (1962) tells the story of an English knight from Herefordshire, called William Briwerr. This landless knight sets out to seek his fortune in 'the East' and comes to the Frankish principality of Achaia, a polity created by Frankish crusaders in the Peloponnesian peninsular of southern Greece following the conquest of Constantinople in 1204 by the Fourth Crusade. Once there William finds service under the baron of Karytaina, the eponymous Geoffrey de Bruyères, one of the twelve chief lords of the principality. Geoffrey invents a kinship tie with William and claims him as a cousin, on account of their similar sounding names (Briwerr and Bruyères). As part of Geoffrey's retinue, William observes and participates in military and political action that takes him not just all over the Peloponnese but also to Nicaea and Constantinople by way of central Greece and Macedonia. *Lord Geoffrey's Fancy* is framed by the life of William, its narrator, beginning with his departure from Herefordshire and ending with his return and quiet retirement there.[1] However, Geoffrey is central to the story. This is not because of the titular love affair, which actually occupies a rather marginal position in the narrative, but rather because his character enables the narration of the wider political and military fate of the principality of Achaia, which the novel tracks from acme through to heroic decline.

In a paratextual authorial note at the end of *Lord Geoffrey's Fancy*, Duggan reveals his understanding of the epistemological status of his narrative.[2]

> This is in outline a true story, even to Sir Geoffrey's address to his tent-pole before the battle of Pelagonie. See Rennell Rodd, *The Princess of Achaia*, Edwin Arnold, 1907, and William Miller, *The Latins in the Levant*, John Murray, 1908. The only entirely imaginary characters are the narrator and his wife, though there was a genuine Briwerr family in England. Public events happened as I have described them, though I have used my imagination in supplying motives and explanations, especially for love affairs.
>
> (Duggan 1962: 254)[3]

Duggan claims the novel to be 'in outline a true story' and specifically affirms the truth of one particular scene, Geoffrey's address to his tent-pole (see the second case study below). Implicitly, Duggan therefore accepts that some elements of the narrative are not true. Two characters are identified as imagined, in opposition to the rest of the cast, who are implicitly assumed to be not imagined (i.e. real). The narrator's plausibility (if not his historicity) is suggested by the 'genuine' existence of a Briwerr family in thirteenth-century England. The claim that only the narrator and his wife are entirely imaginary ignores the host of minor and often unnamed characters in *Lord Geoffrey's Fancy*, most often soldiers, knights and servants, who likewise do not survive in the historical record. 'Public events' are claimed as having 'happened as ... described', a statement that leaves the ontological status of private events ambiguous, but implicitly open to the possibility of having not happened. Duggan is thus revealed to conceive of his novel as possessing a story that is both true and false, characters that are both real and imagined, and events that both happened and did not.[4] The dyadic dissonances revealed in this paratextual note are foundational for historical fiction and are precisely the points of rupture that make it so good to think with, since it blurs precisely the binaries on which the authority of modern historiography depends.

Taking my lead from Duggan, this chapter focuses on the *motives* and particularly the *explanations*, that this authorial note identifies as being supplied by his imagination. Duggan contrasts the descriptive *what* of his story, events and characters with the explanatory *why*, without acknowledging that explanation and motive are baked into historiographical narratives, just as much as they are into realist novels. There is no description of the past, without explanation (Megill 1989).

The Princes of Achaia and *The Latins in the Levant*

Again taking my cue from Duggan's authorial note, I compare *Lord Geoffrey's Fancy* primarily with the two modern historiographical narratives, Rennell Rodd's *The Princes of Achaia* (1907) and William Miller's *The Latins in the Levant* (1908), on which Duggan depends for his claim to a mostly truthful story, predominantly real characters, and public events that actually happened. Miller's text, which as the title suggests engages with the whole Frankish Levant, has both a wider scope and a slightly wider chronological focus. Neither devotes much of their narratives to the events that were later received in *Lord Geoffrey's Fancy*.[5] These are classic works of early twentieth-century historiography and today, they remain the foundational narrative accounts of the period, although they read as somewhat dated.[6]

Neither was exclusively historians. While Miller was primarily a journalist, Rodd was a diplomat and later a politician. Both narratives present an often-contradictory mixture of a positivistic conception of historiography with a philhellenic romanticism also seen in their other works. Throughout, both historians display a tendency to paraphrase their source material. This is especially the case with Rodd, who regularly inserts extended translations from medieval texts (as we shall see below in the case studies), which are assumed to be factual and require no analysis. As the prefatory paratexts of both historians make clear, they understand their histories in narrative terms, despite their positivist orientation.

> ... **the brilliant story** of the Dukes of Athens and the Princes of Achaia, I was enabled to some extent to repeople my mountain castles with their proper tenants and to realise **a new world of dramatic personages on a stage** over which the curtain seemed hitherto to have descended with the Roman conquest of Greece.
> (Rodd 1907: vi, emphasis added)

> **We know now**, year by year—yes, almost month by month—the vicissitudes of Hellas under her Frankish masters, and all that is required now is **to breathe life into the dry bones**, and bring upon **the stage** in flesh and blood that picturesque and motley crowd ... the persons of the romantic **drama** ... Throughout I have

based **the narrative** upon first-hand authorities. I can conscientiously say that I have consulted all the printed books known to me in Greek, Italian, Spanish, French, German, English, and Latin, which deal in any way with the subject … The historian of Frankish Greece is confronted at the outset with the problem of **telling his tale** in the clearest possible manner.

(Miller 1908: vii–viii, emphasis added)

Both Rodd and Miller explicitly conceive of their history writing as telling a story and use extended dramatic metaphors in describing their projects. Miller's claim to be breathing 'life into the dry bones' of what 'we know' – a claim he also makes in another of his historiographical works ([1921] 1964: 57, 85) – is precisely what Alessandro Manzoni identified as the great opportunity of the historical novel. In his seminal study, Manzoni wrote that historical fiction could give 'not just the bare bones of history, but something richer, more complete. In a way you want him [*sic*] to put the flesh back on the skeleton that is history' (1996: 67–68; De Groot 2009: 35) While both Miller and Manzoni deploy a well-worn trope that appears in various places including the book of Ezekiel (37: 1–14), the close alignment in their visions of historiography and historical fiction signpost the potential of the comparative analysis undertaken in this chapter to blur the boundaries between such generically demarcated narratives.

The *Chronicle of the Morea*

All three of the modern narratives introduced so far depend on a group of five medieval historiographical narratives traditionally grouped under the umbrella title of the *Chronicle of Morea*. These texts are understood by scholars to be five different 'versions' – two Greek (the HT and P 'versions'), one old French, one Italian and one Aragonese – of a Greek (or possibly old French) 'original', probably composed in the fourteenth century (Jeffreys 1975; Shawcross 2009: 31–52). According to modern historians, the two versions of the *Chronicle of Morea* considered to be oldest, fullest and closest to the original (namely the Greek HT and the Old French texts), constitute the principal surviving source for Frankish and Byzantine Morea during the thirteenth and fourteenth centuries. The *Chronicle of Morea* has tended to be seen as less reliable than other historiographical narratives that narrate the same period, such as those of George Akropolites, Geoffrey de Villehardouin, George Pachymeres, Ibn Bībī and Nikephoros Gregoras, particularly because of the HT version's low-brow Greek and verse form. Nevertheless, it is often the only (or only detailed) source for much of the history of the principality of Achaia. To dramatically simplify what is an extremely complex collection of narratives, the *Chronicle of Morea* can crudely be thought of as being split into two halves by the battle of Pelagonia (1259). The first half, which begins with the establishment of the principality, focuses on its apogee in the 1250s, while the second half is dominated by its sharp decline after 1259, in the face of Nicaean expansion and the polity's increasing dependence on the Angevin kingdom, formalized by the treaty of Viterbo in 1267.

It is not made explicit in Duggan's paratextual authorial note whether he had read the *Chronicle of Morea* himself. The dependence of both Rodd and Miller's histories on the text may have been enough, although he was capable of reading Greek and the critical edition of John Schmitt (1904) was accessible at the time of composition. Nonetheless, in his review of the 1964 translation of the HT 'version' of the *Chronicle of Morea* by Harold Lurier (1964), which appeared just after Duggan's death, Peter Topping assumed that *Lord Geoffrey's Fancy* was directly influenced by the *Chronicle of Morea*.[7] Regardless of the directness of the relationship between the *Chronicle of Morea* and *Lord Geoffrey's Fancy*, these narratives are related to both each other and *The Princes of Achaia* and *The Latins in the Levant*. Their comparative analysis, in this chapter, seeks to blur the categorical and generic distinction between modern historiography and historical fiction that Topping re-inscribed in his review, carefully dividing, as he does, the reception of the *Chronicle of Morea* into historical significance (noted first) and its influence on literature (cited last).

The battles of Karydi, Pelagonia and Prinitsa

Three battles structure *Lord Geoffrey's Fancy*, dividing the novel into roughly equal parts. These battles illustrate and explain the fate of the principality. This begins with the battle of Karydi (1258), which saw intra-Frankish rivalry play out as chivalric war-as-sport between the principality of Achaia and the duchy of Athens; moves to the battle of Pelagonia (1259), which saw all the Franks defeated by the Byzantines; and culminates in the battle of Prinitsa (1263), in which a heroic fight sees the Franks temporarily halt the Byzantine occupation of the Morea, whilst signposting inexorable Frankish defeat. These battles describe and explain the political history of both the thirteenth-century Morea and the wider Eastern Mediterranean world in more than just Duggan's novel (generally on the use of battles, see Kinloch 2018: 101–20). The battle of Pelagonia in particular is one of the central events in the narratives offered by both the *Chronicle of Morea* and modern scholars of late Byzantium.

The explanatory function of battles in historiographical narrative, combined with the use of battles as canonical examples of indisputable facts of the past (e.g. Carr 1962: 10–11; Marwick 2001: 152), make these three events especially illustrative places to test and blur the binaries offered by Duggan in his authorial note. This exploration will take the form of three case studies, in which I will examine the explanations given for some action that took place during each battle mentioned in these four narratives. In my first example, I will demonstrate the disjuncture between all three modern texts and their 'source material' (i.e. the *Chronicle of Morea*), with a particular focus on the manner in which modern historiographical theory and style sometimes require that historians contradict their sources and imagine action. In the second, I show how the rhetorical form of the *Chronicle of Morea* forces its way into all three modern texts, whether it is naively paraphrased or logically historicized. The third case study extends the argument of the second by tracking the survival of a cliché from a speech in all three modern texts in a way that suggests the potential of the historical novel to playfully subvert historiographical positivism.

1. The battle of Karydi: Inventing Geoffrey's defection

Much of the early part of *Lord Geoffrey's Fancy* (chapters two–four) relates to the rivalry between the principality of Achaia and the duchy of Athens. In chapter two, Geoffrey de Bruyères (nephew of the Prince of Achaia) marries Isabel (daughter of the Duke of Athens) in order to maintain the fragile balance of power between these two Frankish polities. Despite this, conflict breaks out between them in chapter three, over the suzerainty of knightly fees in Euboea. This conflict climaxes in a set-piece battle in chapter four, between armies aligned with the Prince of Achaia (Geoffrey's uncle and suzerain) and the Duke of Athens (Geoffrey's father-in-law). The military confrontation presented in chapter four, known as the battle of Karydi (1258) in modern historiography, has been located in a pass in the hills between Megara and Thebes (Rodd 1907: 194; Miller 1908: 106–08; Ilieva 1991: 150). In this battle, Geoffrey sides with his father-in-law. In so doing he breaks the laws of suzerainty, according to which Geoffrey should have fought for his suzerain (his uncle the prince). Consequently, his defection requires explanation.

Lord Geoffrey's Fancy explains Geoffrey's decision to abandon his uncle and join the Athenians in misogynistic terms. Geoffrey is presented as being nagged into submission by his wife Isabel, who persuades him to side with her father, because she preferred gay Athens, where all her blood relatives were living, to isolation in Geoffrey's more modest and rural castle in Karytaina. Geoffrey's defection is explained in a dialogue between the narrator William and his wife Melisande, after Geoffrey announced to his men his decision to desert his uncle the prince.

> So the lady Isabel has won. I thought she would. Let that be a lesson to you, William. In politics husbands are guided by their wives, and that is true even of the best knight in all Romanie. Poor Isabel, she has been miserable here all summer, with her baby dead and her husband away on campaign.
> (Duggan 1962: 57)

Geoffrey's motivation is wholly explained by his relationship with Isabel. His relationship with the duke himself is entirely absent from Duggan's narrative. This pivotal event in the early narrative is thus explained through one of the 'love affairs', which Duggan's authorial note identifies as being supplied by his imagination (254). *The Princes of Achaia* and *The Latins in the Levant*, in their briefer treatments of Geoffrey's defection, both allocate less agency to Isabel.

> And now in the moment of his need, **Guy sought, through the influence of his daughter Isabella, to detach her husband**, Geoffroi de Bruyères, the foremost soldier of the Morea, from allegiance to the Prince his uncle. **Overcome by the pleading of his wife**, the lord of Carytena, after long searches of the heart and with much misgiving, broke his oath of allegiance.
> (Rodd 1907: 194)

> … Geoffroy de Bruyères, baron of Karytaina, 'the best soldier in all the realm of Romania,' who had fought for his prince in Negroponte, **after a struggle between**

conflicting ties of kinship, deserted his liege lord and uncle, William, for the side of his father-in-law, Guy.

(Miller 1908: 105)

In Rodd's explanation, Isabel is transformed into an agent of the Duke of Athens (Guy). However, she remains a prominent participant in the action and Geoffrey's defection is explained through feminizing language (Isabel's 'pleading'). In Miller's explanation, Isabel drops out of the narrative completely, leaving only an implicit trace in the relationship between Geoffrey and his father-in-law. Both explanations deploy emotive language (i.e. 'searches of the heart', 'pleading', 'struggle' and 'conflicting ties') to explain Geoffrey's motivation and decision and both, to different extents, decentre Isabel, without displacing the importance of her marriage ties.

In the narratives depicting Geoffrey's defection in *Lord Geoffrey's Fancy*, *The Princes of Achaia*, and *The Latins in the Levant* Isabel is understood to be the daughter of the Duke of Athens. However, in the *Chronicle of Morea* she is understood to be Guy's sister, rather than his daughter. She is also, it is worth bearing in mind, never identified by name.[8] Modern historians have argued from texts other than the *Chronicle of Morea* (*Lignages d'outremer* 2003: 90, nn. 144–45 (§333), Sanudo II.125–127) that Isabel was Guy's daughter and not his sister. Consequently, they have identified this as an error in the narrative. Indeed, it is almost impossible to read the *Chronicle of Morea* today in any language without this error being signposted, since most editions and translations of the text include explanatory footnotes (e.g. Buchon 1845: 107, n. 1; Lurier 1964: 167, n. 32; Van Arsdall and Moody 2015: 77, 254). However, the fact that Geoffrey was the prince's brother-in-law is essential to explaining Geoffrey's defection in the *Chronicle of Morea*. In the *Chronicle of Morea*, unlike the three modern texts, it is the Duke of Athens himself who pleads with Geoffrey (Lurier 1964: 167). The interaction of these two characters is framed in completely different terms. In the *Chronicle of Morea*, honour, friendship and brotherhood between two brothers-in-law is offered as the principal explanation for Geoffrey's defection, rather than the relationship between son-in-law and father-in-law. In the long passage in which this explanation unfolds in the HT 'version' of the *Chronicle of Morea*, Geoffrey is described no less than five different times as friend, brother or brother-in-law.

Ὁ κάλλιος φίλος ... παρακαλῶντα ὡς ἀδελφὸν καὶ γνήσιον του ... ὁ ἀδελφός του ... τοῦ γυναικαδελφοῦ του ... Εἶπεν ὅτι καλλίον ἔχει νὰ ἀχάσῃ τὴν τιμήν του,/ παρὰ νὰ λείψῃ ἐκείνοῦ τοῦ γυναικαδελφοῦ του.

[... the very honourable friend ... pleading as his brother and relative ... his brother ... his brother-in-law ... He said that it is more honourable to lose his honour/than to leave his brother-in-law.]

(*Chronicle of Morea*, 3218–36; Lurier 1964: 167)

This focus on the filial bonds between Geoffrey and the Duke of Athens offers a different explanation for Geoffrey's defection, one in which Isabel plays only a marginal role.[9] Since the *Chronicle of Morea* is the only medieval text that narrates the defection of Geoffrey, although other texts mention the battle, all three modern explanations depend either directly or indirectly on the *Chronicle of Morea* at this point. However, since the filial explanation of the *Chronicle of Morea* cannot be used in the modern narratives, all three must imagine an alternative, independent of their 'source material'. Duggan, Rodd and Miller's explanations of Geoffrey's defection offer different emphases on the personal and political. However, despite some formal and stylistic differences between Duggan's novel and the two modern historians (e.g. the use of direct speech), all three explanations are inventions, supplied by these authors in the twentieth century. Since all three modern narratives are equally divorced from the medieval text through which they claim access to the thirteenth-century past, and thus authority, the difference between historiography and historical fiction is revealed to be only at the formal and stylistic level. Comparison of how this novelist and these historians respond to the incompleteness of the historical record highlights the role of imagination and invention in historiography, thus blurring the distinction between the two.

2. The battle of Pelagonia: Explaining Frankish defeat

The battle of Pelagonia (1259) is a central turning point in *Lord Geoffrey's Fancy*, the two modern histories and the *Chronicle of Morea*. In all these narratives, defeat at Pelagonia, the capture of the prince and most of the knights of the principality (including the narrator in *Lord Geoffrey's Fancy*) and the ransom paid for the prince in the form of three key castles are understood to simultaneously precipitate the decline of the principality.[10] Central to the explanation of why this battle occurred in all four narratives is a speech given by Geoffrey de Bruyères. The reception of Geoffrey's speech from the *Chronicle of Morea*, in the two modern histories and *Lord Geoffrey's Fancy*, blurs the distinction between historical fiction and historiography, because there is no qualitative difference in the reception of this speech's explanatory role in the works of the novelist Duggan and the historians Rodd and Miller, despite the canonically suspicious status of speeches in historiography.

A scepticism towards the reliability of speeches, identified as fictive, literary and rhetorical, has been ingrained in the practice of history, since its emergence as a formal and increasingly professionalized discipline in early modernity. Voltaire, for example, identified speeches as one of three ways in which historians draw false characters, in a section of his preface to *The History of the Russian Empire under Peter the Great* alongside a critique of how historians also give false facts.[11]

> Harangues, or set speeches, are another species of oratorical lying, which was anciently allowed to the historians. They made their heroes say what it was possible for them to have said. This liberty indeed might be taken with a person of some antiquity; but now these fictions are no longer tolerated: nay, we go still further; for if a speech were to be put into the mouth of a prince that never pronounced it, we should consider the historian a rhetorician.
>
> (Voltaire 1763: xxii)

The principal locus of this debate, as alluded to by Voltaire, has been antique historiography and especially the speeches of Thucydides (Jebb 1907: 359–445). The legacy of this scepticism is now solidly embedded in modern Byzantine historiography, as has recently been illustrated by a stock-taking article by Ralph-Johannes Lilie (2014: 208).[12] It is therefore noteworthy that narrative elements, such as speeches, traditionally identified as fictive, literary and rhetorical, are presented as true in both *Lord Geoffrey's Fancy* and *The Princes of Achaia*. It is also significant that the explanatory role of speeches persists even when they are excised from 'scientific' modern scholarship, as in *The Latins in the Levant*.

According to the *Chronicle of Morea*, the Frankish army came to the field with an allied force of Epirot Romans to fight the Nicaean Romans. However, the bastard son of the Epirot ruler defected to the Nicaeans before the battle. Upon hearing this, the council of leaders (both Frankish and Epirot) determined to flee and leave their army behind while they made their escape. To this effect they bound all the leaders present with an oath. Geoffrey de Bruyères, however, wishing to warn his men without breaking his oath and to enable them to pressure the prince to stay and fight, gave a loud (direct) speech to his tent-post, intending to be overheard (*Chronicle of Morea*, 3864–72; Lurier 1964: 185–56). His ruse is successful and although the Epirots flee the Franks stay, fight nobly and consequently are defeated by Turkish and Roman trickery.

In Rodd's *The Princes of Achaia*, the speech of Geoffrey from the HT version of the *Chronicle of Morea* is translated and reproduced in full, alongside a paraphrase of the passage preceding it.

> But the lord of Carytena was troubled and perplexed, and pondered how he might save his people, to whom he was devotedly attached, without breaking the oath of secrecy to which he had subscribed. A broken lance was lying in his tent, and with the shaft he loudly struck the tent-pole and addressed it in the epic vein, 'Oh, pole of my tent, a loyal servant hast thou been to me until this day, and were I to fail thee and desert thee now, recreant should I be and lose thy faithful service. Therefore fain would I excuse myself to thee, and have thee to know that the Prince and the Despot and we, the other high barons of the army, have bound ourselves together by oath to fly this night and abandon our people. This may I not discover to any man, because of my oath, but to thee I tell it, that art not a man, affirming that the truth is even so.'
>
> (Rodd 1907: 204)

This relatively loose translation of the *Chronicle of Morea* is presented by Rodd, without caveat, as a true account of what was actually said.[13] In *Lord Geoffrey's Fancy*, Geoffrey also gives a speech to his tent-pole. The speech follows the rough shape of that of the *Chronicle of Morea* and *The Princes of Achaia*, although it differs in tone and length.

> 'Good old tent-pole,' he said loudly, 'on all my campaigns you have been with me, against Grifons and Esclavons and against my dear uncle William. Now I must leave you to fall into the hands of my enemies. And not only you, old tent-pole. I must also abandon my servants and my muleteers and indeed all my dismounted followers. For that matter some of the knights of my mesnie may be left behind.

'The leaders of the host have agreed to flee secretly in the middle of the night, from shameful fear and for no other reason. But the camp must be left standing, to deceive the Sebastocrator so that we get a good start. Therefore we may not warn our faithful followers, to whom we are bound by oaths of mutual fealty. The leaders will escape while their followers perish. O my tent-pole, what baseness, what ingratitude, what felony! A good knight should warn his followers of impending danger. But a good knight cannot break his pledged word. Before he revealed the hideous project the Despot bound me with an oath of secrecy. I swore by my hope of salvation never to reveal the decisions of the council to a living soul. But you, my dear tent-pole, have no soul; though you are more worthy of Heaven than the Despot or even my uncle William, who has consented to this foul treachery. Therefore to you I may open my heart, lamenting the shame to which I am bound by the oath I swore before the council.'

(Duggan 1962: 115–16)

This speech is significantly longer and more detailed. Further, it transforms elements of the action narrated, most notably, by shifting blame for this perceived treachery and cowardice to the Epirot despot and away from the Prince of Achaia.[14] The speech scenario is also different, since it is delivered not for the multitude of men around Geoffrey's tent, as in the *Chronicle of Morea*, but rather just for the narrator William.

Suddenly he stopped in his tracks, staring at me. His eyes wrinkled as though with a smile, though his mouth remained set. 'Don't go right away, cousin William,' he said thoughtfully. 'I have a secret I may not tell to a living soul. But I'm not a leper, you know, there's no need to keep away from my tent. In fact you might take a look at the tent-pegs. These Grifons have fastened the guy-ropes with a cunning knot I should like to see copied in Escorta. No, don't keep away from my tent, though at present I can't invite you inside.'

(Duggan 1962: 113–14)

Despite these transformations, Duggan explicitly states in his paratextual note that this speech was, at least in outline, true (1962: 254). In other words, both Duggan and Rodd offer paraphrases of the speech as true or essentially true accounts of *what actually happened*. It is perhaps unsurprising that this vivid vignette was taken up so enthusiastically by Duggan, but it is more remarkable that Rodd integrates the text in exactly the same way.

Miller's rendition of this episode is, like his narrative of the battle of Karydi, stylistically simpler. He offers no direct speech, does not explicitly mention the story of the tent-pole and is generally much more concise.

For an instant even William's courage seems to have failed him; but the reproaches of that stalwart baron, Geoffroy de Bruyeres, prevailed on him to lead his diminished but now homogeneous army against the heterogeneous host of Greeks, Hungarians, Germans, Slavs, and Turks.

(Miller 1908: 111)

Although Miller's narrative ostensibly excises the speech, its explanatory function remains the same. His description of Geoffrey prevailing on the prince (William) to fight depends on the same speech in the *Chronicle of Morea* that Duggan and Rodd reproduced.[15] Miller transforms the speech to Geoffrey's tent-pole into a direct confrontation/conversation between Geoffrey and the prince, but the speech's explanatory logic remains. Miller's narrative doubtless appears more plausible to modern historians with the sensibilities of Voltaire and Lilie, but if anything this direct confrontation/conversation between Geoffrey and the prince rests on no textual evidence from the *Chronicle of Morea*. It is, in other words, imagined by Miller as the most plausible *historical* explanation of *what actually happened*.

Duggan and Rodd reproduce and adapt the speech of the *Chronicle of Morea*. Miller attempts to excise this problematic textual element from his story and yet despite this is unable to escape the explanatory framework that the speech sets up. His narrative ends up relying on the speech and even being forced to imagine action that is not explicitly presented in the *Chronicle of the Morea*, on which the truth claimed by all three modern narratives ultimately depend. The main discernible difference between historiography and historical fiction turns out to be the style in which they paraphrase and reproduce the *Chronicle of the Morea*. In the end the most formally historiographical narrative (i.e. Miller's) is the least faithful to the medieval *source material*.

3. The battle of Prinitsa: Explaining Frankish victory

The final structuring battle of *Lord Geoffrey's Fancy* is the so-called battle of Prinitsa, in which 312 Frankish knights vanquished a vast army of Nicaeans. According to the *Chronicle of Morea*, before the battle the Frankish leader, Jean de Catabas, the cuckolded husband of Jeanne de Catabas – the eponymous lady with whom Geoffrey de Bruyères had eloped to Italy – gave a long speech to his men. Examination of the reception of this speech in the three modern texts, like the previous case study, demonstrates that there is no qualitative difference in the reception of this speech in the historiography and historical fiction. For all three, the speech is converted into historical fact. If anything, the formal freedom of historical fiction allows Duggan to potentially become a more critical reader of the *Chronicle of Morea* than Rodd and Miller. This reading thus demonstrates the potential of non-historiographical discourse to challenge positivist readings of medieval narratives.

In the *Chronicle of Morea*, Jean mentions a number of topics in a set-piece speech, similar to that constructed in numerous other important passages of the text.[16] After pointing out the disparate and ill-equipped nature of the enemy, he states that their victory would be praised as long as Noah's Ark remains on Mount Ararat.

Ἰδέτε πάλιν δεύτερον, ἀφέντες καὶ συντρόφοι,/ὅτι, ἂν μᾶς δώσῃ ὁ Θεὸς κ' ἡ τύχη μας ἐτοῦτο,/τὸν ἀδελφὸν τοῦ βασιλέως κ' ἐτοῦτα τὰ φουσσᾶτα/μὲ πόλεμον καὶ μὲ σπαθὶ νὰ τοὺς νικήσωμε ὧδε,/**ἕως ὅτου στήκει ἡ κιβωτὸς στὸ Ἀραρὰτ τὸ ὄρος,**/μέλλει στήκει τὸ ἔπαινος τῆς σημερνῆς ἡμέρας,/ὅπου μᾶς θέλουν ἐπαινεῖ ὅσοι τὸ θέλουν ἀκούσει.

> [And in second place, lords and comrades, consider that should God and our fortune grant that we here defeat the brother of the basileus and these armies with battle and with sword **as long as the ark remains on Mount Ararat**, so long will remain the praise of this day, with which all those who will hear of it will praise us.]
>
> (*Chronicle of Morea*, 4740–46; Lurier 1964: 210)

This allusion to Noah's Ark is repeated by both Miller and Rodd as fact.

> Then Messire Jean de Catavas addressed his men. '[…] **so long as the ark of God shall rest on the mountain of Ararat**, shall live the praise of this day on the lips of men.'
>
> (Rodd 1907: 223)

> Despite the smallness of his forces and his own physical infirmity, which prevented him from holding sword or lance, he ordered the prince's standard—the anchored cross of the Villehardouins—to be tied fast to his hand, and, reminding his men that they were Franks and their enemies men of many nations, bade them win fame which would endure **'so long as the ark remains on Ararat.'**
>
> (Miller 1908: 122)

Rodd again translates the whole speech, describing it as how Jean addressed his men, while Miller only quotes this allusion in isolation, but nevertheless as fact. So both include this colourful vignette, adopting it uncritically as fact and with it the explanatory power of a speech which produces a battle in which Western knights won a great victory, motivated by heroic, epic and religious goals. Duggan includes this same vignette, but in a manner that foregrounds the allusive quality of the reference and thus undermines its significance.

> 'We speak one language, we fight in the same way, we know one another, we serve the same lord. The Prince left us at home, thinking us unfit for war. Let's show him his mistake. Let's do a famous deed of arms, something that will be remembered for as long – as long – as long as Noah's Ark rests on Ararat.' **Evidently Sir John had been trying to think of some famous battle of the past, and could not name one**.
>
> (Duggan 1962: 210)

Just as in the previous case study, this speech, and its explanatory logic of a textual element of which modern historians claim to be particularly suspicious, persists in all the modern narratives. The chivalric call of the old knight Jean, as illustrated by this quotation, explains (at least in part) the victory of this tiny Frankish force in all the narratives. Miller and Rodd offer their quotations as straightforward fact, conforming (at least stylistically) to the expectations of modern 'scientific' historical discourse. Duggan, in contrast, places a question mark next to his citation, by quipping that Jean had not been able to think of a sufficiently august battle and thus somewhat undermines the explanatory power of the religio-chivalric speech. Although all three narratives reproduce the quotation, the novel appears to offer a more sceptical reception of the speech than the modern historians. Outside the disciplinarily accepted framework of historiography in which a statement can be either true or false, Duggan is able to highlight and thus question the invented, literary, rhetorical and downright odd quality of this statement, without excising it from his narrative. This moment in the narrative thus hints, albeit somewhat intangibly, at the possibilities of historical fiction providing a framework capable of a less rigid critique than traditional historiography allows.

Preliminary conclusions

Historical fiction represents the threshold between a disciplinary historiography, that refuses to abandon its failed attempt to become a science, and fiction, the repressed other that historiography refuses to become (Certeau 1988: 308–54; White 2005: 147–48; Wake 2016). Historical fiction's attempt to distinguish itself from other realist novels and from historiography proper offers a crack through which to re-examine the assumed categorical and generic distinction that modern disciplinary historiography assumes for itself. Duggan's authorial note highlights several of the dissonances produced by historical fiction's attempt to face in two directions simultaneously, when it claims that *Lord Geoffrey's Fancy* possesses a story that is both true and false, characters that are both real and imagined, and events that both happened and did not. The comparative examination of these dissonances in *Lord Geoffrey's Fancy* highlights similar phenomena in historiography.

Each of the three case studies, in different ways, seek to blur the boundary set up by disciplinary history. The first two case studies illustrate how modern historiographical explanations are both too divergent from their source material to fulfil their claims to an exclusively true story (as in the first case study) and retain too much of their narrative and rhetorical structure (as in the second and third). The first focuses on how historiography ends up being an inventive and imaginative process, while the second and third both demonstrate that there is often no qualitative difference between the ways in which historiography and historical fiction receive medieval texts. In these examples the principal difference in the reception of the *Chronicle of Morea*'s narrative is its formal style of its retelling. Finally, the third case study tentatively suggests that the opportunity to look sideways at historical narration is a potential of historical fiction that has yet to be exploited. Taken as a whole, this chapter seeks to demonstrate that thinking about historiography in terms of reception and engaging with the logics that organize both historiography and historical fiction has the potential to empower alternative and (at least potentially) less disciplinarily straight-jacketed readings, because it starts by acknowledging that historians are also in the business of imagining their stories and that meaning is neither fixed nor singular.

Acknowledgements

This chapter was begun within the framework of the 'Moving Byzantium: Mobility, Microstructures and Personal Agency' project, funded by the Austrian Science Fund (project Z 288 Wittgenstein-Preis). It was completed within the framework of the 'Narrative Hierarchies: Minor Characters in Byzantine and Medieval History Writing' project, funded by the Research Council of Norway (grant no. 324754).

Notes

1. Note that Duggan himself retired to Ross-on-Wye in Herefordshire for the last eleven years of his life and it is there that he wrote *Lord Geoffrey's Fancy* (Waugh 1964).
2. Authorial notes are important loci for the dissonances inherent in historical fiction and have even been suggested as a definitional element for the generic identification of historical fiction: 'It might be a rule of thumb to define the historical novel as something which has an explanatory note from the writer describing their own engagement with the period in question, either through schooling or, more commonly, through their reading and research' (De Groot 2009: 6–8). See also Chapter 15.
3. Duggan finishes this note by stating that 'The narrator's opinion of Greeks, Turks, and other foreigners is his own, and not necessarily that of the author' (Duggan 1962: 254). As this statement suggests, *Lord Geoffrey's Fancy* views Byzantine/ Frankish Greece through an English and Frankish lens. Place names are 'Frankicized' throughout and a glossary of place names is included (Duggan 1962: vii). Athens and Thebes, for example, are rendered as Satines and Estives. The Byzantines/Eastern Romans, including both Nicaeans and Epirots, are consistently called Grifons. The latter are produced as sly and effeminate, while Turkish characters are rendered as barbarous and violent. Both are opposed to the honest martial masculinity of the crusaders. For the gendered production of Byzantines in Western/crusader texts and modern historiography, see respectively Demacopoulos (2019: 13–48) and Neville (2019: 5–21).
4. The realness of events and characters are central to the early understanding of the historical novel: 'We consider (say) the eighteenth century from the purely historical standpoint, and, while we do so, are under no delusion as to our limitations; we know that a few of the leading personages and events have been brought before us in a more or less disjointed fashion, and are perfectly aware that there is room for much discrepancy between the pictures so presented to us (be it with immense skill) and the actual facts as they took place in such and such a year' (Nield 1902: 10).
5. Sixteen pages of Miller's 675-page text (*c.* 2.4 per cent) narrate the period covered in *Lord Geoffrey's Fancy*, in contrast to approximately forty pages of Rodd's 635-page-long monograph (*c.* 6.3 per cent).
6. For the importance of Miller's work, see Paul Hetherington's appraisal: 'It is pre-eminently *The Latins in the Levant* (1908), and *Essays on the Latin Orient* ([1921] 1964) that reveal Miller's capacity for reducing complex and detailed issues to a clear and coherent narrative unity. These masterly studies are his most lasting gifts to medieval scholarship, and of enduring value. When listing his works, he always put them before any others. They are books of their period; but it is still impossible

to study these centuries of Levantine history without having digested them' (Hetherington 2009: 155).
7   'Beyond its historical significance the Greek Chronicle has had an influence on literature, ranging from the Helena episode in the third act of *Faust II* to various dramas and novels in modern Greek and the admirable historical novel, *Lord Geoffrey's Fancy* (1962), by the late Alfred Duggan' (Topping 1965: 737).
8   Concerning the naming (or not) of female characters in Byzantine historiography, see Kinloch (2020).
9   This is consistent across all versions of the *Chronicle of Morea*.
10 Generally on the importance of the battle of Pelagonia in historiography of the thirteenth century, see Kinloch (2018: 155–69).
11 Concerning Voltaire and historiography, see Pierse (2013) and Stern (2015: 14).
12 'The consequence of this is, however, the realization that speeches of this kind, if they were ever delivered, which is quite doubtful, had nothing at all to do with reality' (Lilie 2014: 208).
13 It is worth noting the hypocrisy of Rodd here, since in the preface to his history he patronizingly critiques the history of 'the talented authoress' Diane de Gobineau for having 'followed too closely the narrative of the chronicle [of Morea] for historical accuracy' (Rodd 1907: viii).
14 On the ambiguity of the *Chronicle of Morea* on points of Frankish valour, see Demacopoulos (2019: 103–21).
15 It is not, for example, mentioned in the principal source used by Byzantinists, the *Chronike syngraphe* of George Akropolites (Macrides 2007: 361).
16 On speech acts in the *Chronicle of Morea*, see Shawcross (2009: 131–49).

Bibliography

Buchon, J. A. C. (1845), *Recherches historiques sur la principauté française de Morée et ses hautes baronnies*, 2 vols, Paris: J. Renouard.
Carr, E. H. (1962), *What Is History?*, Harmondsworth: Penguin Books.
Certeau, M. de (1988), *The Writing of History*, New York: Columbia University Press.
De Groot, J. (2009), *The Historical Novel*, London: Routledge.
Demacopoulos, G. E. (2019), *Colonizing Christianity: Greek and Latin Religious Identity in the Era of the Fourth Crusade*, New York: Fordham University Press.
Duggan, A. (1962), *Lord Geoffrey's Fancy*, London: Faber & Faber.
Haldon, J. (1984), '"Jargon" vs. "the Facts"? Byzantine History-Writing and Contemporary Debates', *Byzantine and Modern Greek Studies*, 9: 95–132.
Hetherington, P. (2009), 'William Miller: Medieval Historian and Modern Journalist', *British School at Athens Studies*, 17: 153–61.
Ilieva, A. (1991), *Frankish Morea (1205–1262): Socio-Cultural Interaction between the Franks and the Local Population*, Athens: S. D. Vasilopoulos.
Jebb, R. C. (1907), *Essays and Addresses*, Cambridge: Cambridge University Press.
Jeffreys, E., J. Haldon and R. Cormack (2008), 'Byzantine Studies as an Academic Discipline', in E. Jeffreys, J. Haldon, and R. Cormack (eds.), *The Oxford Handbook of Byzantine Studies*, 3–20, Oxford: Oxford University Press.
Jeffreys, M. (1975), 'The Chronicle of the Morea: Priority of the Greek Version', *Byzantinische Zeitschrift* 68: 304–50.

Kaldellis, A. (2010), 'The Study of Women and Children: Methodological Challenges and New Directions', in P. Stephenson (ed.), *The Byzantine World*, 61-71, Abingdon: Routledge.

Kaldellis, A. (2016), 'The Manufacture of History in the Later Tenth and Eleventh Centuries: Rhetorical Templates and Narrative Ontologies', in S. Marjanović-Dušanić (ed.), *Proceedings of the 23rd International Congress of Byzantine Studies, Belgrade 22-27 August 2016: Plenary Papers*, 293-306, Belgrade: The Serbian National Committee of AIEB.

Kinloch, M. (2018), 'Rethinking Thirteenth-Century Byzantine Historiography: A Postmodern, Narrativist, and Narratological Approach', DPhil diss., University of Oxford.

Kinloch, M. (2020), 'In the Name of the Father, the Husband, or Some Other Man: The Subordination of Female Characters in Byzantine Historiography', *Dumbarton Oaks Papers*, 74: 303-28.

Lilie, R.-J. (2014), 'Reality and Invention: Reflections on Byzantine Historiography', *Dumbarton Oaks Papers*, 68: 157-210.

Lurier, H. E. (1964), *Crusaders as Conquerors: The Chronicle of Morea*, New York: Columbia University Press.

Macrides, R. (2007), *George Akropolites: The History*, Oxford: Oxford University Press.

Macrides, R. (2010), 'Editor's Preface', in R. Macrides (ed.), *History as Literature in Byzantium*, ix-xi, Farnham: Ashgate.

Mango, C. (1975), *Byzantine Literature as a Distorting Mirror: An Inaugural Lecture Delivered before the University of Oxford on 21 May 1974*, Oxford: Clarendon Press.

Manzoni, A. (1996), *On the Historical Novel*, Lincoln: University of Nebraska Press.

Marwick, A. (2001), *The New Nature of History: Knowledge, Evidence, Language*, Basingstoke: Palgrave.

Megill, A. (1989), 'Recounting the Past: "Description," Explanation, and Narrative in Historiography', *The American Historical Review*, 94 (3): 627-53.

Miller, W. (1908), *The Latins in the Levant: A History of Frankish Greece (1204-1566)*, London: J. Murray.

Miller, W. ([1921] 1964), *Essays on the Latin Orient*, Cambridge: Cambridge University Press.

Neville, L. (2019), *Byzantine Gender*, Leeds: Arc Humanities Press.

Nield, J. (1902), *A Guide to the Best Historical Novels and Tales*, London: Elkin Mathews.

Nielen, M.-A. (2003), *Lignages d'outremer*, Paris: Académie des inscriptions et belles-lettres. [*Lignages d'outremer*]

Papadopoulou, E., ed. (2000), *Marinos Sanoudos Torsello, Istoria tis Romanias*, Athens: Ethniko Idryma Erevnon.

Pierse, S. (2013), 'Voltaire: Polemical Possibilities of History', in S. Bourgault and R. Sparling (eds.), *A Companion to Enlightenment Historiography*, 153-87, Leiden: Brill.

Rodd, R. (1907), *The Princes of Achaia and the Chronicles of Morea: A Study of Greece in the Middle Ages*, London: E. Arnold.

Schmitt, J. (1904), *The Chronicle of Morea: A History in Political Verse, Relating the Establishment of Feudalism in Greece by the Franks in the Thirteenth Century*, London: Methuen & Co.

Shawcross, T. (2009), *The Chronicle of Morea: Historiography in Crusader Greece*, Oxford: Oxford University Press.

Stern, F. (2015), *Varieties of History: From Voltaire to the Present*, London: Macmillan International Higher Education.

Topping, P. (1965), 'Review of *Crusaders as Conquerors: The Chronicle of Morea*, by Harold E. Lurier', *Speculum*, 40 (4): 737–42.
Van Arsdall, A. and H. Moody (2015), *The Old French Chronicle of Morea: An Account of Frankish Greece after the Fourth Crusade*, Farnham: Ashgate Publishing.
Voltaire [Arouet, F.-M.] (1763), *The History of the Russian Empire under Peter the Great*, London: J. Nourse and P. Vaillant; L. Davis & C. Reymers.
Wake, P. (2016), '"Except in the Case of Historical Fact": History and the Historical Novel', *Rethinking History*, 20 (1): 80–96.
Waugh, E. (1964), 'Alfred Duggan (10 July 1964)', *The Spectator*, July: 10.
White, H. (2005), 'Introduction: Historical Fiction, Fictional History, and Historical Reality', *Rethinking History*, 9 (2–3): 147–57.

13

The Barbarians Will Always Stay: Rose Macaulay and the Futility of Empire

Olof Heilo

In *The Towers of Trebizond* (1956), Rose Macaulay describes, with a wit that made the novel an immediate success, how a group of British Anglicans set out to establish a foreign mission in Turkey. Written at a time when the British Empire was beginning to lose ground all around the world, the absurdity of their enterprise forms the backdrop for a novel about human vanity and cultural priggishness. The leader of the party, Father Chantry-Pigg, is firmly convinced of his own duty to spread the Word of Christ, but deeply loathes all Christians that are not Anglicans, which happens to be most of them. The narrator's aunt, Dot, pontificates the superiority of the British way of life from the back of a camel, a reminiscence of a colonial past that she insists on bringing with her on the mission. Since neither of them has any knowledge of Turkish, they use a Turkish Anglican convert, Dr Halide Tanpınar, for assistance: a modern Turkish woman who declares her commitment to the Kemalist republic but still shows herself anxious to defend its Ottoman past. Needless to say, both the religious and secular Turks of the 1950s remain unreceptive towards Anglicanism. The party ends up at Trabzon, Trebizond or Trapezunt, the last capital of the Byzantine Comnenian dynasty, where the ruins of the Byzantine palace evoke different feelings among the travellers.

> Father Chantry-Pigg said his piece about Turkish apathy and squalor having let this noble palace and citadel go to ruin, as all antiquities in Turkey went to ruin … Dr. Halide, who had the lowest opinion of the public and private morale of Byzantines, said that it was understandable that the monuments to such vicious, cruel, violent, and murderous profligates and maladministrators as the Byzantine emperors, despots, grand dukes, nobles, bishops, eunuchs, populace, and above all the Trabzon Comnenus dynasty … – it was understandable, said Dr. Halide, that the Osmanlis, taking over this corrupted and vicious empire, should not care to preserve the edifices reared out of the blood of the citizens … aunt Dot did just say that, when it came to bloodthirstiness, murder, torture, violence and all that, it seemed a pretty near thing between Byzantines and Turks; after all, as she pointed out, both the Comneni and their conquerors were Asiatic, and deeply devoted to cruelty … Dr. Halide said, look at the religious tolerance of Sulemein

the Magnificent in sixteenth century Istanbul. 'So much more tolerant was he than the West,' she said, 'that no doubt some of your ancestors fled to Istanbul to escape from persecution at home.' I thought that this would have been very wise of our ancestors, whatever it was they were being persecuted for, because Istanbul would have been a very beautiful and romantic city to flee to.

(Macaulay 1995: 74–75)

The narrator, whose gender remains unknown, is less interested in the civilizing objective of the expedition and more attracted to the exotic sights that it has to offer. She or he is already working on a book about the trip, frequently running into other British people who are doing the same ('They are all writing their Turkey books', as the aunt condescendingly comments). The expedition eventually breaks up somewhere along the border to Armenia, where Father Chantry-Pigg and Aunt Dot finally abandon the project of converting the Turks and instead decide to 'crash the curtain'. That is, they are to make their way across the Iron Curtain into the Soviet Union and save Western Christian civilization from within the innermost bowels of its greatest opponent. The narrator returns to Britain where he or she suffers the loss of a lover who only by the very end is outed as a man.

Rose Macaulay herself, by this time aged seventy-three, had been travelling to Trabzon in 1954, adding another self-ironic metalevel to the novel;[1] and, as we shall see, the passage quoted above contains further clues to its conception. In June 1955, she gave readers of the *Times Literary Supplement* a foretaste of the subject of the novel through a poem in five stanzas called 'Dirge for Trebizond'. But whereas *The Towers of Trebizond* is marked by self-deprecatory distance, told (by the author as well as the narrator) from the safety of home in Britain, the melancholic 'Dirge for Trebizond' rather seems to be borne out of a real-time experience on the journey; perhaps in a scene like one in the novel, where the narrator is found painting among the ruins of the Byzantine palace of Trabzon (Macaulay 1995: 145).

In the following, I would like to devote particular attention to the poem, which I think deserves more attention than it has hitherto received.[2] Its literary qualities are admittedly debatable: laden with cultural clichés, historical tropes, stereotypical imagery, worn-out idioms and sermon quotes in both Greek and Latin, it features a dream-like, somewhat rambling vision of disjointed characters, agencies and motifs: Ovid and Cavafy, Byzantium and modern Turkey. Still, I would argue that precisely Macaulay's way of using static components to create a dynamic whole is what gives 'Dirge for Trebizond' a certain – if I may say so – 'Byzantine' quality (cf. Nilsson 2021: 22-26, 31–32). More specifically, I would like to highlight how the Byzantine interacts with other cultural tropes of the poem in a way that renders them all a significance that goes far beyond simple mechanisms of Western cultural othering.

Byzantinism

A *dirge*, an English word which originally referred to the Latin office of the dead prayer, is a lament. The 'Dirge for Trebizond' begins with the words 'Where is now Byzantium' and ends with the words 'We knew Byzantium once, now no more'. In short, it is a lament for Byzantium.

> Where now is Byzantium, its lost last empire?
> Where the Grand-Comnenus in his palace on the crag?
> Their magnificence the emperors, Alexios, Andronicos?
> They sat beneath the gold roof set with stars,
> The floors were rose marble, the walls bright as flowers.
> They were Byzantines, with libraries and such;
> They talked of homoousion, babbled of the Trinity,
> In the Greek of Trebizond.
> Oh the glitter of the churches, chanting their Masses
> Within the painted walls, where Christ and his emperors
> Stood stiff and bright, like trees!
> The library of Tychius, the marbles, the glory,
> The Trebizond princesses, straight as palms,
> The rich merchant cargoes, tossing up the Euxine
> From the Golden Horn to Trebizond!
>
> (Macaulay 1955, l: 1–15)

The first stanza brings to mind Umberto Eco's description of the movie *Casablanca* (1942) as 'clichés having a ball' (Eco 1985), at least in terms of clichés about Byzantium. First, the melancholic question, which embeds the empire in an inaccessible past: where is the snow of yesteryear? Then, the evocation of the Grand-Comnenus, babbling about the trinity in his palace under the roof set with stars: a fairy-tale-like description that seems to echo Coleridge's rhymes about Kublai Khan in his pleasure-dome. The triumphant culmination sounds like a pastiche on the famous third and fourth stanzas from Yeats's 'Sailing to Byzantium', ending in an ecstatic stacking of historical names and facts with unclear correlation. Tychicus was a scholar in sixth- or seventh-century Trebizond, known from the works of the Armenian natural philosopher Ananias of Shirak (Conybeare 1897); the princesses, 'straight as palms', evoke the fifth-century mosaics of the martyr virgins in Sant'Apollinare Nuovo in Ravenna, a recurring source of imagination about the Byzantine Empire at a time when the Byzantine monuments of Istanbul were still badly researched or inaccessible (Herrin 2020: 387 ff.). Like the word *homoousion*, which mainly belongs to the religious conflicts of the fourth century, all of this paints a picture of a late Antique Byzantium that is, actually, very distant from the late medieval Comnenian Empire that had Trebizond as its capital. But just as in Victorien Sardou's (1831–1908) explanation for why he let his play about the Empress Theodora end by having the protagonist, contrary to historical facts, strangled by a eunuch – he had to give her 'a death more Byzantine than the real one' (Boeck 2015: 124, quoting Hart 1913: 95) – we are, of course, neither in the late ancient nor in the late medieval empire. Byzantium is simply a fantastic place out of this world, a vision of a lost splendour.

'Byzantinism' as a set of Western clichés about Byzantium is often associated with the notion of something ridiculously bureaucratic, ceremonious and traditionalist; in the worst case, false and intrigant (Angelov 2003). It sometimes overlaps with Saïd's definition of orientalism: a world considered 'irrational, depraved (fallen), childlike' (Saïd 1978: 40; Cameron 2003). The main difference is that whereas the oriental is an eternal Other, unchanging and unchangeable, who has never been and will never be anything but an oriental, there is an element of familiarity in the Byzantine: the Westerner seems to know him or her as one would a distant relative that has somehow ended up in a bad place (cf. Boeck 2015: 122–23, 128–31). All classical points of orientation for the modern West were available to the Byzantines, too, so why and where did they get lost?[3] Change, it seems, is as much a part of the problem as a lack of change when talking about Byzantium (Heilo 2018).

Classicism

That the author of 'Dirge for Trebizond' is standing among the same ruins as the narrator of *The Towers of Trebizond* becomes clear in the second and third stanzas of the poem:

> In the fig-grown palace ghosts whisper
> In the Greek of Trebizond.
> Among the broken walls and the brambles
> Feet pass round and about:
>
> (Macaulay 1955, l: 16–19)

> Through Byzantine windows they peer at the harbour,
> Where Turkish ships rock, the crescent on the prow
>
> (Macaulay 1955, l: 34–35)

It is not merely the history of the Byzantine Empire that ends here, overlooking the Black Sea. It might be worth quoting another reflection on past glory made in a ruinous setting:

> It was at Rome, on the fifteenth of October 1764, as I sat musing amidst the ruins of the Capitol, while the barefoot friars were singing vespers in the Temple of Jupiter, that the idea of writing the decline and fall of the city first started to my mind.
>
> (Gibbon 1911: 128)

Charles Lock (2012) uses this Gibbon quote when he discusses Rose Macaulay's essay book *The Pleasure of Ruins* (1953), but the description of the young historian sitting in Rome during his Grand Tour and conceiving *The Decline and Fall of the Roman Empire* is equally useful to bear in mind when reading *The Towers of Trebizond* and 'Dirge for Trebizond', whose descriptions of the Byzantine ruins engender similar tensions between irony and sentiment, distance and closeness, representation and reality (cf. White 1973: 55).

That 'Dirge for Trebizond', too, is not only a poem of Byzantium but also of the decline and fall of the Roman Empire, becomes clear in the last stanza. Here we see Macaulay drop Greek quotations and references in favour of Latin ones and, somewhat surprisingly, cut across the Black Sea from Trabzon-Trebizond to Constanta-Tomis,

> On the Pontic shores, by the bitter lake
> Where Ovid cried in vain to Rome;
> Where, crying and praying, he came at last to terms
> With life and death and Caesar and fate [...]
>
> (Macaulay 1955, l: 59–62)

It might seem a frail arch to strike from the Comnenian emperors in Trebizond to the Roman poet who was exiled to the Danube delta by Emperor Augustus; but again, Gibbon offers a clue; surveying the situation of the Roman Empire in the early fourth century and talking about the Sarmatians that Constantine the Great struggled to keep at bay, Gibbon reflects upon how 'the tender Ovid, after a youth spent in the enjoyment of fame and luxury, was condemned to a hopeless exile on the frozen banks of the Danube, where he was exposed, almost without defence, to the fury of these monsters of the desert' (1906–07, III: 185).

The setting is particularly noteworthy. 'On the shores of the Black Sea', according to Neal Ascherson, writing about the ancient Greek colonists of that place, 'there were born a pair of Siamese twins called "civilization" and "barbarism"':

> In this particular encounter began the idea of 'Europe' with all its arrogance, all its implications of superiority, all its assumptions of priority and antiquity, all its pretensions to a natural right to dominate.
>
> (Ascherson 1996: 49)

Gibbon and Macaulay, too, use the Black Sea as a backdrop for reflections on civilization and barbarism, with the difference that they have seen the end of the story: (Graeco-Roman) civilization is merely a stage between (Pontic) barbarism and (Trapezuntine) Byzantinism (cf. further Gossman 1981: 30–33). Rather than cultural superiority, what they express is a feeling of resignation to the forces of nature. For all his 'cries in vain', Ovid was never recalled to Rome but had to come to terms with the barbarian sea, just as Gibbon had to accept that the 'happiest time for man', the Roman Empire of the second century CE, had succumbed to a change that it already carried within.

Barbarism

Gibbon's mastodont work ends with the fall of Constantinople to the Ottomans in 1453. Macaulay's poem reads almost like a final comment on the same process, describing how 'Mahmud's Janissaries, Mahomet the Sultan' close in on the last remaining city of the empire – Trebizond – in 1461. The 'barbarians howl round the walls like the sea, as if they and the Black Sea are part of the same force of nature; the Byzantines seek support in religion and pray to St. Eugenios, the patron saint of the city, while the emperor, David Comnenos, tries to negotiate with the enemies at the gate. All to no avail: 'The Sultan and his hordes pour through. / The barbarians are in.' (Macaulay 1955, l: 29–30).

At this point, the references are obvious to another avid reader of Gibbon, Konstantin Cavafy, whose poem 'Waiting for the Barbarians' (1898) describes how the decline and fall of the Roman Empire emerge out of an external necessity that, at closer examination, turns out to be a mere pretext for changes that actually come from within:

Why is our emperor up and about so early,
and seated at the grandest gate of our city,
upon the throne, in state, wearing the crown?

>Because the barbarians will arrive today.
>And the emperor expects to receive their leader.
>Indeed, he has prepared to present him
>with a parchment scroll. Thereon he has
>invested him with many names and titles.

Why have our two consuls and praetors come out
today in their purple, embroidered togas;
why did they put on bracelets studded with amethysts,
and rings with resplendent, glittering emeralds;
why are they carrying today precious canes
carved exquisitely in gold and silver?

>Because the barbarians will arrive today
>and such things dazzle the barbarians.

(Cavafy 2007: 14–15)

In Cavafy's poem, the ancient world becomes Byzantine when it tries to fend off an invasion of nameless barbarians. All the stage props of Byzantinism, from an outer appearance studded with gold, jewels, purple and embroideries, to an innate preference for traditions, hierarchies and stagnation, are convenient responses to a threat that, by the end, turns out to be the solution and not the problem. Obsessed with external self-preservation, the empire loses any sense of an inner purpose, and once the barbarians are gone, is left alone with a mortifying void. Whereas the setting appears to be late Roman, Filippomaria Pontani has shown how the poem echoes an episode in Niketas Choniates's *History* in which the Byzantine Emperor Alexios III (r. 1195–1203) tries to impress the envoys of the German Emperor Henry VI (Pontani 2018). Written by a Greek in British-controlled, but still nominally Ottoman Egypt, 'Waiting for the Barbarians' is a multi-layered elegy over a bygone greatness.

Unlike Cavafy's Romans, Macaulay's Byzantines seem quite happy with themselves and somewhat indifferent to the barbarian threat. At least there is no sign that they have changed their way of life due to the appearance of an external enemy. They keep doing what they have been doing for a millennium: babbling about the trinity and praying to St. Eugenios. Their downfall, it is inferred, is not caused by a lack of reverence for tradition, but rather an over-confidence in it:

> The Trapezuntines say
> The barbarians are in, for a while.
> Soon the barbarians will go,
> In a week, in a month, in a year.
> In two years, in five, in ten.
> Or it may be fifty, it may be more …
> Barbarians must always go.
>
> (Macaulay 1955, l: 36–42)

In Niketas's story, the barbarians do not go. The bejewelled Alexios III confirms the Germans in their prejudice that the Byzantines are weak, effeminate and easy to rob of their riches, thus anticipating the Fourth Crusade that will devastate the empire a few years later and leave Constantinople in Western hands for more than fifty years. Macaulay's imagined Trapezuntines turn out to be even more mistaken: the Turks have come to stay far longer than that.

Orientalism

Before she ventures across the Black Sea to reflect upon Ovid, Rose Macaulay takes the conflict between Byzantines and 'Barbarians' straight into her own time:

> Five slow centuries, they still are here,
> No more Masses, no more marvels,
> No more reasoning in the banquet halls
> In the Greek of Trebizond.
> There is no Greek in Trebizond.
> The mouldering marbles, the plastered churches,
> Bright saints and emperors under snow [...]
> Byzantium lost and the last Greek gone,
> Barbarians will always stay.
>
> (Macaulay 1955, l: 44–50, 55–56)

Again, the clichés are dancing. 'Dirge for Trebizond' speaks of 'muffled women', 'sloe-eyed men', 'tall minarets' and 'clamouring bazaars'. It is orientalism, without a doubt, delivered in the same tone as the classical and other cultural references throughout the poem, which can be ironic or sentimental, or both. Yet the power relationship it underlines is diametrically different from the one that Saïd would later address in his post-colonial manifesto. For Saïd, it was essential to show how colonial orientalism strived to maintain a notion of orientals as being unable to rule themselves (Saïd 1978: 31–46, 96–110, 208 ff.). Macaulay, by contrast, depicts the fall of the last remnant of the Roman Empire to orientals that turn out to be not so unable to rule themselves, after all. Rather, the Byzantines who had expected the barbarians to lose their grip sooner or later are the ones that, like Ovid, will forever remain ghostly exiles on the Black Sea coast, their church frescoes and mosaics buried under mosque whitewash.

Saïd does not have much to say about Byzantium.[4] But he does quote Yeats when he wants to illustrate how T. E. Lawrence and Gertrud Bell understood Arab culture (Saïd 1978: 230):

> At midnight on the Emperor's pavement flit
> Flames that no faggot feeds, nor steel has lit,
> Nor storm disturbs, flames begotten of flame,
> Where blood-begotten spirits come
> And all complexities of fury leave,
> Dying into a dance,
> An agony of trance,
> An agony of flame that cannot singe a sleeve
>
> (Yeats 1989: 252)

The orientalism that Saïd addresses, one feels tempted to say, is Byzantinism-orientalism: the literary construction of an Orient in a state of lethargy and powerlessness, where stronger, assurgent nations are called for to take the command – exemplified in the colonial era by the late Ottoman Empire, but already preceded in pre-modern times by a Byzantine Empire in need of Western 'protection' (Heilo and Nilsson 2017). This Byzantine-Oriental should not be confused with the barbarian-oriental as represented by Middle Eastern peoples in a state of conquest and expansion. Gibbon, again, may have established the claim that the Arabs had spread Islam with 'the sword in one hand and the Koran in the other', but he was also eager to note that the Arab prophet

> despised the pomp of royalty: the apostle of God submitted to the menial offices of the family: he kindled the fire, swept the floor, milked the ewes, and mended with his own hands his shoes and his woollen garment.
>
> (Gibbon 1906–7, IX: 86-87)

According to Gibbon, it was not until 'the seat of empire was removed to the Tigris, that the Abbasides [sic] adopted the proud and pompous ceremonial of the Persian and Byzantine courts' (Gibbon 1906–7, IX: 86-87). In other words, the oriental gets corrupted by the Byzantine and the barbarian by the empire – not the other way round (see further Gossman 1981: 55–56). The Ottoman Turks who conquer Trebizond will be in for the same inevitable transformation, repeating the Roman and Byzantine experience and ending up as Byzantine-orientals before giving way to Western colonial powers and the ascending Kemalist republic.

CULTURE

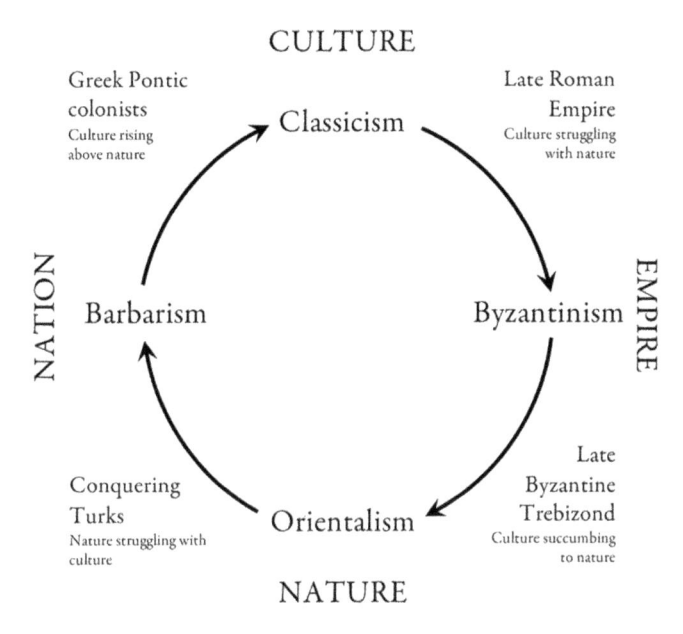

```
      Greek Pontic                          Late Roman
      colonists          Classicism         Empire
      Culture rising                        Culture struggling
      above nature                          with nature

NATION    Barbarism              Byzantinism    EMPIRE

      Conquering                              Late
      Turks                                   Byzantine
      Nature struggling with  Orientalism     Trebizond
      culture                                 Culture succumbing
                                              to nature
```

NATURE

Figure 13.1 Static components engendering a dynamic whole: the interplay of Byzantinism, classicism, orientalism and barbarism in 'Dirge for Trebizond'. Drawing by the author.

As points of (modern Western) orientation and identification, classicism and orientalism are static and impenetrable of each other: the classical represents the highest stage of human progress and achievement through culture, whereas the Orient represents its opposite – unfettered nature, unresponsive to change. Nature in a conquering stage that still has not given in to culture results in barbarism, the state of free nations, which can be noble, savage or both. Culture in a declining stage that has still not given in to nature brings forth Byzantinism, the state of complex empires, which can similarly be sophisticated, cruel or both. The former, still unfettered and free to choose its own fate, is in a stage of creating its own world; the latter, weighed down under the burden of the past, can only try to maintain the existing world. The late Byzantines of Trebizond, who finally succumb to the barbarian sea, are the opposites of the early Greek colonists – only indirectly hinted at in the poem – who once rose above it.

By now, we have reached full circle, where the different cultural components of the poem stand in an inner relationship to each other (Figure 13.1). The main riddle that remains is how they all somehow seem to relate to the present time of the narrator.

The poem in its historical setting

The mid-1950s were critical years for the British Empire. After the loss of India and Pakistan in 1947, imperial hegemony in the Eastern Mediterranean was threatened by the conflict in Israel and Palestine and the rise of Jamal Abd al-Nasser in Egypt. In 1954, led by the charismatic archbishop Makarios III, Greek Orthodox Cypriots proposed

Enosis, unification with Greece, and in the spring of 1955, the Greek paramilitary organization EOKA initiated a series of increasingly violent attacks against British colonial rule on the island.

This was part of the historical backdrop against which 'Dirge for Trebizond' and *The Towers of Trebizond* first appeared. From a purely literary perspective, the poem might be considered inferior to the novel (LeFanu 2003: 270-71),[5] but it still offers important keys to how they can both be read as reflections of decline and renewal. To the Anglican missionaries in *The Towers of Trebizond*, who refuse to see the futility of their ideals, the Byzantine ruins evoke static clichés of peoples, cultures and nations which ultimately reveal their own characters to be clichés: static, etheric and unable to step out into the real world that they have set out to conquer. There is something ghost-like over Father Chantry-Pigg and Aunt Dot as they finally disappear behind the Iron Curtain, much in the same way as there is over the Trapezuntines who say that the barbarians must always leave.

The poem is obviously, almost ostentatiously, laden with clichés as well; but the way these clichés interact and interconnect renders a dynamic, if ultimately cyclic, history of the rise and fall of empires as known from Plato, Ibn Khaldun or Spengler. Once, everyone was a barbarian; one day, everyone will return to a barbarian state. Confirming each of the cultural paradigms in its own static form, the poem ultimately confuses them. It might be worth considering how the narrator in *The Towers of Trebizond* teases the reader by eluding any clear indications of gender. In 'Dirge for Trebizond' the modern Western dichotomy of orientalism ('they' as 'nature') and classicism ('we' as 'culture') is similarly broken down, with barbarism and Byzantinism enabling and engendering their transformation.[6] At Trebizond, the barbarians have not only come to stay; perhaps they never actually left in the first place.

Widely popularized in the nineteenth century by painters like the British-American Thomas Cole, such scenarios have induced inspiration as well as despondence.[7] The imagery of barbarians fighting against an empire represents a new beginning and not just a final end; the Turkish Republic, acting both as a successor to the Ottoman Empire and as a clean break with its multicultural past, might as well stand for many modern nation-states founded on myths about 'barbarian' origins. Polish gentry identified with the Sarmatians, whose language Ovid had struggled to learn; Germans took a pride in having defeated the Romans at the Teutoburger Wald; Swedes claimed descendance from the Goths, Hungarians from the Huns; the French taught children in the colonies of their Gaul origins; and British patriots raised statues to and wrote poems about the ancient Brittonic queen Boudicca, who died as a martyr against the Roman invaders. (Gibbon, it might be added, noted how Britannia finally gained its independence accompanied by the 'Armoricans': 1906-07, V: 280-81.[8])

By 1955, of course, Britain was not a barbarian nation fighting an empire; it was the reminiscence of an empire that was rapidly losing power to nations it considered barbarian. Cyprus was no exception. 'You English', an Israeli journalist tells Lawrence Durrell in *Bitter Lemons* (1957), 'seem to me to be completely under the spell of the Greco-Roman period, and you judge everything without any reference to Byzantium' (Durrell 1957: 159). Durrell assumed that he referred to British policymakers failing to appreciate the importance of the medieval empire to the modern Greek state, but it is tempting to read a more Cavafy-like implication into the comment: obsessed with the idea that it defended classical civilization against barbarism, Britain failed or refused to see how its imperial ambitions turned increasingly Byzantine, and how the alleged Byzantines, orientals and barbarians that it tried to keep under control were now all in the ascent.

One hundred years before the Cyprus crisis, Britain had fought one of its most costly wars under the pretext that it must protect the Ottoman Empire against the 'barbarian' assaults of Orthodox Christians, and it had nervously withdrawn crucial support for Greece when the latter took matters in its own hands and pushed for Constantinople in 1920-22.[9] Macaulay's words 'Byzantium lost and the last Greek gone' in 'Dirge for Trebizond' are not a reference to the distant fifteenth century, but to the population exchanges between Greece and Turkey in the 1920s, which had buried all further hopes for a Byzantine as much as an Ottoman revival. British imperialists in the 1950s, one feels tempted to conclude, resembled the Trapezuntines after the 1453 fall of Constantinople, deludedly believing that their empire, for some reason, would be spared the same fate that had befallen the others.

Final note

'Dirge for Trebizond' appeared in the *Times Literary Supplement* on 24 June 1955. Just a few days prior, the violence of EOKA had taken a rapid turn for the worse, and the new cabinet of Anthony Eden was on edge. In an effort to neutralize Greek claims, the foreign minister Harold Macmillan began to voice concerns for the Turks on the island, courting the government of Adnan Menderes in Ankara and – to the surprise of Athens – suggesting a tripartite conference in London to sort out any disagreements between the countries before the question was presented to the UN. Relations between Greece and Turkey quickly soured (Holland 1998: 59–74). It was not necessarily in the light of the political situation that the press attaché of the Turkish embassy in London wrote a harsh rebuttal of 'Dirge for Trebizond' in which he objected to the description of Turks as 'barbarians', but the timing is still noteworthy. The press attaché reminded both Macaulay and the TLS readers of the religious tolerance of the Ottomans, in almost the exact same words that Macaulay would later put in the mouth of Dr Halide in *The Towers of Trebizond* (LeFanu 2003: 270–71).

Reality would soon surpass the wildest fiction. The London conference broke down at the beginning of September; emboldened by their British host, Turkey refused to support *Enosis* and underlined its determination in a manner that had little in common with any historical precedents of religious tolerance. On the last day of the conference, 6 September 1955, Greek churches, schools, newspapers, businesses and private homes all over Istanbul fell victim to a brutal pogrom that would mark the beginning of the final Turkification of the former Byzantine capital. Staged as a spontaneous outburst of Turkish anger against Greek provocations, the riot seems to have been largely orchestrated by the Menderes government, but there are also indications that the idea may have originated in London (Holland 1998: 75–77).

Enosis disappeared from the UN agenda; insofar as this was the result of any deliberate plan, it might have been a last, Pyrrhic victory of the British Empire. In the following year, the American refusal to support Britain and France in the Suez crisis led to the fall of Eden and initiated a decade and a half of rapid decolonization across the world. Rose Macaulay did not live to witness that: she died in October 1958, having seen her last work enjoy unprecedented success, and eight months after she had been made Dame of the British Empire.

Acknowledgements

I owe my awareness of the existence of 'Dirge for Trebizond' to the essays of the Swedish philologist Sture Linnér (1917–2010), and the opportunity to read it in full to the united efforts of Helena Bodin, Charles Lock and Adrian Marsh, who have also provided me with key information and readings. Special thanks go to Ingela Nilsson, Tonje H Sørensen and George Winter for their helpful comments.

Notes

1. Macaulay had lost her lover of more than twenty years, a married man, in 1942 and was still trying to come to terms with the loss of a life partner and the gossip it had caused at home. Cf. Sullivan (2012: 177–78).
2. To the best of my knowledge, this poem has never been reprinted anywhere else since its publication in *TLS*. It has been briefly discussed by Crawford (1990: 305–06) and LeFanu (2003: 270–71).
3. Hegel (1927) offers perhaps the most articulate critique of this kind.
4. Just as he had remarkably little to say about the Ottoman Empire; cf. Bryce (2013).
5. LeFanu is a bit overcritical: for instance, referring to the Black Sea as 'inhospitable' is merely a classicizing wink to Ovid, a play on the fact that the sea was referred to as both Axeinos (inhospitable) and Euxeinos (hospitable) in Greek.
6. A partly gendered reading of Gibbon's *Decline and Fall* is undertaken by Gossman (1981).
7. In 1834–35 Cole painted a cycle of five large canvases called 'The Course of Empire', which follows a fictitious empire from a savage to an arcadian state and further on to consummation, destruction and desolation.
8. Insofar as this was actually a deliberate attempt to shoehorn the American revolution into an obscure episode of Roman history, it adds a certain irony to it that René Goscinny and Albert Uderzo picked Aremorica as the location of the Gaul village of Asterix (1959), the comic book archetype of 'barbarian' resistance to an empire, conceived at a time when France, just like Britain, found its own empire eclipsed by the American one.
9. See Figes (2010: 147–55) for an overview of the press campaigns leading up to the Crimean War and Fromkin (1989: 543–48) for a summary of the allied handling of the Asia Minor catastrophe.

Bibliography

Angelov, D. (2003), 'Byzantinism: The Imaginary and Real Heritage of Byzantium in Southeastern Europe', in D. Keridis, E. Elis-Bursac and N. Yatromanolakis (eds.), *New Approaches to Balkan Studies*, 3–23, Dulles, VA: Brassey's.

Ascherson, N. (1996), *The Black Sea: The Birthplace of Civilisation and Barbarism*, London: Vintage.

Boeck, H. (2015), 'Archaeology of Decadence: Uncovering Byzantium in Victorien Sardou's Theodora', in R. Betancourt and M. Taroutina, *Byzantium/Modernism: The Byzantine as a Method in Modernity*, 102–32, Leiden and Boston: Brill

Bryce, D. (2013), 'The Absence of Ottoman, Islamic Europe in Edward Said's Orientalism', *Theory, Culture & Society*, 30: 99–121.

Cameron, A. (2003), 'Byzance dans le débat sur l'orientalisme', in M.-F. Auzépy (ed.), *Byzance en Europe*, 235–50, Saint-Denis: Presses Universitaires de Vincennes.

Cavafy, C. P. (2007), 'Waiting for the Barbarians', transl. Evangelos Sachperoglou, in C. P. Cavafy, *The Collected Poems, with Parallel Greek Text*, 15, Oxford: Oxford University Press.

Conybeare, F. C. (1897), 'Ananias of Shirak, Autobiography', transl. F. C. Conybeare, *Byzantinische Zeitschrift*, 6: 572–74.

Crawford, A. (1990), '"The Desire and Pursuit of the Whole": Pattern and Quest in the Novels of Rose Macaulay', PhD thesis, University of Glasgow.

Durrell, L. (1957), *Bitter Lemons*, London: Faber & Faber.

Eco, U. (1985), 'Casablanca, or, the Clichés Are Having a Ball', transl. John Shepley and Barbara Spackman, in M. Blonsky, *On Signs*, 35–38, Baltimore, MD: Johns Hopkins University Press.

Figes, O. (2010), *Crimea: The Last Crusade*, London: Allen Lane.

Fromkin, D. (1989), *A Peace to End All Peace: The Fall of the Ottoman Empire and the Creation of the Modern Middle East*, New York: Holt.

Gibbon, E. (1906–07), *The History of the Decline and Fall of the Roman Empire*, ed. John Bagnell Bury, New York: Fred de Fau.

Gibbon, E. (1911), *Autobiography*, London: Dent.

Gossman, L. (1981), *The Empire Unpossess'd: An Essay on Gibbon's Decline and Fall*, Cambridge: Cambridge University Press.

Hart, J. A. (1913), *Sardou and the Sardou Plays*, Philadelphia, PA: J. B. Lippincot.

Hegel, F. (1927), *Vorlesungen über die Philosophie der Geschichte*, ed. Friedrich Brunstäd, Leipzig: Reclam.

Heilo, O. (2018), 'Between Decline and Renascence: The Late Antiquity of Jacob Burckhardt', in M. Malm and S. S. Cullhed (eds.), *Reading Late Antiquity*, 73–82, Heidelberg: Winter.

Heilo, O. and I. Nilsson (2017), 'Back to Byzantium: Rethinking the Borders of Europe', in A. Stagnell, L. Schou Therkildsen and M. Rosengren (eds.), *Can a Person be Illegal?: Refugees, Migrants and Citizenship in Europe*, 43–52, Uppsala: Uppsala Rhetorical Studies.

Herrin, J. (2020), *Ravenna: Capital of Empire, Crucible of Europe*, Princeton, NJ: Princeton University Press.

Holland, R. (1998), *Britain and the Revolt in Cyprus*, Oxford: Oxford University Press.

LeFanu, S. (2003), *Rose Macaulay*, London: Virago.

Lock, C. (2012), '"Once Was This a Spirit's Dwelling": Rose Macaulay and the Church in Ruins', *International Journal for the Study of the Christian Church*, 12 (3–4): 324–41.

Macaulay, R. (1955), 'Dirge for Trebizond', *Times Literary Supplement*, no. 2782, 2, 24 June.

Macaulay, R. (1995), *The Towers of Trebizond*, London: Flamingo.

Nilsson, I. (2021), 'Imitation as Spoliation, Reception as Translation', in I. Nilsson and I. Jevtic, *Spoliation as Translation: Medieval Worlds in the Eastern Mediterranean, Convivium*, 2: 21–36, Turnhout: Brepols.

Pontani, F. (2018), 'Cavafy and Niketas Choniates: A Possible Source for "Waiting for the barbarians"', *Byzantine and Modern Greek Studies*, 42 (2): 275–86.

Saïd, E. (1978), *Orientalism*, London: Routledge.

Sullivan, M. (2012), 'A Middlebrow Dame Commander: Rose Macaulay, the "Intellectual Aristocracy", and The Towers of Trebizond', *The Yearbook of English Studies*, 42: 168–85.

White, H. (1973), *Metahistory: The Historical Imagination of Nineteenth-Century Europe*, Baltimore, MD/London: John Hopkins University Press.

Yeats, W. B. (1989), 'Byzantium', in *The Collected Poems of W. B. Yeats: A New Edition*, ed. Richard J. Finneran, London: Palgrave Macmillan.

14

M. Karagatsis's Byzantinism in his *Sergios and Bacchos* (1959)

Katerina Liasi

M. Karagatsis is the nom de plume of Demetris Rodopoulos. The initial letter M. of his first name is a conundrum. Some scholars consider that it either refers to Michalis, the name of several of his heroes, or to Mitia, the Russian name of one of titular brothers in the novel by Dostoevsky, Karagatsis's favourite novelist. Karagatsis was a Greek novelist whose work received favourable and unfavourable reviews from the critics during his lifetime and even still today. A prolific and charismatic writer with a rich imagination and the skill to portray lively and realistic characters, he authored a good number of widely read novels inspired by the urban environment of the interwar period. His nonconformist and unconventional writing style put him in a class of his own and singles his work out from that of the other novelists of the so-called 'generation of the 1930s'. That is, the group of authors who contributed to the renewal of modern Greek prose by integrating themes and approaches prevailing in contemporary European literature into their writing.

In the words of another modern novelist, 'Karagatsis builds his authorial world following a personal path' (Douka 2000: 848). He set his course in accordance with his own perception of literature and by transgressing the norms introduced by the writers of his age (Tsiropoulos 1981: 114). He is a novelist par excellence who enlivens situations and facts by using antiheroic and provocative protagonists depicted with masterly finesse and deep sarcasm (Douka 2000: 848–49).

In his novel titled *Sergios and Bacchos*, published in 1959, Karagatsis adopted a new writing method that enabled him to give his audience a new, hybrid work, which did not fall into a precise category of novel-writing nor was it reminiscent of any other literary genre. It is mainly a dense and swift narration of historical facts starting from the third century CE and ending in the year 1951. Nonetheless, this is not a work of historiography for the simple reason that a great many imaginary and unrealistic elements have been fitted in. It is not a historical novel since it ignores quite a few of the conventions of this kind of narrative. It does not in fact, convey the spirit, manners or social conditions of a past age with realistic detail and fidelity, although it remains close to historical facts. It cannot even be categorized as speculative fiction. Moreover, it often and routinely oversteps the limits and rules of natural reality, moving in the direction of a fictional world which, on the one hand, runs parallel or is superior to the real one and, on the other, is ruled by specific and, to some extent, commonly acknowledged and set narrative conventions (Chadzivasiliou 2010: 55).

The two heroes of the novel are saints who, after being martyred, go to heaven and live there for some time among the angels and other saints. This allows the reader to enjoy discussions on numerous diverse issues, such as theology, philosophy, socio-politics and eros. This introductory narrative framework is, from the viewpoint of intertextuality, just a contrivance that harks back to the Byzantine satires of the *Timarion* and *Mazaris's Journey to Hades*, which explore the literary theme of the Descent to Hades (Lampakis 1982: 82–93; Garland 2007). The novel is written mostly in dialogue form and, like the *Timarion*, can also be described as a satirical dialogue, which, generally speaking, is one of the literary forms of the Byzantine satire (Alexiou 1993: 280). As has been also argued, it can be described as a philosophical satire (Kaldellis 2012: 275), something which complies with one of the many descriptions of *Sergios and Bacchos*. Unlike Timarion, the two heroes of Karagatsis's work instead of going down to Hades go up to heaven and, like Timarion, meet many people who are either their contemporaries or ancient philosophers and orators (Kaldellis 2012: 276).

Life in this imaginary paradise follows precise rules, as does their afterlife on earth. It was actually possible for them to return to the world of the living once churches dedicated to them were constructed. Saints Sergios and Bacchos refused to be separated and, as a result, they had to wait until the sixth century and the reign of Justinian when they got their own widely renowned shrine in Constantinople. In what follows, their life on earth is governed by strict rules, which the two saintly heroes quite often break, thus causing amusing and chaotic events. Their mission is purely to help humanity and nudge human history in the direction that best serves the interests of Christianity and Hellenism.

The novel has also been characterized as 'religio-historical and tragicomic' (Karantonis 1981: 133). This definition fails to provide an overall description of the work, since the religious dimension exists in a world of tales and fiction where the principles upon which religion is founded are disputed and the concept of sanctity acquires a new meaning. Moreover, the life of the two saints is enriched with fictitious events to such a degree that it becomes a shocking religious and historical myth.

Another possible description of this work would be 'novelistic chronography', a description that, in a sense, points to the Byzantine literary genre of the chronicle and calls for a comparison with a genre with which Karagatsis's text has quite a few similarities, but also many differences. A common feature is the linear structure of events. It does not start from the creation of the world but from the dawn of Christianity and it concludes in the modern period in which the writer-chronicler lived.

The story relating to the two heroes' – first in physical and then in metaphysical – incorporeal existence, begins in the late Roman period, to which the historical lives of the saints date, and ends in May 1951, the date at which Karagatsis began writing the novel. It took him eight years to complete it, since at the end of the two volumes of *Sergios and Bacchos* the dates of the start and finish of the writing of the work are noted: 'May 1951–May 1959' (2013: 498). It must be also stressed that the life Karagatsis made up for the saintly heroes has very little connection with the hagiography of Saints

Sergios and Bacchos (*BHG* 1624). According to their *vita*, Sergios was a *primicerius scholae gentilium*, that is the highest-ranking officer in the cavalry, as well as a friend of Emperor Maximian, whereas Bacchos was a *secundocurius* in the same unit. The novelist retained some general elements from their life, for instance Sergios's Roman descent (whereas Bacchos is supposed to be Greek in the novel), their military profession and roughly the same historical period as that in which they are reported to have lived (*Vita of Sts Sergios and Bacchos*, chs. 1–2; Fowden 1999: 7–26).

The lives of the two saintly heroes go through all the stages on their way to perfection: from paganism to Christianity, then to monasticism and sanctity. The events that make up the successive stages in their lives are rendered in a shocking fashion. They have the habits, that is the manner and way of life, of people with shortcomings and weaknesses who, more often than not, surrender to all kinds of temptations. What is more, Sergios's martyrdom and death is depicted as a sacrifice made for love rather than on account of his Christian faith.

Byzantine history is reconstructed according to the successive enthronements and dethronements of emperors. In the part of the history that happens after the fall of Constantinople to the Ottomans, the author applies a new device which has the two saintly heroes waking up every ninety-nine years to sum up the main historical events that have occurred. Through their concise monologues, dense dialogues and short episodes of action, readers are informed of the most important events that marked the five centuries extending from 1453 to the mid-twentieth century.

The way Byzantine history is reconstructed, that is, through the emperors' successive enthronements and dethronements, the coronations, or even the scenes of their violent removals from power, constitute an exquisite stage for ironic, satirical, sarcastic and carnivalesque approaches. Numerous incidents in the marketplace, the hippodrome (Karagatsis 2013: 30–45; 2014: 448–53), even in churches are satirized to the point of utter irony, vulgar speech or even blasphemy. The scene in which Patriarch Methodios tries to prove that Emperor Theophilos repented as he lay dying, in response to Empress Theodora's request to remove the name of her husband from the list of iconoclast emperors to be anathematized (cf. Markopoulos 1998: 37–49), is a masterly piece of tragicomedy. The two saints take delight in the whole scene, as if they were spectators having fun at the tragicomic events which accompanied the restoration of 'icon veneration' in 843 (Karagatsis 2014: 466). After listening to a lively and realistic dialogue between Theodora and Methodios, a dialogue that showcases the hypocrisy and corruption of both state and church in Byzantium, Bacchos gets angry, calling them both 'Θεομπαίχτες' (2014: 471), a word that can only be rendered in English periphrastically as 'hypocrites who deceive and make mockery of God'.

Karagatsis uses the history of Paparrigopoulos as a source for referring to events related to the restoration of icon veneration. He also adopts, in his own straight fashion, the view of the nineteenth-century Greek historian as regards the consciences of Empress Theodora and of Patriarch Methodios: 'The religious ideas of these people were so strange that, on the one hand, Theodora did not hesitate to lie knowingly in order to get a pardon for her husband, and, on the other hand, the synod, aware of the lie, did not hesitate to allow the pardon requested' (Paparrigopoulos 1925: 272–74). The satire and sarcasm reach their peak when Patriarch Methodios realizes that his ruse to remove the name of Theophilos from the list of deceased iconoclast emperors has not met with success. The scene that follows, in which he appears screaming that a miracle has happened, and the name of Theophilos has indeed been erased, is completely burlesque. His attempt to conceal that the name had not only been scratched off but mocking words had also been written on the parchment in red ink (Karagatsis 2014: 467–73) constitutes a grotesque joke:

> He stepped down the stairs of the Holy Gate silently walking and having grandiosely stretched out the hand that held the parchment. While walking ahead, he pretended to pay no attention. His hand passed close enough to a candlestick that the parchment came in touch with the flame of a candle and was set alight. Methodios feigned to have been taken aback. He pretended that he wanted to put out the divinely enflamed object that proved Theophilos's innocence. Yet immediately he changed his mind and yelled:
> 'It is God's sign that the loathsome iconoclasts have been condemned to hell!'
> (472–73, author's translation)

The use and reception of Byzantium

As his own work reveals, Karagatsis was not interested in the literary rendering of historical events. His aim was a holistic interpretation of history in all its different aspects: political, social, psychological, religious, ideological and even biological. The way Byzantine history was received and treated in his novel had a precise purpose: the creation of what he called 'a novel that synthesizes everything' ('συνθετικό του παντός μυθιστόρημα') (Karagatsis 1943a, 1943b). Furthermore, it should be taken into account that all the aforementioned issues were at all times viewed through the optics of the ambiguous, dual approach that his heroes adopted. This approach defended or rejected history, ideology and philosophy.

Although the traditional narrative path is by and large followed, the description of historical events is constantly open to contradictory and contrasting views and interpretations. This is achieved by means of the conflicting approaches taken by the two main characters in the narrative vis-à-vis so-called 'national' issues. Roman Sergios is well educated and sophisticated, always trying to interpret all issues rationally. Bacchos, on the other hand, is impulsive and very passionate about his Greek identity. The diametrically opposed positions they adopt in relation to all the different historical issues as well as their frequent arguments eventually lead to a full and devastating condemnation of traditionally accepted historiography (Meraklis 1981: 58–59). This is an antiheroic treatment of history which undermines, subverts and revises the significance of historical events in the development of Byzantium.

Apart from historiography itself, all the parameters previously touched upon are subject to the scrutiny of the strict, ironical and often sarcastic gaze of Karagatsis. Byzantium appears to provide him with the most appropriate backdrop against which to express his own views on the exceptional significance of sex in human relationships and the influence that it has on them. In other words, as a historical period, Byzantium offers the most appropriate stage on which to display the author's personal views on sexuality and its impact on human relations, which in turn exert an influence on social, political and religious situations.

Sergios and Bacchos is a typical example of the amalgamation of all the contradictory and provocative elements that run through Karagatsis's prose. This feature is still predominant today simply because 'it intertwines plot with self-referentiality, the realistic with imaginary element, history and parody, and, last but not least, what is popular with what is regarded as modern' (Tziovas 2010: 313).

Reproduction and subversion of Byzantine clichés and stereotypes

Similarly to other modern Greek novels about Byzantium written in the interwar period and later, *Sergios and Bacchos* repeats clichés regarding the reception of Byzantine history. The narrative focuses on situations in the imperial court, emphasizing the scheming, murdering and blinding that went on, all resulting from the desire to ascend to the imperial throne. The image of the Byzantines as people motivated by their own interests and intrigues and as being active in the imperial court reproduces a stereotype.

The perception of Byzantium as a theocratic society is adopted here from a derisive perspective and presented in a sarcastic tone. Both prelates and monks are treated ironically and criticized by the two protagonists, whose saintly identity adds authority to their judgements. According to them, the icons of the 'Romans' were mere representations of incorporeal bodies lacking bones, flesh and soul (Karagatsis 2013: 193). The Church is equally reprimanded for being responsible for the fact that

> subsequent centuries will fail to know what the shape, expression and bodily appearance of Basil II, the so-called 'Bulgar-slayer' was. By the same token, they will have to rely on their own imagination to figure out the kind of appeal and attraction such empresses as Theophano and Irene the Athenian had; likewise, they will never know the exquisite and unique beauty of Maria of Alania.
>
> (161, my translation)

The contrast between the Western statues and the Eastern icons is another point which contributes to the dialogue carried on through the novel about the differences of the two civilizations.

Similarly, this two-volume novel does not exclude references to the destruction that Greek civilization and culture suffered as a result of the imperial policy that favoured Christianity. The same stereotypes prevail in the description of the character of the Latins and, more particularly, the Franks:

> Knighthood, a code of individual honour, arrogance, false romance eroticism, duels over nothing, jousts and, generally speaking, admiration of a superficially polite behaviour, under which illiteracy and contempt for learning are hiding.
>
> (195–96, my translation)

This passage, which seeks to sum up the character of the Latins, agrees with the image of them constructed in the *Alexiad* of Anna Komnene, whose Franks are so utterly barbarian that she cannot even pronounce their names (Anna Komnene 2001: x, 4, 315). At first sight Karagatsis shares the views of the Byzantine female historian and through Bacchos he describes the Franks: they are 'primitive and coarse, keen on arguing, insatiable talkers, arrogant, audacious, malicious, with the mentality of perverse children' (Karagatsis 2013: 183, my translation). Nonetheless, Sergios stands aloof from this verdict before finally consenting to see them on their own terms. He contends that it is not right to judge solely by the image that the crusaders who had passed through Byzantium had created of themselves. At this point Karagatsis opens up a dialogue with Anna Komnene, pointing out her lack of objectivity in her negative portrayal of the Franks and the Latins in general.

For the history of the reign of Alexios I Komnenos, Karagatsis seems to have taken inspiration from the obvious source, the *Alexiad*. For the events regarding the succession of Alexios he relied on the *Epitome of Histories* (*Epitome Historiarum*), the chronicle written by John Zonaras, as well as the *Chronike Diegesis* of Niketas Choniates. This is confirmed by the episode of Alexios's death in which the version of events provided by those authors rather than that of Anna takes centre stage. According to Ioannes Zonaras, Alexios suffered a bad death as he was abandoned by all and no one was left to wash his body and to ornate him (Büttner-Wobst 1897, XVIII: 28–29, 759–65; Gregoriadis 1995: 57–60).

M. Karagatsis – M. Psellos: Literary convergences

Through the study of Byzantine historians one can find the very interesting contrast between Karagatsis's *Sergios and Bacchos* and Michael Psellos's *Chronographia*. In all the references to him in the novel by the Greek writer, the Byzantine polymath is ridiculed and denigrated for his personality and the role he played in the imperial court. In this case the omniscient narrator of *Sergios and Bacchos*, who often pronounces his views emphatically, treats the multifaceted identity of Psellos in utterly ironic terms, underscoring the characterizations 'blind' and 'idiot' that Sergios usually reserves for politicians (Karagatsis 2013: 154, 158). Among those who 'although they called themselves politicians, were lacking in any political thinking' (154) is 'the prime minister of the new and young emperor: the intellectual and writer Michael Psellos, who, though he had a universal mind, could not find a solution for any kind of a problem!' (158). The irony is subtle and bitter here. However, as mentioned above, a common thread links the two authors and their works in many respects.

Karagatsis must have known Psellos's famous *Chronographia*. To begin with, the historical matters of the period covered by the *Chronographia* are treated in a similar fashion in the novel. An eclectic affinity can be seen in the way historical events are interpreted in both accounts. For example, Basil II and Constantine IX Monomachos alike are denigrated for not having ensured that at least one of their nieces or daughters married in order to secure the succession to the imperial throne (Karagatsis 2013: 136; Psellos 2014, II: 5, 26–27). Moreover, with reference to Zoe and Theodora, the daughters of Emperor Constantine VIII, Karagatsis endorses the view of the average Byzantine that 'neither had sufficient intellectual ability to govern the state' (VI: 5, 108-09). According to Karagatsis, who uses a well-known proverb to describe the low intelligence of the two women, 'they were unable to divide two donkeys' straw' (Karagatsis 2013: 136).

Not unlike Psellos, Karagatsis is characterized by 'intellectual rapaciousness', in the sense that he too dealt with and indulged in all kinds of learning. A polymath, like Psellos, Karagatsis devoted himself to writing prose, poetry and history in order to achieve a holistic interpretation of the latter, as already pointed out previously, exploring all its different dimensions: political, social, psychological, religious, ideological and biological.

Furthermore, common literary elements in terms of form and manner of writing can be identified in the theatricality and dramatization of the two works. In *Sergios and Bacchos*, the dialogical form, lively descriptions by the heroes and the short episodes of plot are typical above all of the theatrical genre. All the characters that are historical figures have both a real and an imaginary life. Not only do each of the two protagonists assume the dual identity of a real and an imaginary person, they also play various other roles, constantly changing personas.

Theatricality is equally present in Psellos's work. His descriptions of imperial ceremonies in the Great Palace are given in minute detail (VI: 3, 107–08), while several historical episodes are rendered in theatrical fashion (Puchner 1999; Papaioannou 2013). A prominent example is the description of the populace's revolt against Michael V Kalaphates. The author reconstructs this historical event in an extensive section of *Chronographia*, which includes an introduction, dialogues, lively accounts, interventions by the narrator and flashback; overall, a conflation of historical and fictional elements (Psellos 2014, V: 24–33, 92–98).

A difference between the two authors can be noted in the way they treat the fictional and the historical elements. *Chronographia* is a rather unreliable piece of historiography since the narration is mostly about the writer and his memories about historical events he witnessed (Hunger 2005: 194). This is something that does not apply to *Sergios and Bacchos*, in which the addition of fiction and the theatricality of action do not affect historical coherence. Both writers aspire to a realistic rendering of events and aim to persuade their readership of its authenticity. Psellos contends that he himself experienced the events that he narrates, while Karagatsis shows himself only towards the conclusion of his novel. Psellos is the protagonist of his own work, giving the reader moments of excellent acting:

> I stood voiceless, with open mouth, as if I were struck by thunder ... And then, as though some fountain gushed forth from my insides, a flood of tears ran from my eyes without stopping and, at the end of my laments, sighs came up to complete my emotion.
>
> (Psellos 2014, V: 41, 101–02, my translation)

Both writers delight in making their heroes persuasive. All the people who populate the books of Karagatsis are flesh and blood creatures (Panagiotopoulos 1981: 13). His heroes are portrayed realistically. At any rate, whether they are imaginary characters or real people, Karagatsis created psychologically detailed characters who give the impression of being 'a person that has existed and has been encountered by the author' (Negrepontis 1981: 91). Likewise, Michael Psellos portrays his heroes as extremely lifelike figures and explores their psychology. As is well known, his descriptions of historical persons are not one-dimensional, painting them black or white, but intentionally present them as full of contradictions. In that respect, Psellos diverges from the common practice of Byzantine historians who liked to draw conventional portraits (Rosenqvist 2008: 146–47). He insists more than any other Byzantine writer on rendering both the external and internal characteristics of his creations. This tendency is well exemplified by his detailed description of the figure and behaviour of Basil II, the only emperor who, according to Psellos, deserved a positive appraisal (Psellos 2014, I: 34–336, 21, 22).

Both *Chronographia* and *Sergios and Bacchos* set their narrative in the imperial court. Their authors are intrigued by the personalities of various emperors, internal politics, usurpations and manoeuvring of all kinds. Moreover, they avoid putting the emphasis on wars, something that differentiates *Chronographia* from all other works categorized as 'historiography'. In fact, *Chronographia*, a misleading title for the kind of text it represents, was a collection of personal memoirs integrated into portraits of historical contexts (Rosenqvist 2008: 144–45). In many cases its objective was to demythify the imperial status quo by applying the literary tools of irony, satire and sarcasm. Needless to say, demythifying history was also the objective of *Sergios and Bacchos*. In order to ridicule and destroy his victims, Psellos was ready to use any possible weapon, including gossip, hints about sex scandals, slander, lies and exaggeration. Not unlike Psellos, Karagatsis has been criticized for seeing history largely through the lens of scurrilous and scandalous stories (Raftopoulos 1960: 66). Both of them were engaged in comprehensive criticism of persons and institutions.

A remarkable novelty in Psellos is his biological vision of the empire, something that coincides with Karagatsis's own biological descriptions of history. Psellos likens the empire to a biological entity, 'a robust animal', which can fall sick at any time (Psellos 2014, VI: 49, 126). Should the first symptoms of the illness appear and not be carefully treated by the most appropriate person, the emperor will suffer some fatal affliction. For instance, Psellos rebukes the insatiable lust that Constantine IX Monomachos treats as his duty, and considers Monomachos responsible for the decline of the empire:

This particular emperor, in failing to care for the state and being interested only in sexual enjoyment and sensual pleasure, was the one who inaugurated all the evils that would in the future exhaust the then still robust body of the empire (Psellos 2014, VI: 49, 126–27, my translation).

In a similar vein, Karagatsis tries to explain the historical course of the Greek nation in terms of biology. For its corruption and decline he suggests putting 'the blame on the degenerate Mediterranean blood, which had not been sufficiently regenerated by mingling with the barbarians' (2013: 162). His explanation of Byzantine decline relies on the same rationale but with the prospect of death bringing forth resurrection: 'They know that the Empire of the Greeks is an organism sentenced to death. They know too, however, that its cells will survive to resurrect the dead organism one day' (203). Both Psellos and Karagatsis deal with time as a catalyst in a process that ends in decline and decay.

To sum up, both writers are interested in interpreting history. Psellos's aim in noting down the acts of historical figures consists in searching for causes and commenting on outcomes (Psellos 2014, VI: 48, 126). The interpretation of historical facts was always at the centre of Karagatsis's prose writing. He always aimed for a comprehensive understanding and interpretation of history as well as of the societies and the individuals who were involved in historical events. Psellos's arrogance, as far as his own testimony and judgement are concerned, is manifest in his declaration that his own well-founded analysis is worth more than anything future historiographers might figure out (Psellos 2014, VI: 48, 126) and has, of course, absolutely nothing in common with the ironic self-deprecation of Karagatsis. In a documentary by Greek national television about his life, Karagatsis makes a sarcastic statement in his own characteristic voice: 'Anyone who dares to portray us as we are is a bad writer. Hence behold, my dear, the reason why I am a bad writer' (*Times and Writers* 2001–02). And later on, in the same tone, he concludes by stating: 'As you may see, my main feature is modesty' (*Times and Writers* 2001–02).

Both writers are distinguished for their provocative pen, their ground-breaking practices as writers, their modern way of considering history, and their portrayal of contemporary heroes. Herbert Hunger's comment on this matter is worth quoting here: 'Every now and then we admire how modern the persons and events that Psellos describes appear' (1978: 379–80). Similarly, one can cite the Neohellenist Dimitris Tziovas's view of Karagatsis: 'Karagatsis possesses a unique advantage in Greek prose-writing: he can be read as a popular and a modernist [author] and can function as a diachronic and a contemporary writer' (2010: 313).

Bibliography

Alexiou, M. (1993), 'Writing against Silence: Antithesis and Ekfrasis in the Prose Fiction of Georgios Vizyenos', *Dumbarton Oaks Papers*, 47: 263–86.
Anna Komnene (2001), *Alexias*, ed. D. R. Reinsch and A. Kambylis, *Annae Comnenae Alexias, Corpus Fontium Historiae Byzantinae* XL/,1, Berlin and New York. Available online: http://archive.ert.gr/8564/ (accessed 10 April 2020).
Büttner-Wobst, T. (ed.) (1897), Ioannes Zonaras, *Epitomae historiarum libri XIII–XVIII* (CSHB), Bonn: E. Weber.
Chadzivasiliou, V. (2008), 'O Karagatsis kai to fantastiko. Afigimatikes technikes, kosmotheoria ka ideologia sto "Chameno nisi" (1943) kai sto "Amri kai mougkou" (1954)', in *M. Karagatsis: Ideologia kai poiitiki, Praktika synedriou*, 55–62, Athens: Benaki Museum.
Douka, M. (2000), 'One Anti-school Writer', *Nea Estia* (1729): 845–49.
Dieten, J. L., van (1975), *Nicetae Choniatae Historia*, 2 vols (CSHB XI/1–2), Berlin and New York: de Gruyter.
Garland, L. (2007) 'Mazaris's Journey to Hades: Further Reflections and Reappraisal', *Dumbarton Oaks Papers*, 61: 183–214.
Gregoriadis, I. (1995), *Linguistic and Literary Studies in the* Epitome Historion *of John Zonaras*, Thessaloniki: Kentron Vyzantinon Erevnon.

Hunger, H. (2005), *Die hochsprachliche profane Literatur der Byzantiner*, transl. Taxiarchis, K. Athens: M.I.E.T.
Kaldellis, A. (2012), 'The *Timarion*: Toward a Literary Interpretation', in P. Odorico (ed.), *La Face cache de la Littérature Byzantine: le Texte en Tant que Message Immediat*, 275–88, Paris: Centres d'études byzantines, néo-helléniques et sud-ouest européenes, École des hautes études en sciences sociales.
Karagatsis, M. (1943a), 'Modern time', *Proia*, 21 April.
Karagatsis, M. (1943b), 'New directions', *Proia*, 7 April.
Karantonis, A. (1981), 'O logotechnis pou eleipse …', in *Epanektimisi tou M. Karagatsi: Eikosi chronia apo ton thanato tou*, 130–34, Athens: Astrolavos/Efthyni.
Karagatsis, M. (2013), *Sergios and Bacchos*, (2) Athens: Bibliopolion tis Estias.
Karagatsis, M. (2014), *Sergios and Bacchos*, (1) Athens: Bibliopolion tis Estias.
Key Fowden, E. (1999), *The Barbarian Plain. Saint Sergius between Rome and Iran*, Berkeley: University of California Press.
Lampakis, S. (1982), 'Oi katabaseis ston Kato Kosmo sti Vyzantini kai sti metavyzantini logotechnia', PhD thesis, University of Ioannina.
Life of Sts Sergios and Bacchos (BHG 1624), ed. I. van den Gheyn *Analecta Bollandiana* 14, 1895, 375–95.
Markopoulos, A. (1998), 'The Rehabilitation of the Emperor Theophilos', in L. Brubaker (ed.), *Byzantium in the Ninth Century: Dead or Alive?*, 37–49, Abingdon: Routledge.
Meraklis, M. G. (1981), 'Threis paragrafoi tiw Karagatsikis pezografias', in *Epanektimisi tou M. Karagatsi: Eikosi chronia apo ton thanato tou*, 53–63, Athens: Astrolavos/Efthyni.
Negrepontis, G. (1981), 'Nyxeis sti leitourgia tou grafia', in *Epanektimisi tou M. Karagatsi: Eikosi chronia apo ton thanato tou*, 65–69, Athens: Astrolavos/Efthyni.
Panagiotopoulos, I. M. (1981), 'Epistrofi ston Karagatsi', in *Epanektimisi tou M. Karagatsi: Eikosi chronia apo ton thanato tou*, 9–15, Athens: Astrolavos/Efthyni.
Papaioannou, S. (2013), *Michael Psellos Rhetoric and Authorship in Byzantium*. Cambridge: Cambridge University Press.
Paparrigopoulos, K. (1925), *Istoria tou Ellinikou ethnous. Apo ton archaiotaton chronon mechri simera*, ed. P. Karollidis, III, B, Athens: Eleftheroudakis.
Psellos, M. (2014), *Chronographia*, ed. D. R. Reinsch, Millennium Studies 51, Berlin and Boston: de Gruyter.
Puchner, W. (1999), 'Theatrologikes paritereseis se byzantinous istoriografous', in *Fainomena kai nooumena: Deka theatrologika meletimata*, Athens: Politeias.
Raftopoulos, D. (1960), 'M. Karagatsi "Sergios and Bachos"', *Epitheorisi Technis*, 67–68: 66–70.
Rosenqvist, J. O. (2008), *Die byzantinische Literatur: Vom 6. Jahrhundert bis zum Fall Konstantinopels 1453*, transl. I. Basis, Athens: Kanakis.
Times and Writers (2001–02), [TV documentary] ERT archive.
Tsiropoulos, K. (1981), 'Gia ton M. Karagatsi', in *Epanektimisi tou M. Karagatsi: Eikosi chronia apo ton thanato tou*, 114–18, Athens: Astrolavos/Efthyni.
Tziovas, D. (2010), 'Laikos kai monternos' (in Greek), in *M. Karagatsis: Ideologia kai poiitiki, Praktika synedriou*, 313–28, Athens: Benaki Museum.

15

Fantastic(al) Byzantium: The Imagery of Byzantium in Speculative Fiction

Przemysław Marciniak

There has been no comprehensive survey of Byzantine motifs in the growing body of popular literature that focuses on the empire until today. Some works have been discussed by Nike Koutrakou (2003, 2004) and more recently by Emir Alışık (2021). Such a situation is understandable because this type of survey would require engagement with a significant number of texts in many different languages.[1] This chapter has no ambition to fill this gap. Instead, it proposes looking at two aspects of modern novels: the portrayal of Byzantium and the Byzantines and the paratextual notes accompanying the novels.

The amount of available material necessitates some limitations and requires making a choice as to what my focus should be here. The sheer number of novels inspired by Byzantium, from historical novels to detective stories to sci-fi and fantasy novels, is enormous.[2] Interestingly, there is also a growing number of authors with a solid background in Byzantine studies, including Harry Turtledove, a master of alternative history, and Arkady Martine (a pen name for AnnaLinden Weller), an award winner of the 2020 and 2022 Hugo Award. In an interview, she explains that her novel *A Memory called Empire* was directly inspired by her work on the relationship between Byzantium and Armenia in the eleventh century.[3]

Although a precise quantitative description is not altogether possible, it seems that two historical periods have received particular interest from authors of novels set in Byzantium – the times of Justinian I and the fall of Byzantium. Moreover, a specific set of emblematic Byzantine phenomena is also familiar for a wider readership, such as iconic chariot races and the Hagia Sophia. For example, in Robert Silverberg's sci-fi novel *Up the Line* (1969), the standard programme for a tour of Byzantium includes 'the coronation of an emperor, a chariot race in the hippodrome, the dedication of Hagia Sophia, the sack of the city by the Fourth Crusade, and the Turkish conquest' (ch. 19). In addition, however, recently, authors have begun to explore lesser-known periods, which mirrors both the development of Byzantine studies and the growing number of books designed to popularize it.

It seemed appropriate to discuss Byzantium and Byzantine rather than Eastern Roman or Roman motifs – even if some scholars insist that this term should be avoided as it is ideologically charged nowadays.[4] The novels discussed in this chapter do not seek to tell the 'truth' about the Eastern Empire. Their vision of Byzantium is that of a creator and not a scholar. Nonetheless, many authors seem to be aware that 'Byzantium' is an exonym, coined only after the fall of Constantinople. And yet the term 'Byzantium', however artificial it may seem to students of Byzantium [*sic*!], has penetrated popular culture through diction and imagination. There are, as always, some exceptions to this rule. Lucille Turner (*The Sultan, the Vampyr, and the Soothsayer*, 2016) chose the appellation 'Greek' (for instance, John VIII is called 'the Greek Emperor') rather than 'Eastern Roman' or 'Byzantine'.[5] Her choice, however, results from juxtaposing Orthodox Greeks with Roman Catholics and thus underscoring the faith of inhabitants of the Eastern Empire. In most cases, 'Byzantium' is used conventionally with no underlying agenda as neither (most) authors nor their readership are aware or interested in scholarly debates on the use of the term 'Byzantium'.

Unlike in historical novels, the degree of the 'Byzantine presence' in speculative fiction can vary. There exists a group of novels in which Byzantium features indirectly. Their plot is not set in any specific period of Byzantine history but either in modern times or in some altered version of reality. However, similarly to other texts, they can build upon stereotypical imagery. In Romuald Pawlak's *Army of the Blind* (2007), the Eternal Byzantium conquers modern-day Poland. Even though technically advanced, Byzantium represents an oppressive, overly bureaucratic state, an antithesis of democracy whose citizens ('Bizs') are new overlords of the subdued populations.[6] In this storyworld, Byzantium is constructed using some easily identifiable, though conveniently nebulous, elements of the Byzantine reality: the Orthodox Church, Byzantine bureaucracy (represented by logothetes) and the Varangians. The Byzantine scenery serves a very concrete purpose – to show how a person behaves when confronted with an authoritarian and all-powerful state. In this sense, Pawlak's novel is a typical example of *social science fiction*, a subgenre of science fiction concerned with commenting on social problems and important issues.[7] The real Byzantium is here unimportant, but Pawlak uses some widely spread clichés to depict it as a paradigmatic authoritarian state. Similarly, in the novel *Immortal* (N. Holder and C. Golden, 2000, set in the Buffyverse),[8] Byzantium is represented by the Empress Theodora, who came to be almost a paradigmatic Byzantine character.[9] Theodora, a reformed prostitute, is duplicitous by nature, a trace commonly ascribed to the Byzantines: 'The beautiful empress shared Veronique's interest in the occult arts, though to the world she attempted to present a different picture altogether – pious in the extreme, a reformed sinner and champion of the state religion' (p. 48).

However, some novels defy simple definitions. Guy Gavriel Kay's duology *The Sarantine Mosaic* (*Sailing to Sarantium*, 1998; *Lord of Emperors*, 2000) depicts a storyworld heavily based on life in Byzantium under Justinian I. Kay shows and acknowledges (in the preface to his novel) a familiarity with many works dealing with Byzantine history. Nonetheless, his novel is by no means an alternative version of the Byzantine Empire; instead, here there is an entirely parallel world (Kay himself speaks of 'a variation'), which is signalled by the fact that this other Earth has two Suns.[10] While readers can recognize the links to both Byzantium and Yeats's poetry relatively quickly,[11] and while certain Byzantine stereotypes undoubtedly influenced the portrayal of the Sarantines, Kay's novel is not about Byzantium but Sarantium, an entirely new world. *The Sultan of Byzantium* by Selçuk Altan (*Bizans Sultani*, 2011) is even more difficult to define. It tells the story of a man who discovers that he is the descendant of Constantine XI Palaiologos and an heir to a vast fortune guarded by a century-old mysterious organization. As one of the reviewers remarked, 'it is kind of a Turkish DaVinci's code'.[12] However, this unbelievable story is just a pretext to the Turkish author's homage to Byzantine culture and history.

This chapter looks at the representation of Byzantium and the Byzantines through the prism of imagology (image studies). Imagology explores national stereotypes and images as expressed in literary discourses. It does not strive to understand a given society, but rather focuses on examining the discourse of representations of that society (Leerssen 2007: 27). In other words, imagology analyses the representations of the Other (in a way, imagology is somewhat like orientalism as it analyses received stereotypes). In his survey chapter on the representation of the Greeks, Gregory Paschalidis briefly mentions a stereotypical representation of the Byzantines (2007: 167). Therefore, it is justified to use imagological tools to study the image of Byzantium and the Byzantines, even if this means studying images of a long-defunct culture. Today's debates (see the Introduction to this volume) on replacing the exonym Byzantium with more appropriate labels are not generally helpful in studying imagery of Byzantine/Medieval Eastern Empire in speculative fiction. Still, they are indicative of how enormous a burden this appellation came to be. The choice of speculative fiction rather than historical novels is also dictated by the fact that such works have more literary freedom when portraying Byzantine characters.

The works discussed in this chapter belong broadly to popular literature and, more precisely, to speculative fiction. Speculative fiction encompasses genres including elements that deviate from or do not exist within reality. In other words, it includes supernatural, ahistorical or futuristic elements. This chapter focuses on sci-fi and fantasy (including subgenres such as alternative history and historical fantasy). The works are mostly written in modern times, except for the fifteenth-century *Tirant the White*, which could be seen as a distant predecessor of the more recent novels. Works chosen for this analysis were written in different languages. However, their authors seem to share, and sometimes challenge, similar stereotypes and misconceptions of Byzantium and its culture.

Some of these novels are similar in their approach to the Byzantine heritage as the same or similar works shaped the approach of the respective authors. Others, on the other hand, stand out and present a highly unconventional approach to Byzantium. My selection is necessarily arbitrary, though most texts selected for this analysis enjoyed or still enjoy some popularity among different readerships. I have decided to discuss works from two, rather different, spheres: the Anglophone world (since they have the biggest impact and influence) and Polish novels (since in Poland Byzantium has never been particularly popular and is perceived as almost paradigmatically 'exotic').

The following chapter is divided into three parts. The first discusses the imagery of the Byzantines in selected novels that belong to the genre of alternative history.

The second briefly explores the depiction of Constantinople and Byzantine culture in speculative fiction. And finally, the third explores paratexts and peritexts, where authorial notes intended for readers of the novels are analysed.

What ifs?

The tradition of writing an alternative history of Byzantium goes back to the fifteenth century and the famous Catalan novel *Tirant el Blanco* (*Tirant the White*) authored by Joanot Martorell (Vaeth 1918). Martorell, who wrote around 1460, a few years after the fall of Constantinople, alters historical facts; Byzantium, with the help of the brave Tirant is saved and restored. While the Byzantine world is 'the centrally "different" culture in this novel' (Doody 1996: 210), it is not the Other it will eventually become in later literature. The Greeks (not the Byzantines as this appellation had yet to be forged) fight boldly (Martorell 1996: 239),[13] and princess Carmesina underscores how well the inhabitants of the country are educated (211).[14] Martorell's version of the Eastern Empire is free of many prejudices, which overflow in later narratives. However, this approach is by no means surprising. Leaving aside possible political overtones (Díaz-Mas 2004: 345) and the author's ideological motivations, the novel's internal logic dictates such a perception of the Empire. Tirant symbolically represents the West summoned to help the East, which in turn automatically creates a binary opposition between the strong (the West) and the weak (the East) (see also González-Casanovas 1991: 112). Byzantium (the East) needs to be saved, but the object of this saving cannot be completely worthless. Tirant's story is exceptional, although it foreshadows to some extent what will become a typical portrayal of Byzantium and the Byzantines in popular literature as being weaker, inferior and in need of rescuing.

Tirant the White is conventionally described as a chivalric romance, but it can also be seen as the precursor of the modern althist ('alternate history') genre. As Karen Hellekson states, 'The alternate history asks questions about time, linearity, determinism, and the implicit link between past and present. It considers the individual's role in making history, and it foregrounds the constructedness and narrativity of history' (2009: 453). One altered episode or one person making a different choice could change the entire historical narrative. This is for instance the case for Harry Turtledove's *Agent of Byzantium* (1987). In the preface to this collection of short stories he offers,

> This book, then, draws heavily on my academic background. It's set in the early fourteenth century of an alternate world where Muhammad, instead of funding Islam, converted to Christianity on a trading mission up into Syria. As a result, the great Arab explosion of the seventh and eighth centuries, which in our world spread Islam from the Atlantic to the frontiers of China, never happened.

In Mieszko Zagańczyk's *Black Icon* (*Czarna Ikona*, 2006), the victory of Roman IV Diogenes at Manzikert (in 1071; in reality, the Byzantine army was defeated, and the emperor himself was captured) created the point of divergence. This change, coupled with some supernatural or magical elements, creates an alternate history of the eleventh-century Byzantine Empire. Similar to Zagańczyk's depiction of the empire is the portrayal in the novel *The Dragon Waiting* by John M. Ford (1983). Though not primarily about Byzantium, it is set in a world where fifteenth-century Byzantium is still a superpower. It is in Byzantium,

> [...] where vampires and wizards are real. The Byzantium where Christianity was suppressed, and Julian's religious pluralism took permanent hold [...] The Byzantium where Islam never developed to apply pressure from the south. The Byzantium where France never really became France, where Gaul was partitioned between the Empire in the east and England in the west. The Byzantium where Rome fell but the Empire kept the party going for another thousand years, at least.[15]

However, an altered storyworld may also be created by including unfamiliar or fantastical elements, such as time travel, supernatural forces, etc. In Chelsea Quinn Yarbro's *A Flame in Byzantium* (1987), such a foreign element is apparent as the novel's main character, Atta Olivia Clemens, happens to be an immortal vampire. Olivia is originally Roman, from the time of Nero, and in the sixth century CE must flee from Rome to the world's new capital – Byzantium. In Sean Munger's *Zombies of Byzantium* (2013), eighth-century Byzantium under the rule of Leo III was attacked by zombies. The undead played an essential role in averting the Saracen siege of 717–718.[16] And finally, in Lucille Turner's *The Sultan, the Vampyr, and the Soothsayer* (2016), Vlad Dracul, whose story is narrated against the final decades of Byzantium, is portrayed as some kind of supernatural creature.

While the general stereotypes (intrigue and luxury) loom over the portrayal of the Byzantines in such novels, there is also a significant degree of creativity. In Turtledove's storyworld, the Romans (he never uses the term 'Byzantines') are 'bustling, cheeky, always on the lookout for the main chance, everlastingly curious, and quick to lose interest in anything new. They are altogether unreliable' (p. 45). Turtledove, a historian by training, toys with the perceived stereotypes of the Byzantines. However, his depiction still favours a negative side more. Yet, instead of being decadent and deceitful (which is characteristic of old culture), the Byzantines behave more like children, which means that they are still vigorous (and therefore young). In Yarbro's novel, Olivia, who flees the old Rome and arrives in the new one, witnesses the shift in importance and power when the ancient capital of the Empire is falling apart, and the new one replaces it entirely. Constantinople or Byzantium is, quite refreshingly, contrasted with Rome, a poised and decadent place. As a friend of Olivia notes in a letter to her, 'Doubtless, since Romans are more lax than we, you have grown accustomed to a level of license that might ill-prepare you for the more decorous and dignified life of this great city [...] What can be thought charming and eccentric in Roma, could give offense in Konstantinoupolis' (p. 29). And Antonina, Belisarios's wife, somewhat ironically (if we remember her unfavourable description by Procopius), states, 'Yes, we do put more value on good conduct than the Romans' (p. 100). These statements echo the vision of Byzantium as overly (and perhaps also falsely) religious. Curiously enough, the inhabitants of the Eastern Empire are never referred to as 'the Byzantines' even though they are often contrasted with 'the Romans' of the old empire. They are something different, something new, yet to be named.

In Turner's novel, the Byzantines are portrayed as keepers of knowledge and protectors of the Christian faith. The future Emperor Constantine XI Palaiologos says to Dracul, Vlad's father, when showing him the library of Constantinople, 'What we have here – what we still have – is nothing less than the greatest store of knowledge mankind has ever possessed, perhaps the greatest he will *ever* possess' (p. 199). This perception of the Byzantines as sophisticated librarians is by no means a new idea. Jules Zeller, in his 1871 *Entretiens sur l'histoire. Antiquité et Moyen Age*, called the Byzantines 'the librarians of humankind'.[17] However, there is a significant difference between these two statements. For Zeller, the Byzantines were just passive 'librarians', while Turner sees them as active curators and keepers. Undoubtedly, the authors of althist novels, who by definition do not need to respect historical realities, are more at liberty to manipulate the Byzantine past. And yet, they both subsume and alter the perceived stereotypes.

In Byzantium, that is to say, Nowhere

Alfred Jarry's drama *King Ubu* (1888) is said to be set 'en Pologne, c'est-à-dire nulle part' (in Poland, that is to say, Nowhere). Paradoxically, the most salient feature of many novels set in Byzantium is a lack of Byzantium. Or, more precisely, a lack of Byzantine features in the detailed descriptions of architecture, costumes, customs, etc. Panagiotis Agapitos argues that the Middle Ages of contemporary crime fiction are 'a unified imaginary space that is being primarily shaped and reshaped by means of literary conventions rather than by medievalist scholarship' (2021: 51). Obviously, sci-fi stories do not need to engage with reality to the same degree as historical novels. Mapping a contemporary mentality onto 'medieval' societies is also much less surprising – in a world where demons and witches exist, some purely logical laws are simply suspended.

Certain authors attempted to construct the language of their medieval protagonists. Interestingly, Zagańczyk and Munger's novels are set apart from other texts by the style of language that they employ. Munger 'deconstructs' Byzantium's otherness and remoteness by making his protagonists speak a very low-brow language.[18] Zagańczyk, on the other hand, attempts to use various Polish registers to render different idiolects used by multiple groups in Byzantium. He also makes his protagonists use various Greek words (*ugro pyr, malaka*). Yarbro explains in the Author's Note that 'Greek usage is based on the usage of the period and on the social position of the characters: it is not modern Greek, nor it is the Greek of Homer' (p. IX).[19] Interestingly, such experiments, which were supposed to render Byzantine Greek in modern languages, are not recent inventions. They date back to Jean Lombard's *Byzance* (1901), whose language was heavily criticized by the Byzantinists.[20]

However, the authors do not remove their storyworlds from the Byzantine reality altogether. Usually, the setting of speculative fiction novels is limited to what is familiar to the potential readers of the novels, mainly buildings and places that have survived until today. They represent 'the familiar' and something with which a potential reader can identify. The authors often refer to items perceived as emblematic of Byzantium culture: icons and mosaics. In *Up the Line,* the protagonist notes that upon seeing the inhabitants of Constantinople, 'Figures in colorful robes, looking like fugitives from Byzantine mosaics, sauntered through the spacious square' (ch. 20). The imperial palace in the *Sultan, the Vampyr, and the Soothsayer* is decorated with mosaics (p. 193). The main character in the *Zombies of Byzantium* is a monk who is an icon painter (which certainly has additional connotations during the iconoclasm).

The distinction between various periods of Byzantine history is virtually absent. There is usually some shade of difference between the novels set in the early period (more precisely in Justinian's Constantinople) and those set in later times. There is one notable exception to the rule – the internal logic of Silverberg's *Up the Line* dictates that since the chrono-travellers visit various periods, there must be a variance shown between these different times. So, Constantinople in the year 408 'was still as much a Roman city as it was Greek' (ch. 20), which makes its inhabitants more Roman than Byzantine ('In the distance there appeared a procession of nobles, clean-cut and close-cropped in the Roman fashion', ch. 20). But in later periods, Constantinople has changed, which is evidenced by the emergence of Byzantine fashion and appearance.[21]

Various elements of the Byzantine reality are usually described in a very opaque manner. In *A Flame of Byzantium,* Olivia is served the food that 'was not the spiced pork and wine of Roma but something more exotic – grilled lamb with onion and cinnamon and pepper – than the fare of ancient Roma' (p. 101). While the inspiration for the dish was probably modern Greek rather than Byzantine cuisine, there is a clear juxtaposition of old Rome and exotic *qua* oriental Constantinople. The food served by Antonina, as well as '[t]he fabric, too, was cotton and silk, not linen and wool as it had been so long ago' (p. 101), signifies the exoticness attributed to Byzantium. Leo III in the *Zombies of Byzantium* eats 'the trout in the *gakos* sauce' (p. 41). *Gakos* is probably an erroneous form of the *garos* (a fish sauce), which the Byzantines inherited from their ancient ancestors and which most likely signifies something odd and luxurious at the same time. Food can be employed to create the oriental-like scenery of Constantinople, 'Once it became obvious to the other peddlers in the vicinity that we were susceptible customers, they crowded around by the dozens, offering us souvenirs, candied sweets, elderly-looking hard-boiled eggs, pans of salted nuts, trays of miscellaneous animal organs, eyeballs and other balls' (*Up the Line*, ch. 20). The description of the Emperor Diogenes IV's clothing in Zagańczyk's novel, which includes a luxurious *paludamentum*, dalmatic and a lot of gold and pearls (p. 58), does not intend to be historically accurate but rather builds on the stereotype of Byzantine luxury and sumptuousness.

Most of the sci-fi/althist novels mention a few Constantinople focal points, such as the hippodrome.[22] Interestingly, some authors offer more details than others. In *Up the Line,* the tourists from the future visit the pre-Justinian city, 'And then we emerged on the Mese, the grand processional street, lined by arcaded shops, and on this day, in honor of the baptism of the prince, decked with silk hangings adorned with gold' (ch. 20). The description in the *Agent of Byzantium* is even more specific, 'Darkness was falling as he lurched into the Augusteion, the main square of the city, which was flanked by Hagia Sophia, the palace district, and the hippodrome' (p. 201). This relative attention to detail is unsurprising, as Harry Turtledove is a Byzantinist by training. In addition, Zagańczyk's Constantinople is constructed by listing the most iconic places (Hagia Sophia, Mese, the Theodosian Walls, Blachernae and Galata).

However, as previously noted, such descriptions are mostly limited to places whose remnants can still be found in Istanbul today. Munger, in *Zombies,* mentions Blachernae, the Church of Christ Pantepoptes, and Walls – all these still survive in modern Istanbul. Even if the authors are aware of a growing body of literature on the city's urban space (and the more recent novels contain more detailed information), they seem to choose not to overwhelm their readers. Some of these architectural details are supposed to make the scenery more familiar and believable, but others build on the preconceived knowledge of Constantinople (and more broadly Byzantium) as an exotic, opulent city. And yet, this generalization can also be challenged as Munger's Constantinople is stereotypically 'dazzling, vibrant, opulent and lavish', but it is also 'intensely boring' (p. 50).

Paratexts and peritexts

Peritexts are a sub-category of paratexts; they are all elements written in a book that do not constitute the main text but rather complete it. Gérard Genette divides peritexts into 'publishing' and 'authorial'. Authorial peritexts include elements such as prefaces, glossaries, etc.[23] Interestingly, peritexts feature abundantly in the 'Byzantine' sci-fi novels. Their presence signifies that the authors are aware that the Eastern Empire or Byzantium needs to be explained to potential readers. There are, of course, varying levels of success, as Ford details in his Historical Notes about the Fourth Crusade of 1404 and the Emperor Julian called Apostata [sic].

In most cases, authorial peritexts are represented by authorial notes, prefaces or glossaries. Some authors limit themselves to listing scholarly publications they have consulted (as does Kay in Acknowledgements). Still, others embark on explaining the events from which they drew inspiration in more detail. Turner's 'Historical Note' is a short essay discussing the religious quarrels between the East and the West. Similarly, Yarbro's note is designed as a micro-introduction to the history of the Eastern Empire. Ford's notes (or the parts about Byzantium) focus on two emperors, Julian the Apostate (who created the point of divergence by suppressing Christianity) and Justinian I. The knowledge about the latter is taken, unsurprisingly, primarily from Procopius's works.

Authorial peritexts also testify to the fact that many authors are well aware that what we call 'Byzantium' was the 'Roman Empire'. Some authors, especially the older generation, use the anachronistic term 'Byzantium'. Yarbro's 'Author's Note' speaks about 'Byzantine civilization' and 'Byzantine empire'. Still, she also offers: 'Although the Byzantines spoke Greek and were strictly and repressively monotheistic Christians, they considered themselves to be the political and cultural descendants of Imperial Rome and were very proud of this heritage ...' (p. vii). Even Munger, who uses the appellation 'Byzantine' throughout his novel, makes a terse note prefacing his novel

'Byzantium – the Eastern Roman Empire'. However, many other authors are more careful with the terminology. Turtledove, in the preface to the *Agent of Byzantium*, states explicitly, 'The Roman Empire (which in its medieval, eastern guise we usually call the Byzantine Empire) …' (p. 4). Undoubtedly, Turtledove's case is, as already mentioned, peculiar because, as he himself says, 'I'm a science-fiction writer and a historian' (p. 4).

In her introduction and explanatory notes, Turner focuses heavily on religious issues – here it can be seen that she is primarily interested in Byzantium as the protector of Christianity and the Orthodox faith. As a result, Turtledove accentuates the religious aspects of the Eastern Empire. In the glossary of historical names and terms, the entries relating to Byzantium include Hagia Sophia, explained as the Greek Christian Orthodox Basilica, and Manicheans. Her 'Historical Notes', as mentioned above, deal with the schism between the East and the West. Yet, Byzantium is not the leading actor in her novel; it is primarily reduced to two roles – the *fidei defensor* and the curator of past wisdom, with the former, visibly underscored in the peritext. The religion of Byzantium and, more precisely, religious persecutions and a strict religious 'order' are also singled out as key factors defining Byzantine civilization in Yarbro's introduction.

Curiously, none of the peritexts included in the novels under consideration mention the usual Byzantine stereotype; there is no discussion of the Byzantine decadence. This stands in sharp contrast to nineteenth-century 'Byzantine' novels where decadence was the defining feature, and paradoxically also the most interesting feature of this civilization. Instead, the authors pursue their individual agendas but their novels are ultimately founded on some original source material (rarely) and scholarly literature (more often).

Epilogue

Speculative fiction shows that particular fascinations do not disappear easily – Theodora (re)discovered by Victorien Sardou at the beginning of the twentieth century does not cease to intrigue modern authors. She either features in the novels set in her time or is evoked as the iconic empress. In the *Immortal,* she strived toward immortality with a vampire. In *The Dragon Waiting,* she is mentioned as Theodora of Byzantium who 'turned vampire to save herself from death' (p. 121; Theodora seems to be identified as a vampire in many novels). Cyril Mango argued that sixth-century Byzantium was attractive for writers because it was relatively the best researched period of Byzantine history (Mango 1981: 337). Yet today, the situation has changed. Even if Theodora and Justinian are still popular, authors look for inspiration elsewhere, searching for different periods and events.

What is apparent from this analysis is that the imagery of Byzantium is not a simple hotpot of clichés and preconceived conceptions. Although the authors evoke specific ideas attributed to Byzantium, such as luxury, richness and refinement, they project an image, which is both nuanced and complex. Even less successful books challenge the paradigm and no longer convey a simplified (and simplistic) image of Byzantium as a decadent state. In *A Byzantine Werewolf*, one of the characters describes Constantinople to the main protagonist saying (p. 58),

> You're in Syria lad, well within of Constantinople. Could you not have heard of it? The second incarnation of Rome, vast with wealth and rich in culture. Her armies renowned, and her generals feared. Her influence is felt throughout the west, and her churches spring up across the land like flowers following rain. Surely you've heard of the great city?

The Byzantium of popular literature is still golden, exotic and mysterious, and its inhabitants can be duplicitous and complicated. But it is also sophisticated and culturally rich. A recurring motif is its attachment to religion. However, it is no longer Gibbonian Christianity, which ultimately destroyed the Roman Empire; it is something important, valued and worth defending. The sample of works analysed in this chapter might perhaps be too few, but it is tempting to conclude that the imagery utilized to represent Byzantium has evolved. And it is only logical to presume that it has done so because Byzantine studies are a growing discipline in higher education. These two areas continue to influence each other to their mutual benefit.

Acknowledgements

Publication co-financed by the funds granted under the Research Excellence Initiative of the University of Silesia in Katowice.

Notes

1. I have been able to identify only a handful of texts written in languages other than English and Polish. For instance, G. V. Abgarovich and O. V. Aleksandrovich penned a novel *Byzantium* (Византия), which is set simultaneously in modern Moscow and in Byzantium.
2. In the Polish language alone, there has recently been a surge of novels drawing on Byzantine themes.
3. 'But the short version of how Byzantine history informed this book is as follows: in the year 1044 AD, the Byzantine Empire annexed the small Armenian kingdom of Ani. The empire was able to do this for a lot of reasons—political, historical, military—but the precipitating incident involved the Catholicos of the Armenian Apostolic Church, a man named Petros Getadarj, who was determined to prevent the forced conversion of the Armenians to the Byzantine form of Christianity. He did this by trading the physical sovereignty of Ani to the Byzantine emperor in exchange for promises of spiritual sovereignty. When I started writing *A Memory Called Empire*, my inciting question was: what's it like to be that guy? To betray your culture's freedom in order to save your culture?' (http://strangehorizons.com/non-fiction/articles/an-interview-with-arkady-martine/ (accessed 15 November 2021)).
4. One of course could wonder to what extent one ideology is simply replaced with another one. See also the Introduction to this volume.

5   This choice, however, is not entirely surprising as earlier texts often used this appellation.
6   At the end of the novel its protagonist says, 'In a week there will be an anniversary of liberating us from the yoke of democracy' (p. 246).
7   This genre was very popular and very successful in Poland where various authors used it to comment on the societal problems under communism when the criticism of the regime was fraught with persecutions.
8   That is exploring the storyworld of *Buffy the Vampire Slayer*.
9   Theodora has made it to videogames as is leading the Byzantine civilization in the videogame *Civilization III*. See Chapter 7 in this volume.
10 For a thorough discussion, see Malosse (2007: 229–35).
11 See, for instance, 'Sailing to Sarantium by Guy Gavriel Kay (The Sarantine Mosaic #1)', Fantasy Book Review, https://www.fantasybookreview.co.uk/Guy-Gavriel-Kay/Sailing-to-Sarantium.html (accessed 18 November 2021).
12 See the reviews of this book on Amazon: https://www.amazon.com/Sultan-Byzantium-Selcuk-Altun/dp/1846591481 (accessed 19 November 2021).
13 'When the men in ambush saw the *Greeks fighting so boldly* (emphasis, PTM), they came out furiously and fell into the thick of the Christians, spilling their blood. The duke could not take the fierce battle any longer and he secretly fled without doing much harm to the enemy. And those who were able to escape went with him.'
14 '"What makes you think Greek ladies are less clever than French ones?" asked the princess. "We shall understand your Latin, no matter how obscurely you speak it".'
15 From the 'Introduction' by Scott Lynch.
16 Munger's novel to some extent belongs to the genre of *secret history*; see ch. 16, p. 238: 'No history books mention the role of the undead ghouls in the Saracen siege of 717.'
17 Zeller (1871: 393): 'les Byzantins deviennent seulement […] les bibliothécaires du genre humain'.
18 Examples include 'Most of my military commanders are whimpering idiots' (p. 45); 'I'll proclaim you Grand God-Emperor Messiah with the Biggest Cock in the Universe' (pp. 45–46).
19 I have to admit that I have failed to notice many passages exemplifying this claim. Perhaps it is meant rather as a general information for readers about the Greek spoken by the protagonists of the novel.
20 See, for instance, reviews by Zichy (1902: 202) and also by Diehl (1926: 238–39).
21 'I saw Nicephorus himself emerge in his chariot for his noontime drive: a stately figure with a long, ornately braided black beard and elaborate gold-trimmed robes. On his breast he wore a pendant cross, gilded and studded with huge jewels; his fingers glistened with rings. A crowd had gathered to watch the noble Nicephorus leave his palace' (ch. 32).
22 *A Flame in Byzantium*: 'The Hippodrome resembled the Circus Maximus, though it was not as boisterous or as crowded as the huge amphitheater in Roma had been' (p. 100).
23 On paratexts and their relationship to the text, see Genette (1991: 261–72).

Bibliography

Agapitos, P. (2021), 'Visually Demolished and Textually Reconstructed: Performing the Middle Ages in Contemporary Crime Fiction', in L. James, O. Nicholson and R. Scott (eds.), *After the Text: Byzantine Enquiries in Honour of Margaret Mullett*, 41–55, London: Routledge.

Alışık, E. (2021), 'Towards an Unearthly Byzantium: Mapping Out Topoi of Byzantinisms in Speculative Fiction', in E. Alışık, *'What is This Byzantinism in Istanbul!': Byzantium in Popular Culture*, 290–317, Istanbul: Kasım.

Díaz-Mas, P. (2004), 'El eco de la caída de Constantinopla en las literaturas hispánicas', in P. Bádenas and I. Pérez-Martin (eds.), *Constantinopla 1453. Mitos y realidades*, 317–49, Madrid: CSIC.

Diehl, C. (1926), 'Byzance dans la littérature', in C. Diehl, *Choses et gens de Byzance*, 231–48, Paris: De Boccard.

Doody, A. M. (1996), *The True Story of the Novel*, New Brunswick NJ: Rutgers University Press.

González-Casanovas, R. J. (1991), 'Religious and Cultural Politics in Tirant lo Blanc: The Mediterranean Contexts of Chivalry', *Catalan Review*, 5.1: 95–120.

Hellekson, K. (2009), 'Alternate History', in M. Bould, A. Butler, A. Roberts and S. Vint (eds.), *The Routledge Companion to Science Fiction*, 453–57, London: Routledge.

Koutrakou, N. (2003), 'L'image de Byzance dans la littérature fantastique et policière', in M-F. Auzépy (ed.), *Byzance en Europe*, 193–213, Saint-Denis: Presses Universitaires de Vincennes.

Koutrakou, N. (2004), 'L'impero rivisitato. Bisanzio nel romanzo fantastico e nel giallo', in G. Cavallo (ed.), *Lo spazio letterario del Medioevo.3: Leculture circostanti, 1: La cultura bizantina*, 765–96, Roma: Salerno Editrice.

Leerssen J. (2007), 'Imagology: History and Method', in M. Beller and J. Leerssen (eds.), *Imagology: The Cultural Construction and Literary Representation of National Characters. A Critical Survey*, 17–32, Amsterdam and New York: Rodopi.

Malosse, P.-L. (2007), 'Justinien visité et revisité', *Anabases. Traditions et Réceptions de l'Antiquité*, 5: 229–35.

Mango, C. (1981), 'Daily Life in Byzantium', *Jahrbuch der Österreichischen Byzanitnistik*, 31 (1): 327–53.

Martorell, J. and Galba, J. M. de (1996), *Tirant Lo Blanch*, transl. D. Rosenthal, Boston, MD: Johns Hopkins University Press.

Paschalidis, G. (2007), 'Greeks', in M. Beller and J. Leerssen (eds.), *Imagology: The Cultural Construction and Literary Representation of National Characters. A Critical Survey*, 166–71, Amsterdam and New York: Rodopi.

Vaeth, J. A. (1918), *Tirant lo Blanch. A Study of its Authorship, Principal Sources and Historical Setting*, Columbia, NY: Columbia University Press.

Zeller, J. (1871), *Entretiens sur l'histoire. Antiquité et Moyen Age*, Paris: Didier et cie.

Zichy, T. (1902), 'Jean Lombard. Byzance' (review), *Byzantinische Zeitschrift*, 11: 202–03.

Conclusion: No Longer a Forgotten Empire?

Przemysław Marciniak

One of the common descriptors of Byzantium is the phrase 'the forgotten Empire', but how is Byzantium 'forgotten' if there are over a thousand results in the books department on Amazon.com? Undoubtedly, its presence and influence are far less prominent than those of classical antiquity. Its history is taught at schools only fragmentarily; its secular architecture was only scarcely preserved. However, its heritage is still tangible in many countries, not only those linked to the Eastern Empire by a shared history or the same religious denomination. Norman Davies, in the chapter on Byzantium in his book *The Vanished Kingdoms*, remarked: 'The "Byzantine Empire," in contrast, is no more than an intellectual construct, an abstraction, some might say, that never really existed' (2012: 312). Yet such a statement could be applied to all civilizations that perished, and whose history and culture are reconstructed by scholars prone to perceiving them through the lenses of their contemporary fears and fashions. However, Byzantium seems to differ from many other 'vanished kingdoms' because of its political and religious legacy and importance. Byzantium, as an intellectual and scholarly construct, is a domain of ambiguity and opposition: it is both important (for Greece, Russia and in a highly complex way also Turkey) and unimportant (for many countries outside the Byzantine 'commonwealth'). It is simultaneously ours, and it represents 'the Other'. It 'belongs' to Western tradition (in fact it was responsible for preserving ancient heritage), and yet it is often perceived, geographically and culturally, as oriental.

These issues have been addressed by scholars in the past, who analysed the place of Byzantium in political discourses and scholarly debates. The editors of this volume intended to change the perspective and offer some initial glimpses into shaping Byzantine imagery in the modern period and the more popular media. This picture is far from complete and – purposefully – far from entirely cohesive. Some chapters are more analytical and others more descriptive, especially those meant to provide the reader with unknown or difficult-to-access material. The section devoted to literature is thematically and geographically varied, but all texts discussed therein belong to popular literature rather than the high-brow one, and thus, mirror the 'popular' view of the empire.

The chapters in this volume reveal how the imagery of Byzantium/the Eastern Empire functions in popular imagination. Their authors attempted to provide answers to questions that may arise in connection with the reception of Byzantium in our times: did the broad and instant access to sources coupled with a growing body of scholarly literature change how modern creators conceive Byzantium? Can modern media themselves influence the way of representing and understanding Byzantium?

Access to knowledge about Byzantium is much more egalitarian these days; although still a relatively small discipline, it has a solid internet presence. There are Facebook groups for Byzantine history and art; YouTube offers plenty of films on various aspects of the Eastern Empire. Internet forums teem with discussants arguing who was the best, or worst, emperor. This relatively easy access to what used to be scholarly knowledge results in more widespread awareness of the empire. Still, it can contribute to simplified imagery since various sources offer unverified and unchecked information.

Byzantium and Byzantinism are still used for political purposes, but it appears that the imagery of the Eastern Empire in videogames, speculative fiction and TV shows can transgress geographical and political boundaries; it does not have to be connected to a specific political ideology. In this sense, the traditional view of Byzantinism 'As a discourse of "otherness"', which 'evolves from, and reflects upon, the West's worst dreams and nightmares about its own self', is no longer – in my view – the dominant narrative (Angelov 2003: 3).

However, I would argue that the reception of Byzantium remains spotty: it is limited to several key characters and events, and while the traditional repertoire is growing, the narrative potential of Byzantium is still underused. There is no big Hollywood movie about the fall of the city, Basil II, no rom-com about Leo VI and his wives. The only high-budget film on the fall was shot in Turkey and was a by-product of Neo-Ottoman ideology. On the one hand, this lack of interest in Byzantium probably results from uncertainty as to whether a Byzantine story would have the potential to interest enough viewers to make such an enterprise profitable.

However, on the other hand, this relative pop cultural lack of interest results partly from a fluctuating Byzantine 'identity'. Unlike antiquity, the Byzantine period is not seen as an irreplaceable part of the culture and history of Europe (however we want to define 'Europe'). Paradoxically, Byzantium belongs to the many (because of the religious and political heritage) and to no one (because it has no obvious direct cultural heirs).

Yet still, a relative unawareness of Byzantium and any stereotypes connected with its culture make the empire even more interesting. Perhaps today's culture is more open about exploring unfamiliar phenomena and revisiting received stereotypes. The Byzantine presence manifests itself big and small. Fashion houses show collections based on Byzantine icons; ice manufacturers offer flavours called Byzantine, there are Byzantium-scented candles and perfumes called 'Byzantium'. The Byzantium image in the popular imagination is, by all means, the sum of both efforts by Byzantinists and people from outside academia. Coco Chanel has reportedly said, 'Why does all I do become Byzantine?' ('Pourquoi est-ce que tout ce que je fais devient byzantin?'). It is still far from it, but the modern imagery of Byzantium is becoming more widespread. And this volume has provided just a taste of this fascinating issue.

Bibliography

Angelov, D. G. (2003), 'Byzantinism: The Imaginary and Real Heritage of Byzantium in Southeastern Europe', in D. Keridis, E. Elias-Bursac and N. Yatromalakis (eds.), *New Approaches to Balkan Studies*, 3–23, Dulles, VA: Brassey's.

Davies, N. (2012), *Vanished Kingdoms: The History of Half-Forgotten Europe*, London: Penguin Books.

Afterword: Forging Textual Realities, or How to Write a 'Byzantine Mystery Story'

Panagiotis Agapitos

The writing of afterwords is often a boring exercise for writers and readers alike. Besides, what should one write about Neobyzantinism in the popular imagination, when this fine volume is opening up a window into an as yet uncharted territory. As far as I am concerned, I find myself in a Dr Jekyll and Mr Hyde dichotomy, given that I am a professional Byzantinist as well as a writer of historical crime fiction. Though I have published two or three papers on the image and use of Byzantium in modern Greek culture, I was asked by the editors of the volume to write about my own creative writing and the image of Byzantium therein. What follows, then, are my thoughts on my novels, the way in which I approached their drafting and writing, some comments on crime fiction and history, and how Byzantium can fit in this polarity as a creative spatiotemporal setting and not just as a Neobyzantinist fantasy. The essay, therefore, does not meet the expectations of a typical broad afterword as it is rather narrow and blended with a few 'autobiographical' reminiscences.

In June 1991 I had been recently released from my military service and had returned to Athens from a short stay at the Dumbarton Oaks Research Library and Collection in Washington. I had participated in a workshop on 'Byzantium as a Familiar Stranger' where a number of scholars talked about the image of Byzantium in scholarship. I was without a job and had a lot of free time, so I decided to put aside my teenage infatuation with poetry and started reading crime fiction. Two months later, I was sitting with a friend of mine on a beach in Sounion, at the southernmost tip of Attica, and profusely praising a historical crime novel that I had just read. It was Robert van Gulik's *Poets and Murder*, acted out in seventh-century China at the time of the Tang Dynasty. The protagonist was the impressive Judge Dee who solved simultaneously three apparently unrelated cases. I was saying to my friend that I particularly liked how medieval China was convincingly represented through the plot and did not give the impression that it was just an exotic scenery for some additional colour in an otherwise typical Western European narrative.

'What a pity that nothing similar has been written for Byzantium', I added.

'Why don't you write something?' my friend asked who was not a Byzantinist.

For a moment I remained speechless. This idea had never crossed my mind. A strong enthusiasm got hold of me, I bought a large notebook and, without really thinking about it, I saw in front of me three things: the title of the novel would be *The Ebony Lute*, the plot would be placed during the reign of Emperor Theophilos (829–841) and the sleuth would be called Leo. I started collecting material, translating and reworking Byzantine and Arabic prose and verse texts, drafting various characters that could become part of the plot. But the few pages I tried to write were awful and I threw them away.

The truth is that I never had a natural inclination for writing. At school I neither wrote poems nor good essays, though I liked to tell stories, transforming an ordinary incident into a funny adventure, improvising imaginary stories to fool my teachers when they caught me unprepared in class, narrating to my mother the dreams of the previous night. Moreover, at the beginning of my career as a professional Byzantinist I believed that scholarly discourse and, consequently, the kind of writing that presented the results of research was a communicative and utilitarian necessity primarily (if not exclusively) involving the academic community. Until then, but also later, I had not been concerned with how such a scholarly discourse could step out of the narrow circle of researchers to reach out (if such a thing would have been ever possible) to a broader public. In 1992 I was appointed at the University of Cyprus and I put my notebook of *The Ebony Lute* into a drawer.

Five years later, on a hot day in August 1997, I was looking in Athens' English bookshop for the last novel of Philip Kerr's superb crime trilogy set in the Berlin of the Nazi era. As I was browsing through a shelf, I met a famous Greek Byzantinist who had just picked up the latest police procedural of Ed MacBain.

'I very much like police novels', he said in his deep voice. 'What about you?'

'So, do I! I just found Philip Kerr's *German Requiem*.'

'But, my dear Mr. Agapitos, these young writers do not write police novels', he remarked. 'They try to write literature and their books are utterly unreadable.'

I was taken aback and, in order to save the situation, I asked him what he would think of a crime novel set in Byzantium. He looked at me gravely behind his thick glasses. 'The Byzantines knew very well how to kill, but they had no idea how to narrate!' he proclaimed ponderously and left holding his MacBain novel under his arm.

What a blow. How could a Byzantinist say such a thing? Byzantine historiography, for example, is full of magnificent narratives. Furthermore, there survive twelve love romances, but, above all, we have the lives of saints and the collections of their miracles. Many of these texts are among the most powerful narratives of medieval literature. It was then that I realized what I had not grasped before. Our attitude towards Byzantium is that of a negation: Byzantium is not ancient Greece, Byzantium does not have secular art, Byzantium does not have readable literature, and so on. 'The Byzantines knew very well how to kill, but they had *no* idea how to narrate.'

I was irritated at this pompous attitude and, upon my return to Nicosia, I pulled my notebook out of the drawer, started drafting the novel's plot and sketching more carefully the cast of characters. In the years since my appointment at UCY, I begun finding a more personal style in my scholarly texts, especially because I was forced to present longer talks that gave me the opportunity to test my skills at interpretive essay writing. Therefore, I thought that the composition of a crime novel with the elements that in my inexperienced and prejudiced mind were the characteristics of its writing – logical plot, clear structure, focus on the essentials of the story, unadorned style – resembled the way in which I approached the writing of a research paper: an intellectual rather than an emotional process. Unexpectedly, on a clear winter's morning in Nicosia – it was January 2002 – I started writing the opening sequence of *The Ebony Lute* and I immediately realized that I had erred in my appreciation of writing. The narrative had claimed an independence that surprised me because in the representation of the execution scaffold and the ensuing dialogue between the *protospatharios* Leo and his young secretary Photios I recognized things that concerned me as a person even if they had been filtered through my experience of Byzantine culture. My intellectual involvement with the spatiotemporal character of history found its counterweight in the emotional relation I developed with the fictional characters of the story. This balancing made the writing much harder for me, yet it offered me the possibility to create a long and comprehensive narrative composition, something I had not achieved until then in my scholarly work.

Before moving to my own novels, let me spend here a few words on crime fiction more generally. As a genre, crime fiction was gradually shaped by a set of extremely pronounced conventions that were fully formed by the 1920s, defining what many critics and readers saw as a 'non-literary genre', or as W. H. Auden put it, 'an escape from literature' – exactly the attitude reflected in the remarks of my august colleague twenty-six years ago. What are these conventions? The detective is mostly alone and is exclusively male up to the 1980s, with the exception of Agatha Christie's Miss Marple, who represents a sleuth category of her own. The detective is mostly depicted as an eccentric (often highly cultured) genius (Sherlock Holms and Hercule Poirot) or as an experienced 'man about town' (Sam Spade and Philip Marlowe) or, again, as an intelligent and perceptive representative of the middle class (Inspector Maigret). He might get involved in an amorous, sometimes fatal, affair during the development of the story. He usually operates in a fixed (spatial or social) environment, while his own psychological persona is equally fixed. The central crime of the plot either has a very 'staged' character (as in the British pre-Second-World-War murder mystery) or it appears to be almost coincidental (as in the American crime story). The detection of the crime is based on two kinds of fictional logic: that of the crossword riddle and its complex evidence in the British type or of the improvised narrative and its haphazard ramifications in the American type. At any rate, 'literary writing' (whatever that might mean) is by definition excluded. However, these conventions (paradigmatically codified in the works of Arthur Conan Doyle, Agatha Christie, Dashiel Hammett, Raymond Chandler and George Simenon) were being left behind by the late 1950s, for example, in the novels of Patricia Highsmith, Friedrich Dürrenmat and Ruth Rendell, whose demanding writing attracted the attention of critics and public. The role of the detective ceases to be clear cut, 'good' and 'evil' lose their well-defined borders and begin to blend, style becomes much more individual, the characters take on a psychological depth unknown before, violence and sex are depicted more explicitly.

Here, then, comes along a professional Byzantinist who wants to write a crime novel set in ninth-century Byzantium. Where lies the problem? No police or crime detection existed in Byzantium, nor was there any literary tradition of narratives concerning crime and institutional justice as we find them in China of the seventeenth century, and on which van Gulik based his novels. Thus, the conventions of the twentieth-century mystery genre have to be transposed to a world foreign to the social, economic and cultural environment in which they had been created. In my opinion, such a transposition, if executed in a mechanical manner, will not be able to create a fictive make-believe spatiotemporality because it imports to a pre-modern historical period and its very different mentalities, notions so modern that they cancel the historicity of the plot setting. As a result, the remote past either appears as a tame, two-dimensional representation of a setting known to the broader public through school education, for example, in the 'medieval mysteries' of Elis Peters and other British writers of the so-called 'cosy style'. Or, again, it might become an exaggerated, equally two-dimensional, burlesque that recreates a distorted modern image of that specific past, as in the Roman novels of Lindsay Davis, where the characters speak and act as if they were in a Chandler novel. In other words, the past is presented as a romanticized or de-romanticized tragicomedy on a parodic theatre stage. I decided to tackle the problem differently. To the basic conventions of the traditional genre, I tried to find a corresponding version that would reflect some equivalent Byzantine practice or mental attitude.

My detective, the *protospatharios* Leo (his court-hierarchy title means 'senior swordbearer'), thirty-two years old in *The Ebony Lute*, lives alone in his grand family house in the capital with his trusted old servant. He is a learned Constantinopolitan gentleman who plays the lute and is an enthusiastic reader of ancient Greek love romances. He comes from a family of judges and heads as *protoasikritis* (i.e. 'senior secretary') the imperial chancellery, being responsible for drafting laws, decrees and other important documents. He is not married because he was forced, after the death of his elder brother, to enter the service of the state, but also because he was rejected by the woman he had fallen in love with at the age of sixteen and suffers in the pathetic manner of the heroes in the Greek romances. All of this allows to a certain extent the conventions around the 'lonely detective' to function in a Byzantine context, though the strangeness of an unmarried man who is not a monk is commented by various characters in the novels, for example, in chapter 5 of *The Ebony Lute*. This staging also suggests that Leo lives, initially at least, in a world of literary assumptions, rather than of real-life experience – an attitude that we, mistakenly, believe many Byzantines had.

Out of the thousand years of Byzantine history I chose as the setting for my plots the second period of the iconoclastic controversy, that is, from the accession of Leo the Armenian in 813 until the death of Theophilos in 842. Leo was fictitiously born on 15 September 800. Thus, his life and the lives of his immediate ancestors are embedded in the tumultuous years between 750 and 850. But why choose this particular era? For one, it is a period practically unknown to the broader public. But, most importantly, it is an age of social and administrative changes, a period where important reforms in the judicial system were taking place, and where Emperor Theophilos himself insisted on justice as a major component in the proper function of society. It was also an age of scholarly and literary renewal, of experimentation and confrontation with the scientific and cultural achievements of the Abbasid Califate in Baghdad – the Muslim superpower facing Byzantium in the Near East. Finally, it was the time of an important theological debate about the character of icons, in other words, the painted depictions of divine and holy figures, such as Christ, his mother Mary and the saints. This debate played a role in the understanding and function of the visual arts within Byzantine society from the eighth century onwards. In this sense, an intelligent, juridically educated and cultured man of iconoclast tendencies around the year 830 would be able to view a criminal act and its social context as an intellectual problem to be solved on many different levels. To make the criminal core of the story fit into a broader context, political history is drawn into the plot by making the detective an ambassador of the emperor on different kinds of diplomatic missions.

Crime novels most often set their plots in an urban landscape; thus, the city as a space generates itself the conditions of crime. One thinks of Raymond Chandler's Los Angeles and its historicized mutations in James Ellroy and Walter Mosley, who write respectively about the 'white' and the 'black' LA in the late 1950s and early 1960s. Contrastively, I use each time a different setting, though it would have been easy to use Constantinople as the crime-breeding urban space of my plots. But modern historical literary works and scholarship about Byzantium focus to an excessive degree on Constantinople, equating the capital with the empire itself, an image that the Byzantines themselves cultivated after the age of Justinian to an equally excessive extent – a stance similar to the gradual creation of Paris as the absolute centre or even the life-giving heart of France. The device of removing the setting from the capital and having it change allows me to present the readers with different socio-political, cultural and even ethnic situations within the empire from a close-up perspective, countering in this way the master narrative of Byzantine Studies. The settings are Cappadocian Caesarea (in modern-day Turkey) and the embattled eastern borders during a hot May of 832; Macedonian Thessaloniki in an ice-cold January of 833; the inhospitable island of Skyros in the Aegean Sea during a rainy November of 835. Leo always travels as the emperor's emissary and he dislikes it – yet another attitude expressed openly by the Byzantines. He is therefore a stranger to each of these places, someone who looks at the *locus criminis* from the outside and who has to fight his way through the local community and the specific mentalities of its members.

While working on the plot of *The Ebony Lute*, I started sketching Leo's fictional life in relative detail in order to draw the outline of a series of five novels. I decided to have Leo's psychological persona deepen emotionally and mature intellectually. This change takes place gradually as he discovers for himself, primarily through his mistakes, the mechanisms of crime detection. This, obviously, is a process involving critical self-reflection. Certainly, there existed no such thing as psychoanalysis or an understanding of the subconscious in pre-modern cultures, though educated Byzantines were fully aware of the various philosophical and theological aspects concerning the operations of a human being's soul – his or her psyche. However, the Byzantine had a practical model for observing and categorizing human behaviour, and that model was provided by astrology and the signs of the zodiac circle. Much of the psychological background in my Byzantine mystery stories is based on these ancient astral patterns. Leo, for example, is a Virgo and behaves very much in accordance with what the Byzantine considered the chief elements of this zodiac sign; Leo's friend, Prince Moutasim, is a Gemini, and Leo even comments in *The Ebony Lute* on Mutasim's typically Gemini behaviour.

In this way, I was able to explore what many Byzantines perceived as a clash between a person's inner and outer self, or, in our terminology, between the private sphere and the various public social roles. Could one be 'simple', in other words, be the same person inside and outside him/herself? Or would one have to be 'double' in order to go through the vicissitudes of life? Was 'simplicity' equal to honesty and truth, while 'duplicity' equal to dishonesty and falsehood? Leo engages with the search for his true self, as he is confronted with situations and emotions outside the protected world of his aristocratic household and high office. He gradually discovers and reluctantly accepts the suppressed, darker sides of his psyche and the rejected desires of his body. It is a process that helps him, even if in a painful way, to understand the crime he is each time faced with and to apply justice in a manner appropriate to that crime and its motives, even if sometimes not in accordance to the letter of the law.

A crime is patently essential to a crime novel, but beyond colouring the narrative with blood, what does a crime represent? In the older forms of the genre, the crime committed was rarely depicted in action and certainly not in a raw manner, while it never violated societal order as a system. It might, for a very brief moment, have disturbed some part of this order (more so in the American and Central European versions, than in the old British ones), but it never criticized the status quo in its entirety; crime was a private matter between individual people. Recent crime novels, however, starting with French writers in the 1970s like Jean Patrick Manchette, have questioned this conformist and escapist attitude, and have placed crime in a broader context of societal disorder and institutional corruption. It is society itself and its problematic condition that generate crime, creating along the way a new manner of narrating this crime. On the one hand, character as a formative element of crime becomes of secondary importance because crime is a societal, not a personal, matter. On the other hand, narrative now allots much more space to the depiction of violence and sex, while it has become far more cinematic in its use of an action-packed plot and related description techniques. Recent English writers of medieval crime novels, like Susannah Gregory and Michael Jecks, integrate this attitude into their plots. As a result, medieval crime and sex look blatantly modern. Once again, I chose a different path. Instead of inventing crimes on my own, I created them out of the material offered by the Byzantine sources taking as my starting point the penal chapters of law collections. For example, all crimes committed in *The Ebony Lute* and judged by Leo in chapter 22 can be matched with specific crimes punished in the *Ecloga*, the juridical compendium issued by Emperors Leon III and Constantine V in 741 and used in Byzantine courts up to the tenth century. I further used stories of crime and lust reported in historical and hagiographical works of the period, while I also copied acts of violence depicted in illuminated manuscripts, like the scene of flagellation in chapter 1 of *The Bronze Eye*. As strange as some of the crimes or sexual behaviours in my novels might appear, they, in fact, reflect to a substantial extent the Byzantine criminal and sexual *imaginaire*.

In this way, the plots are drawn from within Byzantine culture and, in my opinion, are not Neobyzantinist constructs. In order to give depth to this perspective from within, I have employed Byzantine narrative techniques in various parts of the plots. Let me mention just one example. The opening chapters of all three of my novels start out as an *ekphrasis*, that is, a fully developed narrative description of a large 'painting': the huge execution scaffold with mutilated corpses in the middle of an arid Anatolian plain seen by Leo, the marketplace of Thessaloniki seen through the eyes of an old stylite monk perched on his column, a black warship crossing the Aegean on an autumn evening before a storm described by the third-person narrator. For most readers the narrator's perspective resembles that of a film camera and, so, the Byzantine rhetorical technique of 'translucent discourse' (*enargeia*) is perceived as something very modern, though it is not so in the least. The Byzantines called this kind of 'imitative' writing *mimesis*. The term referred to a complex system of recreating the literary devices and the rhetorical style (but not necessarily the actual words) of a specific author. Beyond stylistics, I also applied *mimesis* to the narrative structure of my novels. Each one of them 'imitates' the structural techniques of a different twentieth-century mystery author: Robert van Gulik and his Chinese historical novels in *The Ebony Lute*, the urban slow-paced novels of P. D. James in *The Bronze Eye* and Agatha Christie's 'remote-place-and-many-suspects' riddle-plots in *The Enamel Medusa*. For those readers who know the mystery genre and its variations, there is an added pleasure in discovering the imitative dialogue (sometimes wholly subversive) that takes place between my novels and those of my illustrious predecessors. For example, the 'Chinese' plot structure in *The Ebony Lute* is hinted at by the presence of a young woman who is taken to be Chinese and is dressed up exactly like the attractive and often good-hearted whores in van Gulik's novels. This is a typical Byzantine attitude to literary composition.

We see, then, the professional Byzantinist selecting all the necessary scientific material from his laboratory to construct his 'Byzantine mystery stories'. The use of this material gives a strong flavour of authenticity to the plots. But what about the overall depiction of the past? Is what the reader sees the 'real' Byzantium of the ninth century? We should be reminded that it is practically impossible to reconstitute even the early years of our own lives, much less to reconstruct a past age in its totality, because we rely in our comprehension of the past on memory and order. Memory operates through a complex system of selection, while order imposes on the selected material a sort of uniformity and coherence that the past did not have. History is more of a layered co-existence of disorderly discontinuities rather than a flowing progression of orderly continuities. I turned this situation into a declared stance of my writing by thinking of myself as a creator of forged paintings. I collected all the authentic source material through my professional knowledge but I have put it together according to interpretive perspectives of the age to which I belong. Thus, I have woven into the plots of my novels such issues as psychological character formation, the construction of social roles and gender issues, sexuality and interpersonal relations, representations of alterity and deviation and finally, criticism of institutions and socio-political corruption.

This broader attitude to the mystery genre I owe to my readings in postmodern fiction which, in my opinion, bears strong cultural and literary similarities to Byzantine textual production. For example, a number of important devices developed by postmodernist writers can be massively found in Byzantine literature; for example, rejection of a normative literary canon and its worn-off forms, experimentation with non-literary or even counter-literary expression, use of textual collage and parodic style, organization of narrative along paratactic rather than hypotactic structures, extreme presence of digression and loose association, artistic creation as a mechanical process, open criticism of originality. This artistic attitude is finely captured by a triad of Italian novels published almost simultaneously in 1979/80, very different from each other in style and perspective, yet very similar in their subversive approach to narrative and its literary past: *At What Point Is The Night* by Carlo Fruttero and Franco Lucentini, Italo Calvino's *If On a Winter Night a Traveller* and Umberto Eco's *The Name Of The Rose*. All three, while taking a criminal act as their starting point, deal with writing, reading, narrating and interpreting the arts of fiction and detection. At the same time, all three novels continuously evoke memories of the novelistic genre and its great texts. They resemble large, discursively painted canvases of great complexity inviting the readers to get lost in their enticing labyrinths.

As for the visual aspect of my novels, I owe a particular debt to the cinematic techniques of Akira Kurosawa. Many of his most famous movies take place in Japan of the sixteenth century, an age of brutal civil strife and clashes between the samurai feudal world and a new military order, such as *The Throne of Blood* and *Rebellion*, adaptations of Shakespeare's *Macbeth* and *King Lear* respectively. Kurosawa's approach to history was modernist and archaic at the same time, as he used the archaic worlds of Shakespearean mythical tragedy for his plots and medieval Japanese Kabuki plays for his aesthetics, while employing cinematic devices developed by American western and gangster movies.

What to a certain extent I attempted to create in my own Byzantine mystery stories is a narrative painting of history that is both forged and true – 'forged' in that it never existed as such, 'true' in that it is a conscious reinterpretation of the past through the present and an artistic dialogue with past and present stories along the path of a blood-stained narrative. To phrase it concisely, postmodern European literary fabrication is the prerequisite for Byzantine fictional truth.

Index

Locators in *italics* refer to figures

accuracy, historical 134–5, 150, 199
administrando imperio, De 193
Agapitos, Panagiotis 5, 254
Agathos, T. 182–3, 187
Age of Empires series 125, 127–9, 137
Agent of Byzantium 252, 255–6, 257
Ahl, David H. 126–7
Alışık, Emir 249
Akalabeth: World of Doom 127
Alexiad 244
Allegory 185
Altan, Selçuk 251
althist 252–3
Amiroutzes, George 154
ancestors, heroic 69
Anglo-Saxons *see* identity, British
Antonopoulos, Konstantinos 188
Apocryphal Tales 194–5
Arakon, Aydin 165
architecture 4, 40–1
    Byzantine 52–3
    Byzantine and French Medieval 33–4
    Byzantium in France 38–40
    Constantinople 255–6, 258
    Frenchmen 36–8
    terminology 34–6
        see also Paris World Exhibition 1900; Vladimir, Prince
architecture byzantine en France. Saint-Front de Périgueux et les églises à coupoles de l'Aquitaine, L' 38
Arena Kıraliçesi 163
Ahrweiler, G. H. 93
Armenia 5, 55–6, 136, 226, 249
Army of the Blind 250
Arnold, J. J. 85
art, Byzantine 52
art historians 196
Ascherson, Neal 229

Asimov, Isaac 5
Assassin's Creed: Revelation 125
authoritarianism 149
authority, imperial 52

Bacchae 186
Bakradze, Dimitri 56
Baptism of Vladimir 69, *70*
Barbarism 229–31, 236
Baronius, Cardinal 5
Basil II, Emperor 68
Battal Gazi Destani 156, 162–3
Battal Gazi Destani (novel) 166
Battal Gazi'nin İntikamı 167
Battal Gazi'nin Oğlu 167
Battalname 160–3
Beretti, Alexander 69
Bildergeschichten 113
Bitter Lemons 234
Bjornlie, S. M. 85
Black Icon 252
Blood on the Ground 182
Boisserée, Sulpiz 38
Bosnia-Herzegovina 12
boyars 152
Braudel, F. 93
British Museum 82, 83–4
    Byzantium 84–5
    Germanist theme 88–91
    Western Kingdoms 85–8
Bryer, A. A. M. 132
Bulgaria 12, 19–23, 58–9, 132–3
Bull, Hedley 3
Bulychev, Kir 3
Buslajev, Fëdor 52
Byzance après Byzance 151, 155
Byzantine revival style 52, *53*
Byzantine Werewolf, A 257
Byzantinism 2–4, 125, 154, 226–8
Byzantinoslavica 58, 196

Calends 183–4
Campbell, J. 90
Čapek, Karel 194–6, 202
Captain Meïdanos 185
Casablanca 227
Catherine the Great 49
Caucasus 55–6
Cavafy, Konstantin 230–1
censorship 148, 149
Chalkokondyles, Laonikos 148, 155
characters 152–3
Chateaubriand, François-René 33–4
children 110–11, 197
China Mountain Zhang 4
Chirac, Jacques 159
Choisy, Auguste 52
Choix d'églises byzantines en Gréce 36
Choniates, Niketas 230–1, 244
Christianity 153
    architecture 36–7, 40
    Greek identity 91–8
    literature 240, 243
    modern media 179, 186
    Paris World Exhibition 15, 20, 23
    political tool 46, 55–6
    Prince Vladimir 69, 72, 74
Chronicle of Morea: A History in Political Verse, Relating the Establishment of Feudalism in Greece by the Franks in the Thirteenth Century, The see Morea, Chronicle of
Chronike Diegesis 244
Chronographia 244–7
churches 70–1
Cimický, Jan 198–9, 202
cinema 1
    Greek 177–9 see also Greece (Greeks)
    Romanian 150–4
citizens 125
Classicism 228–9, 235
Classics Illustrated 110–12
clichés, Byzantine 243–4
Clodt, Peter von Jürgensburg 69
Cold War 114, 154, 155
Coleridge, Samuel Taylor 227
colonialism 13, 46, 54, 56–8, 95, 134
    Macaulay 225, 233–5
    see also Nations

colonies 12–13
comics, graphic 1, 109, 124
    soft power 110–12
consciousness, national 112, 161–3
Constantinople 164
    see also Istanbul
Couchaud, André 36–7
courts, imperial 246
Creative Assembly 129
Crimea 72
Cross Against Cross 196
cultural heritage, national 21–3
cultures 1, 4–5, 56–9, *233*, 268
    European 82–4
    Indigenous 12
    Russian 49
Czechoslovakia 58
    see also historical fiction, Czech

Danileviskij, Nikolaj 51
Day of National Unity 72
Death of the Empire: A lesson from Byzantium, The 71
decadence 257–8
Decline and Fall of the Roman Empire 5
Demut-Malinovsky 69
Derrida, J. 81, 90
Despot, The 199
diasporas, transnational 58
Diehl, Charles 2, 162
Dimitriadis, Nikol(as) 114–16
Dirge of Tribizond see Macaulay, Rose
Dog, Cat, and the Orphan 200
Dostálová, R. 199
Doukas 148, 155
Doxobus 184–5, 187
Dragon Waiting, The 253, 257
du Cange, Charles du Fresne, Sieur 47–9
Duggan, Alfred 209–10, 212, 213, 215, 217–18, 220
Dunant, Henri 52
Dungeons & Dragons 127
Durrell, Lawrence 234
Dyment, David 126

Eco, Umberto 227
Ekkehard 114
elites 49–50, 58, 169
emperors 246

Empire of Constantinople 50, 52–3, 54, 57–8
empires 134, 170, *233*, 246
Entretiens sur l'histoire. Antiquité et Moyen Age 254
environments, social 202
Epitome of Histories 244
Erbakan, Necmettin 170
Erdoğan, Recep Tayyip 169–70
ethnic groups 163
Europa Universalis series 125, 134, 137
European Union (EU) 82, 170
events, chronology of 151
events, historical 59, 128, 169
    literature 195, 199, 241–2, 244–5, 247
    propaganda 147, 150

facts, historical 179–80, 247
Fatih Feneri 165
fiction 1
    historical *see* historical fiction, Czech; Morea, Chronicle of
    speculative *see* imagery
films (movies)
    comics 110, 114, 116
    political tool 69, 71
    propaganda 148–50
    Turkey 160, 165–70
    videogames 124–5
    see also cinema, Romanian
Fischer, S. 86
Flame in Byzantium, A 253, 255
food 255
Ford, John M. 253, 256
Formigé, Jean-Camille 18–19
Foskolos, Nikos 182–3, 188
France (Frankes) 2, 38–40
    literature 236, 253, 268
    political tool 46, 52, 58
Franco-Prussian War 52
Franks, (term?) 243–4
Frații Jderi 148, 150, 152–3, 155

Gagarin, Grigorij 55
Garriot, Richard 127
Genette, Gérard 256
Georgia 55–6
Germany (German Democratic Republic (GDR/DDR)) 38, 40, 54, 59, 74, 112, 114–16
Ghazi, Battal 160–1, 163

Gibbon, Edward 5, 131, 162, 228, 229, 232
Girault, Charles 41
globalism 57–59
    see also Nations
Grabar, André 57, 58
Grammatas, Theodoros 112
Great Britain 57
Greece (Greeks) 37, 81, 94–8, 265
    1960–1971 179–82
    1973–1976 182–4
    1987–2003 184–7
    cinema and television 177–9
    literature 200, 208–9, 234–5
    modern media 110, 114–16, 125, 166
    Paris World Exhibition 16–17, 20
    past and future 187–8
    political tool 46, 49
    see also Vladimir, Prince
Griffin, Sean 68, 73
Griveaoud, M. 82
Grünbart, Michael 114

Haiducii 148
Hegen, Hannes 112–13, 114, 116
Hellekson, Karen 252
Heller, Michel 49
heroes 111, 197
    national 147–8, 155
    saintly 240–1, 245–6
    Turkey 161, 163, 165–8, 170
    see also superheroes
Histoire de l'Empire de Constantinople sous les empereurs français 47
Historia Constantinopolitana 197
historical fiction, Czech 193–4, 201–2
    Čapek 194–6
    Cimický 198–9
    Kalenda 199–201
    Šimáček 196–8
Histories of Greek Cinema 180
historiography *see* Morea, Chronicle of
History 230
History of the Brave Czech Peoples, The 194
History of the Decline and Fall of the Roman Empire, The 131
history, Russian 71
Hungary 12, 147–8, 150
Hunger, Herbert 247

I gyftopoula 182
iconoclasm, Greek 184–7
icons 96, 255
identity 151, 161
   Anglo-Saxons 88–91
   British 84–5
   Romanian 149
   Turkish 165
   see also museums, interpretations of Byzantium
identity, Greek 91–3
   after fall of Byzantium 94–6
   lost territories 93–4
Iliogenniti 181–2
imagery 249–52
   in Byzantium, Nowhere 254–6
   epilogue 257–8
   paratexts and peritexts 256–7
   what ifs 252–4
imagology 251
Immortal 257
Imperiale 180–1
imperialism 86, 151, 162, 267
   literature 233–5, 243–6, 255
   political tool 52, 54, 58–9
   Prince Vladimir 67, 69, 74, 77
   videogames 128–9, 132–5, 137
inaccuracies 129–30, 132–3, 137, 182
inspiration 1
Institutum Kondakovianum 57, 58–9
International Congress of Byzantine Studies, Xth (1955) 165
intertextuality 240
Iorga, Nicolae 151
Islam 165, 168
Istanbul 164, 167
   see also Constantinople; superheroes
Italy 55, 153
   architecture 37–8, 40
   museums 86, 97
   Paris World Exhibition 12, 15

Jarry, Alfred 254
Journal of the Bulgarian Engineering-Architectural Society (BIAD) 21–2
journals 57, 58

Kaiser-Wilhelm Memorial Church 54
Kalenda, František 199–201, 202
Kambanellis, Iakovos 183
Kanellis, Elias 112
Kantakouzenos, Manuel 199
Karagatsis, M. 239–42
   Byzantine clichés and stereotypes 243–4
   and Psellos 244–7
   use and reception of Byzantium 242–3
Karagiannis, A. 111
Karalis, Vrasidas 181
Karydi, battle of 212–15, 217
Kassiani Hymnographer 179–80
Katavolinos, Thomas 154
Kavtaradze, Sergey 75
Kay, Guy Gavriel 250–1
King Ubu 254
King's Flute, The 180
Klinkmann, Sven-Erik 2
Komnene, Anna 244
Kondakov, Nikodim 52, 56–7
Kondakov Seminar 196
Konstantinou, Panagiotis 181
Koutrakou, Nike 249
Koychev, P. 22
Kozanoğlu, Abdullah Ziya 160, 162–4
Kramer, T. 114
Kritoboulos of Imbros 148, 155
Kubinka Cathedral 74–8
Kyrias, Kostas 183

Labarte, Jules 52
Laborde, Alexandre de 35
Labrinos, Fotos 184–5
Laisi, Katerina 4
Latins in the Levant, The 210–11, 212, 214, 216
Legend of Zelda, The 127
Lenoir, Albert 36
Leontiev, Konstantin 51
Lieutenant Natasha 182
Lilie, Ralph-Johannes 216
literature 5, 170
   children's 111–12
   see also historical fiction, Czech; Morea, Chronicle of
Lock, Charles 228
Lombard, Jean 254
Lord Geoffrey's Fancy 209–10, 212–14, 216, 220

Lord of the Rings, The 127
Lurier, Harold 212

Maastricht Treaty 82
Macaulay, Rose 225–6, 234–6
    Barbarism 229–31
    Byzantinism 226–8
    Classicism 228–9
    historical context of poem 233–4
    Orientalism 231–3
Macmillan, Harold 234
magazines *see* comics, graphic
Magne, Lucien 17–18
Mango, Cyril 257
Manzoni, Alessandro 211
Martorell, Joanot 252
Masaryk, Tomáš Garrique 58, 196
Matine, Arkady 5
Mavroeidi-Papadaki, Sophia 111–12
Mazaris's Journey to Hades 240
McHugh, Maureen 4
media 71, 75, 159
Medieval II: Total War 125
Medievalism 124
Medvedec, Dmitry 71
Mehmed II, Sultan 46, 47, 149, 152, 163
Memory Called Empire, A 5
memory, national 74
Menderes, Adnan 234–5
Mérimée, Prosper 34, 38
Microsoft 127
Middle Ages 123–6
Miller, William 210, 212, 214, 215, 217–19
Million Adventures, A 2
Miserables, Les 110
missionaries 234
Mitropoulou, A. 181
Miyamoto, Shigeru 127
Moldavia 149, 151
Montesquieu, Charles-Louis de 131
Moravia (Great Moravia) 193–4
Morea 135, 137
Morea, chronicle of 207–8, 220
    battles of Karydi, Pelagonia and
        Prinitsa 212–20
    Chronicle of Morea 211–12
    Lord Geoffrey's Fancy 209–10
    Princes of Achaia and *The Latins in the
        Levant* 210–11

mosaics 76, 255
    see also Vladimir, Prince
Mosaik 112–116
multilingualism 163
Munger, Sean 253, 254, 256
museums 4
museums, interpretations of Byzantium
        81–3, 98–100
    British Museum rooms 41 and 40
        83–91
    Christian museums 91–8

Napoleon III 52
narratives, national 74, 83, 162, 169, 171,
        193–4
national-communism 149
Nationalisms, Balkan
    defining cultural heritage 21–3
    Paris World Exhibition 14–21
Nations 45–6, 59–60
    Byzantine 46–54
    colonies 55–7
    without borders 57–9
Neamul Șoimăreștilor 148
newspapers 159
Niketas Choniates 230–1
novels 160, 168, 249
    young-adult 196
novels, fantasy 124
novels, graphic 5
novels, Turkish 160–3
Nowhere 254–6
Nye, J. 110

Obolensky, Dimitri 56–7
Orientalism 231–3, 235
*1000 years ago: The Feast of Calends in
        976 AD* 183–4, 188
Ostrogoths 84–5, 88
Othering (Otherness) 12–13, 23, 251–2
Ottoman Empire 46, 49, 147–8, 162–3,
        169, 233–4, 241

Palamas, Costis 180
Papadiamantis, Alexandros 182
Papadopoulos, Y. C. S. 182–3, 187
Paparigopoulus, C. 96, 112
Paparrigopoulos, K. 241
Paradox Interactive 134

Paraskevas, Ilias 179
paratexts and peritexts 256–7
Paris World Exhibition 1900 11–14
    aftermath 21–3
    Balkan States 14–21
Patriot Park 74–5
patriotism 155
Pawlak, Romuald 250
peasants 152–3
Pechlivanidia brothers 110
    Kostas 115
Peers, Glenn 3
Pelagonia, battle of 211, 212, 215–18
Pera Museum 1
periodicals *see* comics, graphic
Peter the Great 49
Pleasure of Ruins, The 228
Poland 147–8, 153, 250–1, 254
politicians 244
Pong 126
Porphyra and Blood 183
Portokalakis, Panagiotis 187
power, soft 110–12
prejudices 124, 131, 138, 197, 200, 252
press 234
Prince Vladimir 71
Princes of Achaia, The 210–11, 212, 214, 216
Prinitsa, battle of 212, 218–20
propaganda 50, 52, 59, 113, 194
propaganda, political 4
propaganda, Romanian 147–9
    cinema 150–4
    movies 149–50
    reference sources 154–6
Prussia 52
Psellos, Michael 244–7
Pullan, Richard Popplewell 38
Putin, Vladimir 71, 72, 74, 75

reference sources, propaganda 154–6
relations, human 242–3
religion 164, 186, 240, 257
Renaissance, Italian 97–8
Reynaud, Léonce 40
Rise of the Tomb Raider 125
Rodd, Rennell 210, 212, 213–14, 215, 217–19
Rodopoulos, Demetris *see* Karagatsis, M.

Romania 4, 12, 14–15, 18–21, 23
    see also propaganda, Romanian
Romanos Diogenis 183
Rosenqvist, Jan Olof 3
Rotas, Vassilis 111
Rus Iznachalnaya 69
Russell, Steve 126
Russia (Russian Empire) 46, 49–50, 52, 54–9, 132, 134–5
    see also Vladimir, Prince
Russian Military Historical Society 72
Russo-Byzantine style 50–1
Russo-Turkish War 50–1

Sadoveanu, Mihail 148
Saïd, E. 232
Saint-Simon, Henri de 36
Saint Vladimir *see* Vladimir, Prince
Saladin, Henri 19–20
Sarantine Mosaic, The 250
Sardou, Victorien 227, 257
satire 240
Savulun Battal Gazi Geliyor 167
Scheffel, Joseph Victor 114
Scherbakov, Salavat 72, 73–4, 78
Schmidt, John 212
sculpture *see* Vladimir, Prince
Second World War 59, 74, 75, 76
Séelinges, Henri de 19–20
Serbia 16–17, 23, 201
Sergios and Bacchos see Karagatsis, M.
Sertoğlu, Murat 167
Sessa, K. 85
settings, physical (locations) 151–2, 167
    see also Constantinople
sexuality 242–3
Sfikas, Kostas 185
Sicily, Norman 54
Silverberg, Robert 249
Šimáček, Radovan 196–8, 202
Skalenakis, Giorgos 180
social media 159, 170–1
soft power 110–12
Soldatos, Y. 181
Spacewar! 126
speeches 111, 125, 200, 241
    Chronicle of Morea 212, 215–19, 220
    propaganda 148, 152
Sphrantzes, Georgios 155

Spieser, Jean-Michel 48
Stage Actresses, The 187–8
Stamboulopoulos, Giorgos 185–6, 187
Ștefan cel Mare 148, 149, 152–3
Stephen III (Stephen the Great) 147
stereotypes 129, 250, 251, 253, 255, 257
    Byzantine 243–4
stories, illustrated *see* comics, graphic
Sultan of Byzantium, The 251
Sultan, the Vampyr, and the Soothsayer, The 253, 255
Sumer Game, The (Hamurabi) 126
superheroes 165–168, 169
    see also heroes

technologies 129, 134–5, 136
television 116, 168, 170, 194
    Greek 177–9, 247 *see also* Greece (Greeks)
Tennis for Two 126
Texier, Charles 37–8
textbooks 149, 194
    Prince Vladimir 72, 74, 78
    videogames 124, 129
Tezuka, Takashi 127
theatre 187
theatricality 245
Theoderic 86–7
Theos, Dimos 185
Thessaloniki Film Festival, 28th 185
Thibaut, Philippe 134
Thon, Konstantin 50
Tikhon, Archimandrite (Shevkunov) 71
Timarion 240
Times Literary Supplement 226, 234
Tirant the White 251–2
Topping, Peter 212
Toswell, M. J. 4
Total War series 129–34, 137
Towers of Trebizond, The see Macaulay, Rose
Trabzon (Trebizond/Trapezunt) *see* Macaulay, Rose
traditions, imperial 74
translators 155
treason 150
Tudor 148
Turkey 169–70
    1990s and 2000s 168–9
    Byzantine women 164–5

Byzantium 163–4
    Constantinople 164
    literature and cinema 159–60
    novels 160–3
    superhero films 165–8
Turner, Lucille 250, 253, 254, 256, 257
Turtledove, Harry 252, 253, 256, 257
Two Suns in the Sky 185–6, 187–8
Tziovas, Dimitris 247

Ukraine 72
Ultima series 127
United States of America (USA) 110
Unknown War 182
Up the Line 249, 255

Vasnetsov, Viktor 69, 73, 76–7
Venice 39
Verneilh, Félix de 38–40
Veselovsji, Alexander 52
videogames 4–5
    Middle Ages 123–6
    strategy 126–38
videos games 1
Vienna 14–15
Vitberg, Alexander L. 50
Vitet, Ludovic 38, 39
Vlad III Drăculea (*Vlad Țepeș*/Vlad the Impaler/Dracula) 147, *148*, 148, *150*, *152*, *154*, 253
Vladimir, Prince 67–8
    Kubinka Cathedral 74–8
    rise and fall, 988 to 1988 68–70
    strikes back, new millennium 70–4
Voltaire 215

Wallachia 151
Walton, Jo 4
Weller, AnnaLinden 5
women, Byzantine 164–5, 167
World Exhibition, USA 21

Yarbro, Chelsea Quinn 253, 256
Yarnley, C. J. 132
Yeats, W. B. 227, 232, 250

Zagańczyk, Mieszko 252, 254, 256
Zeller, Jules 254
Zombies of Byzantium 253, 255, 256
Zonaras, John 244